TWILIGHT OF EMPIRE

The Brest-Litovsk Conference and the Remaking of East-Central Europe, 1917–1918

Twilight of Empire is the first book in English to examine the Brest-Litovsk Peace Conference during the later stages of the First World War with the use of extensive archival sources. Two separate peace treaties were signed at Brest-Litovsk – the first between the Central Powers and Ukraine and the second between the Central Powers and Bolshevik Russia.

Borislav Chernev, through an insightful and in-depth analysis of primary sources and archival material, argues that although its duration was short lived, the Brest-Litovsk settlement significantly affected the post-Imperial transformation of East Central Europe. The conference became a focal point for the interrelated processes of peacemaking, revolution, imperial collapse, and nation-state creation in the multi-ethnic, entangled spaces of East Central Europe. Chernev's analysis expands beyond the traditional focus on the German-Russian relationship, paying special attention to the policies of Austria-Hungary, Bulgaria, and Ukraine. The transformations initiated by the Brest-Litovsk conferences ushered in the twilight of empire as the Habsburg, Hohenzollern, and Ottoman Empires all shared the fate of their Romanov counterpart at the end of the First World War.

BORISLAV CHERNEV is Lecturer in Modern European History at the University of Exeter.

BORISLAV CHERNEV

Twilight of Empire

The Brest-Litovsk Conference and the Remaking of East-Central Europe, 1917–1918

UNIVERSITY OF TORONTO PRESS
Toronto Buffalo London

© University of Toronto Press 2017
Toronto Buffalo London
utorontopress.com
Printed in the U.S.A.

Reprinted in paperback 2019

ISBN 978-1-4875-0149-5 (cloth)   ISBN 978-1-4875-2449-4 (paper)

♾ Printed on acid-free, 100% post-consumer recycled paper.

Library and Archives Canada Cataloguing in Publication

Title: Twilight of empire : the Brest-Litovsk Conference and the remaking of East-Central Europe, 1917-1918 / Borislav Chernev.
Names: Chernev, Borislav, author.
Description: Paperback reprint. Originally published in hardcover in 2017. | Includes bibliographical references and index.
Identifiers: Canadiana 20190097132 | ISBN 9781487524494 (softcover)
Subjects: LCSH: Brest-Litovsk Peace Conference (1917-1918) | LCSH: Treaties of Brest-Litovsk (1918) | LCSH: World War, 1914–1918 – Peace. | LCSH: World War, 1914–1918 – Europe, Eastern. | LCSH: World War, 1914–1918 – Europe, Central.
Classification: LCC D613 .C54 2019 | DDC 940.5—dc23

University of Toronto Press acknowledges the financial assistance to its publishing program of the Canada Council for the Arts and the Ontario Arts Council, an agency of the Government of Ontario.

For my parents

Contents

List of Illustrations   ix
Acknowledgments   xi
Note on Transliteration and Place Names   xiii
Glossary   xv

Introduction: A Forgotten Peace   3

1 *Ostpolitik* Meets World Revolution   12

2 Peacemaking and Self-Determination at Brest-Litovsk   41

3 The Great January Strike as a Prelude to Revolution in Austria   79

4 The Brest-Litovsk System and Modern Ukrainian Statehood   120

5 Brest-Litovsk and the Elusive Bulgarian "Dream of Byzantium"   158

6 The Second Treaty of Brest-Litovsk and After   183

Conclusion: Brest-Litovsk and Europe's Twentieth Century   221

Notes   225
Bibliography   273
Index   287

Illustrations

Maps

Map 1 Approximate extent of the Eastern Front at the conclusion of the armistice in December 1917 and the main centres of the Great January Strike in January 1918 xix
Map 2 Territorial settlement in East Central Europe established by the two treaties of Brest-Litovsk xx

Figures

1 The Russian delegation arrives at Brest-Litovsk 23
2 Leaders of the delegations of the Central Powers 71
3 The Ukrainian delegation in Brest-Litovsk 113
4 The peace with Ukraine 136
5 The first two pages of the Russian treaty 212

Acknowledgments

I would not have been able to complete this project without the invaluable help and support I received from a large number of people and institutions. This book began as a doctoral dissertation at the American University in Washington, DC, and I would like to thank my academic advisor and dissertation committee chair, Eric Lohr, for encouraging me to pursue this project from the beginning of my doctoral studies. Max Paul Friedman, James Shedel, and Joshua Sanborn provided regular feedback during the writing phase, which improved the quality of my work substantially. Several friends and colleagues were kind enough to offer feedback on different parts of the manuscript; I am especially grateful to Sarah Thelen and Jayne Cosson. The archival research necessary for this book was made possible in part by a CES Pre-Dissertation Fellowship from the Council for European Studies at Columbia University in 2012, and by several fellowships and grants from the Department of History and the College of Arts and Sciences at the American University in 2011–12. I would also like to thank the archivists and librarians at the National Archives and Records Administration in College Park, Maryland; Harvard University's Houghton Library in Cambridge, Massachusetts; the Austrian State Archives and Labour History Society in Vienna, Austria; the Bulgarian Central State Archives in Sofia, Bulgaria; and the British Library in London, England for their kind assistance. At the University of Toronto Press, Richard Ratzlaff has been an engaged, supportive, and extremely helpful editor. Last but certainly not least, I would like to thank my parents, Veselina and Viktor, for their moral support and unconditional love.

Note on Transliteration and Place Names

I have used the Library of Congress systems of transliteration for Russian and Ukrainian names and a modified Library of Congress system of transliteration for Bulgarian names (where 'â' appears as 'a' and so on). Most East Central European towns have different names in different languages, some as many as six. I have used the version most commonly found in the documents relating to the country in control of a particular settlement during this period rather than the present-day name (thus Dvinsk rather than Daugavpils and Cattaro rather than Kotor), unless there is a commonly established English name (thus Cracow rather than Kraków and Kiev rather than Kyiv). In the case of the Austrian half of the Dual Monarchy, where linguistic particularism was common at the crownland (provincial) level, I have used German place names, German being the language of the central bureaucracy in Vienna (thus Lemberg rather than Lwów and Brünn rather than Brno). I have also used Constantinople and Ottoman Empire rather than Istanbul and Turkey, except when quoting a document.

Glossary

Adler, Viktor – leading Austrian social-democrat

Altvater, Admiral Vasilii – military consultant in the Russian delegation

AOK – *Armee Oberkommando* (Austro-Hungarian High Command)

Arbeiterheim – Austrian labour council. The term refers to an association of labour unions or union branches in a given area and is not to be confused with *Arbeiterrat* (workers' council), the Austrian equivalent of Russian *soviets* which emerged during the Great January Strike

Arz von Straußenburg, General Arthur – Austro-Hungarian chief of staff 1917–18

Bauer, Otto – radical Austrian social-democrat

Bethmann-Hollweg, Theobald von – German Imperial Chancellor 1909–17

Bukharin, Nikolai – leading Bolshevik and member of the Left Communist faction

Chaprashikov, Stefan – Bulgarian minister plenipotentiary in Petrograd and Moscow 1917–18

Czernin von und zu Chudenitz, Count Ottokar – Austro-Hungarian foreign minister 1916–18

Czernin, Otto – Austro-Hungarian minister plenipotentiary in Sofia; Ottokar's younger brother

Demblin, Count August – Austro-Hungarian foreign ministry liaison at the Imperial Court

Eichhorn, Fieldmarshal Hermann von – commander-in-chief of the German forces in Ukraine in 1918

Ellenbogen, Wilhelm – leading Austrian social-democrat

Ferdinand Maximilian Karl – Prince Regent, subsequently king of Bulgaria 1887–1918

Ganchev, Colonel Petur – Bulgarian liaison at the OHL and military consultant in the Bulgarian delegation

Fokke, Colonel Dzhon – military consultant in the Russian delegation

Forgách von Ghymes und Gacs, Count Johann – Austro-Hungarian ambassador in Kiev in 1918

Hádik, János – Hungarian food minister 1917–18

Hakki Pasha, Prince Ibrahim – Ottoman diplomat

Hertling, Count Georg Friedrich von – German Imperial Chancellor 1917–18

Hindenburg, Fieldmarshal Paul von – German chief of staff of the commander-in-chief of *Ober Ost* 1914–16; chief of staff of the German Army 1916–18

Hoffmann, Major-General Max von – German chief of staff of the commander-in-chief of *Ober Ost* 1916–18

Höfer, General Anton – Austrian food minister 1917–18

Hohenlohe-Schillingsfürst, Prince Gottfried zu – Austro-Hungarian ambassador in Berlin 1914–18

Holubovych, Vsevolod – Ukrainian minister of commerce and industry and prime minister in 1918

Ioffe, Adolf – Bolshevik diplomat; leader of the Russian delegation in Trotsky's absence

Karl Franz Joseph – emperor of Austria and apostolic king of Hungary 1916–18

Kucharzewski, Jan – Polish prime minister 1917–18

Kühlmann, Baron Richard von – German state secretary for foreign affairs 1917–18

Landwehr von Pragenau, General Ottokar – Austro-Hungarian chairman of the joint food committee 1917–18

Lenin, Vladimir Il'ich – Bolshevik leader and Russian chairman of the *Sovnarkom* 1917–24

Leopold, Prince of Bavaria – German commander-in-chief of Ober Ost 1916–18

Ludendorff, General Erich – German first-quartermaster general of the OHL 1916–18

Mérey von Kapos-Mére, Kajetan – Austro-Hungarian diplomat; leader of the Austro-Hungarian delegation in Czernin's absence

Mirbach, Count Wilhelm von – German ambassador in Petrograd and Moscow in 1918

Narkomindel – *Narodnyi komissar inostrannykh del* (Russian people's commissar for foreign affairs); the term was also used to refer to the institution as a whole

Narodno Subraine – Bulgarian people's assembly (parliament)

Ober Ost – *Oberbefehlshaber Ost* (German commander-in-chief in the East); the term was also used to refer to the territory under German military administration on the Eastern Front

OHL – *Oberste Heeresleitung* (German supreme high command)

Pallavicini, Margrave Johann von – Austro-Hungarian ambassador in Constantinople 1906–18

Popov, Hristo – Bulgarian minister of justice 1913–18; leader of the Bulgarian delegation in Radoslavov's absence

Rada – Ukrainian council; the Ukrainian word *rada* is the equivalent of the Russian word *soviet*; the Central (*Tsentral'na*) Rada was the highest governing organ of the Ukrainian People's Republic in 1917–18

Radek, Karl – leading Bolshevik and member of the Left Communist faction

Radoslavov, Vasil – Bulgarian prime minister 1886–7, 1913–18

Reichsrat – Austrian Imperial council (parliament), a bicameral legislature which consisted of the House of Lords (*Herrenhaus*) and the House of Representatives (*Abgeordnetenhaus*)

Renner, Karl – leading Austrian social-democrat

Rosenberg, Friedrich Hans von – German diplomat; leader of the German delegation in Kühlmann's absence

SDAPÖ – *Sozialdemokratische Arbeiterpartei Österreichs* (Social-democratic Workers' Party of Austria)

Seidler von Feuchtenegg, Ernst – Austrian prime minister 1917–18

Seitz, Karl – leading Austrian social-democrat

Skoropadskyi, Pavlo – Hetman (leader) of Ukraine in 1918

Sovnarkom – *Sovet narodnykh kommissarov* (Council of People's Commissars); constitutionally, the highest governing body of the Russian Socialist Federative Soviet Republic 1917–22 and of the Soviet Union 1922–46

Toshev, Andrei – Bulgarian minister plenipotentiary in Vienna 1917–20

Trotsky, Leon (Lev) Davidovich – Russian people's commissar for foreign affairs 1917–18; people's commissar for military and naval affairs 1918–25

USS – *Ukrains'ki Sichovi Stril'tsi* (Ukrainian Sich Sharpshooters). Ukrainian unit within the Austro-Hungarian army 1914–18

Vynnychenko, Volodymyr – Ukrainian prime minister 1917–18

Wekerle, Sándor – Hungarian prime minister 1892–5, 1906–10, 1917–18

Wilhelm, Archduke von Habsburg – Austro-Hungarian commander of the USS 1915–18 and pretender to the Ukrainian throne

Wilhelm von Hohenzollern – German kaiser and king of Prussia 1888-1918

Map 1: Approximate extent of the Eastern Front at the conclusion of the armistice in December 1917 and the main centres of the Great January Strike in January 1918.

Source: Adapted from William R. Shepherd, *Historical Atlas*. New York: Henry Holt, 1911.

Map 2: Territorial settlement in East Central Europe established by the two treaties of Brest-Litovsk.

Source: George H. Allen, *The Great War, Volume 5: The Triumph of Democracy*. Philadephia: George Barrie's Sons, 1921. Wikimedia.

TWILIGHT OF EMPIRE

The Brest-Litovsk Conference and the Remaking
of East-Central Europe, 1917–1918

Introduction: A Forgotten Peace

The old order changeth, yielding place to new.
                    Alfred, Lord Tennyson, *Morte d'Arthur*

The dynastic empires of the Romanovs, Habsburgs, Ottomans, and Hohenzollerns, amongst themselves, had controlled for many centuries East Central Europe, that vast region between the Elbe and Dnieper rivers.[1] The system of imperial dynasticism first began to weaken over the course of the nineteenth century with the emergence of nation states in the Balkans, as Ottoman power declined and independent states premised on the preservation and enhancement of a specific ethnicity rather than a particular dynasty gradually emerged. Ultimately, however, it was the Great War which shattered this intricate imperial system across East Central Europe.

In Winston Churchill's famous multi-volume history of the Great War entitled *The World Crisis*, he referred to the war in the east as "the unknown war." There was much truth in this. While the Great War had broken out in the east with the Austro-Hungarian declaration of war on Serbia, Russian mobilization, and the German ultimatum to St. Petersburg, the subsequent escalation of the conflict meant that the strategic importance of the Western Front overshadowed events elsewhere. The fighting on the Eastern Front, however, was every bit as intense as that in the trenches of the Western Front. It destroyed millions of lives and spread famine and revolution throughout East Central Europe, as the warring dynastic empires and newer, smaller states were pushed to exhaustion.

The Brest-Litovsk Peace Conference of December 1917 – March 1918 between the Central Powers (Germany, Austria-Hungary, the Ottoman

Empire, and Bulgaria), Bolshevik Russia, and Ukraine became the first step in the long, drawn-out process to end the tremendous bloodletting of the Great War, first in the east and then elsewhere. The two peace treaties signed by the Central Powers, first with Ukraine on 9 February 1918 and then Russia on 3 March 1918, were its direct outcome. This book examines peacemaking at the conference and consequent implications across East Central Europe, with a particular emphasis on the interdependence of diplomatic negotiations at Brest-Litovsk and domestic developments. It suggests that, although the duration of the Brest-Litovsk settlement was short-lived, it played an important if underappreciated role in early twentieth-century European history, becoming a focal point of the interrelated processes of peacemaking, revolution, imperial collapse, and nation state creation in the multi-ethnic, entangled spaces of East Central Europe during a decade-long continuum of violence between 1914 and 1923. One of the main aims of the book is to go beyond the traditional notion of Brest-Litovsk as a draconian, dictated settlement imposed by a ruthlessly militaristic Germany on a prostrate Russia at the barrel of a gun. Although I address the merits of the Russian Treaty of Brest-Litovsk in the final chapter – especially in comparison with the Paris settlement of 1919–20 – I am less interested in establishing relative degrees of severity or apportioning blame than in demonstrating how the settlement came about and how the multifarious implications of Brest-Litovsk transcended the dominant Russo-German dynamic.

Consequently, this book proposes that the peace negotiations at Brest-Litovsk had a profound impact which outlasted the immediate collapse of the territorial and political-economic framework established by the two peace treaties in the wake of the defeat of the Central Powers in the autumn of 1918. The settlement occupies an important position halfway through a decade-long period that Peter Holquist has dubbed a "continuum of upheaval and crisis,"[2] which remade East Central Europe beyond all recognition. "When the war in the east ... ended," explains Mark von Hagen, "the pressures and constraints of the various entanglements also resulted in a much more radical postwar reconfiguration of borders and populations than was the case in the west."[3] The fact that the Brest-Litovsk negotiations were the first in the history of international relations to be conducted in the open, with the world press receiving each session's proceedings within a few days, meant that the rhetoric emanating from the green table received an immediate response throughout the region aptly described by Iván T. Berend as the "crisis zone of Europe."[4] Thus, the brief duration of the settlement notwithstanding, Brest-Litovsk helped to condition the nature of the second phase of the continuum of violence in East Central Europe in important ways, ways which had lasting implications for twentieth-century European history as a whole.

Brest-Litovsk marked the international debut of the Bolshevik dual foreign policy of ideological warfare and formal negotiations, which played an enormous role in the development of international relations over the course of the short twentieth century. The Bolsheviks, encouraged by their successful revolutionary seizure of power in Petrograd in November 1917, sought to use the negotiating table as a platform from which to spread proletarian revolution – first to the countries of the Central Powers and then to the world at large. The policy of the Central Powers at Brest-Litovsk, therefore, reflects the first concerted attempt to deal with the particular type of violent social revolution Bolshevism championed and to terminate the continuum of violence unleashed in 1914. In practice, this meant ending the war in the east, accommodating imperial collapse in Russia and the territorial fragmentation inherent in that process, consolidating the imperial-dynastic framework in East Central Europe by setting-up a *cordon sanitaire* of buffer states in the western borderlands of the former Russian Empire, and providing the war-weary, starving populations of East Central Europe, Austria-Hungary in particular, with much needed foodstuffs and the hope of imminent general peace.

In addition to marking the first stage of international Bolshevik revolutionary policy and the response it engendered, Brest-Litovsk saw the advent of the critical concept of self-determination. The discussions of this novel principle, particularly those between the German and Russian delegations in January 1918, led to the first application of this concept in a major peace settlement. These debates are generally dismissed as offering mere lip service to the idea, while the emergence of self-determination as a leading concept of international relations is usually placed within the framework of the Paris Peace Conference and the liberal internationalist ideology developed by American President Woodrow Wilson. However, the debates in Brest-Litovsk and their immediate resonance across East Central Europe meant that diverse organs of government and state – ranging from the Bulgarian and Ukrainian delegations in Brest-Litovsk, to the Polish prime minister, to actual and would-be provincial councils in contested territories as widely separated as the Baltic Duchy of Courland and the Black Sea province of

Dobrudja – routinely invoked the right of national self-determination in the pursuit of their respective political agendas. Consequently, the concept was firmly ensconced in the vocabulary of twentieth-century international relations long before it became the subject of heated debates in Paris and the source of anti-colonial resistance outside Europe.

Finally, the Brest-Litovsk negotiations shed light on the nature of coalition warfare, one of the most important aspects of the Great War, and one which prolonged it beyond all expectations and made a negotiated peace extremely difficult if not virtually impossible to achieve. As Patricia Weitsman convincingly argues, alliance cohesion "is a function not only of the level of external threat but also of threat within an alliance."[5] The introduction of Bulgarian and some largely overlooked Austrian government records helps to reconstruct Bulgarian and, to a lesser extent, Ottoman policy at Brest-Litovsk, thereby broadening the narrower focus on the nature of the relationship between Germany and Austria-Hungary which is more prevalent in the literature. The emerging picture is of a much less united, less German-dominated Central Powers alliance, with a greater divergence of individual policies and multiple foci of agency. While the German High Command remained the single most important actor, it was not the sole policymaker in the alliance. Conflicts between the German High Command in Kreuznach, the German government in the Wilhelmstraße, the Austro-Hungarian Foreign Ministry in the Ballhausplatz, and the growing antagonism between Sofia and Constantinople conditioned the internal dynamics of the alliance and severely tested its integrity during the course of the Brest-Litovsk peace negotiations.

Owing to these diverse factors, the implications of Brest-Litovsk varied enormously across the crisis zone of Europe. In the Habsburg Empire, where conditions in the winter of 1917–18 resembled those in the Romanov Empire during the lead-up to the February Revolution of 1917, Brest-Litovsk affected the nature and the course of revolution. At the time of the conference, the food crisis in the Austrian half of the Dual Monarchy was acute, especially in the Imperial capital of Vienna and the principal cities of Prague, Trieste, and Cracow. In January 1918, the negative news coming from Brest-Litovsk about the stalling of the negotiations led to food riots, industrial strikes, and the spontaneous emergence of workers' councils on the model of Russian *soviets*.

As a genuine revolutionary crisis unfolded, Austria-Hungary appeared on the edge of the abyss, with the Habsburg authorities and the leaders of Austrian social-democracy unanimous that proletarian revolution would be inevitable if peace were not concluded at Brest-Litovsk soon. A combination of skilful negotiations with the striking workers on the part of the Habsburg authorities, a temporary relief of the precarious food situation through imports from Germany and Romania, and the successful negotiations with the Ukrainian delegation in Brest-Litovsk, which led to the conclusion of peace between the Central Powers and Ukraine in early February 1918, averted the looming catastrophe. However, the socio-economic situation in Habsburg Central Europe remained precarious, and the so-called Great January Strike in effect became a prelude to the Central European revolutions, which eventually swept away the imposing Habsburg and Hohenzollern Imperial-dynastic establishments. When these revolutions occurred in the winter of 1918–19, they were of a qualitatively different kind than the proletarian revolution on the Bolshevik model which had threatened to engulf the region in January–February 1918.

Further east, the Brest-Litovsk settlement fostered the twin processes of Imperial collapse and nation state emergence, thus playing an important role in the early stages of modern Ukrainian statehood in particular. The diplomatic, political, and economic arrangements established by the peace conference in the southwestern parts of the former Russian Empire provided the framework for the Ukrainization policies carried out by a succession of actual and would-be Ukrainian governments between the spring and autumn of 1918. The experience of Brest-Litovsk ultimately convinced Lenin that nationalism had to be accommodated within the system of Soviet rule, and thus contributed to the origins of the indigenization [*korenizatsiia*] policy of the 1920s.

Austro-German military intervention in Ukraine on behalf of the government of the Central Rada (council) prevented a full Bolshevik takeover of Ukraine in February 1918. It also enabled the Rada to attempt to strengthen the foundations of the fledgling Ukrainian nation state by pursuing agrarian-socialist Ukrainization under a revolutionary republican government. Hetman Pavlo Skoropadskyi, who succeeded the Rada after a successful coup carried out with German approval at the end of April 1918, sought to establish a conservative monarchy based on the restoration of private property and the support of a Ukrainian army. Archduke Wilhelm von Habsburg, a self-Ukrainized prince who became one of the leaders of the Ukrainian national movement and a prospective candidate for the throne, worked towards the creation of a populist monarchy under Habsburg suzerainty, which prioritized the cultural Ukrainization of the peasantry as well as the socialization of the land economy. The Brest-Litovsk settlement both enabled and constrained these policies but did not determine them, as it cannot be reduced to a simple military occupation. Ukrainian elites, Imperial legacies, and revolutionary developments all combined to shape multiple, at times competing, Ukrainization policies and to set their limitations along the entangled Eastern Front of the First World War. Even though the Brest-Litovsk settlement was formally abolished in November 1918, an independent Ukrainian state continued to exist until 1920, following which Ukraine became a union republic of the Soviet Union. Ukrainization policies continued under the Soviets in the 1920s.

Whereas Imperial collapse in the northern part of East Central Europe only began after the February Revolution of 1917 destroyed the Imperial centre in Petrograd and unleashed strong centrifugal forces in the multi-ethnic borderlands of the Russian Empire, it was more or less an accomplished fact in the south by 1913, given that the Ottoman Empire, the erstwhile Imperial overlord, had been reduced to a mere foothold in Eastern Thrace protecting the capital of Constantinople. Thus, Brest-Litovsk affected not so much the process of nation state formation as the subsequent process of nation state consolidation in the region, demonstrated by the case of Bulgaria. Pursuing what I refer to as the "dream of Byzantium" – regional hegemony and minor Great Power status as the only possible form of nation state consolidation – the Bulgarian delegation in Brest-Litovsk sought to bring about the legal recognition of large-scale territorial annexations under the guise of national self-determination. The failure of this policy led to widespread domestic disaffection, the fall of the government in June, and the abdication of the king in October, thereby demonstrating the unfeasibility of the pursuit of regional domination in the Balkans and the inherent perils with which the process of nation state consolidation is fraught.

Early studies of Brest-Litovsk usually glossed over these multiple aspects and impacts of the conference and focused primarily on the nature of the second/Russian Treaty of Brest-Litovsk, much like early studies of the Paris Peace Conference of 1919–20 which tended to revolve around the merits of the Treaty of Versailles.[6] The result was an often implicit comparison between the two, pitting the allegedly more equitable if imperfect peace of Versailles against the Carthaginian, dictated peace of Brest-Litovsk. This is most clearly evident in John W. Wheeler-Bennett's *The Forgotten Peace: Brest-Litovsk, March 1918*, the first monograph to explore Brest-Litovsk at some depth on the basis of published sources, participants' memoirs and personal interviews. The eminent

Introduction: A Forgotten Peace 9

British historian focused on the Russo-German dynamic, portraying the negotiations as a duel between the German first-quartermaster general, Erich Ludendorff, and the Bolshevik leader, Vladimir Lenin, neither of whom was actually present in Brest-Litovsk. According to Wheeler-Bennett, Ludendorff endeavoured to knock Russia out of the war by infiltrating it with the virus of Bolshevism. This strategy seemed to work initially, as the Germans imposed a harsh settlement on their vanquished Russian foes. A Pyrrhic victory, it ultimately resulted in the revolutionary virus turning westwards and fatally infecting Germany in October–November 1918.[7]

Although Wheeler-Bennett's pioneering effort has been superseded by more thorough studies based on a constantly growing number of archival sources, the view of Brest-Litovsk as a dictated peace has proved remarkably enduring. In one of the first German-language monographs on the subject after the Second World War, Werner Hahlweg criticized the rapacious annexationism of the German High Command and condemned the peace as a *Diktatfriede* (dictated peace).[8] Following Hahlweg's early effort, German studies in the 1960s and 1970s revolved around the so-called Fischer Controversy, which began with the publication of Fritz Fischer's monumental work *Germany's Aims in the First World War*, originally published in German as *Griff nach der Weltmacht* in 1961. Rejecting the notion of a defensive war, the Fischer School argued that the civilian government, industrial elites, and a wide cross section of German society were essentially in agreement with the military authorities on the need for an annexationist policy for the duration of the war, with Brest-Litovsk representing an important case in point.[9]

On the other side of the debate, Wolfgang Steglich analysed the Brest-Litovsk negotiations within the framework of Austro-German peace policy, suggesting that total war made the Bolshevik-proposed peace without annexations and indemnities unrealistic.[10] Another prominent conservative German historian, Gerhard Ritter, opposed Fischer's thesis vehemently, arguing that Fischer had overestimated the influence of annexationist interest groups and the importance of Chancellor Bethmann-Hollweg's September 1914 program. Although he agreed that it was not "a treaty of reconciliation," Ritter concluded that "[a]ll in all, the treaty of Brest-Litovsk was rather better than its reputation, and despite its harshness, it was not really a treaty of force."[11] Also among those who disagreed with the Fischer School was Winfried Baumgart who emphasized the lack of coordination between the civilian and military authorities, concluding that, "instead of working together to facilitate the war effort, the *Auswärtiges Amt* and the OHL clashed bitterly over eastern policy."[12] In the circumstances, Austria-Hungary's role at Brest-Litovsk was at best an unbrilliant second, compromised as it was by internal weaknesses and the food crisis in particular, which made it desperate to sign a "bread peace" [*Brotfrieden*] with Ukraine.[13]

The eastern policy of the Central Powers had its greatest impact on the Ukrainian provinces of the former Russian Empire, affecting the course of the Ukrainian Revolution. Émigré Ukrainian historians like Oleh S. Fedyshyn and Stephan M. Horak have emphasized the importance of the Ukrainian treaty of Brest-Litovsk and the Central Powers' subsequent military intervention for Ukrainian statehood, while Soviet Ukrainian historians maintained that these events were a betrayal of the revolution.[14] Most recently, Russian historian Irina Mikhutina has modified this interpretation, suggesting that the Ukrainian treaty was a stab in the back for Russia.[15]

Soviet and post-Soviet historiography of Brest-Litovsk has rarely entered into debates with German- or English-language counterparts.[16] For several decades, scholars had to abide by the official Party interpretation outlined by Stalin in his 1938 *Short Course in the History of the All-Union Communist Party (Bolsheviks)*. Soviet historians invariably portrayed Brest-Litovsk as a strategic victory for Lenin, who was able to secure a "breathing spell [*peredyshka*]" for the revolution. At the same time, they deplored the "treacherous" behaviour of Trotsky, arguing that he was in league with Austro-German imperialism.[17] This evaluation of Brest-Litovsk was also accepted by non-Soviet socialist historians, with one Yugoslav scholar going as far as to describe the peace as the "crucial moment [*prijelomni trenutak*] of the October Revolution" which almost singlehandedly ensured its long-term survival.[18]

Critical reappraisals of the Brest-Litovsk negotiations and the Bolshevik role in them became possible only with the advent of the policy of *glasnost* in the Soviet Union in the late 1980s. The appearance of revised accounts coincided with the official rehabilitation of Trotsky and Bukharin. They attempted to re-evaluate the role of Trotsky in the making of Soviet policy, admitting that his views largely coincided with those of Lenin. Another subject these works focused on was the failure of world revolution, which quickly became apparent in the immediate aftermath of the conference.[19] The last decade has seen a multiplying of interpretations, with Russian scholars viewing Brest-Litovsk variously as Lenin's "trap" [*lovushka*] for Germany, a demonstration of the failure of the Bolshevik dual foreign policy, or even Russia's "shame" [*pozor*].[20]

Recent works by Belarusian and Bulgarian historians have addressed the impact Brest-Litovsk had on their respective countries' statehood.[21]

This book suggests that the implications of Brest-Litovsk go far beyond influencing any single nation, affecting rather the wider region of East Central Europe thus ushering in an era of unparalleled ideological struggle which dominated Europe's twentieth century. The ongoing twin processes of Imperial collapse and nation state creation fuelled by the growing resonance of national self-determination – facilitated by the negotiations – meant that Brest-Litovsk became, in effect, the twilight of empire in East Central Europe, as the Habsburg, Hohenzollern, and Ottoman empires all vanished like their Romanov counterpart at the end of the Great War.

Chapter One

Ostpolitik Meets World Revolution

The Great War pitted against each other two alliances of very different capabilities. Even before the entry of the United States into the war in April 1917 as an Associated Power, the Entente enjoyed clear superiority in manpower and materiel. It therefore quickly subjected the Central Powers, also known as the Quadruple Alliance (after October 1915), to a stifling blockade and forced them to fight on several fronts against overwhelming odds. Outgunned and outnumbered, the Central Powers sought to split the enemy coalition in order to regain the initiative. Having identified Russia as the weakest link in the enemy chain after the failure of the Schlieffen Plan and the war of movement in the west, and after the resounding victories at Tannenberg and the Masurian Lakes in the east in the autumn of 1914, the Central Powers endeavoured to weaken Russia further through a combination of strategic pressure and propaganda in order to force it to conclude a separate peace. However, even as it lost its important western territories of Congress Poland, Courland, and Lithuania as a result of the Great Retreat that followed the Austro-German breakthrough at Gorlice-Tarnów in May 1915,[1] the Imperial Russian establishment resolutely rebuffed all approaches by the Central Powers, notwithstanding ubiquitous contemporary rumors to the contrary. "[T]he Imperial Government made no moves towards a separate peace," convincingly argues Sergei Melgunov. "[T]here were no organized social groups working on a specific plan to conclude a separate peace with Germany prior to the revolution; there were no secret negotiations behind closed doors."[2]

This chapter is derived in part from an article published in *The International History Review* on 21 Aug 2013, available online: http://dx.doi.org/10.1080/07075332.2013.817465

The February Revolution of 1917, which forced the weak and ineffectual Emperor Nicholas II to abdicate and replaced the authoritarian empire with a democratic republic under a Provisional Government, bolstered Austro-German hopes of splitting Russia from its Entente partners. During an interview with the American ambassador in Vienna, Frederick C. Penfield, on 31 March 1917, the Austro-Hungarian foreign minister, Count Ottokar Czernin von und zu Chudenitz, admitted that "he could not prophesy whether the new regime in Russia would recognize that continuation of war would be criminal and that they [the Provisional Government] could conclude an honorable peace as any of the entente [sic] powers could at any moment."[3] The *grand seigneur* of cabinet diplomacy and scion of one of the most important Bohemian noble families dating back to the thirteenth century was in fact deeply impressed at the ease with which the erstwhile policeman of Europe had succumbed to revolution. Subsequently, he warned his emperor in April of the same year that "[i]f the Monarchs of the Central Powers are not able to conclude peace within the next few months, it will be done for them by their people, and then will the tide of revolution sweep away all that for which our sons and brothers fought and died."[4] The revolutionary turmoil in Russia appeared to present challenges as well as opportunities, infusing with greater urgency the Central Powers' quest for a separate peace in the east.

Going beyond tentative statements of intent, Imperial German Chancellor Theobald von Bethmann-Hollweg outlined the draft terms for a separate peace with Russia on 7 May 1917. According to his notes, Russia was to renounce Courland and Lithuania, already under German occupation. The two provinces would become formally sovereign duchies enjoying substantial internal autonomy; however, they would be militarily, politically, and economically associated with Germany. The chancellor proposed the Baltic port of Mitau or some other city "between the lines" (territories currently under Austro-German military occupation) as a possible venue for negotiations.[5] The chancellor's notes indicated the German government's resolve to use Russia's destabilization to make negotiated gains in the east.

While the civilians considered the political terms of a possible peace treaty, the German (*Oberste Heeresleitung*, OHL) and Austro-Hungarian (*Armee Oberkommando*, AOK) High Commands prepared a detailed draft of an armistice between the Central Powers on the one hand, and Russia and Romania on the other, which would end the hostilities on the Eastern Front in preparation for a formal peace conference. The text of this armistice covered purely military matters and carefully avoided any political implications; it bore a close resemblance to the one the Central Powers eventually presented to the Bolsheviks at Brest-Litovsk several months later.[6] However, the diplomatic and military preparations of the Central Powers were premature, as the Provisional Government in Petrograd obstinately refused to countenance a separate peace and proceeded to launch an ultimately disastrous offensive in the southern sector of the Eastern Front in June 1917. There appeared to be no way out of the impasse, notwithstanding the failure of the Kerensky Offensive, the Russian retreat from East Galicia, and the German capture of the important Baltic port of Riga in September 1917.

The situation changed dramatically after the Bolsheviks seized power in Petrograd on 7 November 1917 in a bloodless coup. During the preceding months, they had broadened their appeal campaigning extensively under the slogan "Land, Bread, and Peace." In an article published in *Rabochii i Soldat* on 1 November, on the eve of the seizure of power, noted Bolshevik theorist and leader Leon Trotsky had emphasized that only a "genuinely revolutionary government" could bring peace. "Such a government," he wrote, "would address the German troops directly, going over the heads of allied and enemy diplomats." The message would be straightforward: "In the name of the Russian people, the Russian Government offers you, Germans, an immediate peace."[7] Once in power, Bolshevik leaders Lenin and Trotsky felt compelled to extricate themselves from the tentacles of what they described as an imperialist war, fearing that their fate (and, more importantly, that of the revolution) might mirror that of the Provisional Government should they refuse to do so. In the preface to the French and German editions of *Imperialism: The Highest State of Capitalism,* published in 1920, Lenin subsequently elaborated that "the war of 1914–18 was imperialist (that is, an annexationist, predatory, war of plunder) on the part of both sides; it was a war for the division of the world, for the partition and repartition of colonies and spheres of influence of finance capital, etc."[8] A genuinely revolutionary government would eliminate finance capital, thereby destroying the corresponding superstructure of imperialist colonial conquest.[9] Thus, it logically followed that such a government would have no incentive to continue fighting a war whose sole premise was the pursuit of a new division of the world's spoils favourable to either of the two warring camps. This attitude created the opening the Central Powers were looking for.

A Fractured Alliance: The Central Powers and the Bolshevik Peace Offer

On 8 November, the day after the successful Bolshevik coup, the new Russian government released its (in)famous "Decree on Peace," wherein it abolished secret diplomacy, proposed an immediate general peace without annexations and indemnities, and demanded that each nation be granted the right to self-determination (defined as "the right [of a nation] of choosing freely – the troops of the annexing or, generally, the more powerful nation being completely withdrawn and without any pressure being brought to bear – the constitutional form of its national existence ...").[10] Given their strategic priorities and meticulous preparation, it might have appeared logical for the Central Powers to seize this opportunity immediately. They did nothing of the sort. The exchanges between their governments over the next two weeks highlight the extent to which the members of the Quadruple Alliance differed on important questions of war and peace.[11]

During the deliberations over the Bolshevik proposal, German stalling was a major contributing factor to the initial deadlock. It was also emblematic of the larger problems which plagued the Central Powers alliance, such as poor coordination of peace policy and a lack of consensus on war aims and how best to achieve them. "In shaping its strategy," Hew Strachan asserts, "Germany had identified its enemies' alliance as a source of weakness, not strength: it was to prove a fatal miscalculation but it was an accurate reflection of Germany's own experience of coalition warfare."[12] This most pertinent observation overlooks the fact that Germany itself was often guilty of causing a fair amount of interallied friction and confusion. In this case, German hesitation meant that the Austrians took the lead, as the exhausted Dual Monarchy was desperate for a peace that would allow it to address its precarious domestic situation. But even the appearance of endorsing a peace proposal based on national self-determination was fraught with danger for the multinational Habsburg Empire, whose own increasingly disaffected nationalities would be likely to claim the right to self-determination for themselves. This dilemma would become an important factor in Austro-Hungarian peace policy over the following months.

On 9 November Emperor Karl noted that, in view of the most recent events in Petrograd, this was an opportune moment to extend formal peace feelers.[13] In a letter to Imperial German Chancellor Count Georg von Hertling on 10 November, Czernin emphasized the ways in which

Vienna and Berlin could use the Bolshevik insistence on the right to self-determination to their own advantage. By effectively co-opting the formula of "peace without annexations and indemnities," the Central Powers could insist on self-determination for the non-Russian nationalities in the western borderlands of the empire in order to permanently detach Congress Poland, Courland, and Lithuania from Russia. "It would be our business to ensure that the desire for separation from Russia and for political and economic dependence on the Central Powers be voiced from within these nations," concluded the foreign minister.[14]

Czernin elaborated his ideas further in a detailed memorandum, instructing Habsburg ambassadors in Berlin, Constantinople, Sofia, and Munich[15] to inform the respective governments of his proposed course of action. He prefaced the memorandum with the remark that it was absolutely clear that the Russian offer was utopian and that no one would take it seriously at face value. However, if the Central Powers played their cards right, it offered them the opportunity to conclude a separate peace with Russia. In order to present the Entente with a *fait accompli*, Czernin proposed that the Quadruple Alliance quickly agree on and make public an answer. It was an elegant attempt to skirt the thorny issue of national self-determination by reinforcing the primacy of the principle of non-interference in other states' domestic affairs, which had been one of the key aspects of the Westphalian System of international relations since 1648:

1 We recognize the new Russian Government and are prepared to negotiate with it.
2 We recognize the sovereign right of the Russian Government to regulate the internal affairs of Russia, and note that Russia has extended the right of self-determination to all its peoples.
3 We reserve for ourselves the same sovereign right to regulate our internal affairs.
4 We accept the Russian proposal to conclude a peace without annexations or indemnities.
5 We accept the Russian proposal for a three-month long armistice beginning on [a designated date] and are prepared to send representatives for the negotiations to a neutral venue.

It was perfectly clear that the Entente would never accept the Russian proposal, Czernin concluded, and that following its refusal the Russians would probably sign a separate peace with the Central Powers.

In conclusion, he added that the Ottomans were likely to support his standpoint, as their interests of protecting the territorial integrity of their empire against foreign encroachment were ostensibly almost identical with those of the Habsburgs. Elsewhere, it would have to be made absolutely clear to Sofia that the Bulgarians risked nothing by agreeing to a peace without annexations and indemnities; as they did not intend to annex any territories from Russia, they would be free to pursue their territorial aspirations elsewhere (Macedonia and the Dobrudja) in the wake of the expected Russian withdrawal from the war.[16]

Why was the Habsburg foreign minister so keen on a quick answer to the Russian proposal? The reasons, which he outlined in a telegram to the Austro-Hungarian ambassador in Berlin, Prince Gottfried zu Hohenlohe-Schillingsfürst, were primarily of a domestic character. The Austrian minister of the interior had reported that news of the Russian proposal had had an enormous effect across the empire. People eagerly awaited the Central Powers' answer. The excitement had already reached dangerous proportions in certain areas; the Austrian war minister believed the government would have to deploy all available forces to combat possible strikes.[17] Nor were these fears groundless. "Russian democracy asks the proletariats of all countries to fight for its peace offer," reported the *Arbeiter Zeitung*, official organ of the Social Democratic Workers' Party of Austria (*Sozialdemokratische Arbeiterpartei Österreichs*, SDAPÖ) on 11 November. "The workers of Austria will fulfill their duty [to do so]."[18] Responding to the call, approximately 10 000 Viennese workers gathered in front of Concert Hall on the same day to demonstrate for peace and show solidarity "with their Russian brothers." They also adopted a resolution that urged the government to begin peace negotiations with Petrograd right away.[19] Similar demonstrations took place throughout the empire, showing that even unelected Imperial leaders could no longer afford to completely disregard popular sentiment in important matters of foreign policy.

Eager to prevent widespread disturbances of this kind, Czernin had instructed the morning papers to state that the Russians had dispatched no official armistice offer yet. However, he expected them to do so soon, at which point the Central Powers would have to accept the offer in order to prevent domestic upheaval. He reiterated that this would still allow them to pursue a favourable policy towards the occupied territories through the use of "national self-determination for Russia's peoples." In conclusion, the foreign minister asked the ambassador to inform the German government of the internal conditions in

Austria-Hungary and implore the Germans to do everything possible to allow the two countries to continue working together and not force Vienna to resort to a separate arrangement [*nicht zu einem selbständigen Schritt gezwungen waren*].[20] Czernin hoped to overcome German resistance by combining the spectre of revolution with the subtle threat of a separate Habsburg peace with the Russians. He would return to these two themes repeatedly over the course of the following months.

Czernin was right to expect objections from the leading power in the Quadruple Alliance. Hertling was in general agreement with the Austrian proposal but considered it more prudent to wait for the Entente's refusal before presenting the Russians with an answer.[21] In general, the elderly imperial chancellor tended to defer on most matters of foreign policy to the state secretary for foreign relations, Baron Richard von Kühlmann, a fellow Bavarian in a government dominated by Prussians and an experienced diplomat who had enjoyed a fruitful career in the German Embassy in London before the war.[22] Kühlmann objected to swift action on the grounds that the power struggle in Russia was far from over, and hence it would be premature to deal with the Bolsheviks at this stage.[23] In a subsequent communication, Kühlmann assured Czernin that he would continue to follow the policy guidelines the two of them had set but emphasized that it would be a mistake to appear overzealous over the Decree on Peace. The French press had already decried the Bolsheviks as German agents, and the Central Powers ought to be careful not to compromise themselves.[24] Erich Ludendorff, first quartermaster-general in the OHL, seemed even less convinced, enquiring of General Max Hoffmann, the influential chief of staff of the commander of German forces in the east (*Oberbefehlshaber Ost, Ober Ost*), whether it was possible to "negotiate with these fellows" at all. Hoffmann's answer was an unequivocal yes, in light of the need to transfer troops to the Western Front in preparation for the upcoming spring offensive.[25] Still, the Germans remained content to await further developments and do nothing in the meantime.

As Czernin had expected, the Ottoman government raised no significant objections to his plan. However, the Sublime Porte expressed concern over possible German and Bulgarian disagreement with the point of "no annexations." The Austro-Hungarian ambassador in Constantinople, Margrave Johan von Pallavicini, came out of his conversations with the Ottoman leadership with the impression that Constantinople feared the Germans might use Bulgarian opposition as an excuse for not participating. If this were the case, there could be absolutely no talk of the Ottoman Empire joining in such a démarche.[26] The need to secure a Great Power ally had played a major part in the Ottoman decision to enter the war, and Constantinople did not wish to endanger its German alliance, considered indispensable to the empire's continued existence, by endorsing a peace initiative to which Berlin was opposed.[27]

Bulgaria might have been the smallest member of the alliance, and the most negligible, both militarily and economically, but this in no way prevented it from being one of the more vocal and demanding. The Bulgarian minister plenipotentiary, Andrei Toshev, having conferred with the German Ambassador in Vienna, Count Botho von Wedel, advised the prime minister, Vasil Radoslavov, that any quick action in the matter was unwelcome, since it might be interpreted as a sign of weakness or could perhaps even compromise the integrity of the Quadruple Alliance. He suggested that any future reply include the proviso that "the national unification of the Bulgarian tribe [*pleme*] has nothing in common with the actual meaning of the term 'annexation.'"[28] This would become a constant Bulgarian refrain during the subsequent course of negotiations, to the great irritation of the other members of the alliance. In the meantime, Radoslavov listened to Czernin's ideas "with great interest" and enquired whether Vienna had received an official peace note. However, he told Czernin's younger brother, Otto, who was the Austro-Hungarian minister plenipotentiary in Sofia, that he could not give an official answer on behalf of the government in the absence of King Ferdinand, who was presently visiting the Italian Front as a guest of Emperor Karl. Personally, he was doubtful Germany would relinquish all occupied territories in the east. He did not mind the application of the "no annexations" clause to a Russian treaty, but he was convinced the Central Powers ought to present the Russians with a "dictated" (!) peace. Otherwise, Britain and France would use a non-annexationist peace with Russia to their advantage[29] and presumably demand that the clause be extended to all other theatres of war, including the Balkans.

While the Central Powers were wrangling over how best to respond to the Russian overture, the Bolsheviks decided to break the deadlock on 21 November by sending an open invitation to the German government to commence armistice negotiations and instructing the commander-in-chief, General Nikolai Dukhonin, to see to the matter.[30] This offer finally spurred the Germans into action, leading Ludendorff to work hurriedly on revisions of the draft armistice treaty from the spring and Kühlmann to outline a formal response along the lines of Czernin's earlier suggestions.[31] General Dukhonin refused to obey the order, but he was relieved from his post and subsequently beaten to death by the angry, radicalized troops in General Headquarters in Mogilev. Petrograd further announced that Ensign Nikolai Krylenko, Dukhonin's replacement as commander-in-chief, would personally travel to the front on 24 November in order to engage the Germans directly in *pourparler*.[32]

Even before Krylenko could make himself known locally, however, Russian troops had taken matters into their own hands and concluded local armistices with their German counterparts at Lake Narocz, Złoczów, Dvinsk, Baranovichi, and elsewhere along the front.[33] Unlike the celebrated Christmas Truce on the Western Front in 1914, involving German and British troops crossing the trenches into no man's land to chat and play a game of association football (soccer), which was duly celebrated in Britain as part of the centenary of the Great War, the local armistices in the east have remained largely unknown.[34] Yet, they had an arguably greater effect on the subsequent course of events by demonstrating the unwillingness of ordinary Russian soldiers and the increasing reluctance of German soldiers to continue the bloodletting. Nor was this dynamic necessarily limited to areas of the front where Bolshevik influence was pre-eminent. The commander of Ottoman forces in the Caucasus reported in mid-December that the Russian troops opposite him, who had refused to recognize Lenin's government, were also willing to conduct separate negotiations and eventually concluded an armistice not much different from the one in Brest-Litovsk.[35]

In what was now a mere formality, at 5 p.m. on 27 November three Russian delegates crossed the German lines outside the city of Dvinsk and proposed an armistice on all fronts, to be followed by the conclusion of a general peace. Following a lengthy discussion between the two sides in French, German, and Russian, and the authentication of the Russian document, at 12:20 a.m. on 28 November General von Hofmeister produced an official letter accepting the Russian invitation. The two sides agreed to commence formal armistice negotiations at the headquarters of *Ober Ost* in the half-burnt and completely deserted Russian fortress of Brest-Litovsk on 2 December.[36]

Even though Austro-German plans for armistice negotiations in the east had included Romania alongside Russia from the spring of 1917 on as a matter of course, the final agreement made no mention of the former country. The formal reason for this was the lack of official Romanian communication.[37] However, it was perfectly clear to everyone in

Berlin and Vienna that the Romanians would be unable to continue fighting once the Russians had exited the war. Thus, Romania would have had no choice but to accept an Austro-German invitation to Brest-Litovsk. The real reason was, yet again, inter-allied wrangling over war aims. This time, the disagreements involved Bulgarian claims to the whole of the Romanian-held province of Dobrudja and the Ottoman wish for commensurate compensation elsewhere (see chapter 5). Unable to bridge the divide between their Balkan allies, Germany and Austria-Hungary decided the Quadruple Alliance should hold separate negotiations with Romania instead. The Bulgarians agreed. "If Romanian delegates do arrive [in Brest-Litovsk], we shall demand that the Romanian government make a formal proposal. Only then will we negotiate with them," averred the Bulgarian military representative in Brest-Litovsk.[38] Consequently, separate armistice talks took place in the Romanian town of Focşani in December 1917, followed by a peace conference in German-occupied Bucharest in February–March 1918. Even without the Romanians present in Brest-Litovsk, however, inter-allied tensions would play a major part in the negotiations.

The Armistice Negotiations: 3 December 1917–15 December 1917

A forgotten armistice preceded the forgotten peace of Brest-Litovsk. Unlike the much more celebrated armistice of 11 November 1918, which ended fighting on the Western Front and is typically (if erroneously) considered to mark the end of the Great War, the armistice of December 1917 did not bring about a complete end to military operations in the east. The fighting on the Eastern Front and in the Caucasus, however, from February 1918 onwards bears only superficial resemblance to the fighting preceding December 1917. Whereas the years 1914–17 had witnessed a relatively straightforward Imperial clash along more or less stable frontlines, the transformed continuum of violence through the years 1918–23 was a much messier affair, involving nascent nation states, ideological warriors, and insurgents as well as empires. The armistice of December 1917 thus marks an important turning point. The armistice of 11 November has acquired a highly symbolic meaning in much of Western Europe and North America, in part because its import was (and is) easier to comprehend: this is when the guns finally fell silent, on the eleventh hour of the eleventh day of the eleventh month. The armistice of December 1917, on the other hand, contributed to the transformation of an already complicated military situation into a logistical nightmare. Whereas the former armistice brought the fighting in the west to a brisk end, the latter heralded the beginning of an entirely new period of uncertainty in the east. In the words of Polish leader Józef Piłsudski in 1919, "[h]ere there are doors which open and close and it depends on who will force them open and how far."[39]

The Central Powers' representatives arrived at Brest-Litovsk in the last few days of November. As chief of staff to the commander-in-chief of *Ober Ost*, the capable General Hoffmann was the OHL's natural choice for a military representative, while the AOK designated Lieutenant Colonel Hermann Pokorny. In addition, the Wilhelmstraße selected Ambassador Friedrich Hans von Rosenberg as an unofficial political representative, while the Ballhausplatz dispatched Ambassador Kajetan Mérey von Kapos-Mére and Legation Secretary Count Emerich Csáky von Kererzek und Adorjan. The Ottomans and Bulgarians also sent representatives, respectively General Zekki Pasha and Colonel Petur Ganchev. The diplomats' role was to be purely advisory; as the armistice negotiations were expected to be only about military matters and last but a short time, Berlin and Vienna decided to leave them mostly in the hands of the military experts, Hoffmann in particular. "Our first goal during the negotiations with the Russians would be to sign an armistice," wrote Rosenberg to the Foreign Office. "Until then, we should avoid conversations about peace on the grounds that the military representatives have no authorization to discuss these matters."[40] Rosenberg told Csáky privately that only after the signing of the armistice could he state off the record that the peace conference should take place in Brest-Litovsk immediately.[41]

In the event, however, the Central Powers found it very difficult to restrict the armistice negotiations solely to the customary military affairs. Before a single Russian delegate had set foot in Brest-Litovsk, the Bolsheviks were raising political questions. "In today's [telephone] conversation, the Russians spoke more about peace than about the armistice," Lieutenant Colonel Pokorny telegrammed on 29 November. "The latter, it appears, is of secondary importance to them, since a peace treaty is seemingly a matter of life and death for Lenin's government."[42] This was merely a taste of things to come. One look at the composition of the Russian delegation is enough to realize where its priorities lay. All three chief delegates – chairman Adolf Ioffe, Trotsky's brother-in-law Lev Kamenev, and Grigorii Sokolnikov – were professional revolutionaries with no previous military, diplomatic, or political experience. Their primary occupation was subversion and propaganda, and they

1. The Russian delegation arrives at Brest-Litovsk. Trotsky is in the centre.
Source: Wikimedia Commons.

revelled in it. Lieutenant Colonel Dzhon Fokke, a military expert in the Russian delegation, described their arrival in Dvinsk, *en route* to Brest-Litovsk, in the following manner:

> Around 11 a.m. [on 2 December] the delegates' train finally arrived, a chariot for the forthcoming funeral rites. The whole train was decorated with red banners and red cloth, the bloody symbols of mourning of the revolution.
> It was impossible to get anywhere near the train. The anticipating crowd surrounded it entirely: the train was for the crowd, and the crowd was for the train. A spontaneous demonstration broke out. They [the delegates] began to deliver speeches even before they could leave the train, shouting words from the windows.[43]

A spectacular revolutionary spectacle, this ostentatious cavalcade highlighted the extreme naïveté of early Bolshevik foreign policy, which presumed that a few well-made speeches were all that stood between Lenin's party and world revolution.

In contrast to the well-prepared, authoritative Hoffmann, the Russian military delegates were there just to fill the numbers; when Fokke asked Admiral Vasilii Altvater, the senior military expert, what their guidelines were, he was told that there were none. "Quite simply," explained Altvater, "we are not to sign anything, just listen to what the comrade-delegates from the Central Committee are going to discuss with the Germans .... The *actual* delegates, Ioffe and Kamenev, have apparently received some instructions."[44] Even this was beyond the Bolshevik delegation, however. According to Irina Mikhutina, it had "failed to prepare even standard documents for such an occasion," owing to lack of time and qualified personnel.[45]

The prevailing atmosphere of distrust and tension between the Bolshevik delegates and the military experts was quite understandable. The latter were drawn exclusively from the higher officer ranks of the Imperial Russian Army, one of the main bulwarks of the Old Regime (along with the civil service and the clergy), which the professional Bolshevik revolutionaries had worked so hard to subvert with propaganda after the February Revolution. While some of these former Imperial officers – most notably Altvater, who became commander-in-chief of the Soviet Naval Forces in 1918 – would ultimately rally to the Bolshevik cause, they could not so easily be reconciled to their erstwhile Bolshevik adversaries at the time of the Brest-Litovsk armistice negotiations, as Altvater's private conversations with General Hoffmann demonstrated. Many more – like Fokke, who later moved to newly independent Estonia – would end up joining the Whites during the Russian Civil War. The fact that some of these officers, including Altvater, were descendants of noble Baltic German families also made them potentially untrustworthy on the basis of their nationality and social class.

Finally, four "representatives of the revolutionary classes" – a worker, a peasant, a soldier, and a sailor – completed the twenty-eight member strong Russian delegation, which arrived at Brest-Litovsk on the morning of 3 December.[46] Rosenberg diplomatically described the Russians as "in part extremely interesting personalities, partly intimidated and naïve."[47] Less gracefully, the bewildered German general who greeted the delegation at the front enquired *"Ist das auch ein Delegat?"* (is 'this' also a delegate) upon observing Anastasia Bitsenko, a Left Socialist Revolutionary (SR) terrorist who had previously served time in Siberia for the assassination of an Imperial Russian general.[48] It was the first curious encounter of two vastly different worlds.

The opening session of the armistice proceedings took place in the afternoon of 3 December. After a short opening speech in which he welcomed his Russian guests, the commander-in-chief of *Ober Ost*, Prince Leopold of Bavaria, handed the reins over to his chief of staff, General Hoffmann. Ioffe set the tone for the Bolsheviks' subsequent approach with his reply: "We have come here as the representatives of the peoples of Revolutionary Russia, which is filled with a firm resolve to put an end to the general war that shall correspond to the just yearnings of the masses of the democracies of all the belligerent countries."[49] It was an historic moment, which marked the entry of Bolshevism into the sphere of international relations. As John W. Wheeler-Bennett wrote over seven decades ago, "with the opening of the negotiations, there emerged that new and potent factor in world diplomacy, Bolshevik propaganda; propaganda carried on by the party which formed the Government of the Soviet State, but of whose activities that Government professed official ignorance."[50] It was precisely for purposes of propaganda that the Russian delegation insisted on making the proceedings public. The representatives of the Central Powers raised no objections, and the two sides meticulously kept minutes (the Germans and, occasionally, the Austrians, did this on behalf of their allies), which they compared and immediately released to the world press after each session. This unprecedented publicity was a major contributing factor to the international resonance of Brest-Litovsk.

Vague declarations of intent aside, Ioffe initially proposed to discuss a general armistice on all fronts, in an attempt to steer the discussion towards the topic of the general peace he declared to be indispensable to his government. Since the Bolsheviks had already expressed this view in the Decree on Peace, the Central Powers knew what to expect and had prepared accordingly. Hoffmann capitalized on the one major flaw of Ioffe's proposal when he enquired whether the Russian delegation had been authorized by its absent Entente allies to discuss a general armistice on all fronts. Upon receiving a negative answer, he stated that he also did not have such authorization and declared the matter settled until further notice. The general also added that he had licence to discuss only military matters; political issues would have to wait until the peace conference itself. Ioffe had probably expected this rebuttal, as he did not raise any objections. Since it was important for propaganda purposes to convey to the working classes of Europe the Bolsheviks' unwavering commitment to a general peace from the very beginning of the Brest-Litovsk negotiations, Ioffe's opening salvo had served its purpose. The Russians then asked for and received an adjournment in order to go over the technical aspects of their armistice proposal.[51]

A curious incident involving the Bulgarian military representative occurred just before the adjournment, inadvertently giving the Russians a helping hand. Without prior consultation, Colonel Ganchev frivolously suggested that the Central Powers present their draft armistice straight away in order to save time. With the Bolsheviks also in support of the proposal, Hoffmann had no choice but to accept it, albeit with great displeasure. The general managed not to reveal his cards, reading out only the headings of the points the military representatives of the Central Powers wanted to discuss.[52] This incident set the stage for a series of *faux pas* on the part of the Bulgarian delegation over the course of the conference.

According to Fokke, the Russian delegation had to compose an armistice proposal from scratch, no preparations of any kind having been made prior to their arrival. Thanks to Colonel Ganchev's "favor," they were able to use the Austro-German headings, which gave them something to work with. On this occasion, the Bolshevik delegates largely deferred to the expertise of the military experts, as their own was virtually non-existent.[53] During the session of 4 January, Admiral Altvater read out the Russian proposal, whose main points were:

1 The length of the armistice is six months. A seventy-two hour advance notice is required for its cancellation.
2 No troops can be moved from one front to another or to different sections of the same front.
3 The German army and navy shall evacuate the Moonsound islands of Dagö, Ösel, and Moon in the Gulf of Riga.[54]

These were shrewd conditions. A six-month armistice could enable Russia to restore its fighting capabilities, receive military aid from its allies, and re-enter the war in case the peace negotiations with the Central Powers broke down. Evacuation of the Moonsound Islands would remove the German strategic threat to Petrograd, thereby increasing Russia's defensive options. Finally, the prohibition of troop transfers would make a German offensive in the west the following spring unfeasible. The conditions bore the clear mark of the Russian military experts, who reasoned in terms of inter-allied strategic planning and fighting capabilities. Given the overwhelming military superiority enjoyed by the Central Powers on the Eastern Front in the autumn of 1917, however, the terms amounted to wishful thinking more than anything else. The ongoing decay of their armies, partially induced by Bolshevik propaganda, meant that the Russians had no way of compelling the Central Powers to agree to such terms.

The representatives of the Quadruple Alliance were not amused in the least. Hoffmann "bristled [*oshchetinilsia*]" at this proposal, which had the effect of a "physical blow" on the Austrian and Bulgarian colonels.[55] The *Ober Ost* chief of staff declared the conditions "in part quite astonishingly far-reaching in view of the Russian military situation" and insisted they could only be addressed to a conquered country. He proposed an armistice of fourteen days, lengthened on Russian insistence to twenty-eight days, along the present frontlines extending from the Baltic to the Black sea and in the Caucasus. Altvater refused to concede the point about the evacuation of the Moonsound islands, while Ioffe once again suggested working on the text of a general armistice on all fronts. With no compromise in sight and no direct line of communication to Petrograd, on 5 December the Russian delegates secured a seven-day adjournment that would allow them to travel to the capital and consult with higher authority. A temporary, twelve-day ceasefire came into effect.[56] Far from the mere technicality the Germans and Austrians envisaged them to be, the armistice negotiations were developing into something else entirely.

On a lighter note, the behaviour of the "representatives of the revolutionary classes" during the first stage of the armistice negotiations provided considerable amusement for the military representatives on both sides, while embarrassing the Bolshevik delegates. "I shall never forget the first dinner we had with the Russians," wrote Hoffmann. "Opposite me was the workman, who was evidently caused much trouble by the various implements that he found on his table. He tried to seize the food on his plate first with one thing and then with another ...." The bulky peasant Stashkov, who had his own objective of drinking as much as possible at dinnertime, "drew a smile from the orderly who was serving the wine, and had asked him whether he would take claret or hock, when he inquired which was stronger, as he would prefer to have that."[57] Having evidently enjoyed his stay in Brest-Litovsk, Stashkov asked for a "parting drink [*shkalik na proshchanie*]" on the day the Russian delegation was preparing to leave for Petrograd. After quickly draining the bottle of punch his accommodating German hosts had provided him with, Stashkov proved unable to sign the temporary armistice agreement and even refused to leave of his own accord, bellowing: "Home?

I don't want to go home! I'm fine here!" His blushing fellow delegates had to carry the protesting peasant away, as the smirking Germans looked on, making snide remarks ("Is the delegate ill? Oh dear! Perhaps we better call an ambulance."). "And thus, the first formal agreement [of the conference] lacked the signature of the person who was the sole representative of over a hundred million Russian peasants," noted Fokke sarcastically.[58] The amusement of both the German and Russian military delegates at the behaviour of the "representatives of the working classes" was to a large extent a consequence of the constraints of their similar socio-political backgrounds. The frivolous actions of the peasant turned representative were hardly more shocking than those of the professional revolutionaries and terrorists turned diplomats. They were two sides of the same coin – both demonstrated inexorably if somewhat grotesquely that European diplomacy was no longer a gentlemen's sport, the sole preserve of the high aristocracy.

What did the Central Powers' delegates make of their first brief encounter with the Bolsheviks? From a soldier's point of view, Hoffmann was incensed at the Bolshevik distribution of socialist brochures at the front, which called on German soldiers to mutiny and engage in revolutionary activities. The general lodged an official complaint with Karakhan, the secretary of the Russian delegation who had stayed behind in Brest-Litovsk, in which he accused Petrograd of "unloyal actions against [his] government" and "involvement in internal German affairs."[59] If Hoffmann had expected to embarrass the Petrograd government with this stern note, his endeavour failed most miserably, as the Bolshevik leadership did not have the slightest intention of complying. Hoffmann had in fact received repeated warnings from Admiral Altvater about the potency of the preferred Bolshevik weapon of subversion during their private conversations, but he refused to take them seriously. "The influence of Bolshevik propaganda on the masses is enormous," the admiral had emphasized. "I have already often talked with you about it, and complained that at the time I was defending Ösel the troops actually melted away before my eyes. It was the same with the whole army, and I warn you the same will happen in your army."[60] Hoffmann laughed; it proved impossible for a high-ranking Prussian officer to realize that the Bolsheviks considered involvement in other countries' internal affairs a perfectly acceptable means of conducting foreign relations, and that it might affect even the fabled German sense of order and discipline. As suggested earlier, the private conversations between Hoffmann and Altvater were also a clear sign of the serious differences between the Bolshevik delegates and their military experts. At times, it appeared as if there were two separate Russian delegations at the armistice talks, working against each other.

The diplomats' impressions were far more subtle than Hoffmann's. Kajetan Mérey explained to Czernin that there were several reasons for the adjournment of the negotiations – the uncertain internal situation in Russia, the unreliable communications between Brest-Litovsk and Petrograd, the desire to give the Entente another chance to join the negotiations, the possibility of a new international socialist conference in Stockholm, and the news that Ukraine would sign a separate armistice and peace (see chapter 4). His personal opinion, which he believed the German diplomats shared, was that the Russians would return to Brest-Litovsk in a few days and sign the armistice, their prior objections notwithstanding. It was difficult to say whether peace negotiations would follow, although Mérey was fairly certain the Entente would do everything possible to nip them in the bud. While the Russians would be unable to continue fighting, they would pursue their main goal of general peace, not through diplomatic means but by encouraging revolutionary upheavals among the populations of the belligerent states. *Only when their hope in this outcome and these methods has been extinguished will they sign a separate peace with the Central Powers*, he emphasized. In any event, that would be merely the appearance of peace rather than a substantive peace, an agreement filled with catchphrases rather than specific content.[61]

Mérey's evaluation of the Bolsheviks' objectives and preferred means of action was remarkably prescient. He had quickly grasped that the Central Powers were dealing with the proponents of a radically new type of ideologically-driven diplomacy and that the Bolsheviks' views and conduct of international relations could not have been more different from the traditional chancery diplomacy practised by the Central European empires. After having had several conversations with members of the Habsburg delegation, Emperor Karl expressed the opinion that a peace treaty with the Bolsheviks would be *"va banque* play" (i.e., placing everything at stake). If the Central Powers signed the peace, the Bolsheviks would attempt to spread their revolutionary ideas to East Central Europe. In the absence of peace, it would be impossible to contain local socialists. The emperor was convinced the only way out of this conundrum was to make peace with the Bolsheviks while employing every means possible to oppose their revolutionary attempts, including sealing the border. He also realized that state rights

[*Staatsrechte*], with the possible exception of national autonomy and national self-determination, had no meaning for them. "We should of course remain adamant about non-interference in our internal affairs," he advised Czernin.[62]

As Mérey had surmised, back in Petrograd People's Commissar for Foreign Affairs (*Narodnyi komissar inostrannykh del, Narkomindel*) Trotsky decided to use the adjournment to make one last appeal to Russia's allies. On 6 December he sent a telegram to the ambassadors of Britain, France, the United States, Italy, and the other allies, demanding that they "take part in the negotiations for an armistice and peace ... [or] declare clearly and definitively before all mankind the aims for which the peoples of Europe may have to lose their blood during a fourth year of war."[63] With no answer forthcoming, Trotsky summoned Ioffe, Kamenev, Fokke, Altvater, Commander-in-Chief Krylenko, and Major General Vladimir Skalon to his office in Smolny for a debriefing on the day the delegation was scheduled to head back to Brest-Litovsk, 10 December. According to Fokke's memoirs, Ioffe delivered an oddly optimistic report on the course of negotiations, while Altvater emphasized the need to remain firm on the evacuation of the Moonsound Islands. Trotsky concurred but cautioned against undue optimism, warning that the Germans might prove obdurate yet. However, he proffered no new instructions, merely asking Ioffe to take the matter to him should the Germans refuse to sign the armistice. Finally, the *Narkomindel* authorized changes of personnel in the delegation: probably owing to Stashkov's antics, the "representatives of the revolutionary classes" were out, and Major General Skalon was in as a representative of General Headquarters.[64]

The return of the Russian delegation to Brest-Litovsk on 12 December was overshadowed by an unfortunate incident, which once again highlighted the differences between the Bolshevik delegates and their military experts – the suicide of the newly-appointed military adviser, Skalon. The general had momentarily stepped out of the meeting of the Russian military experts discussing the demarcation line along the southern section of the Eastern Front, when Lieutenant Müller, the interpreter, barged in unannounced and shouted that the general had shot himself. The terrified Russians ran to Skalon's room, only to find the general lying on the floor fatally wounded. A suicide note addressed to his wife, which stated cryptically that he "could not live anymore," was left on the table. The Germans adjourned the afternoon session and brought in an Orthodox priest from nearby Białystok for the funeral service (the priest, who was unaware of the revolutionary events in Russia, apparently mistook Admiral Altvater for Emperor Nicholas II). Everyone present was understandably rather shaken but, according to Fokke, Skalon's actions struck a note with several of the Russian military experts: "'I envy him!' Thus spoke some, and nobody could raise any objections. Shattered nerves apart, there was plenty of supporting evidence for a hidden logic behind the suicide. The Great Russian Revolution had destroyed the basis of normal, every-day life [*podrubila korni privychnoi zhizni*] quite mercilessly."[65] For the Russian military experts present in Brest-Litovsk, the general term "revolution" had suddenly acquired a very specific, personal meaning.

Whether the general's tragic demise influenced the rest of the delegates in any appreciable way is impossible to ascertain, but the proceedings on 13 December and 15 December were decidedly low key. The Russians raised some objections about the exact demarcation line in the Baltic Sea, and the typically unrelenting Hoffmann this time agreed to a compromise. The Russians then suddenly dropped their demands for a German evacuation of the Moonsound Islands, which paved the way for an agreement. On the evening of 15 December the representatives of the Central Powers and Russia signed an armistice largely along the lines of General Hoffmann's earlier suggestion. The armistice would come into effect on 17 December and last until 14 January, whereupon it would be automatically renewed unless either side elected to revoke it by submitting a written note seven days in advance. The Central Powers appeared to have won the opening duel, but the Russians had not done too badly either, bearing in mind their poor preparation, absence of clear instructions from Petrograd, lack of cohesion within the delegation, and personnel troubles. They had failed to compel the Germans to evacuate certain territories in the Baltic, but neither had they had to withdraw from the Ottoman districts in Eastern Anatolia and the Caucasus they were occupying. Most of the remaining armistice provisions merely reflected the status quo in the east in December 1917.

War Aims and Diplomatic Methods

The decision to negotiate with the Bolsheviks prompted the clarification of the specific aims of the Central Powers' *Ostpolitik* (eastern policy). While General Hoffmann was conducting armistice negotiations with the Russian representatives during the first two weeks of December, German and Austrian leaders were busy debating these aims.

On 7 December Czernin attended a meeting of the Habsburg Crown Council. He envisioned grave difficulties arising from the expected excessive annexationist demands of the OHL, which he believed the German government would be unable to oppose. Under such circumstances, Austria-Hungary could hope to acquire little if anything. In fact, Czernin was prepared to offer the Russians peace on the basis of the *status quo ante*, stating that failure of the negotiations due to German obstinacy would have grave consequences for the exhausted Dual Monarchy. As a last resort, he would even sign a separate peace. Although the council approved Czernin's policy, the Hungarian prime minister, Sándor Wekerle, warned against endangering the German alliance.[66] In spite of his strong words, Czernin did not wish to break with the Germans either, as he considered a separate peace "suicide for fear of death," which would leave the weakened Habsburg Empire isolated and vulnerable.[67] Instead, he wanted to impress the Germans with the threat of a separate peace, inducing them to curtail their territorial aspirations.

Czernin's gloomy overview of the situation at the council notwithstanding, there is substantial evidence to suggest the foreign minister hoped Austria-Hungary might be able to make some impressive gains at the conference by way of securing the so-called Austro-Polish Solution, which would have seen Congress Poland join Galicia and become an equal partner in a reformed trialist Habsburg Monarchy. However, the specific implementation of the Austro-Polish Solution would have to wait, due to opposition from the German High Command and from Budapest, both on strategic grounds. Although opposed to any significant structural reorganization of the Dual Monarchy for fear of upsetting the fragile German-Magyar equilibrium, the Hungarians were in fact willing to accept the incorporation of Congress Poland into Austria as a crownland rather than as a third sub-imperial entity.[68] Suffering from ill health on the eve of the peace negotiations, Czernin wired Mérey the following list of Austrian conditions, in case the conference started in his absence:

1 Military certainty that the peace will hold.
2 Receipt of foodstuffs from Russia.
3 Possibility to retain the military occupation of Poland before achieving its future accession to the Monarchy. A military cordon covering the present frontline should remain extant in order to allow us to block revolutionary intrusions. The [Austro-German]

condominium in Poland might remain intact for the immediate future.
4 Zero tolerance of any interference in our internal affairs.
5 Insurance that the "limitless ambitions" [*masslosen Begierden*] of the OHL not endanger the peace, to be achieved by way of a subtle implication at the opportune moment. Peace with Russia must come under any circumstances, and all eventualities are possible except the break-up of negotiations due to the Central Powers' actions.
6 Prompt communication of all developments pending instructions via Hughes telegraph.[69]

Czernin's conviction of the need to push through the Austro-Polish Solution against mounting German opposition only grew at the beginning of the conference. On 24 December he wrote to Emperor Karl that Germany would probably make enormous gains in Courland and Lithuania as a result of the expected separate peace with Russia. In this case, it would not be possible for Austria-Hungary to remain empty-handed and to be in the situation of having fought three years so that Germany can profit. "Your Majesty must receive Poland in order to maintain parity," insisted the foreign minister [*E.M. müssen daher Polen erhalten, um paritätisch dazustehen*].[70]

It is quite clear from the above that the Austro-Hungarian foreign minister had formulated both minimum and maximum aims in order to retain a flexible position and be able to navigate successfully the difficult diplomatic situation he expected to encounter in Brest-Litovsk. He believed this would allow him to circumvent the Scylla and Charybdis of German cynical avarice and Bolshevik revolutionary idealism and emerge as a mediator not just in Brest-Litovsk, but at a future general peace conference as well, very much in the proud Habsburg tradition of Prince Metternich at the Congress of Vienna in 1814–1815 and (somewhat less prominently) Count Gyula Andrássy the Elder at the Congress of Berlin in 1878.

Czernin's fears of the "limitless ambitions" of the OHL were not altogether unfounded. At a preliminary meeting held in Berlin on 6–7 December, members of the German government and the OHL agreed to instruct Hoffmann to insist on Russian withdrawal from Livonia and Estonia, as yet unoccupied by German troops.[71] The military's desire to involve itself in the affairs of these two Baltic provinces was not a mere whim. As Olavi Arens has demonstrated, it stemmed in large part from the lobbying of the Baltic German nobles, whose substantial landed estates and traditional privileges were under threat from the revolutionary developments in Russia and from the rise of Estonian and Latvian national movements.[72] During a subsequent conference held at General Headquarters in Kreuznach on 18 December, however, Kühlmann and Hertling advised against extending the German sphere of influence to Livonia and Estonia in order not to jeopardize future long-term relations with Russia. General Chief of Staff Field Marshal Paul von Hindenburg countered by emphasizing the military necessity to secure the eastern border and advocated personal union of the two provinces with Germany.

Kaiser Wilhelm II, in typical fashion when faced with disagreement between the civilian and military leadership, prevaricated, remarking vaguely that Germany ought to assist Russia in directing its justifiable desire to have access to the open sea towards the Persian Gulf, as the Baltic is an inland sea.[73] The Kaiser's vacillations and his inability to resolve disputes whenever they arose meant that German policy-making remained profoundly dysfunctional during the entire period under consideration. Time and again, each participant left the conference table with his own idea of what course of action had been adopted and how best to pursue it.

The issue of Livonia and Estonia remained unresolved, therefore, as did the Polish Question. During previous debates on Germany's war aims in the east, the question of a Polish border strip [*Grenzstreifen*], to be annexed and Germanized with the twin aims of strengthening the defences of Silesia and East Prussia and acquiring living space [*Lebensraum*], had always been high on the agenda.[74] When the size of the border strip came up on this occasion, Kühlmann and Hertling once again urged moderation, citing possible trouble in the Reichstag as well as the opposition of the Prussian Ministry of State to a large influx of Poles. Kaiser Wilhelm II insisted that Germany had the right to secure its borders in Poland (presumably against Austrian demands), as it alone had liberated that country. Once again, a final decision was postponed indefinitely. In contrast, there was no disagreement over the future status of Courland and Lithuania, as Hertling raised no objections to a personal union with Germany, a policy also favoured by his predecessor, Bethmann-Hollweg. The Kaiser dismissed the possibility of separate rulers but acknowledged the necessity of allowing the two duchies substantial internal autonomy and of governing them "with a loose rein [*mit langem Zügel*]," so they could develop their special character

[*Eigenart*]. German leaders, having thus outlined, however vaguely, their territorial policy for the upcoming conference, failed however to specify how it was to be pursued, presumably allowing Kühlmann considerable leeway in his negotiating strategy.[75]

A striking characteristic of the minutes of the December conferences is the repeated use of the phrases "military necessity" (or its equivalent, "on military grounds") and "state/border security." Isabel Hull has argued persuasively that the former was a byword for a German operational military culture, a set of "habitual practices, default programs, hidden assumptions, and unreflected cognitive frames," which relied on exponentially increasing levels of violence in the pursuit of total military victory.[76] This is an important observation, as Hindenburg and Ludendorff in fact employed the phrase with the same implication of escalating the war on a number of different occasions, from forced labour to unrestricted submarine warfare.

The generals' use of the term "security" also revolved around purely military considerations and differed markedly from Kühlmann's usage, which took into account multiple factors including economic and trade relations with Germany's neighbours and the other Great Powers.[77] This more flexible concept of security necessitated making limited negotiated gains while simultaneously re-establishing cordial relations with Russia, a priority which the state secretary emphasized on a number of occasions. Unlike the generals, trapped in their military culture, Kühlmann did not believe in a total victory on all fronts.[78] In his mind, certain gains in the east would offset the sacrifices Germany would have to make in the west in order to secure peace there.[79]

Imperialist designs *per se* were not necessarily engendered by military culture, however. The prevailing consensus among the German leadership was that Germany had gone to war in 1914, at least in part, in order to break away from the unfavourable strategic position to which the Triple Entente's *Einkreisung* (encirclement) had supposedly subjected it. A return to the *status quo ante* meant a return to (relative) isolation and to an increasing disparity of forces, as Russia recovered from the defeats of the Russo-Japanese War of 1904–05 and completed the reorganization of its military, an act which had so frightened German strategists in the years leading up to 1914. These considerations provide a classic example of what one scholar has recently termed the "'tension of empire,' [meaning] the aspiration to imperialist expansion and the simultaneous fear of dissolution at the hands of its imperialist rivals."[80] The term "imperialist expansion" need not necessarily involve the violent conquest of certain territories. In the case of Germany, it is best associated with pre-war *Weltpolitik*, an incoherent, vague concept which meant different things to different people (Kühlmann himself had written a pamphlet on the subject, *Deutsche Weltpolitik und kein Krieg*, in 1913) and which aimed to secure Germany's allegedly rightful "place in the sun." While the Pan-Germans envisioned outright annexations both in the west and in the east in the pursuit of a continental empire, their views never received official government sanction.[81]

It was with these considerations in mind, out of a sense of weakness rather than strength, that Ludendorff subsequently insisted: "If Germany makes peace without profit, then Germany has lost the war."[82] Furthermore, the first quartermaster-general was never entirely clear on what this "profit" should amount to. He did not suggest annexing substantial territories on the model of the Polish Partitions of the late eighteenth century, nor did he disagree with the Kaiser's insistence that Courland and Lithuania enjoy internal autonomy under a personal union with Prussia/Germany. Given that most peoples in the area were not "historic nations" in the sense that they had never had their own states (with the notable exception of the Poles), the belief that they ought to be associated with a Great Power *by default* was widely shared and not viewed as entirely unreasonable. Administrative divisions in much of the Baltic littoral ran along the long-outdated borders of historic principalities which in no way reflected nationality. These nations, therefore, did not possess the ready-made organs of state – clearly defined state borders, a national diet, law code, civil service, army, and currency – which smoothed Finland's path to independence.[83] As one scholar reminds us, "no observer of pre-war politics anticipated that Estonia would be independent by 1920 ...."[84]

The period of structural transformation away from Imperial dynasticism in Eastern Europe, precipitated by the Russian Revolutions of 1917, seemed to offer a way out of encirclement. It is impossible to say whether German leaders would have been willing to return some of the occupied territories to an extant Imperial Russian establishment in exchange for a separate peace and a future alliance. Given the uncertainty of the situation in the east and the partial collapse of the seemingly impregnable Imperial-dynastic framework, they endeavoured to tie the border states to the Central Powers in some form or fashion at least temporarily in order to utilize their resources for the ongoing war effort elsewhere rather than risk their falling within the sphere of the revolutionary radicals in Petrograd. Indeed, these radicals had no genuine desire for a moderate peace either, as would soon become abundantly clear.

Conversely, Ottoman war aims were much more restrained and practical. On 13 December an Extraordinary Ministerial Council in Constantinople discussed Ottoman policy at Brest-Litovsk. Items on the agenda included Russian evacuation of Ottoman territory in Eastern Anatolia and regulation of sailing in the Black Sea. Grand Vizier Talaat Pasha told the Austro-Hungarian ambassador, Margrave Pallavicini, that the main concern of the Quadruple Alliance must be to reach an agreement with Russia as soon as possible and assured him that the Ottomans would make no difficulties.[85] The final terms authorized by the council were Russian evacuation of occupied Ottoman provinces and abolition of the much-hated capitulations system, which the Great Powers had used to interfere in the empire's domestic affairs and effectively undermine its sovereignty. If the Russians brought up the question of the regulation of the Black Sea straits, which had played such a prominent role in international diplomacy in the decades leading up to the Great War, the Ottoman delegates could consult with their allies, but otherwise they would not broach the subject.[86] The Sublime Porte would also have liked to recover the Caucasian provinces of Kars, Ardahan, and Batum, which it had lost to the Russians as a result of the 1877–78 war. According to Michael Reynolds, however, this was only "an outside hope," as the Ottomans were well aware of their weak bargaining position as the only member of the Quadruple Alliance whose territories were under foreign occupation.[87]

The Central Powers were not alone in trying to exploit the partial structural collapse in East Central Europe. So, too, did the Bolsheviks, who intended to use the upcoming peace conference as a platform from which to spread their revolutionary ideas, thereby replacing the Imperial framework with one of permanent revolution. According to this theory, first developed by Leon Trotsky in 1905, "the socialist revolution begins on the national arena, it unfolds on the international arena, and is completed on the world arena."[88] The Bolshevik Party, as a "party of the new type" – a concept Lenin formulated in his programmatic 1902 pamphlet *What Is to Be Done?* – was supposed to play a special role in this process. Unlike traditional political parties, including the large German and Austrian social-democratic parties, which strove to represent faithfully the wishes of their constituents and pursued incremental change through democratic parliamentary process, the Bolshevik Party was a small, self-appointed, ideological elite of professional revolutionaries that sought to lead the masses by example, becoming in effect the "vanguard of the proletariat."[89]

In theory, at least, this did not entail dictatorial methods, due to the special dialectic relationship between the Party and the workers. Thanks in part to the social welfare measures of the Bismarckian type many European governments had undertaken in the three decades leading up to the Great War, the working class had developed a false, "trade union consciousness," which limited its activity to petty economic demands about work conditions and pay. However, as the proletariat remained the only objectively revolutionary class that embodied historical progress, the Party emerged as the material manifestation of its latent revolutionary potential. Under the astute leadership of the Party, the masses would be able to discard their false consciousness and realize their dormant revolutionary potential. The collusion (or synthesis, in Hegelian dialectical terms) of Party and proletariat would thus result in revolution. As Trotsky described this phenomenon:

> Marxism considers itself the conscious expression of the unconscious historical process. But the "unconscious" process, in the historico-philosophical sense of the term – not in the psychological, – coincides with its conscious expression only at its highest point, when the masses, by sheer elemental pressure, break through the social routine and give victorious expression to the deepest needs of historical development. And at such moments the highest theoretical consciousness of the epoch [i.e. the Party] merges with the immediate action of those oppressed masses who are farthest away from theory. *The creative union of the conscious with the unconscious is what one usually calls "inspiration." Revolution is the inspired frenzy of history.*[90]

This dialectic relationship was expressed at its simplest in Trotsky's famous remark upon assumption of the post of *Narkomindel*: "What diplomatic work are we apt to have? I will issue a few revolutionary proclamations to the peoples of the world, and then shut up shop."[91] In effect, the Bolsheviks would make a revolutionary call to the proletariat of East Central Europe, awakening them from their bourgeois-induced slumber. The reinvigorated workers would then take matters in their own hands and start a revolution, which in turn would limit the role of the Bolshevik Party to directing and channelling their endeavours. The successful Petrograd coup of 7 November appeared to Bolshevik leaders to be undeniable proof (not that any was needed) of the correctness of this theory on the national arena. Brest-Litovsk would provide the stage for its extension to the international arena. While there were differences between Trotsky and Lenin on the tactics to be employed in Brest-Litovsk, both agreed on the necessity to foster world revolution.[92] Contrary to the claims of Soviet historians, the subsequently exiled Trotsky was correct in maintaining that during this early period "the theory of Permanent Revolution, in contradiction to the theory of Socialism in one country, was recognized by the entire Bolshevik party."[93]

The Bolsheviks made no secret of the fact that they aimed at no less than a wholesale structural transformation of international relations. Their openly provocative diplomacy was in stark contrast to the deferential restraint the Austro-German cabinet diplomats practised. During his first conversation with Czernin, Ioffe told the astonished Austro-Hungarian foreign minister: "I hope we may yet be able to raise the revolution in your country too."[94] Czernin was appalled at what he described as the Russian delegate's "utopian revolutionary position," which made compromise based on a rational *quid pro quo* an extremely remote possibility.[95] Nor was this empty banter. When news of the ongoing strikes in Austria-Hungary (see chapter 3) reached him in late January 1918, Ioffe impertinently asked Count Csáky to solicit Czernin's permission to travel to Vienna in order to meet with the workers.[96] Upon receiving a polite but firm refusal, he proceeded to add insult to injury by accusing the Austro-Hungarian foreign minister of "refusing to allow direct negotiations between the representatives of the Workers' and Peasants' Government of Russia and the Austrian proletariat." His government had expressly authorized him to pursue such negotiations, Ioffe added, lest there be the slightest shadow of a doubt over the legitimacy of his humble request.[97] The delegates of the Central Powers were understandably irked at such repeated provocations and unprecedented meddling in their countries' internal affairs.

In addition to the ultimate goal of world revolution, the Bolshevik delegation had a set of more specific aims, which Lenin penned on 10 December. Russia would accept only a peace based on the principles of no annexations and indemnities, and the recognition of the right of self-determination, extended to nations which had not enjoyed that right up to this point (i.e., European colonies in Asia and Africa). Furthermore, Lenin expanded the meaning of the term annexations to include "any territory ... whose population, *over the last few decades* ... has expressed dissatisfaction with the integration of their [sic] territory into another state ..."[98] This program was much more far-reaching than anything the Central Powers hoped to achieve, as its full realization would have entailed the wholesale elimination of the Imperial paradigm of international relations. It was also predicated on the spread of the revolution westwards, which would either replace the bourgeois imperialist governments of Central and Western Europe with proletarian ones or weaken them substantially to force their acquiescence, as Soviet Russia lacked the vast military and economic power necessary to induce such a global transformation.

Conclusion

The Central Powers spent much of the war trying to split the enemy coalition and sign a separate peace with one of its principal members, preferably Russia. However, after the Bolshevik coup of 7 November 1917, Petrograd rather than Berlin or Vienna was in the driver's seat. Brimming with confidence and utterly convinced they were on the right side of history, the Bolsheviks released a sweeping Decree on Peace demanding an end to hostilities in all theatres of war and, as the Central Powers bickered and wondered how to respond to this overture, initiated armistice talks on the Eastern Front. Two vastly different worlds met at the negotiating table in Brest-Litovsk in early December 1917, as revolutionary tactics crossed swords with Imperial cabinet diplomacy for the first time. Making their debut on the international stage, the Bolsheviks pursued the utopian goal of world proletarian revolution by means of propaganda and consequently attempted to transform the purely military armistice talks into a wide-ranging public political debate. In contrast, the Central Powers sought to avoid any political commitments at this early stage and focused on eliminating their Eastern and Caucasian Fronts in preparation for a final offensive in the west. They also formulated an *Ostpolitik* that pursued negotiated territorial gains in the multi-ethnic western borderlands of the former Russian Empire, which they had occupied in 1915. In light of these mutually exclusive goals, the armistice negotiations provided a glimpse into the clash of mutually exclusive *Weltanschauungen* (world views) and ideological imperatives that would come to dominate the peace conference and affect the complicated dynamics on the ground in East Central Europe in the following months.

Chapter Two

Peacemaking and Self-Determination at Brest-Litovsk

Brest-Litovsk appeared to be a particularly inauspicious venue for a peace conference in the winter of 1917–18. In the summer of 1915, retreating Russian troops had elected to deport the entire urban population, the usual western borderlands mixture of Poles, Jews, Germans, and Russian administrators, and burn to the ground this strategic military fortress and key railway hub on the Bug River rather than let it fall intact into the hands of the enemy. By the time the Germans arrived, the town as such had ceased to exist. Having nonetheless chosen Brest-Litovsk as its headquarters, the *Ober Ost* staff moved into the austere but adequate Russian officers' barracks and garrison lodgings, located half an hour's drive from the remains of the town.[1] "This is a curious place – melancholy, yet with a beauty of its own," Czernin mused in his diary after a long, solitary walk in late December. "An endless flat, with just a slight swelling of the ground, like an ocean set fast, wave behind wave as far as the eye can see. And all things grey, dead grey, to where this dead sea meets the grey horizon. Clouds race across the sky, the wind lashing them on."[2]

This was the bleak setting the delegations encountered upon their arrival in mid-December 1917. Czernin had recovered sufficiently from a sudden illness to lead the Habsburg delegation. Even though he was aware of Trotsky's decision not to come to Brest-Litovsk straight

---

This chapter is derived in part from an article published in *Diplomacy & Statecraft* on 07 Sep 2011, available online: http://dx.doi.org/10.1080/09592296.2011.599635'; and in part from an article published in *The International History Review* on 21 Aug 2013, available online: http://dx.doi.org/10.1080/07075332.2013.817465.

away and leave Ioffe in charge of the Russian delegation, the Austro-Hungarian foreign minister was adamant that he and Kühlmann ought to attend the conference from the very beginning. Czernin expected the negotiations to be prolonged, in which case personal contact between the two leading diplomats of the Central Powers would expedite their common work considerably.[3] In addition, he hoped to use his close working relationship with Kühlmann as a restraining influence on the OHL. For his part, Kühlmann was equally interested in cooperating closely with his Austrian colleague. "I endeavored with Count Czernin, who was perhaps the best Austro-Hungarian foreign minister, to establish personally a relationship of confidence [*Vertrauensverhältnis*], which would permit the smooth conduct of our common work," he wrote in his memoirs.[4] Ambassador Rosenberg and General Hoffmann were also present, the latter as a representative of the OHL. Ahmed Nessimy Bey, the foreign minister, was the chairman of the Ottoman delegation, and Hristo Popov, the minister of justice, led the Bulgarian delegation. In Trotsky's absence, Ioffe remained the leading Russian delegate.

Even though the first two phases of the Brest-Litovsk Peace Conference in December 1917–January 1918 marked the debut of the concept of self-determination in international relations, the effects of the Brest-Litovsk proceedings on the discourse of self-determination have been left virtually unexplored by historians, with the notable exception of Arno J. Mayer. Basing his analysis on the earlier writings of Alfred Cobban, Mayer highlighted the role Brest-Litovsk played in the emergence of the New Diplomacy during the last phase of the Great War. He argued that "[i]t was through Bolshevik insistence at Brest-Litovsk that self-determination became a 'dominant interest' for the diplomacy of the war."[5] Even Mayer, however, focused primarily on the Ioffe Program and the reactions it engendered amongst the Entente powers. He paid little attention to the subsequent course of discussions on the subject and altogether ignored the stance of the Central Powers. But the Bolsheviks were not alone in the half-burnt remains of the former Imperial Russian fortress on the River Bug, and a fuller understanding of the importance of Brest-Litovsk on the issue necessitates re-evaluation of these debates.

During the first phase of the peace conference, the two sides attempted to square their opposing views on the concept of self-determination – described by Erez Manela as "the center of the discourse of legitimacy in international relations [in the twentieth century]"[6] – in the (largely hypothetical) context of a general peace conference, one in which the

Western Entente Powers would eventually participate as well. The Bolshevik position, outlined in the Ioffe Program of 22 December, reiterated the main tenets of the Decree on Peace from early November, which posited a general peace without annexations or indemnities, with state borders defined according to the free will of all populations concerned. The Central Power's position, expressed in Czernin's Christmas Speech of 25 December, proposed to agree guardedly with Bolshevik conditions in the case of a general peace being achieved but also raised important qualifications on the application of self-determination, stressing continuity with existing constitutional and state frameworks. Early debates about such application exposed the differing perspectives of Germany and Austria-Hungary, as Czernin briefly threatened to conclude a separate peace with Russia if the Germans proved unwilling to compromise.

Although it subsequently became a celebrated and prominent concept in international relations, self-determination in its specific historical origins has been the subject of remarkably few studies. Historians of American foreign relations typically examine it through the prism of Wilsonianism, identifying self-determination as one of the three or four central aspects of the president's New Diplomacy and the new theory of international relations, known as liberal internationalism, which he helped to develop.[7] Studies of the early application of the concept thus tend to examine it in the context of Wilson's foreign policy, especially as conducted during the last stage of the Great War (spring 1917 – autumn 1918) and in the crucial opening six months of the Paris Peace Conference (January 1919 – June 1919).[8] Only very recently has there been an attempt to disassociate the concept of self-determination from Wilson's vision of a liberal international order.[9] The emphasis on Woodrow Wilson as the oracle of self-determination and on the Paris Peace Conference as centre stage for the prophet's grand entry obscures the specific historical circumstances at the end of the Great War which conditioned the rise of self-determination and propelled it from relative obscurity to paramount importance in international relations.

This chapter suggests that self-determination became the "center of the discourse of legitimacy in international relations" as a result of a *dynamic process* involving multiple actors. This process might have culminated in a "Wilsonian moment" contributing to the international origins of anti-colonial nationalism from Cairo to Seoul, as Manela demonstrates, but it did not begin there or with Woodrow Wilson. It was Lenin rather than Wilson who first picked up the banner of self-determination in the middle phase of the Great War, operationalized it, and elevated it to the level of official state policy after the successful Bolshevik seizure of power. Self-determination discourse gained further momentum at Brest-Litovsk, as both Bolshevik Russia and the Central Powers appeared to agree, for their own reasons, to abide by this principle. Debates on the nature and application of the increasingly important concept of self-determination came to utterly dominate the second phase of the conference in January 1918, as the newly-arrived Trotsky engaged Kühlmann in long-winded, theoretical deliberations on the subject in order to delay the proceedings and expose the allegedly duplicitous nature of the Hohenzollern and Habsburg governments. Albeit ultimately fruitless, these debates on the nature and application of self-determination marked the first attempt to define what would ultimately become one of the leading concepts of international relations in the twentieth century.

The Origins of Self-Determination

Self-determination was originally a concept used by Enlightenment thinkers such as Immanuel Kant in reference to individual rather than collective rights. German socialists, including Karl Marx and Moses Hess, later wrote about "freedom as a process of individual *Selbstbestimmung*."[10] The modern usage of the term dates back to the middle stage of the First World War, specifically to three articles by Lenin. The first one, entitled "The Revolutionary Proletariat and the Right of Nations to Self-Determination," written in German probably in late October–early November 1915, was intended as a response to two articles by Polish socialist Karl Radek (alias Parabellum) published in the *Berner Tagwacht*. In it, Lenin insisted that "we must *link* the revolutionary struggle for socialism with a revolutionary program on the national question," thereby establishing a conceptual connection between proletarian revolution and national self-determination to which he would return repeatedly in the coming years.[11]

The second article, "The Socialist Revolution and the Right of Nations to Self-Determination," published in April 1916, outlined the revolutionary program in greater detail. In opposition to Austro-Marxists, who had clamoured for greater cultural autonomy for the nations of the Danubian basin within the borders of a democratized Greater Austria, Lenin defined self-determination as *"exclusively* the right to independence in the *political sense*, the right to free political secession from the oppressor nation. Specifically, this demand for political democracy implies complete freedom to agitate for secession and for a *referendum* on secession by the seceding nation."[12] This was the ideological origin of the Bolshevik insistence at Brest-Litovsk on referenda for the occupied Russian western borderlands.

Although opposed to nationalism in principle, Lenin tried to reconcile the Marxist dismissal of the phenomenon as a transient, insignificant state of historical development and a bourgeois sham with the prevailing realities of the Great War. Far from corroborating the Marxist assertion that the working man has no country, the outbreak of hostilities in August 1914 had created a social truce in all belligerent countries. Until all peoples could achieve liberation by means of national self-determination, Lenin argued, proletarian internationalism would remain a meaningless phrase owing to the double oppression of the subject/colonial peoples' working class by their own bourgeoisie as well as by that of the dominant nation. Only complete national liberation could pave the way for the elimination of national antagonisms between the different proletariats and the subsequent disappearance of nationalism.[13]

Lenin further outlined three groups of countries to illustrate the principle of self-determination of nations – the advanced capitalist countries of Western Europe and North America where self-determination had been fully realized, the developing Eastern European countries and multi-national empires (Austria-Hungary, Russia, the Balkans) where the right to self-determination needed to be championed, and lastly, the semi-colonial (Persia, China, the Ottoman Empire) and colonial countries (in Africa and Asia) whose revolutionary classes needed to pursue self-determination even in temporary alliance with the bourgeoisie.[14]

Finally, in the July 1916 polemic against Polish Social Democrats titled "The Discussion on Self-Determination Summed Up," Lenin outlined the relationship between self-determination and annexation by defining the latter as *"violation of the self-determination of a nation, it is the establishment of state frontiers contrary to the will of the population."*[15] He also further clarified his views on the application of self-determination in the Russian Empire by drawing a distinction between the more developed, European nations of the western borderlands (specifically Poles, Finns, and Ukrainians) and the less developed, "colonial" peoples of Turkestan, largely based on the fact that under imperialism the former had much greater access to finance capital than the latter.[16] Foreshadowing Trotsky's line of argument in January 1918, when the leader of the Russian delegation at Brest-Litovsk dismissed the proclamations of autonomous association with Germany issued by the "undemocratic" land assemblies of German-occupied Courland and Lithuania as incompatible with genuine self-determination, Lenin maintained that under imperialism "an 'autonomous' nation does not enjoy rights equal to those of the 'ruling' nation."[17] The opposite would be true under socialism, where the liberated nations would strive for free amalgamation. The Bolshevik leader was thus able to operationalize the concept of self-determination in its modern meaning and provide the ideological foundation for the Bolshevik stance on self-determination at Brest-Litovsk during the January 1918 debates.

Self-determination discourse received a further boost by the February Revolution in Russia. While affirming the country's adherence to the cause of the Entente, the Provisional Government issued a statement outlining the main aspects of revolutionary diplomacy on 9 April 1917. This statement sought to distance the foreign policy of the revolutionary government from the imperialist policy of the deposed Romanov dynasty and enunciate morally just war aims.

> [T]he purpose of free Russia [is] not domination over foreign peoples, nor spoliation of their national possessions, nor the violent occupation of foreign territories, but the establishment of a *permanent peace on the basis of the self-determination of peoples*. The Russian people [are] not aiming to increase their power abroad at the expense of other people, they [have] no aim to enslave or oppress anybody.[18]

The manifesto of the Provisional Government generated renewed diplomatic activity between the two belligerent camps regarding the related issues of war aims and a negotiated peace. However, the inconclusiveness of these exchanges showed the unwillingness of crucial members of the rival alliances to contemplate a separate peace or compromise on the war aims they thought might still be achievable through decisive military victory.[19] The failure of the peace by negotiation in 1917 notwithstanding, the impetus provided by the manifesto of the February Revolution ensured that self-determination, albeit still a decidedly vague principle, was increasingly becoming a central aspect of war diplomacy by the early months of 1918. Admittedly, by this point, the October Revolution had introduced a radically new factor into the diplomatic arena. The Bolsheviks, as already noted, made the worldwide extension of self-determination a central tenet of their diplomacy and of Russia's war aims, as expressed in the Decree on Peace. They would reiterate their alleged commitment to this cause immediately after the official opening of the Brest-Litovsk Peace Conference in late December 1917.

The First Phase of Negotiations: 22 December – 28 December 1917

The peace conference officially opened on the afternoon of 22 December with a welcoming speech by Prince Leopold of Bavaria. Following the customary pleasantries expressed by Prince Ibrahim Hakki Pasha, whose title made him the most senior representative, and by Kühlmann, who was presiding, Ioffe suggested that the two sides continue the procedure, already tested successfully during the armistice talks, of releasing the session minutes to the world press. While everyone else agreed, the elderly Hakki Pasha, perhaps the most obvious proponent of traditional cabinet diplomacy, objected on the grounds that daily press releases might engender newspaper polemics and raise obstacles to the smooth conduct of work at the conference. Fearing that Ioffe might try to entangle the Ottoman delegate in his clever propagandist web of deception, Kühlmann felt compelled to intervene and suggest that Hakki Pasha was not opposed to publicity *per se* but rather favoured a few days' delay between each session and the respective press report. Ioffe pointed out that the issue of publicity was of paramount importance to the Russian delegation but conceded that such a delay was in fact unavoidable, as a special joint committee had to compare and adjust accordingly the German- and Russian-language reports before they could be released.[20] On a different day, he may have chosen to go on the offensive and hurl accusations of duplicity at the Ottoman delegation (and, by extension, its allies), but he was apparently eager to proceed with a speech outlining Russian peace conditions. This speech, which has commonly become known as the Ioffe Program, naturally bore a close resemblance to the draft Lenin had outlined earlier in December; it articulated the following six points:

1 Annexation of territories conquered during the war will not be tolerated. These territories ought to be evacuated without delay.
2 The political independence of peoples taken away over the course of the war should be restored.
3 Nationalities which did not enjoy political independence before the war should be accorded this right, by "deciding freely ... whether

they should belong to one State or another, or shall enjoy national independence by means of a referendum." Refugees should be allowed to vote in these referenda.
4 Minority rights should be extended to multi-ethnic territories, "with special rights of national independence regarding culture and administrative autonomy."
5 There will be no indemnities of any kind. War loans between allies will be repaid. Indemnities on private persons (i.e., expropriations of enemy alien property) will be settled by a special international commission and a joint fund.
6 Colonial matters will be settled in accordance with points one through four.

In addition to these main points, Ioffe declared that Russia was opposed to economic blockades, unequal commercial treaties, and special customs unions.[21] In essence, points one through four substantiated the concept of "no annexations" from the Decree on Peace, while point six provided for its application outside Europe. Point five elaborated the concept of "no indemnities," and the supplementary conditions called for an end to economic warfare and special economic spheres (such as closed colonial systems), and the extension of free trade to the entire world. The insistence on national self-determination and minority rights, a hallmark of Wilsonianism at the subsequent Paris Peace Conference, largely informed the January debates between Kühlmann and Trotsky, which would come to dominate the peace conference. The other two issues, while less prominent, also affected the subsequent course of negotiations. Lastly, Ioffe's proposal envisaged a general peace, not a separate arrangement between the Central Powers and Russia.

If we look at the Ioffe Program in isolation, it does not appear to be much different from Woodrow Wilson's famous Fourteen Points program, which the American president enunciated a few weeks later, after the British prime minister, David Lloyd George, had also given a speech that was in effect a response to events in Brest-Litovsk, promoting a peace settlement "based on the right to self-determination or the consent of the governed."[22] Both Wilson's Fourteen Points and the Ioffe Program espoused an ideological commitment to vague, general principles such as national autonomy and self-determination, economic freedom, and a new, open diplomacy, while also emphasizing the transformative effect of moral suasion. Both demonstrated a complete disinterest in details, especially the small matter of practical implementation.

The world views behind this allegedly common ideological commitment, however, could not be more dissimilar. Wilson approached matters from the relatively benign perspective of American liberal internationalism, an approach to international relations based on progressive history and social science rooted in the American experience, which emphasized cooperation. Admittedly, the president's foreign policy was often contradictory, combining idealism with practicality – especially when it came to American interests in the Western Hemisphere. Nevertheless, Wilson genuinely pursued the realization of the principle of collective security, even when it "failed to provide adequate guidance for a postwar settlement," as Lloyd E. Ambrosius has argued.[23]

In contrast, the Bolsheviks saw the world in black and white colours through Marxist eyes, espousing the ruthless suppression of the ruling classes by the proletariat at home and abroad as a prelude to permanent revolution. "Lenin, Trotsky, and the other Bolshevik leaders shared the belief that the fate of the revolution in Russia depended on its spread to the remainder of Europe," elaborates Richard K. Debo. "The war of nation against nation would have to be converted into an international struggle of class against class if the revolution was to survive."[24] At its most basic level, therefore, the Ioffe Program could not really be reconciled with the overriding Bolshevik commitment to world revolution. The diplomats of the Central Powers quickly picked up on this discrepancy. "They are strange creatures, these Bolsheviks," mused Czernin in his diary. "They talk of freedom and reconciliation of the peoples of the world, of peace and unity, and withal they are said to be the most cruel tyrants history has ever known. They are simply exterminating the bourgeoisie, and their arguments are machine guns and the gallows."[25] In the minds of Bolshevik leaders, Marxist-Leninist dialectics could actually reconcile the widespread use of violence in the pursuit of paradise on earth in an ends-justify-the-means scenario. Advocacy of national self-determination played a similar role in that political liberation of nations oppressed under imperialism would ultimately lead to voluntary association under socialism, as Lenin had maintained earlier in "The Discussion on Self-Determination Summed Up." The Austro-Hungarian foreign minister, on the other hand, could not bridge the gap; hence, he concluded that the Bolsheviks were dishonest, and that they could not be trusted.

For the time being, however, the diplomats of the Central Powers refused to become embroiled in a wide-ranging political debate on the implications of the Ioffe Program. They had expected a similar pronouncement, and they asked for and received an adjournment of the afternoon session of 22 December, promising to present the Russians with a detailed response as soon as possible. Czernin and Kühlmann, who generally saw eye to eye on most matters, quickly agreed to play along in an attempt to embarrass Russia's allies and drafted a reply accordingly on 23 December. However, they ran into unexpected trouble from their own allies. The Ottomans insisted that Russian troops evacuate the occupied territories in Eastern Anatolia immediately upon the conclusion of peace. This ran counter to Austro-German plans to retain a military presence in Congress Poland, Courland, and Lithuania, as the Central Powers could not demand with a straight face the unilateral withdrawal of Russian troops while their own remained deep in pre-1914 Russian territory. Such a position would destroy any possibility, however remote, of conciliation; this was something Czernin and Kühlmann could not accept. Ottoman delegates eventually relented, but they did so only "after a hard struggle and repeated efforts." They then objected that Russia had not committed to non-interference in the Central Powers' internal affairs. This time, the usually diplomatic Czernin employed a different tactic – he bluntly told the Ottoman foreign minister, Nessimy Bey, that Austria-Hungary's internal situation was far more precarious than that of the Ottoman Empire. "If I had no hesitation in accepting, he also could be content," concluded Czernin. This brutal logic finally convinced Nessimy Bey.[26] With the Ottomans seemingly satisfied, at least in part, it was time for the Bulgarians to make trouble. The minister of justice, Popov, insisted that Bulgaria be exempted from the "no annexations" clause, as it intended to annex substantial parts of Serbia, Romania, and Greece. After long and heated conversations, which took up most of 24 December, and furious telegram exchanges between Brest-Litovsk and Sofia, the Bulgarians finally acquiesced (see chapter five), thus paving the way for the Central Powers to proceed with their reply to the Russian proposal with at least the semblance of a united front.

With inter-allied wrangling subsiding, albeit temporarily, Prince Leopold invited the delegates to join his staff in a humble Christmas Eve celebration. A decorated Christmas tree, small presents, and the singing of traditional Christmas carols, in which Prince Leopold, General Hoffmann, and Kühlmann merrily participated ("Silent Night,

Holy Night" proved a particular favourite), enhanced the yuletide spirit that briefly animated the dry, official negotiations. The Russians, who for the time being continued to take their meals together with the other delegates, surprisingly contributed to the festivities by bringing in a barrel of caviar – sent from Petrograd specifically for this purpose – a rare delicacy amidst the scarcity of wartime. Russian military expert Fokke, who described the evening in colourful detail in his memoirs, is silent on whether the officially atheist Bolshevik representatives took active part in the celebration of this most emblematic of Christian holidays; presumably, they did not, as the colonel never missed an opportunity for a snide remark aimed at the "comrade-delegates." For his part, Fokke noted approvingly the sense of "patriarchal tradition and spiritual exhortation," as well as his adversaries' sincere adherence to the "traditions of Old Germany," something the Russian Revolution had destroyed.[27]

As negotiations resumed late in the afternoon on 25 December, Christmas Day, Czernin delivered the speech he and Kühlmann had been working on. The representatives of the Central Powers considered the main lines of the Russian proposal suitable for the conclusion of a *general* and just peace, the Austro-Hungarian foreign minister began, thereby emphasizing that acceptance was conditional on the future actions of Russia's allies. The Entente would have to come out unequivocally in support of the Ioffe Program, "for it would not do for the Powers of the Quadruple Alliance ... one-sidedly to tie themselves to these conditions without a guarantee that Russia's Allies will recognize and will carry out these conditions honestly and without reserve also as regards the Quadruple Alliance."[28] With respect to the six main points of the Russian proposal, Czernin gave the following stipulations:

1 The Central Powers do not intend to annex forcibly occupied territories. Occupying troops should be withdrawn.
2 The Central Powers do not intend to deprive of political independence any nations that have lost said independence during the war.
3 The state allegiance of national groups that do not have a state should be settled in a constitutional manner by these national groups alone.
4 "[P]rotection of the rights of national minorities forms an essential component part of the constitutional right of peoples to self-determination." The Central Powers believe it should be applicable wherever practically possible.

5 The Central Powers are in favour of renouncing all indemnities, with the exception of reimbursement for Prisoner of War (POW) costs and enemy alien expropriations.
6 As the only member of the alliance with overseas colonies, Germany believes that the Entente should evacuate captured colonies. The Russian proposal to hold referenda is impractical and unnecessary, as the natives' adherence to the German cause should be ample proof of their desire to remain "with their German friends."

Lastly, the Central Powers agreed unconditionally with the Russian principle of economic freedom, which was hardly surprising given the damage the stifling British blockade was inflicting on the economies of the Central European empires.[29]

While largely in agreement with the Russian proposal, Czernin's speech differed in its interpretation of points three and five in subtle yet extremely important ways. The formulation of point three would render direct German-Russian discussions over the status of the occupied western borderlands obsolete, while simultaneously allowing the existing constitutional organs of Congress Poland (Polish Regency), Courland, and Lithuania (provincial assemblies), conveniently established under Austro-German military occupation, to express their desire for economic and/or political adherence to the Central Powers. Similarly, the seemingly innocuous insistence on reimbursement for POW costs in point six (living expenses and lodgings) took on much greater significance when the huge disparity in the numbers of POWs the two sides had captured (four million by Germany and Austria-Hungary versus just over two million by Russia) came into consideration. Not being privy to diplomatic subtlety, however, Ioffe simply noted these provisos as reservations and declared Czernin's reply to be on the whole satisfactory. He further proposed a ten days' adjournment, which would allow the Entente countries to join the peace conference, but made no objection to the suggestion that Russia and the Central Powers discuss matters pertaining to their specific relations in the meantime.[30]

Things appeared to be moving along smoothly, if somewhat slowly, on the main stage after the first two plenary sessions. "There is no hurry apparently in this place," complained Czernin in his diary on 26 December. "Now it is the Turks who are not ready, now the Bulgarians, then it is the Russians' turn – and the sitting is again postponed or broken off almost as soon as commenced." To pass the time, the foreign minister read memoirs from the French Revolution, "[a] most appropriate reading at the present time, in view of what is happening in Russia and may perhaps come throughout Europe."³¹ He also wrote to the Foreign Ministry to instruct the press to imply that Austria-Hungary had been the first country to bring up the formula of "no annexations and indemnities," which stood at the heart of the present negotiations, nearly a year ago. Czernin also wished to remind the readers of the difficulties he had encountered with the German government when he had first adopted the formula.³² In view of the ostensibly favourable course of negotiations, this press campaign would draw a subtle yet important distinction between the peace policies of Austria-Hungary and Germany in a way calculated to boost Czernin's popular appeal among war-weary ordinary Germans as well as Austro-Hungarians – thus enabling him to cement a place as the leading diplomat of the Central Powers. However, events were soon about to take a turn for the worse.

The appearance of cooperation was merely the calm before the storm. All was not well behind the scenes. The OHL had clearly not received the memo on the diplomats' preferred strategy, which is not surprising given the seemingly inconclusive outcome of the earlier December conferences in Berlin and Kreuznach. Besides, the generals were just as loath to follow proper diplomatic procedure and etiquette as were the Bolsheviks. "From the negotiations one gets the impression that the Russians, not we, are the demandants," Hindenburg telegraphed indignantly from Kreuznach.³³ Kühlmann had to assure him that there was not the slightest risk of Russia's allies actually calling the Central Powers' bluff and agreeing to join the negotiations on the basis of no annexations and indemnities.³⁴ Ludendorff was even more critical of the diplomats' approach, fuming about the confusing application of the right of self-determination instead of "simple and plain demands." These diplomatic tricks had accomplished nothing of substance and clearly left the Russians with false expectations. Hence, the first quartermaster-general urged Hoffmann to set the record straight.³⁵

As Hoffmann also disliked what he perceived to be a duplicitous declaration, he persuaded the diplomats to acquiesce to his telling the Russians off the record that the term annexations would not apply to Poland, Lithuania, and Courland, due to the fact that these territories had already declared their formal independence from Russia. Ioffe, who had clearly failed to grasp the implications of the Austro-German interpretation of point three, was utterly astonished at this frank admission and "looked as if he had received a blow on the head."³⁶ With the Bolsheviks then threatening to break off negotiations, Czernin allegedly lost his nerve and sent his chief military adviser, Lieutenant Field-Marshal Maximilian von Csicserics, to threaten Hoffmann with a separate peace between Austria-Hungary and Russia. The *Ober Ost* chief of staff was decidedly unimpressed. "Well, that is delightful," he told Csicserics, "I shall have twenty-five divisions freed. Austria-Hungary will protect our flank for me after her separate peace, and I shall be able to dispose of the twenty-five divisions elsewhere."[37] Czernin's own description of these events is rather less melodramatic. The situation had exacerbated considerably [*sehr verschlechtert*], he wrote in a telegram to the emperor and the two prime ministers. He had told the Germans that it was absolutely impossible [*ganz unmöglich*] for him to see the potential peace with Russia ruined as a result of annexationist demands and that, in such a case, he would be forced to come to a separate arrangement with Russia. However, he refused to rule out further negotiations.[38]

What can we make of the Austro-Hungarian foreign minister's sudden decision to use his *ultima ratio* at the first sight of trouble, thereby threatening the integrity of the entire alliance? Given his ability to anticipate trouble and predict fairly accurately the general course of events, did he not realize that Hoffmann's clarification, to which he had personally consented, would greatly disturb the Russians? There was precedent for this, as Emperor Karl – who had specifically appointed Czernin with a mandate to conduct active foreign policy – had pursued a peace policy since his coronation and extended peace feelers towards the Entente in an attempt to reassert Austria-Hungary's status as a Great Power. For a variety of reasons, these came to naught; as Manfried Rauchensteiner explains, "[t]hose in Austria-Hungary who wanted to pursue a policy of peace [in the spring and summer of 1917] got repeatedly caught up in the intricacies of alliance politics and in the snares of domestic affairs."[39] This conundrum remained at the forefront of Habsburg policymaking during the Brest-Litovsk negotiations.

General Hoffmann considered Czernin's shattered nerves to be the cause of his erratic behaviour.[40] This was no doubt true to some extent, but there had to be additional reasons. Czernin was not alone in displaying agitated behaviour during the course of the negotiations. So, too, did Ioffe, Ludendorff, Hoffmann, and even the elderly and typically calm Hertling and Hindenburg. Every principal policymaker recognized the importance of the occasion and believed he was playing for high stakes, standing to gain much or lose everything should he choose the wrong course of action. While there was little chance of the Russians actually leaving the negotiating table or of the Austrians going through with their threat, the overall situation remained profoundly obscure as well as emotionally charged.

In an alternative interpretation, Karl Friedrich Nowak has described the threat of a separate peace as a shrewd gambit, a "chess move in the diplomatic technique of Count Czernin, who thereby made it possible for the Secretary [Kühlmann] to take a firmer stand in his own dealings with the Supreme Command [OHL]."[41] There is ample evidence to support this explanation, not least Kühlmann's response and the OHL's subsequent suspicions of having been had for fools.[42] As composed as ever, the state secretary immediately asked Czernin to put his threat in writing, as it would strengthen his position.[43] Thereupon, he duly forwarded the note to the Imperial chancellor.[44] Hoffmann, who was also present during the exchange, came out with the impression that Kühlmann "was not loath to have in his hands such a proof if the wishes of the General Headquarters [OHL] went too far."[45] Orchestrated or not, Czernin's threat of a separate peace seemed to strengthen the position of the diplomats vis-à-vis the OHL, even if Ludendorff thought it unlikely that Czernin would actually go through with it.[46] Fighting against overwhelming odds, Germany could ill afford to completely alienate its closest ally, even if at times it felt it was shackled to a corpse.

Hindenburg and Ludendorff were in fact not alone in disagreeing with the diplomats' course of action. In a long conversation with Emperor Karl on 27 December, the Hungarian prime minister, Wekerle, objected to points three and four of Czernin's speech, as self-determination and minority rights had the potential to undermine Magyar dominance in the Kingdom of Hungary. Emperor Karl defended his foreign minister vehemently, and Wekerle eventually backed down. Wekerle also questioned, however, the advisability of point five (reimbursement for POW costs) on the grounds that the Dual Monarchy had captured fewer Russian POWs than Russia had Austro-Hungarian ones, which was a sensible enough observation.[47] In response, Czernin pointed out that Wekerle had personally told him that it was essential that Austria-Hungary not allow the peace with Russia to fall through, as "it would be a catastrophe." Without the formula of self-determination, Czernin insisted, the Russians would have broken off negotiations, an outcome for which he refused to take responsibility. As far as point five was concerned, he assured Wekerle that the number of POWs was not the only factor determining payment. According to the War Ministry, the relatively higher costs the Habsburgs had borne (presumably due to the higher cost of living in Austria-Hungary relative to that in Russia) would ensure they got a tidy sum indeed from the Russians.[48] Wekerle had no alternative but to acquiesce; as long as the foreign minister had the emperor's ear, his objections had no chance of success. Even more importantly, Kaiser Wilhelm also extended a vote of confidence to Kühlmann.[49] The approval of the two emperors thus vindicated the diplomats' handling of the negotiations.

This was not the last time the Austro-Hungarian foreign minister would cross swords with the German generals more openly than either the Imperial German chancellor or the state secretary thought prudent. Czernin was mindful of the fact that the Habsburg Empire had largely achieved its war aims by the end of 1917 – it had subdued Serbia and Montenegro, neutralized Romania, and prepared the ground for a future implementation of the Austro-Polish Solution. At the same time, it desperately needed peace, as its increasingly beleaguered armies, fractured society, and strained war economy could not withstand the immense pressures of total war much longer. Czernin thus had to perform a delicate balancing act, because Austria-Hungary's security needs required the preservation of the German alliance in addition to the conclusion of peace in the east.[50] The Dual Monarchy was too weak to oppose on its own the dismemberment the Entente had threatened to carry out in the 1915 Treaty of London, which had promised Tyrol, the Küstenland, and Dalmatia to Italy; and Bosnia-Herzegovina and Croatia-Slavonia to Serbia (subsequent secret agreements assigned Transylvania to Romania). Furthermore, as Martin Dean reminds us, "to Austria, alliances were deemed necessary for her continued survival, as opposed to the more independent traditions of Prussian foreign policy."[51] A separate peace with an unreliable, revolutionary government in Petrograd was a poor substitute. As the stronger partner, Germany could afford to take greater chances.

In the event, the whole matter became moot, as the Russians did not follow up with their threat to break off negotiations. During the early afternoon session on 28 December, Kühlmann brought up a sixteen-article draft treaty for deliberation, which Ioffe refused to discuss before the end of the adjournment.[52] Speeches by Popov, who hailed the peace conference as having ushered in "an entirely new era in the development of international law," due to the fact that it had endorsed the political independence and freedom of all states in the world, and by Hakki Pasha, who expressed his enormous satisfaction at the swift course of negotiations, the first phase of the Brest-Litovsk peace conference came to an official end at 6:40 pm on 28 December 1917.[53] The following day, the chief delegates travelled back to their respective capitals in order to report and receive new instructions from higher authority.

Interlude: Fear and Loathing in Petrograd

Since world revolution was one of the main ideological imperatives of Marxism-Leninism, the Bolsheviks naturally attempted to recruit foreign agents in order to spread revolutionary turmoil in their respective countries. This policy received a formal structural framework in the spring of 1919 with the inauguration of the Third International, more commonly known as the Comintern (Communist International). During its heyday in the mid-to-late 1930s, the Comintern controlled most European communist parties and enjoyed considerable international acclaim under its Bulgarian general secretary, Georgi Dimitrov.[54] Brest-Litovsk provided an ideal opportunity to test this policy in embryo. Due to the cultural proximities between Russians and Bulgarians, the latter became a natural target for Bolshevik agitation.

In a shrewd move, the Russian delegation had proposed that separate delegations in Petrograd deal with a variety of non-political matters, such as the living conditions of POWs and the resumption of economic relations even before the formal signing of the armistice. In Brest-Litovsk, the Bolsheviks were in the lair of the beast, surrounded by *Ober Ost* staff, which severely limited their freedom of movement and action. This meant that Bolshevik propaganda was by necessity limited to speeches at the negotiating table. Red Petrograd, on the other hand, was an entirely different proposition. It was the heart and soul of the revolution, and the Bolsheviks could use every trick in the bag to attempt to influence, perhaps even recruit, delegates from the commissions of the Central Powers, who could then be pumped for information and/or used as agents of subversion back in their home countries. For the Central Powers, the negotiations offered an invaluable opportunity to obtain first-hand information about events in Russia and see what the Bolshevik revolution was really about. The German and Austro-Hungarian delegations set off for Petrograd together on 26 December.[55]

The miserable conditions the delegates of the Central Powers had to live and work under in Petrograd were in stark contrast with the austere but adequate surroundings of Brest-Litovsk. The Germans were quartered in the Grand Hotel, and the Austro-Hungarians, Ottomans, and Bulgarians in the Angleterre. These had been premium hotels ranking among Europe's finest before 1914, but the revolution and economic collapse had taken a heavy toll. "Both are filthy, fifth-rate establishments," complained the Bulgarian minister plenipotentiary, Stefan Chaprashikov. "The rooms are cold, without any heating. The food is poor and entirely insufficient – we always leave the dinner table hungry." To make matters worse, one of Trotsky's deputies had told the delegates they were not to leave the hotel alone; a Red Army soldier had to accompany them everywhere they went, allegedly for their own protection. Telegraph communication with their respective governments was very difficult. Last but not least, prices in Petrograd were phenomenally high, at approximately twenty-five times those of 1914 – a shave cost 15 rubles, lunch at a fairly decent restaurant 40–50, a cab ride from the railway station to the hotel 40, and a regular cab ride was 10 rubles.[56] It was anything but a pleasant stay.

In spite of the restrictions the Bolsheviks tried to impose, the delegates of the Central Powers were able to obtain valuable firsthand information. Soon after his arrival, Count Wilhelm von Mirbach, the leader of the German delegation, compiled a detailed report on conditions in Russia. He began by summarizing his overall impression with the single word "chaos," which appeared centred on the first page of his report, following the introductory remarks, as a sort of title as well as a sombre foreboding. The chief reason for the chaos was the "incredible giant leap [*phantastische Riesensprung*] from tsarism to the commune," which had circumvented several intermediary stages of historical development. Mirbach used the phrase *Sturm und Drang* (storm and stress) – a late-eighteenth century German proto-Romantic artistic movement characterized by extremes of emotion as well as an outright rejection of rationalism and other Enlightenment principles – to describe the process, a particularly ironic choice given the Bolsheviks' claim to possessing the ultimate scientific truth. He also warned that this movement was entering its wildest phase, driven by the "hysterical enthusiasm for the gigantic task to rebuild Russia." Owing to these developments, Petrograd itself had changed greatly, albeit not beyond recognition. The level of destruction was not nearly as high as the newspapers had reported, although plundered shops were a common sight. Unsurprisingly, the German aristocrat found the social aspects of revolutionary change most disturbing. "Fellows who earlier used to live in the dodgy parts of town are now crowding the main avenues and all of a sudden want to play gentlemen," he noted disapprovingly. The inability to get easy access to Lenin and Trotsky only served to make Mirbach's irritation worse.[57]

Similar reports, which emphasized the chaotic conditions and near complete societal collapse in Russia could only strengthen the Central Powers' resolve to hold on to the occupied borderlands in order to prevent the westward spread of revolutionary turmoil. Around the same time that Mirbach was recording his observations, the Austro-Hungarian foreign ministry liaison at the imperial court, Count August Demblin, expressed a similar sentiment in a conversation with Emperor Karl on the subject of Poland. "His Majesty was a bit skeptical on [acquiring] Poland," he reported to the foreign minister. "I told him Poland must be Austrian; otherwise, it will be Prussian or Russian. In the latter case, there will be revolution at the gates of Cracow."[58] The occupied western borderlands would thus become either a conduit for Bolshevik-style social revolution or a *cordon sanitaire* for the Central Powers; there did not appear to be a third way. This line of reasoning undoubtedly resonated with Czernin.

The circulation of first-hand information about prevailing conditions in Russia did not remain limited to the highest decision-making government circles in Berlin and Vienna for long. In mid-February, it became public knowledge, after the *Berliner Lokal Anzeiger* published a detailed account by an anonymous member of the German delegation who had just returned from Petrograd. The article described at some length the communalization of private lodgings, widespread famine, virtual absence of public safety, and popular longing for "German order, organization, and discipline." The delegate, who had ostensibly received permission from the Bolsheviks to explore the city on his own due to his decent knowledge of the Russian language, concluded on an ominous note: "I was asked not alone by well-to-do people but also by waiters and chambermaids when the Germans are going to come."[59] The message was clear – beware of the westward spread of Bolshevik-style social revolution – it is uncivilized and un-German.

The Austrian and German delegates, apart from collecting information, quickly uncovered the Bolsheviks' plans for the Petrograd negotiations. In early January, von Hempel, chairman of the Austro-Hungarian delegation, informed Vienna that the early course of proceedings had given him the impression that the Russians were not so much trying to influence public opinion at home as spread socialist-internationalist propaganda in the countries of the Quadruple Alliance. To this effect, agitational speeches often interrupted the proceedings.[60] "The Russians have so far refused to begin economic negotiations," Count Mirbach reported to Berlin on 16 January,[61] even though swift resumption of economic relations was the reason given by the Russians for setting up the Petrograd commissions in the first place. As these negotiations were of secondary importance, the Central Powers could have broken them off at any given time without serious danger to the main conference in Brest-Litovsk; that they chose not to do so demonstrates how highly they valued having a presence in Petrograd.

In the event, the Bolsheviks seem to have been largely ineffectual in their approaches to the German and Austro-Hungarian delegations, if any were attempted. They did, however, achieve remarkable success with several members of the Bulgarian commission. On 22 January, Chaprashikov informed Prime Minister Radoslavov that he had "serious reasons to believe three members of our delegation are conducting dangerous socialist propaganda here, in full accord with the Bolsheviks." As a precautionary measure, he suggested that all personal letters from the delegates Roman Avramov, I. Nedialkov, and B. Simidov which had been dispatched via courier the previous week be inspected closely upon arrival.[62]

Radoslavov had decided to include in the delegation the socialist Avramov, an employee of the State Agency for Agricultural Affairs and Social Vigilance (*Direktsiia za stopanski grizhi i obshtestvena predpazlivost*, DSGOP), in the hope that his previous contacts with the Bolsheviks, including Lenin, might be helpful in securing the purchase of agricultural goods from Russia. However, Avramov seems to have been a double agent, working for the Bulgarian government while also using his frequent trips to Central Europe on behalf of the DSGOP as cover to complete various missions for the Bolsheviks. According to his own admission, he met Lenin at least once during his stay in Petrograd, for lunch, ostensibly to discuss Russian food exports to Bulgaria. He failed in this endeavour, possibly on purpose.[63]

Neither Avramov nor any of his fellow conspirators took any precautions to disguise their subversive activity. The three delegates did not bother to conceal the fact that they sympathized with the revolution, Chaprashikov elaborated in a subsequent report. They met with Bolshevik functionaries daily and informed them at great length about internal conditions in the countries of the Quadruple Alliance. The minister plenipotentiary feared they might attempt to get in touch with local Bolshevik circles upon their return to Bulgaria. On one occasion, Roman Avramov, evidently the leader of this small group, had dinner with famous socialist-realist writer and Bolshevik fellow-traveller Maxim Gorky; the following day, Gorky's newspaper, *Novaia Zhizn'*, printed sensitive documents concerning King Ferdinand. Chaprashikov urged Radoslavov to recall the three delegates, adding that he would not be held responsible for their actions should they remain in Petrograd.[64] The Bolsheviks were trying to spark revolution in the countries of the Quadruple Alliance, he warned, and they were using all their ideological friends to that purpose.[65] The prime minister reacted by asking the minister plenipotentiary to send the ringleader Avramov to Berlin, where he would meet him personally *en route* to Brest-Litovsk, and the other two straight back to Sofia.[66]

Proof of the three Bulgarian delegates' collaboration with the Bolsheviks seemed to appear soon after. "My suspicions have been confirmed," Chaprashikov reported on 3 February. According to the evening edition of *Novaia Vedomost'*, the *Sovnarkom* (*Sovet narodnykh kommissarov*, Council of People's Commissars) had created an autonomous Supreme College for Russian, Romanian, Bessarabian, and Bulgarian Matters, whose members were preparing to head south to Romania and commence propaganda and subversion work forthwith. "It is unclear who the Bulgarian members of this college are," Chaprashikov added, "but I am utterly convinced those three are involved." He reiterated his plea that they be recalled to Sofia as soon as possible, while also suggesting that Avramov not be allowed to travel to Berlin, as he might attempt to become a conduit between the Bolsheviks and German Independent Socialists. In order to nip this dangerous association in the bud, the minister plenipotentiary proposed to warn Count Mirbach not to accept any letters from the three implicated Bulgarians.[67]

The affair finally came to an end in mid-February. At first, Avramov refused to return to Sofia, asking for permission to remain in Petrograd or travel to Stockholm, where the Bolsheviks had plenty of established agents, both Russian and foreign.[68] Chaprashikov did not budge and eventually persuaded him to leave, along with the other Bulgarian delegates, on the night train on 19 February, although Avramov was defiant to the last. Chaprashikov himself left Petrograd a few days later, as did the German, Austro-Hungarian, and Ottoman delegations, due to the resumption of hostilities between the Central Powers and Russia (see chapter six).[69] In subsequent years, Avramov moved to the Soviet Union and was apparently a useful mid-level Party functionary.[70] The Bolsheviks continued refining their methods and successfully recruiting international functionaries in Russia and abroad in the elusive pursuit of world revolution.

Interlude: Constitutional Crisis in Berlin

The dysfunctional nature of German decision making at the top level had played a major role in sparking the first major inter-allied crisis in Brest-Litovsk, over the Czernin-Kühlmann tactic of appearing to go along with the Russian proposal of a peace without annexations and indemnities as articulated in Czernin's Christmas Speech. The lack of clear-cut resolutions in the December policy conferences and the growing impatience of the OHL meant that this incident would not remain an isolated event. Another contributing factor was confusion regarding the constitutional responsibilities of the OHL and of the civilian government. This crisis highlights the interdependence of internal developments and diplomatic action in Brest-Litovsk, in that the crisis was fueled partly by developments at the conference, yet its unfolding also affected the future course of negotiations. It is also demonstrative of two other patterns. First, even as late as the winter of 1917–18, Germany was not quite the military dictatorship described in most studies.[71] While one cannot deny the fact that the OHL was one of the most important players in the making of German policy, it was by no means the sole determining factor. Nor could it always have its way on every single issue. Second, the so-called military faction was not a monolithic bloc. There were serious differences of opinion within it, as there were differences of opinion in the civilian government, and General Hoffmann's behaviour during the Berlin incident and later during the Brest-Litovsk negotiations demonstrates that there was much more fluidity here than one usually imagines.

The constitutional crisis broke out at an Imperial Council held at Bellevue Palace in Berlin on 2 January 1918. Trouble had already begun to brew during the lead-up to the council. In a private meeting, an icy Ludendorff reproached Hoffmann for allowing Czernin's Christmas Speech to go through. Hofmann insisted that "the general outline of the negotiations [should have] been discussed and settled between the General Headquarters and the Chancellor of the Empire and the Secretary of State during their conference in Kreuznach [on 18 December]."[72] As Hoffmann himself had not been present at Kreuznach, this was a sensible line of defence. It also implied that, if anyone was to blame, it was in fact Ludendorff. "It is impossible to settle the lines for so difficult a task as a Treaty of Peace by making all sorts of general conversations on both sides," Hoffmann noted critically in his memoirs.[73] Although Ludendorff deemed Hoffmann's excuse acceptable, this exchange marked the beginning of a serious worsening of relations between the vengeful first quartermaster-general and the *Ober Ost* chief of staff.

Hoffmann did not wish to deliberately provoke his mercurial superior and risk incurring Ludendorff's wrath, but his independent mindset soon got him into trouble. During the lead-up to the council, Kaiser Wilhelm summoned Hoffmann on 1 January and asked him for a debriefing on the Brest-Litovsk conference as well as for his personal opinion on the Polish Question. Hoffmann, whose view differed substantially from Ludendorff's on the proposed Polish border strip to be annexed, initially refused to speak, but Wilhelm's insistence meant that the general had no choice but to comply. He unveiled a map showing his own, rather modest proposal for border rectifications to improve the defences of Thorn, Soldau, and the Upper Silesian coal mines. The Kaiser declared himself completely satisfied with this solution. It is worth noting, however, that the general's moderate proposal stemmed less from an innate reasonableness and/or opposition to annexations *per se* and more from a typically Prussian dislike of Poles as an alien, unassimilable population in the Prussian east. "I was an enemy of any settlement of the Polish question which would increase in Germany the number of subjects of Polish nationality. Notwithstanding the measures that Prussia had taken during many decades, we had not been able to manage the Poles we have, and I could not see the advantage of any addition to the number of citizens of that nationality," Hoffmann wrote in his memoirs.[74] As Vejas G. Liulevicius has demonstrated, this disparaging attitude towards nationalities in the east was characteristic of the *Ober Ost* administration in Lithuania and the Baltic littoral, which sought to transform the allegedly backward, chaotic borderlands into modern, productive, organized spaces where "German work" set a shining example for the locals to emulate.[75] It is also symptomatic of the multiple, often contradictory strands of *Ostpolitik* German decision-makers pursued during the war, including at Brest-Litovsk.

No official protocol of the Imperial Council of 2 January appears to exist, which means that one has to rely on the personal writings of the attendants and the comments they made to others for a reconstruction of events.[76] The council began calmly enough, with Kühlmann delivering a report on the Brest-Litovsk negotiations and his plan for their continuation, which the Kaiser approved. Thereupon, things took a turn for the worse. Previously, sensing what lay ahead, Kühlmann had privately pleaded with Wilhelm not to bring up the Polish Question or even invite Hoffmann to the council, in order to prevent the situation from escalating unnecessarily. Characteristically, the Kaiser ignored the state secretary's cautious advice and proceeded to unveil a large map that reflected Hoffmann's proposed borders, asserting that this was the Polish border-strip he wanted.[77] To compound the situation, he morally reprimanded the generals, who were seemingly unaware of the existence of this project in the first place. Upon hearing this, Ludendorff allegedly lost his nerve and shouted at Wilhelm.[78] Hertling's son and secretary noted in his diary that the general was merely "jealous [*eifersüchtig*] of Hoffmann," due to the fact that the Kaiser had come out in favour of his proposal.[79] An additional explanation is that Ludendorff's domineering personality did not take criticism at all well, even if it was of the constructive kind. During the earlier debates, he had already quarrelled with the state secretary for no apparent reason. Kühlmann later told Czernin that "Ludendorff himself was not clear as to what he wanted," refusing his [Kühlmann's] suggestion to travel to Brest-Litovsk and take part in the negotiations because "he would only spoil things if he did."[80] Crossed for the second time in quick succession, Ludendorff simply lost control and lashed out.

In his typically vacillating manner, Kaiser Wilhelm postponed indefinitely a final settling of the Polish Question, pending his review of the OHL's counter-proposal. This finally brought the painful scene to an end. Beyond himself with rage, Ludendorff later demanded Hoffmann's resignation. The Kaiser, who seems to have warmed to Hoffmann's direct, honest personality, for once decided to stand up to the imperious first quartermaster-general and refused outright.[81] Unused to defeat, Ludendorff pressed on and had Hindenburg send the Kaiser a letter on the question of responsibility for foreign policy on 7 January. This initiated a series of extremely interesting exchanges between Wilhelm, Hertling, and the OHL. Hertling asserted that, according to the Imperial Constitution, the Imperial chancellor alone was responsible for the conduct of foreign policy in general and for the Brest-Litovsk peace negotiations in particular. In contrast, Hindenburg and Ludendorff insisted that they had a moral responsibility for these matters, even if this contravened the letter of the law. "[I]n our position, as it has developed – without any conscious action on our part," wrote Hindenburg to Hertling, "[W]e feel ourselves jointly responsible to the German nation, history and our own conscience for the form which the peace takes. No formal declaration can relieve us of that sense of responsibility."[82]

Unsurprisingly, the Kaiser refused to make a definitive ruling and tried to reconcile the opposing views of the OHL and the Wilhelmstraße.

Neither side was satisfied with the result. The crisis, however, had roots much deeper than the events of the Imperial Council of 2 January 1918. The great successes of the wars of German unification in the 1860s and early 1870s had made the General Staff extremely popular, and cemented its position free from civilian oversight. It took great cunning on the part of Bismarck to keep the military in check and prevent it from interfering in government policy. The Iron Chancellor's successors were not nearly as artful, and even the highly capable Bethmann-Hollweg found himself unseated by the military faction in July 1917.

How did the German constitutional crisis affect the course of the Brest-Litovsk negotiations? While the Hindenburg-Ludendorff tandem locked horns with Hertling over the theoretical issue of constitutional responsibility, Kühlmann emerged as a moderate winner on the specific question of his policy at the conference. Even though there had been no directives, the Kaiser's tacit support meant that the state secretary now had greater leeway in his negotiations with the Russians and was not pressed for time. Hoffmann, on the other hand, had been discredited in Ludendorff's eyes, which meant that any attempts to ameliorate the first quartermaster-general's demands by appealing to reason would henceforth be met with suspicion. But Kühlmann's was a Pyrrhic victory with unintended consequences. His decision to engage in long-winded debates with Trotsky on the question of self-determination would drive a wedge between Czernin and himself and play straight into the hands of both the Bolsheviks and the OHL.

The Second Phase of Negotiations: 9 January – 18 January 1918

The delegations of the Central Powers returned to Brest-Litovsk early on 4 January, 1918, and Czernin's first order of business was to confer with Kühlmann over breakfast.[83] Although there had been no official answers to the proposal to join the peace conference from the Entente powers, the French foreign minister, Stéphen Pichon, had made their uncompromising stance clear in a speech in the Chamber of Deputies on 31 December, in which he had stated: "There is no disagreement among us. Russia may treat for a separate peace with our enemies or not. In either case, the war for us continues."[84] This meant that the negotiations would henceforth be about a separate peace between Russia and the Central Powers. Entente statesmen had suddenly found themselves on the defensive on the issue of self-determination as a result of the early pronouncements at Brest-Litovsk and the Bolshevik publication of the decidedly annexationist secret treaties. They were also coming under increasing fire from liberal and leftist circles in their own countries. As a consequence of Ioffe's and Czernin's declarations and the seeming acceptance of self-determination as a central principle of the negotiations by the two sides, the leading Entente politicians felt the need to crystallize their own ideas on the subject. The British prime minister, David Lloyd George, took the lead in an address to the British Trades Union League at Caxton Hall on 5 January 1918, outlining British war aims in the following terms:

> Firstly, the sanctity of treaties must be re-established; secondly, a territorial settlement must be secured based on the right to self-determination or the consent of the governed; and, lastsome, we must seek by the creation of some international organisation to limit the burden of armaments and diminish the probability of war.[85]

Curiously, Lloyd George used the term "consent of the governed," a favourite of Woodrow Wilson's, synonymously with self-determination. The president, who had been planning his own counter-statement for some time, sought to regain the initiative immediately. On 8 January 1918 he delivered his celebrated Fourteen Points speech to Congress, followed by the so-called Four Points speech three days later in which he used the term self-determination for the first time in a public pronouncement.[86] This declaration meant that the Allies, the Central Powers, and the Bolsheviks had all accepted self-determination as a guiding principle of the peace, at least in theory. The German High Command and important sectors of German society would continue to harbor annexationist aims, but on the level of official discourse there was no denying the paramountcy of self-determination after January 1918.

In an attempt to muddy the waters, on 2 January Ioffe dispatched a telegram suggesting a transfer of venue to neutral Stockholm and explained that the Russian government considered Czernin's Christmas Day speech not entirely satisfactory.[87] In his address to the Reichstag Main Committee on 3 January, Imperial Chancellor Hertling refused to entertain Ioffe's proposal, stating simply that he expected the Russians to honour the agreement to resume negotiations in Brest-Litovsk.[88] Bolshevik leaders had obviously not been very hopeful, as they replied that the Russian delegation, now headed by *Narkomindel* Trotsky, would indeed do so.[89] With the ten-day adjournment officially at an end, on 5 January a joint telegram signed by the chairmen of the four delegations of the Central Powers informed the Russians that the failure of the Entente to join the conference had ruined the prospects for an immediate general peace and thus invalidated the provisions of Czernin's speech. In light of this development, the Quadruple Alliance intended to reclaim freedom of action during the subsequent negotiations.[90] In effect, this meant that the entire Ioffe Program was now obsolete. With general peace out of the question, the two sides would have to restrict themselves to discussing the specific settlement in East Central Europe and the Caucasus, which of course had been Czernin's and Kühlmann's intention all along.

The second phase of negotiations brought few overall positive developments, even as the opposing delegations' respective strategies became increasingly clear. In a *volte-face*, Austria-Hungary and Germany, whose invasions of Serbia and Belgium in August 1914 had precipitated the descent into general European war, would now pose as liberators and protectors of small nations in the east. "My plan was to involve Trotsky in an academic discussion about the right of national self-determination and its possible practical application, in order to bring about whatever territorial concessions we absolutely required," Kühlmann explained in his memoirs.[91] Czernin summarized this strategy in a memorandum to the OHL, which he subsequently forwarded to Ambassador Hohenlohe in Berlin, stating that he and Kühlmann would pursue no direct annexations. "Their plan was to use the Russian government's catchphrase of 'national self-determination for Russia's peoples' in order to bring about the accession of these [occupied territories] to the two empires."[92] In accordance with this plan, Kühlmann would argue that the border states had already exercised their right to self-determination in separating from Russia and were currently under German protection.[93] The Russians would have to recognize this or risk appearing hypocritical, as they themselves had insisted on the inviolability of the right to national self-determination. This policy, if successful, would transfer the western borderlands of the former Russian Empire to the Central Powers' sphere of influence, since the viability of these regions as (at least nominally) independent states would depend upon Austro-German military support, when faced with Bolshevik hostility.

The seeming consensus between German civilian and military factions on the need to detach certain territories from Russia has led Peter Borowsky to argue that Kühlmann's imperialism differed from Ludendorff's only to the extent that it relied on the more flexible and diplomatic methods of indirect rule. Borowsky further dismissed the concepts of "autonomy" and "right to self-determination," which the diplomats brought up repeatedly, as mere "catchphrases" [*Schlagworten*].[94] These terms, however, were brought to the negotiating table by the Bolshevik delegation, even if they conveniently suited Germany's strategy of employing revolutionary tools against the colonial empires of the Entente, in places as diverse as India, Persia, Egypt, and Ireland. The concepts, furthermore, were very much open to interpretation at the time, as the subsequent Paris Peace Conferences also showed. Kühlmann did not leave the future status of the border states deliberately vague in an act of artifice. He did it because he knew all too well that there was no agreement between the German government, the OHL, and Vienna. Seeking to define their status would have amounted to opening the proverbial can of worms, leading to endless bickering, thus exposing the cracks in the Central Powers alliance.

In the event, Kühlmann got more than he had bargained for. The unwillingness of the Entente to attend the peace conference had clarified the situation for the Bolsheviks, who realized they would be unable to compel any of the imperialist governments of the two warring alliances to conclude a "democratic" peace by moral suasion alone. "The Russian revolutionaries never had illusions about the possibility of an accord with the imperialists," Ioffe noted guardedly in his notes to the official Bolshevik publication of the proceedings in 1920. The Entente's refusal to participate and the excessive German demands led him to add, "further negotiations could only be for show [*demonstrativnyi kharakter*]."[95] Consequently, Trotsky was perfectly happy to delay the course of negotiations indefinitely in the hope that revolution would break out in East Central Europe, and he considered the debate regarding self-determination as good as any for that purpose. "The delay in negotiations was to our interest," he noted in his memoirs. "That was my real object in going to Brest-Litovsk."[96]

The January debates between Kühlmann and Trotsky did not bring about any concrete results, which is why they are often dismissed as mere "lip service" to the concept of self-determination.[97] This is not entirely so. Both the conservative German state secretary and the revolutionary Russian *Narkomindel* vied to become the leading authority on the application of the increasingly important concept of self-determination, at least in the immediate framework of the East Central European settlement. This duel entailed a discursive power struggle over the various theoretical underpinnings, practical considerations, and procedural aspects of self-determination. The debates between Kühlmann and Trotsky are therefore important in being one of the first attempts, however hypothetical and divorced from actual policy, to go beyond the use of self-determination as a slogan and to seek to apply it to the peacemaking process.

As Woodrow Wilson would also find out, when dealing with self-determination the devil lay in the details. Who was the "self"? Was it an administrative, historical, or economic entity, such as the antiquated Baltic duchies of Courland, Estonia, and Livonia? This is not as outrageous a suggestion as it might appear at first glance – at the Paris Peace Conference in 1919, Czech leaders Thomáš Masaryk and Edvard Beneš argued successfully that the historical-economic unity of the former Habsburg Kingdom of Bohemia trumped national distinctions, thereby incorporating three million reluctant Bohemian and Moravian Germans into the new state of Czechoslovakia. Was it a specific class, such as the proletariat or the peasantry, as Trotsky insisted? Was it the nation? This last concept was extremely vague in large parts of East Central Europe, where ethnic and linguistic diversity was the order of the day. Who could realistically claim to represent the nation? In the Baltic littoral, social and urban-rural divisions often tended to coincide with ethnic divisions, with Baltic Germans the traditional governing and land-owning elite. Along with Jews and ethnic Russians, they represented a large percentage of the urban population, whereas largely illiterate Latvian and Estonian peasants were a vast majority in the countryside. The *Ober Ost* administration helped the Baltic German population enhance their privileges and formulate political demands in the territories under its control, although the two groups did not always see eye to eye.[98]

In an illustration of this pattern, an estate-based constituent assembly for Courland convened in the ceremonial throne room of the old ducal palace in Mitau between 21 September and 23 September 1917 in order to elect a *Landesrat* (provincial council), to serve as a representative body of the duchy. The seventy-nine-member constituent assembly included twenty-seven large landowners, twenty-seven small landowners, sixteen townsmen, five clergymen, and four hereditary knights [*Ritterschaft*].[99] Of these, forty-nine were German, twenty-eight Latvian, and one Lithuanian. The make-up of the *Landesrat* reflected the estate breakdown of the assembly, but every one of its twenty members was German. Its first order of business was to issue a unilateral declaration of independence from Russia and call for affiliation [*Angliederung*] with Germany in order to "work together for the reconstruction of Courland."[100] On 3 January 1918, the Estonian *Ritterschaft* issued a similar plea for union [*Anschluss*] with Germany, claiming that unoccupied Estonia had suffered badly under the rule of "the armed thugs [*Soldateska*]" since the beginning of the revolution.[101]

Property qualification and/or estate affiliation had been a prerequisite for enfranchisement in the old order and as such helped shape wartime politics in Prussia and Hungary. If the principle of property qualification were to be retained, one could consider the Baltic German-dominated *Landesräte* in Courland, Estonia, and Livonia as legitimate representative bodies. This, in turn, would render their declarations of independence legal acts of international law. Kühlmann made precisely this argument during the session of 11 January:

> The Russian Government, in accordance with its principles, has proclaimed for all peoples without exception living in Russia the right of self-determination, even going as far as complete separation. We maintain that the regions now occupied by us, the de facto plenipotentiary bodies representing these peoples in question [i.e., the *Landesräte*] have exercised the right of self-determination in the sense of separation from Russia, so that in our view these regions can no longer be considered as belonging to the Russian Empire in its former shape.[102]

In contrast, Trotsky, who naturally viewed self-determination through a Marxist lens, objected to the *Landesräte* not so much on the basis of nationality as on the basis of class. The councils were made up entirely of feudal and bourgeois elements and were hence reactionary. Only *soviets*, as genuinely democratic councils of workers, peasants, and soldiers, could claim to represent the people of the occupied territories.

> We fully maintain our declaration that peoples inhabiting Russian territory have the right to self-determination, without external influence, even to the point of separation. We cannot, however, recognize the application of this principle otherwise than in regard to *the people themselves, and not in regard to certain privileged parts of them*.... [T]hese de facto plenipotentiary bodies could not appeal to the principles proclaimed by us.[103]

Further discussions touched on preconditions for the holding of plebiscites. Whereas Trotsky insisted on the evacuation of the occupied territories prior to the conduct of elections, Kühlmann rejected this on account of military necessity, as military operations were still ongoing

2. Leaders of the delegations of the Central Powers. From left to right: the chief of staff of *Ober Ost*, Major-General Max von Hoffmann; the Austro-Hungarian foreign minister, Count Ottokar Czernin; the Ottoman grand vizier, Talaat Pasha; the German state secretary for foreign affairs, Baron Richard von Kühlmann; the Bulgarian minister of justice, Hristo Popov.
Source: F. von Bruckmann, *Grosser Bilderatlas des Weltkrieges*. Wikimedia Commons.

on several fronts. The German delegation issued a counter proposal, pledging to guarantee plebiscites to be held after the conclusion of a general peace and with German troops still present to preserve order. The Bolshevik representatives found this unsatisfactory.[104]

Neither Kühlmann's *Landesräte* nor Trotsky's *soviets* were fully inclusive representative bodies, notwithstanding claims to the contrary by both parties. Despite espousing the right of self-determination, these councils excluded large sectors of the population on the basis of their ethno-national or socio-economic background. Such inconsistency, however, was not unique to the negotiations at Brest-Litovsk. Self-determination was an ideal concept, with origins going back to the principles of the Enlightenment, presupposing popular unanimity in favour of a specific form of government engendered by rational choice. Since this was not how the dynastic empires of East Central Europe functioned (or the colonial empires of Britain and France, for that matter), the application of such an ideal concept was bound to run into difficulties when confronted with the confusing situation on the ground, where multiple foci of loyalty (nation, region, religion, language, dynasty, class, estate) coexisted in a delicate equilibrium. It would prove to be immensely difficult, therefore, to apply the principle of self-determination faithfully even in the best of circumstances, and the last phase of the Great War offered anything but an ideal setting for such an endeavour. The British prime minister, David Lloyd George, who was heavily involved in the deliberations on the application of self-determination at the Paris Peace Conference, described the overwhelming magnitude of the task in the following manner in his memoirs:

> It is easy to lay down general principles such as "self-determination" or "government with the consent of the governed." How are these principles to be applied in the delineation of boundaries under confusions of this kind [i.e., famine, local wars, etc.]? These conditions affected the frontiers of over a score of separate States, new and old, from the Rhine to the Euphrates. Above all, how was it to be done when the exigencies of dangerous world conditions imposed a time limit on the decisions of the negotiators?[105]

Back in Brest-Litovsk, the morning session of 11 January concluded with a long, fruitless exchange between Kühlmann and Trotsky on the nature of genuine representative bodies, the effects occupying troops had on the selection process, and the necessary juridical prerequisites for the formation of a legal state entity, especially as these applied to Courland and Lithuania.[106] During the afternoon session, their discussion continued with respect to Poland. For a number of reasons, the Polish Question was even more complicated than the Baltic one. First, unlike most other ethnic groups in the western borderlands, the Poles were a historic nation with a long history of statehood (the Polish-Lithuanian Commonwealth had been a Great European Power between the sixteenth and eighteenth centuries) and a well-developed national movement (as well as a profound sense of their own importance).

Second, Germany and Austria-Hungary ruled over substantial Polish populations in Poznania and Galicia, which made the issue a sensitive one domestically. Third, between 1914 and 1917, the competing Imperial regimes had developed elaborate Polish policies that aimed to win Polish support for their cause, an outstanding example of what Mark von Hagen has described as an Imperial project to mobilize ethnicity for the war effort.[107] In September 1914, the commander-in-chief of the Russian Army, Grand Duke Nikolai Nikolaevich, promised to create an autonomous, unified Poland, including Poznania and Galicia, within the Russian Empire at the end of the war. The Austrians responded by sponsoring the formation of a Polish Legion within the Habsburg Army. In November 1916, Berlin and Vienna upped the ante by proclaiming an independent Kingdom of Poland on territory captured from the Russians. This amorphous entity had a prime minister, a regency council pending the election of a king, and a German-issued currency (*marka*), but no defined borders and no independent administrative structure. Most of Congress Poland was in fact under an Austro-German condominium, which included the civilian German Government-General Warsaw to the north and the Austrian Military-Government Lublin to the south.[108] Both administrations tried to court the Polish national movement.

These actions whetted the appetite of Polish government officials. Emboldened by the earlier concessions, on 18 December 1917 the Polish prime minister, Jan Kucharzewski, wrote to the Imperial German chancellor, Hertling, to request Polish representation at the Brest-Litovsk peace conference in accordance with the principle of self-determination.[109] Since Poland was technically an independent state, this was a sensible request. At the same time, a separate Polish delegation might attempt to navigate between the Russians and the Central Powers, thereby making life even more difficult for Berlin and Vienna. Hertling, as was his habit when faced with a particularly complicated foreign policy problem, sought Kühlmann's advice. The state secretary responded by stressing the extreme delicacy of the question of Polish international representation. According to Article V of the Patent of 12 September 1917, the Polish government could not conclude international agreements for the duration of the Austro-German occupation. Furthermore, Kühlmann pointed out, only belligerent powers – which Poland was definitely not – were supposed to be represented at Brest-Litovsk. Perhaps Germany and Austria-Hungary could present the Polish position at the conference in order to placate the Poles.[110] Czernin was likewise reluctant to accept Polish delegates, making vague promises of possible consultation.[111]

As the second phase of negotiations commenced in January and the question of self-determination came to dominate the proceedings, Kucharzewski reiterated his demand, insisting that Polish representation in Brest-Litovsk was indispensable for Warsaw's continued cooperation with the Central Powers and for the prospects of general peace.[112] By this point, however, Trotsky's refusal to accept the various councils in the occupied borderlands as legitimate state organs had presented Kühlmann with a face-saving formula. He completely understood and sympathized with the Polish request for representation at the conference, the state secretary wrote to Kucharzewski. Unfortunately, it could not be granted, "as the Russian delegation recognizes neither the independence of the Polish state nor the legitimacy [*Rechtmäßigkeit*] of its present government."[113] Kucharzewski had no alternative but to acquiesce, albeit with great displeasure. There the matter rested, at least for the time being. The refusal of the Central Powers to admit a Polish delegation to Brest-Litovsk, however, marked the beginning of Polish estrangement from their cause.

Trotsky was highly dismissive of the Kingdom of Poland backed by the Central Powers. "We accept the right of the Polish people to independence," he declared, "but we cannot accept some or other territorial combinations of the current Polish Ministry, not represented here, as the genuine expression of the will of the Polish people." The Russian government would therefore refuse to countenance any decision taken under German occupation. Kühlmann pointed out that it was illogical for Trotsky to object to the fact that the Polish government was not represented at the conference while simultaneously refusing to recognize it. Czernin enquired by what means the Russians intended to solicit "genuine" Polish representation, since holding a plebiscite in Brest-Litovsk was obviously impractical. Trotsky refused to comment, asking for an adjournment of the session.[114] He considered the Polish regency to be the most egregious example of a puppet government propped up by Austro-German imperialism. Czernin and Kühlmann, on the other hand, insisted that it was the only legitimate government of Poland. It certainly was the *only* Polish government at the time, and it was sufficiently independent-minded to cause occasional concern and mild irritation in Berlin and Vienna. However, Trotsky would recognize only a government "of the people," a phrase he repeatedly refused to elaborate on, to the utter desperation of Czernin and Kühlmann. There could be no agreement. Characteristically, no one actually bothered to ask the Poles themselves.

Kühlmann and Trotsky continued to reiterate more or less the same points over the next few days. As the negotiations dragged on agonizingly, Czernin, whose nerves were not particularly strong in the best of circumstances, began to lose patience. The same was true of Hoffmann, who was constantly being urged by Ludendorff to shorten the purposeless philosophizing. In a meeting with the diplomats, the general suggested that he use the next opportunity to make a statement of intent in order to force the issue. Kühlmann, who by this point was beginning to realize that his theoretical debates with Trotsky led to a dead end, agreed. Czernin raised half-hearted objections but eventually gave way. During the plenary session of 12 January, Hoffmann delivered what Czernin described in his diary as "his unfortunate speech." With forthright, soldier-like austerity, the general proceeded to remind the Bolsheviks that the victorious German army occupied Russian territory, and that the hypocritical Russian delegation had no right to demand "for the occupied territories the application of a right of self-determination of peoples in a manner and to an extent which its Government does not apply to its own country." In addition, the OHL must refuse to evacuate any of the occupied territories on account of military necessity.[115]

Trotsky seized the unexpected opportunity for a tirade, and "[f]or a few minutes, the peace conference was transformed into a Marxian propagandist class for beginners," as the *Narkomindel* pointed out the qualitative difference between using violence against capitalists and violence against the proletariat. "There was something delightfully piquant in this discussion of the revolutionary use of force in that gathering of Hohenzollern, Hapsburg, Sultanic, and Coburg diplomatists, generals, and admirals," he noted with satisfaction in his memoirs.[116] Harking back to Lenin's definition of self-determination from 1916 and following the Bolshevik agenda to treat the peace conference as a propaganda forum, he was actually prepared to acknowledge German annexationist demands and overwhelming force, as long as these were expressed clearly in the straightforward language of a Prussian general rather than the sophistry of a Bavarian or Bohemian diplomat. "We are revolutionaries, but we are also realists," he had averred, "and we prefer to speak directly about annexations rather than substitute the genuine term with a euphemism," Trotsky said at the proceedings.[117] He also took pleasure in the "extent of the disagreement between German diplomacy and the high command."[118] Kühlmann and Czernin, however, could not talk about annexations, even if they so wished (they did not), since that would cause agitation at home and make a negotiated peace with the Entente at a later date a virtual impossibility.

Czernin and Hoffmann were not the only two people despairing at the lack of progress. As the OHL's patience began to wear thin, Hindenburg telegraphed Hertling with the newly-acquired information that Trotsky allegedly had no intention to sign a peace treaty. As the fruitless prolongation of the negotiations only worsened Germany's military situation, he argued, the Central Powers should present the Bolsheviks with an ultimatum in order to clarify the situation and regain the option of reaching a military decision in the east, if necessary.[119] This time, the OHL met with the combined opposition of Kühlmann and Hoffmann, which demonstrates that individuals could and did look beyond the civilian-military divide when they thought the situation warranted such an approach. The state secretary and the *Ober Ost* chief of staff warned that delivering an ultimatum to the Russians before the conclusion of the simultaneously ongoing negotiations with the Ukrainians would constitute a "grave political error."[120]

This was neither the first nor the last time Hoffmann would side with the diplomats, incurring the displeasure of his direct superiors in the process. In late December, he had had a revealing conversation with Baron Gautsch, a member of the Austrian delegation, about the differences between Germany and Austria-Hungary. The general asked Gautsch for a description of the Dual Monarchy's present economic situation and of morale among the population, expressing the hope that the Habsburgs would not break with Germany, Czernin's threat of a separate peace notwithstanding. He had great sympathy for Czernin personally and was grateful for his friendly attitude towards Germany. Thanks to his interaction with the Austro-Hungarian foreign minister, Hoffmann added, he had learnt to appreciate the political as well as the military side of things. Finally, he promised to use his considerable influence with Ludendorff in the common interest of the two countries.[121] Having found himself at odds with Ludendorff after the altercation at the Imperial Council at Bellevue on 2 January, Hoffmann moved even closer to the diplomats.

For the time being, however, the deadlock could not be broken, as the gulf between the positions of Russia and the Central Powers on the application of self-determination in the disputed borderlands seemed unbridgeable. On 18 January, the two sides agreed to a second ten-day adjournment, but not before Trotsky delivered yet another propagandist speech in which he accused the Central Powers of outright robbery, as they tried to detach 150 000 square kilometers of territory from Russia under false pretenses.[122] During the adjournment, the domestic crisis in Austria-Hungary deepened. Trotsky was jubilant, as events in Central Europe seemingly vindicated his dilatory approach. "In the interval, which lasted ten days," he wrote, "serious disturbances broke out in Austria and strikes took place among the laboring masses there – the first act of recognition of our methods of conducting the peace negotiations on the part of the proletariat of the Central Powers in the face of the annexationist demands of German Imperialism."[123] For a few memorable days in January 1918, it seemed world revolution might not be a pipedream after all.

Conclusion

Debates on the nature and application of the increasingly important concept of self-determination dominated the first two phases of the Brest-Litovsk peace conference, between late December 1917 and mid-January 1918. During the opening session of 22 December, the Russians announced their peace program, which called for a general peace without annexations and indemnities in accordance with the right to national self-determination. On 25 December, the Central Powers agreed with the Russian proposition on the condition that the Entente join the conference. With no additional participation forthcoming, the two sides reconvened in early January in order to discuss a separate peace. The Central Powers hoped to use Russian insistence on the implementation of national self-determination as a means to gain long-term control of the occupied western borderlands of the former Russian Empire, by insisting that the representative bodies of Congress Poland, Courland, and Lithuania had declared independence and asked for Austro-German protection. In contrast, the Bolsheviks maintained that these councils were illegitimate and called for the withdrawal of German troops in the lead-up to referenda on the future status of these territories. As the negotiations dragged on, the German High Command began urging the diplomats to issue an ultimatum in order to clarify the situation, which contributed to a minor constitutional crisis in Germany at the beginning of January.

Once they realized they could not compel the imperialist governments of the Entente and the Quadruple Alliance to sign a democratic peace by moral suasion alone, the Bolsheviks' main goal during the conference was to delay proceedings for as long as possible, in the hope that revolution would break out in East Central Europe and obliterate the Imperial edifice. To that end, they engaged the representatives of the Central Powers in endless theoretical debates peppered with propagandist speeches whose aim was to foment revolutionary turmoil. They also tried to recruit some Central Powers delegates during separate negotiations held in Petrograd on the resumption of economic relations, with mixed success. As huge strikes and disturbances broke out throughout East Central Europe in mid-January 1918, it seemed that the Bolshevik approach to the peace conference might be about to bear fruit.

Chapter Three

The Great January Strike as a Prelude to Revolution in Austria

Economic Problems and Social Disturbances in Austria before January 1918

The Dual Monarchy functioned remarkably well as a coherent economic whole, whatever national problems it might have had before the outbreak of the war. The heavy industry of Bohemia, Upper and Lower Austria, the oil of Galicia, the shipbuilding industry of the Küstenland, the coal of Moravia and Silesia, and the grain and wheat of Hungary and Galicia made the empire more or less economically self-sufficient. However, the delicate economic balance that existed in peacetime between the more urban, industrialized Austrian half and the more rural, agricultural Hungarian half began to unravel under the pressures of total war. The loss of much of the grain-producing region of Galicia in 1914 and 1916, combined with a series of poor harvests and an increasing reluctance on the part of Hungary to ship large amounts of wheat to its beleaguered partner, made Austria's food supply extremely precarious. Even as Austria and Hungary established Food Ministries over the course of October 1916 and a supervisory Joint Food Committee in February 1917, it proved very difficult for the two constituent states of the Dual Monarchy to coordinate food policy without impinging on each other's sovereignty.[1] The intricate structure of the monarchy made the food question a political as well as an economic one. This, in turn, was symptomatic of the larger structural deficiencies of Dualism, which vested sole authority for such matters in the Austrian and Hungarian governments rather than in the joint Imperial and Royal Government. As Clifford F. Wargelin has argued persuasively, "the disastrous supply situation in Austria represented more than the outcome of declining wartime harvests. It represented the failure of Dualism."² Admittedly, it was a failure under the extraordinary pressures of total war mobilization – and Austria-Hungary was not alone in failing to fully mobilize its economy for total war – but it was a failure nonetheless.

As the economic situation deteriorated steadily, food riots eventually took place in Vienna on 11 May 1916. American Ambassador Penfield gave the following description of what would become an increasingly common sight in the Imperial capital over the next two and a half years:

> In a spontaneous manner a congregation of women and children appeared in the streets of the X. Bezirk [district] and proceeded to smash windows and pillage shoe stores, milk shops and bakeries, a great deal of harm being caused before the police learnt of it and before they could interfere. The excitement grew rapidly, and before the police had an idea of the turmoil, large parties marched in the direction of City Hall shouting and firing stones at stores and windows on their way ..., shouting "We are starving, we are starving."³

The food riots were ominous for two reasons. First, in the virtual absence of a traditional sphere of political activity and expression (the *Reichsrat* had been prorogued in March 1914 and did not reconvene until the spring of 1917), people began taking their frustrations to the streets and engaging in spontaneous direct action, without any reference to organized political parties. Second, traditionally non-political actors, such as women and children, were being transformed into increasingly vocal activists, which meant that issues previously consigned to the private, domestic sphere (such as food) now entered the public sphere and became politicized. Consequently, the food riots represented the first phase of the radicalization of the home front that played such a prominent part in the deliberations of Trotsky and Czernin, among others, during the Brest-Litovsk Peace Conference. As Maureen Healy has pointed out, "[i]f we compare these incidents to the 'workers" strikes of 1918, which historians have pinpointed as a crucial turning point in wartime domestic politics, we see that Viennese food rioters had in fact set the stage and shaped the discourse of Viennese politics."⁴

One other related incident anticipated the events of January 1918. While lunching at a restaurant on 21 October 1916, the notorious Austrian prime minister, Count Karl von Stürgkh, was rather rudely interrupted when Friedrich "Fritz" Adler, son of prominent socialist leader Viktor Adler, barged in unannounced and fired at him three times at point blank range. Ostensibly an isolated act of political terrorism, the spectacular shooting of the prime minister struck a chord with ordinary people who were chafing under the double burden of food shortage (Stürgkh's last meal became the subject of acrimonious debates and puns in the press) and political repression. As Penfield reported to Washington, the word on the street was that the assassination "was the direct outcome of the stern and long continued suppression of free speech" and that "it is but the first of a series of protests which may be expected and which will stop at nothing in order to force a hearing of their grievances and if possible a rectification ... of at least the food troubles, which are growing daily more acute."[5]

Fritz Adler's subsequent trial became a matter of national debate, which further radicalized the nascent popular protest movement. In late May 1917, between forty thousand and sixty thousand Viennese workers spontaneously went on strike without the knowledge or approval of the SDAPÖ Trade Union Committee. Concerned they were losing control of the popular movement, the Trade Union Committee and the party executive convened on 31 May and 1 June to discuss what changes needed to be implemented in order to prevent future repetition of similar events. The union delegates raised the question of a clear party stance towards the so-called radicals, a fringe movement within the SDAPÖ not dissimilar to the German Independent Socialists (USPD), which advocated direct action against the government in defiance of the official party policy of cooperation. During the party executive meeting, Franz Domes emphasized the adverse effects of the increasing politicization of the home front on the party's relationship with its constituents. Frivolous actions only undermined the authority of the trade unions and the party leadership, he warned. If the party leadership did not take energetic measures against this "odious radicalism," the workers would brush aside party representatives and take matters into their own hands. The two meetings adopted a resolution to engage the workers directly and organize regular sessions in which they would debate the burning questions of the day.[6] This scare served as a wake-up call for the social-democratic leadership, greatly influencing their actions during the winter of 1917–18.

As the Viennese food riots and the popular excitement that accompanied Stürgkh's assassination and Adler's trial demonstrate, the so-called Great January Strike [*der große Jännerstreik*] of 1918, which briefly threatened to engulf East Central Europe in the tide of revolution, was not the first case of domestic disturbance affecting the Habsburg home front. However, it was by far the most serious and consequential. The events of January 1918 were described by one historian as "the greatest revolutionary strike action in the whole history of the Austrian labour movement."[7] This perception has made it the subject of greater scholarly scrutiny than any other previous incident. The most widespread interpretation views the strike as an extension of the 1916–17 food riots. While war-weariness and desire for peace among the populace played a certain role, this argument goes, the actions in January 1918 were, in effect, a food riot on a grander scale.[8] In a contrasting narrative, scholars and publications associated either directly or indirectly with socialist and social-democratic parties have tended to portray the great strike as a mass movement for peace, driven by the example of the Bolshevik Revolution and the stalemate in Brest-Litovsk it allegedly engendered.[9] Historians examining the relationship between the January strike and Brest-Litovsk have largely confined themselves to an analysis of the effect of the strike on Czernin's negotiations with the Ukrainian delegation in pursuit of a "bread peace," which would eventually alleviate the domestic grievances and stem the tide of revolution.[10]

While these interpretations have much to recommend them, they tend to present a slightly one-sided view of January 1918, which does not do justice to the complexity of the situation. The strike began over the reduction of the flour ration, and a focus on factors purely ideological and class-related omits the important earlier lessons of the politicization of the home front and the gravity of the food crisis. Moreover, a focus on economic factors alone, disregarding the widespread resonance of Brest-Litovsk, cannot explain the dynamics of the movement, especially its expansion to parts of the Dual Monarchy which had relatively fewer problems with food provisioning, such as central Hungary. In the succinct words of Manfried Rauchensteiner, "it all began in Brest-Litovsk."[11]

In East Central Europe, suffering under blockade in 1917–18, bread and peace were, for all intents and purposes, two sides of the same coin. The war-weary working men and women across the region expected their immense contribution to the war effort to be rewarded with the return of economic prosperity and a greater say in politics, once peace was concluded. The Bolsheviks had realized this in 1917, which is why their surge in popularity owed much to the *promise* of bread and peace. As far as the Habsburg Empire was concerned, "in wartime Vienna, food *was* the political arena," writes Maureen Healy. "At all levels of society ... food dwarfed matters of public concern."[12] Once the food crisis had established a direct link between the home front and the politics of the war, there could be no bread without peace, especially the *general* peace that the strikers demanded. The Great January Strike therefore exemplified a general East Central European shift towards greater democratization and popular participation in domestic politics and foreign policy, both of which had been largely the preserve of an unaccountable Imperial establishment and bureaucratic and military elites prior to the Great War. By combining these issues, the Great January Strike anticipated the Central European revolutions of 1918–19.

Immediate Background and Outbreak of the Strike

The Austrian harvest in 1917 had been exceptionally poor, with wheat at 47 per cent of the 1913 figure, rye at 43 per cent, and barley at a catastrophic 29 per cent.[13] The harsh winter of 1917–18 exacerbated an already hazardous situation. By mid-December 1917, Czernin was trying desperately to figure out how the Dual Monarchy had found itself in such dire economic straits, given that the year's Hungarian harvest had been fairly reasonable. Wekerle had informed him that Budapest had flour only for a few days, and the same was true of Vienna. The chief reason, Czernin suspected, was the unregulated vending of foodstuffs which Count Móric Esterházy, Wekerle's predecessor as prime minister of Hungary, had unwisely sanctioned after the unexpectedly good harvest. This huge mistake could lead to dangerous consequences if the two governments did not attempt to make swift and effective amends, Czernin warned the emperor. The prospective peace with Russia would be poor consolation if Austria-Hungary proved unable to hold out until the next harvest. Furthermore, the expected Russian supplies were problematic, and the foreign minister doubted whether the Central Powers would receive anything at all. "It is perfectly clear that we cannot conduct foreign policy if there is starvation and revolution in the hinterland," Czernin concluded, imploring Emperor Karl to intervene personally and replace the Hungarian food minister, János Hádik, "with a more energetic person who has the will to act before it is too late," in order to requisition privately held supplies and deliver grain to Austrian cities.[14] However, little seems to have been done to address the matter over the following three weeks.

Contrary to what some socialist publications have asserted, the October Revolution appears to have had little immediate effect on the workers of Habsburg East Central Europe. The *Arbeiter Zeitung* welcomed the Bolshevik seizure of power as "an event of enormous meaning [*ein Ereigniss von gewaltigster Bedeutung*]" in a page-two editorial from 9 November entitled "A Revolution for Peace," but added the following qualification: "In Petersburg [sic], the proletarian revolution has won. But Petersburg is not Russia. How the provinces and the army are going to react to the Government of Workers and Soldiers, or whether the bourgeoisie, the aristocracy, and the officer corps will overthrow the democratic government, no one can say at the present moment."[15] More importantly, the 7 November coup elicited no official discussions of any kind within the SDAPÖ leadership over the course of the next two weeks.[16] The "event with enormous meaning" received a similarly muted response outside the capital, judging by the lack of reports of any unusual agitation among local workers from SDAPÖ crownland branches. The case of Linz, the provincial capital of Upper Austria, is perhaps not untypical of German-Austria as a whole for the period November–December 1917. Following the Russian example, some radical workers from the bigger industrial enterprises in Linz had begun to set up workers' councils in secret. According to one report, the inaugural meeting to elect council leaders took place on 12 December 1917 at an inn. The functionaries' subsequent actions consisted of popularizing the council system through covert propaganda and getting in touch with the Russian POWs stationed in the city. However, the influence of the Linz councils on the surrounding population was apparently minuscule, and no further activity reports were submitted until the end of October 1918.[17]

Thus, there appeared to exist little popular desire to emulate the revolutionary seizure of power in Russia if peace, and therefore bread, could be obtained in an orderly manner at the negotiating table, without further disruption to everyday life at home. As the food situation in the Dual Monarchy continued to deteriorate steadily, however, the Brest-Litovsk conference quickly captured the popular imagination, with one contemporary social-democratic publication observing that "the Austrian workers followed attentively the peace negotiations."[18] Where else would peace come from if one could not come to terms with the most peace-loving government in the world, the government of the Russian proletariat, the anonymous author asked rhetorically.[19] As we have already seen, the Bolshevik government was not in fact particularly peace-loving, but it presented itself as such brilliantly.

More importantly, reports of popular agitation and suggestions for peace action streamed into SDAPÖ headquarters from the provinces.

In early December, the Moravian party leadership in Brünn proposed starting a brief strike intended to serve as a peace demonstration.[20] Some two weeks later, SDAPÖ leaders Viktor Adler, Wilhelm Ellenbogen, and Karl Seitz received invitations to a conference in Budapest, at which German, Austrian, and Hungarian social democrats would discuss how best to work together for a quick peace. The party leadership debated accepting the invitation but eventually decided to undertake independent action in the near future.[21] However, they continued to drag their feet until Ellenbogen, no radical himself, urged the party to take an open position on the peace negotiations on 3 January. This finally resulted in concrete action, as the executive decided to convene three large gatherings in Vienna on 13 January in order to discuss the peace negotiations openly with the workers and put the government under pressure.[22]

In the meantime, calls for active social-democratic involvement in the peacemaking process continued to arrive from Austrian crownland party organizations and from across the Leitha. On 6 January, four thousand angry Hungarian workers protested in front of the German Consulate in Budapest against the Central Powers' refutation of the Ioffe Program because of the Entente's refusal to participate. The crowd hurled accusations at Kaiser Wilhelm and, more to the point, stones that smashed several of the consulate's windows.[23] Czernin instructed Ambassador Hohenlohe to apologize to the Imperial German chancellor, Hertling, but also to imply that such incidents were likely to recur if the negotiations broke down due to German obduracy.[24] German sources noted the great outrage over Austro-German policy in Brest-Litovsk expressed among radical Hungarian circles in Budapest, whose members had dispatched couriers to Berlin and Vienna to discuss the situation with German and Austrian radicals and coordinate possible revolutionary action.[25]

Elsewhere, on 7 January the Styrian social-democratic party leadership in Graz warned Vienna of great indignation [*Empörung*] with events in Brest-Litovsk among local workers. They proposed an immediate convocation of a meeting of the SDAPÖ central leadership and crownland representatives in order to organize a joint demonstration that would take place throughout all of German-Austria on the same day.[26] The Viennese invited the Styrians to send representatives to the session of the party executive on 12 January, where the issue would be debated, and informed them about the proposed gatherings for the following day.[27] On 12 January, the War Ministry reported dangerous excitement and dissatisfaction brewing among the workers of the Daimler Motor Works in Wiener Neustadt and singled out the subversive agitation activities of one Eduard Schönfeld, district secretary of the metal workers' union.[28]

The SDAPÖ leadership had once again underestimated the extent of popular enthusiasm. On Sunday, 13 January, five large meetings took place in halls in different districts of Vienna instead of the three planned. "The Peace Negotiations in Brest-Litovsk and Social Democracy" was the sole item on the agenda. Approximately five thousand people attended altogether, according to a police report. Ellenbogen, Domes, and Karl Renner delivered speeches that criticized the behaviour of the Central Powers' delegates in Brest-Litovsk, dismissed a "victorious peace [*Siegfrieden*]" as an impossibility, and demanded a peace without annexations and indemnities. Portentously, socialist leaders themselves came under fire from radical workers. As the discussions became more heated, cries of "Long live the revolution!" and "Long live the Austrian Revolution!" interrupted at least two of the gatherings.[29] The main speakers asked the workers to await the government's answer to their demands and remain calm. However, it was quite clear that the slightest catalyst could set a disturbance in motion, socialist observers noted soon after the fact.[30] Although no major incidents occurred, the overall situation had reached a critical point.

On Monday, 14 January, the Austrian government announced that the already low daily flour ration would be reduced in half. This was the last straw. That morning, the workers of the Daimler Motor Works in Wiener Neustadt walked out in protest, gathered in the factory yard, and sent delegates to the enterprise directors to demand the revocation of the government decree.[31] Sensing the gravity of the situation, the directors agreed to dispatch a representative who would convey the workers' demands to the Austrian food minister, General Anton Höfer, in Vienna. In exchange, they asked for the resumption of work in expectation of a reply from the government. However, the workers had had enough, and they indignantly refused to entertain the notion. Instead, they marched to the city centre and began protesting in front of City Hall with brochures and placards that declared: "Fight for an immediate general peace! Fight for political and social freedom! Down with the war! Down with the government!"

Word of the actions of Daimler's workforce spread throughout Wiener Neustadt and the surrounding area like wildfire, and workers from the locomotive and airplane factories, and the radiator and munitions works quickly joined the procession, swelling the crowd's size to between five and six thousand. The protesters categorically stated that they would not resume work until the flour ration was raised or suitable food substitutes were provided. The local authorities telephoned the Austrian Food Ministry in panic and asked them to delay the reduction of the flour quota, at least until the end of the week. The answer was negative, but the minister declared himself willing to confer with a protesters' delegation the next day. The workers stated they would dispatch a deputation to Vienna while also upholding the strike. In the afternoon the crowd, now ten thousand strong, relocated to the *Arbeiterheim* (labour council), where the convocation of the first workers' council [*Arbeiterrat*] in Austria duly took place, with the aforementioned Schönfeld elected as its chairman. In the meantime, a group of between five and six hundred youth who, according to the *Arbeiter Zeitung*'s subsequent report, had nothing to do with the earlier demonstration, clashed with the small detachment of Bosnian troops (two hundred men) the authorities had dispatched to secure the town square. In the ensuing fracas, most of the windows of City Hall were smashed. This minor incident notwithstanding, the outbreak of the great January strike was a remarkably peaceful affair, especially given the degree of latent tension that had accumulated over the preceding months.

Why did the great Austrian strike break out in Wiener Neustadt, a seemingly small and insignificant industrial centre in Lower Austria, of all places? It was by no means a coincidence. As Karl Flanner has argued, Wiener Neustadt had a strong, organized labour movement going back to the 1860s. The town had a high concentration of radical workers employed in heavy industry. Local socialist leaders had become battle-hardened through constant economic clashes with industrialists before the war. Furthermore, the presence of a significant number of non-German workers meant that proletarian internationalism was not merely a catchphrase for the Wiener Neustadt workforce. (A young Josip Broz Tito, the future communist dictator of Yugoslavia, who worked at the Daimler Works in 1912–13, was notably among these.) Last but not least, the large number of military establishments (barracks, military academy, munitions depot, military airport) in this smaller industrial centre brought the war to the home front in a way that was not paralleled in the Imperial capital or other larger cities.[32]

While this is perhaps a slightly idealized view of the situation on the ground, the documentary evidence suggests that the Wiener Neustadt workforce played a catalytic role for the Great January Strike similar to the role played by the *Putilovtsy* (workers in the Putilov Works in Petrograd, a large industrial complex primarily involved in armaments production) in the February Revolution in Russia. "The Putilov Works ... enjoyed prestige far beyond the Petergof District and even the capital," explains David Mandel. "Its participation in any collective action, by virtue of its numbers alone, made success so much more certain."[33] Like the *Putilovtsy*, the *Wiener Neustädter* were consistently more radical than their counterparts elsewhere, and their actions transformed ostensibly vague economic demands into clearly articulated political ones, even if this was not their initial intention. They also enunciated a radical program of revolutionary action and resolutely refused to return to the factories even after the central party leadership had repeatedly urged them to do so, thereby indicating that the strike could have taken a very different course from the one it eventually did.

Growth and Spread of the Strike I

The Wiener Neustadt delegation, accompanied by Renner, met with the food minister, Höfer, in the House of Representatives of the *Reichsrat* and presented him with two demands on the morning of 15 January. First, the government should increase the flour ration. Second, the government should give a solemn pledge of a favourable outcome of the ongoing peace negotiations in Brest-Litovsk. One social democrat Member of Parliament (MP) emphasized that the swift conclusion of peace was the paramount condition for the resumption of work. Other MPs added that the workers would no longer be satisfied with empty promises. As tensions rose, the negotiations were transferred to the Food Ministry in the afternoon. Höfer promised to send ministry officials to Wiener Neustadt to assess the situation and, if possible, provide assistance. He also called Baron Flotow in the Foreign Ministry for help on the second point. The predictable reply was that it would be impossible to resolve quickly the numerous international problems that had accumulated over almost four years of war. The Austro-Hungarian government had made its peaceful intentions clear on several occasions, and it was working hard to realize them at the negotiating table. Höfer later told Flotow that the workers had demonstrated a deep distrust of Germany's Brest-Litovsk policy, emphasizing that similar revolutionary developments were likely to occur throughout the monarchy if the peace negotiations continued to stall.[34]

Throughout that day, the situation in Vienna remained relatively quiet, even as the movement was already spreading throughout Lower Austria. In Leobersdorf near Baden around 8 000 workers took to the streets in protest, the driving force behind the gathering, according to authorities, being the by now familiar demands for bread and peace. Demonstrations continued in Wiener Neustadt, even as the military authorities tried to close off the main town square. Approximately 2 000 workers from the munitions factory and the printing press in the region also stopped work. Workers numbering close to 10 000 from Neunkirchen and its nearby towns demonstrated at the main town square calling for an immediate peace, denouncing the lackadaisical policy of the Austro-Hungarian delegation in Brest-Litovsk. A second, relatively peaceful meeting of some 3 000 workers took place that evening in the *Arbeiterheim* in Neunkirchen. In Baden, rumors circulated of a planned walkout for the following morning.[35] Disturbances also began to spread to the non-German parts of Austria on the same day (15 January) exemplified by the food riots which took place in Cracow. The provisioning situation in the Küstenland was catastrophic, and the principal city of Trieste could only be supplied by having the navy transport grain from the depot of the nearby naval base in Pola. Even so, the bread ration had to be cut in half, which sparked further workers' demonstrations. Local authorities feared the broadening of the movement.[36]

Up to this point, the SDAPÖ central leadership at party headquarters in the Vorwärts-Haus in Vienna had observed the course of events passively from the sidelines. They maintained that the strike had broken out spontaneously, without their knowledge or involvement. A brief report from Wiener Neustadt outlining the day's events had arrived on the evening of 14 January, but its publication in the *Arbeiter Zeitung* was forbidden by the censors. The party executive decided to send Adler and Seitz to talk to the prime minister, Ernst Seidler von Feuchtenegg, on the evening of 15 January and demand the publication of the report, which then was allowed to appear in the issue for 16 January of the *Arbeiter Zeitung*.[37]

Much more significant for the further growth of the strike was a revolutionary manifesto addressed to the workers which appeared on page one of the *Arbeiter Zeitung* on 16 January, escalating the situation considerably. It is unclear why the censors allowed it to go through, especially given Czernin's subsequent bitter complaints. There seems to be no official documentation on the subject; most likely, it was an oversight on the part of the censors, who passed it on, without paying too much attention to the details, as an addendum to the fairly neutral report of the strike in Wiener Neustadt, the publication of which report had already been agreed upon by the Austrian prime minister and the social democrats. Whatever the case, the manifesto, entitled "Working Men and Women," subjected Austro-German policy in Brest-Litovsk to devastating critique. Russia was demanding nothing from the Central Powers and was even prepared to give Congress Poland, Courland, and Lithuania independence in case the common people (not the upper classes, the article emphasized, which was a direct reference to the *Landesräte* in the Baltic presently the subject of debates between Kühlmann and Trotsky) were in favour of separation. "What interest have we got in the privileged classes deciding the state situation in these lands?" the author enquired, before answering his own question with a pithy "None." If the negotiations were allowed to break down on this issue, the war would go on, so that the Emperor of Austria may become King of Poland and the King of Prussia may control Courland and Lithuania militarily and economically. The people had made immeasurable sacrifices because they had been assured the Central Powers were fighting a defensive war. However, the public could now clearly see that this was no longer the case and that a war of conquest had commenced. It was essential that the ruling classes be made to realize that they alone were responsible for all the sacrifices the continuation of the war would require. Therefore, the manifesto concluded, "we ask you, working men and women, to make your voices heard and fight with us for the quickest possible end to the war! For a peace without open or hidden annexations. For a peace on the basis of genuine national self-determination."[38]

The manifesto was signed "the leadership of the Austrian Social-Democratic Party and the Parliamentary Club of German Social-Democrats," and Plaschka, Haselsteiner, and Suppan do not discuss the question of authorship any further.[39] However, neither Adler and Renner nor Ellenbogen and Seitz seem to have been directly involved in its composition, as the tone and intention of the manifesto are markedly different from those of all other lead articles on the subject in the *Arbeiter Zeitung* from this period. The likeliest suspect is Otto Bauer, one of the most prominent leaders and theoreticians of the left radicals within the party. While he did not claim authorship outright, Bauer emphasized the importance of the manifesto in his subsequent study of the Austrian Revolution. "It testified to the profound change that had already taken place that the party executive issued the manifesto and that the censorship ... did not dare to suppress it," he wrote a few years later.[40] Bauer had spent much of the war in captivity in Russia, which had further radicalized his ideas, and only returned to Austria in the autumn of 1917. In the months after his arrival, he led a double life as an officer in the Austro-Hungarian Army and leader of the radical left.[41] He soon made clear his displeasure with the policy of the SDAPÖ towards the government in a programmatic article entitled "Würzburg and Vienna," which he published in the social democratic journal *Der Kampf* under the decidedly uninspired alias O. B.

In the article, Bauer began by postulating that the social democratic party had always been a revolutionary party, and he criticized the current revisionism, specifically as practiced by the German majority socialists (SPD). This revisionism stipulated that the workers could achieve their goal of socialism through the peaceful overthrow of capitalism in the form of parliamentary reform rather than revolution. Bauer regretted that the majority of German-Austrian social democrats shared the views of "Scheidemann & co" and warned that the red internationalism of the old social-democratic party, which called on the proletarians of all countries to unite, had been replaced by a "black-yellow internationalism," whose aim was the union of all nations under the Habsburg scepter. The Russian Revolution had changed things dramatically, however, substantiating the accusations of revisionism hurled previously at the party leadership by Fritz Adler. The party executive, Bauer went on, consisted of "a couple of comrades who refused to hear alternative views and stifled discussion [i.e., Adler, Renner, Ellenbogen, and Seitz]." Nevertheless, he concluded that the Austrian left must carry out its mission within the old party rather than emulate the German left in splitting from the SPD in order to set up a separate organization (the USPD or German Independent Socialists).[42]

Events in Wiener Neustadt, then, presented Bauer and other likeminded radicals with the perfect opportunity to stir the people to action and shake the party out of its self-induced slumber. As Herbert Steiner has argued, the January strike was the logical outcome of the demands of the radical left.[43] While the Austrian radical left seemed genuinely inspired by the Russian Revolution, it is far from clear that they wished to go as far as the Bolsheviks in carrying out a concerted policy of red terror. For his part, Lenin had been dismissive of many tenets of Austro-Marxism, including Bauer's ideas of national self-determination. He was even more contemptuous of the moderate

Austrian social-democratic leadership, describing Karl Renner in January 1917 as "one of the most servile lackeys of German imperialism."[44] Consequently, as already discussed in chapter one, when Ioffe and Trotsky decided to intervene directly in the course of the Great January Strike, they requested permission from Czernin to travel to Vienna in order to meet with "representatives of the Austrian proletariat" [*predstaviteliami Avstriiskogo proletariata*] rather than any specific Austrian left radicals or members of the party executive.[45]

The strike arrived in Vienna with the publication of the manifesto in the *Arbeiter Zeitung* on 16 January. The workers of the Fiat Works in Floridsdorf (XXI. *Bezirk*) and the arsenal in Favoriten (X. *Bezirk*) were the first to walk out that morning in the Imperial capital, after word of mouth had arrived from Wiener Neustadt.[46] By early afternoon, fifteen thousand workers had gone on strike in Floridsdorf, including two thousand from the Fiat Works. Several hundred people protested in front of the Food Ministry. As the situation progressively deteriorated, the Vienna city commandant informed the chiefs of police that several enterprises had asked for military protection and that he had provided fifteen companies of one hundred men each.[47] A further four companies were expected to arrive over the course of the day from nearby Bruck an der Leitha. An infantry brigade was also en route, but it was expected to take several days to arrive.[48]

The police estimated the number of strikers in Vienna to be 55 080 in the early afternoon. In Simmering (XI. *Bezirk*), female workers intercepted an automobile transporting bread and stole twenty-five loaves. The police located them and arrested two of the women in order to discourage similar incidents.[49] However, this was merely a taste of things to come. All over the city, street cars came to a standstill as workers took to the streets to join the protest. Women and young people made up the majority of protesters in the city centre (*Innere Stadt*, I. *Bezirk*), Wieden (IV. *Bezirk*), and Favoriten, where twenty-one people were arrested.[50] The total number of strikers had risen to 84 300 by the evening. The afternoon also witnessed a new wave of demonstrations, which often took place in the *Arbeiterheime* of each district, with evidence of unanimous resolve to continue the strike. The speakers explained that the purpose of the strike was to force the conclusion of swift peace in Brest-Litovsk and improve the provisioning situation. In the gathering in Landstraße (III. *Bezirk*), one social-democrat MP criticized sharply the speech General Hoffmann had delivered in Brest-Litovsk on 12 January. In Brigittenau (XX. *Bezirk*), there was even a suggestion made to dispatch representatives of organized labour to Brest-Litovsk. Over the course of the afternoon, large crowds made up primarily of young men and women attempted to march from Favoriten to the city centre. While the police were successful in intercepting the majority, several hundred were able to reach the City Opera on the Ringstraße. Once there, they smashed the windows of a fashionable café and of the local tram to Baden. The perpetrators were detained.[51]

Most social-democratic leaders were taken aback by the scale of the disturbances. The party executive meeting on 16 January heard a report from Seitz about his talk with the prime minister the previous evening and about events in Floridsdorf. Tomschik elaborated on the mood of the Southern Railway workers, who had joined the strike after reading the front-page manifesto in the *Arbeiter Zeitung*. Domes explained that there were 61 000 workers currently on strike in Vienna; since this number is considerably lower than the figure reported by the police that evening, it is clear that events on the ground had caught the party leadership unawares. After a long discussion, they decided to issue a manifesto to the workers in the *Arbeiter Zeitung* the next morning in an attempt to reassert control of the popular movement.[52]

Previously the same day, Renner attended the scheduled conference of the representatives of the Food Ministry and the protesters in Wiener Neustadt, over which the town mayor presided. The representative of the Food Ministry described at some length the gravity of the overall food situation, while the workers acknowledged the government's efforts to handle the crisis as sincere but insufficient. All of the social-democratic speakers were unanimous in their belief that the cutting of the flour ration had not played a decisive role in the outbreak of the strike – it had been the Brest-Litovsk negotiations and the desire for general peace.[53] The workers were fully aware that the comprehensive resolution of the food question was inextricably linked with the conclusion of peace – first in the east, which would enable the arrival of foodstuffs from Russia, and then in the west, which would result in the lifting of the Entente blockade of the Central Powers. The irony that the importation of grain from the east would be possible only by way of forced requisitions and thus largely at the expense of others' suffering, especially that of Ukrainian workers, was probably lost on the Austrian workers who thought of Ukraine stereotypically as the breadbasket of the Russian Empire. In the meantime, there could be no mention of resumption of work in Wiener Neustadt or elsewhere. The movement continued to grow throughout Lower Austria, with 25 000 people estimated to be on strike in the district of Baden alone.[54]

On 17 January, the *Arbeiter Zeitung* published the manifesto the party leadership had agreed on the previous evening, which presented a set of conditions for ending the strike:

1 The government will provide a solemn guarantee that the peace negotiations in Brest-Litovsk will not break down as a result of territorial demands by the Central Powers. The government will inform the workers' representatives truthfully about the course of negotiations and will listen to their suggestions.
2 The government will reorganize the Food Ministry.
3 The government will agree to democratize local elections by introducing the universal, secret, direct ballot.
4 The government will end the militarization of industry.

The order in which these demands appeared reflected the workers' belief in the close correlation between the Brest-Litovsk Peace Conference and the food question. The reorganization of the Food Ministry could only be a stop-gap measure, pending the resumption of peacetime socio-economic relations and international trade. In conclusion, the manifesto stressed that the masses would cease their demonstrations and return to work only if the government acknowledged the voice of the workers and agreed to put an end to their suffering by bringing the war to a quick end.[55]

Apart from the list of demands, which the party leadership hoped might help stem the more radical undercurrents of the movement and engage the government in a dialogue, the *Arbeiter Zeitung* published a second article on the strike seeking to explain its origins. After relaying the events in Wiener Neustadt on Monday and their impact in Lower Austria since then, the article emphasized that there had been no concerted efforts to urge the workers to go on strike. The rising of the masses was elemental; hence, no power could have prevented it. The article went on to criticize Count Czernin's methods in Brest-Litovsk but conceded that the latest news from the peace conference were more positive than they had been for some time. They were hopeful that there would be a way to reach an agreement with the Russians and the Ukrainians. "But one cannot keep the masses calm with such promises!" the article warned. The government must honestly, scrupulously, and in the clearest possible way assure the masses that the peace conference would not break down as a result of annexationist demands.[56] With these two articles, the social-democratic leadership opened the door for direct negotiations and cooperation with the authorities in order to prevent the radical left from hijacking the popular movement. The ball was now in the government's court.

Government Attempts to Address the Food Crisis

The close relationship between food supply and domestic unrest was hardly unique to the Dual Monarchy. According to Charles Tilly, "the sudden failure of the government to meet specific obligations which members of the subject populations regard as well established and crucial to their own welfare" is an important cause of revolutionary situations.[57] During the Great War, food supply became *the* principal government obligation. The catastrophic breakdown in the provisioning system in Russia in the autumn of 1916 demonstrated the gross incompetency of the Imperial establishment and magnified its many shortcomings, destabilizing its already shaky hold over the country. There had in fact been plenty of grain in the countryside, but due to a breakdown in infrastructure and a shortage of rolling stock the authorities proved woefully inefficient in transporting it to large urban centers, especially Petrograd. Ordinary people blamed the government rather than middlemen or the bad harvests, and a women's demonstration against the shortage of bread in Petrograd held on International Women's Day was one of the important expressions of popular dissent that helped to spark the February Revolution.[58]

The breakdown of the relationship between rural and urban Russia in late 1916 had many parallels in the growing estrangement between rural Hungary and urban Austria in late 1917. This breakdown was also fuelled by an overly complicated political edifice that made urgent relief action extremely problematic. As we have already seen, the Habsburg authorities' inability to provide for their populations' most basic needs played an important role in the politicization of the home front and in the outbreak of the January strike. The looming collapse of the provisioning system threatened to completely delegitimize the Imperial and Royal Government and exacerbate considerably an already precarious revolutionary situation.

By the time the SDAPÖ leadership decided to reach out to the authorities on 17 January, the Austrian government had in fact been trying desperately to address the food situation for the previous two days.

On 15 January, Czernin received a letter from the governor of Bohemia, Count Max von Coudenhove, which he immediately forwarded to the Foreign Ministry for transmission to Emperor Karl and Prime Minister Seidler. According to this missive, which set all sorts of alarm bells ringing, Austria had received only limited quantities of foodstuffs from Hungary and 10 000 wagons of maize from Romania, resulting in a deficit of at least 30 000 wagons. Coudenhove had already warned the prime minister that in a few weeks Austria's war industry would grind to a halt, railway transportation would be made untenable, and army supply would break down. This catastrophe would lead to the collapse of Austria and subsequently of Hungary. Seidler had apparently answered only with a cryptic "Yes, so it is." No one seemed to be able to do anything about it, Coudenhove complained, and he could only hope that some *deus ex machina* would intervene to save the Dual Monarchy from the worst at the last moment.

This letter only seemed to confirm Czernin's worst fears. He blamed the prime minister's "frivolity and unreliability" for the dangerous situation, adding that he feared it was perhaps too late to avert a complete collapse [*Niederbruch*], which might be expected in the next few weeks. "Words fail me to describe Seidler's apathetic attitude," Czernin raged, while urging energetic action. First, he declared, the chairman of the Joint Food Committee, General Ottokar Landwehr von Pragenau, should immediately visit Kaiser Wilhelm with a personal letter from Emperor Karl. Without a direct appeal to the Kaiser, nothing would come of it, Czernin explained. Second, expropriations should take place in Hungary right away. Although government storehouses were empty, due to the Esterházy-Hádik Administration's grave error of allowing the unregulated selling of foodstuffs, it appeared that merchants, industries, factories, and villages had substantial stocks of supplies which could be used. The hapless Hádik would have to go. Third, the daily ration must remain cut indefinitely. Fourth, the government should determine whether Poland could send supplies. The situation was undoubtedly better in Lublin, Czernin opined. Fifth, Czernin himself would continue to make every effort to obtain supplies from Ukraine. This might be possible, but only in very low quantities, he cautioned, and only late in the spring. He finished by imploring Emperor Karl to take the food question extremely seriously. If economic policy were allowed to continue in the same clueless manner, the Habsburg Empire would undoubtedly experience revolutionary upheaval and collapse in the upcoming weeks.[59]

The conversation held between Count Demblin, the foreign ministry liaison at the Imperial Court, and Emperor Karl on 16 January to go over Czernin's suggestions highlighted the enormous institutional difficulties Dualism placed in the way of a successful government intervention. The emperor explained that he did not have the slightest illusion about the gravity of the situation. Requisitions would be carried out in Hungary in the most draconian manner. Demblin protested that requisitions were already happening, but in the wrong places. The peasants in the countryside had little, whereas the stocks of the middlemen and speculators had remained untouched. The authorities had to make sure the supplies reached the consumers quickly, before they spoiled. Emperor Karl consented but added it was too late to alter the entire system. The only way to fix the problem would be to create an extraordinary post of joint food dictator with unlimited powers. However, before he could take such a drastic measure, he would have to send both the Austrian and Hungarian parliaments packing, as they would never willingly consent to the curtailment of their respective powers such a plan entailed. As this was likely to precipitate a huge political crisis, the cure might prove to be worse than the disease and kill the patient. Demblin suggested that it might be possible to remedy the situation without such constitutional experiments, as long as the Hungarian food minister could set aside the separate interests of the Hungarian markets in the name of the survival of the Dual Monarchy and apply the necessary pressure. Since Hádik was not that man, he would have to be replaced with someone more reliable and more energetic. The emperor agreed to think matters over. In the meantime, he telephoned Ambassador Hohenlohe and dispatched General Landwehr to Berlin.[60]

Even as he advocated stern action, Czernin continued to be inundated with pleas for help. On 16 January, General Landwehr informed him that 450 wagons of flour must be sent to Vienna as soon as possible, as supplies would be completely depleted within the week.[61] Germany appeared to be the only immediate source of relief for the Dual Monarchy, and Czernin had no choice but to explain the situation to Kühlmann in every depressing detail and ask for 2 000 wagons of grain. Kühlmann relayed the request to the Imperial chancellor; however, as Germany was also suffering from food shortages, he doubted any relief would be forthcoming from Berlin.[62] Needless to say, this weakened Czernin's bargaining position in Brest-Litovsk considerably. The foreign minister complained bitterly that it was impossible to conduct foreign policy when the home front was in such disarray;[63] he could not be the mendicant and the demandant at the same time. "I am unable to remedy all your mistakes," Czernin wrote angrily to Prime Minister Seidler. Germany could not help, as it had too little for itself. The prime minister should see into the possibility of transporting Romanian supplies and confer with the Hungarian government about the expropriation of stocks "in the most brutal manner [*durch brutalste Gewalt*]" and their immediate shipment to Austria.[64]

Sending supplies from the Austro-Hungarian occupation zone in Poland was also problematic though not altogether impossible. The governor general, Stanisław Szeptycki, told the foreign ministry liaison in Lublin, Baron Hönning, that any requisitions would have an adverse political effect and make survival until the new harvest difficult.[65] Nevertheless, Czernin instructed him to stop all food shipments to Warsaw and reroute them immediately to the Dual Monarchy.[66] The Foreign Ministry representative in Warsaw also met with the Polish food minister, who explained that it might be possible to provide 4 200 wagons of rye, wheat, and oats, 12 000 wagons of potatoes, 400 wagons of legumes, and 200 wagons of seeds, albeit with great difficulty. While additional quantities might be raised through requisitions, this was likely to be met with popular resentment,[67] which would have the added drawback of endangering the future implementation of the Austro-Polish Solution further.

Startled by the extent of the crisis in Austria and the frightening possibility of the utter collapse of the Habsburg war effort, the Germans also decided to lend a hand. At a conference with Ambassador Hohenlohe and General Landwehr on 18 January in Berlin, the German government pledged to provide Austria with 4 500 tons of flour forthwith. In exchange, Hungary would pay Germany the same amount of flour or 5 600 tons of maize under Austrian supervision by 15 March. German shipments would commence as soon as the Austro-Hungarian Foreign Ministry had secured the acceptance of the Austrian and Hungarian governments. After the Austro-Hungarian minister plenipotentiary, Count Duglas von Thurn, pleaded with the government in Munich, Bavaria also promised to provide between 2 000 and 3 000 wagons of potatoes pending approval from the Imperial Potato Office and assurance that Bavaria's provision quota to the German Army would be reduced by the same amount.[68]

However, even the Germans' extraordinary 4 500 ton shipment would not suffice, the Austrian authorities informed Czernin, as this still left a 1 300 ton daily shortage; they asked the foreign minister to reroute to Austria the bread supplies, between 4 000 and 4 500 tons, in the Romanian Danubian ports of Orşova and Turnu Severin currently earmarked for Germany. In addition, the German-run Military Government Romania would have to do everything possible to provide Austria with at least 1 000 tons daily. Whereas during the previous year 300 000 tons of barley had been collected in Austria, the 1917 harvest had yielded no more than 142 000 tons. The recovered districts of East Galicia and Bukovina, partly fallow, had been plundered by Habsburg and Russian armies. Hungary had so far sent 44 000 tons. As far as the Romanian harvest was concerned, the Dual Monarchy had received 176 000 out of a total of 405 000 tons, 30 per cent of which had been appropriated by the army. Thus, only 70 per cent or 124 000 tons remained for the civilian population. Consequently, the food situation in Carinthia, Carniola, Trieste, and the Küstenland remained critical.[69]

With respect to negotiations on the remaining Romanian harvest, the Germans and the Austrians agreed that the Dual Monarchy should receive 125 000 tons of maize and 8 000 tons of wheat. As the harsh winter weather rendered shipment along the partly-frozen Danube almost impossible, these supplies would have to be transported with the use of Habsburg rolling stock.[70] Requisitions also took place in earnest in Hungary, after Prince Lajos Windischgrätz replaced Hádik as food minister in a cabinet reshuffle on 26 January, with the emperor's nod of approval. Windischgrätz was sufficiently "black-yellow" to look after the needs of the Dual Monarchy as a whole rather than solely those of the Kingdom of Hungary. He also understood better than most the close correlation between peacemaking in Brest-Litovsk and the social disturbances at home. "Internal confusion, foreign policy, food problem, these three were now one," he wrote in his memoirs. After the AOK provided him with three infantry divisions, he employed draconian measures to requisition all available supplies from Hungary to provide for Austrian cities.[71]

Lastly, Czernin instructed his younger brother in Sofia to check whether the Bulgarians might be able to send something. "Your Excellency can go as far as to assure the Bulgarian Government that we are prepared to bind ourselves to a treaty supporting their claim to the entire Dobrudja."[72] The elder Czernin's entreaty seemed reasonable enough, as Bulgaria was primarily an agricultural country whose core territory had been spared the devastation of the fighting; furthermore, the Bulgarians had occupied rich agricultural lands in Macedonia, old

Serbia east of the Morava River, and in the Dobrudja. In theory, at least, they were supposed to have plentiful supplies. However, as previously discussed (see chapter two), the Bulgarian government was looking to import food from Russia, which made it less than sympathetic to Austria's plight. Nevertheless, Otto Czernin promised to arrange a meeting with Prime Minister Radoslavov and King Ferdinand. He would impress upon the prime minister the danger of the spread of revolution throughout East Central Europe and play the "Dobrudja trump card [*Dobrudscha-Trumpf*]" carefully.[73]

In his meeting with Radoslavov on 16 January, Otto Czernin painted the situation in the darkest colours without, however, resorting to the "chief trump" of the Dobrudja. Justifiably alarmed, the prime minister consulted the king and immediately telegraphed the Bulgarian representative in Bucharest, General Tantilov, enquiring how much from its part of the Romanian harvest Bulgaria could offer. Nonetheless, he was doubtful more than 100 wagons would be available. As for sending grain from Bulgaria itself, Radoslavov was adamant this was absolutely impossible. General Protogerov, head of the DSGOP (Bulgarian food agency), had recently informed him that the slowly diminishing reserves would run out in April, "and what will happen then no one knows."[74] The following day, Otto Czernin warned the Foreign Ministry that there was serious danger of Bulgaria "attempting to jump the sinking ship" and signing a separate peace if the situation continued to deteriorate.[75] The revolutionary situation in Austria thus posed a severe threat to the diminishing cohesion of the Central Powers alliance.

On 18 January, Radoslavov informed the Austro-Hungarian minister plenipotentiary that Tantilov had no rolling stock to send the apparently available supplies. Worse still, the Danube would be unfit for shipping for another month and a half.[76] Things appeared to move along smoothly from there; by 21 January, Tantilov had prepared a few hundred wagons of flour and maize and promised to try his best to increase this number to about one thousand, as Czernin had requested. Radoslavov intimated that he was hopeful Austria-Hungary would stand fast by Bulgaria in its hour of need "like a true alliance partner." Otto Czernin thanked him graciously, adding that the Dual Monarchy's gratitude would make itself known in every situation.[77] In effect, this amounted to a tacit promise of Austrian political support for Bulgarian territorial aspirations in the Dobrudja. Radoslavov further explained that he was well informed about the disturbances in Austria thanks to Minister Plenipotentiary Andrei Toshev's dispatches from Vienna. The prime minister believed the strikes were fuelled by Bolshevik revolutionary propaganda, which was unfortunately making its way through the frontline. Such propaganda in the countries of the Quadruple Alliance could not lead to the same revolutionary outcome, he argued, since the political atmosphere across East Central Europe was rather different from that in absolutist Russia. In particular, the armies were more reliable; the Bulgarian army was *könig-treu*, Radoslavov reassured Otto Czernin.[78]

However, it soon transpired that the Bulgarians had been making their calculations based on wishful thinking more than anything else. On 21 January, the Austro-Hungarian representative in Romania, General von Sendler, telegraphed that nobody in Bucharest knew anything about supplies that belonged to Bulgaria or about locomotives and wagons being dispatched from the Dual Monarchy. Bulgaria had received a single shipment of 400 tons and a further exclusive shipment of 1600 tons from German supplies in Romania. In contrast, Radoslavov insisted that Bulgaria did have a claim to a part of the Romanian harvest.[79] General von Sendler confronted General Tantilov, who apparently replied that Bulgaria did not have a right to any Romanian supplies north of the Danube. The Bulgarians *may* have had a claim to the harvest in the Northern Dobrudja, formerly part of the Kingdom of Romania but not included in the military government, but this was never spelled out. The quantities of flour and maize Tantilov had dispatched to Austria could not, therefore, be part of a non-existent Bulgarian stockpile. In fact, Sendler concluded, they were *identical* with the Habsburg contingent Austria was scheduled to receive by default.[80] This farcical incident drove home the dysfunctional nature of the Quadruple Alliance with irresistible force. If there was no clarity on the ostensibly straightforward matter of who had what claims to the food supply of occupied Romania, how could the Central Powers coordinate their peace policies successfully in Brest-Litovsk? Confusion remained the order of the day.

Given the extent of the food crisis and inter-allied wrangling, however, the Habsburg authorities' actions were remarkably successful in averting a complete breakdown in January–February 1918. While Czernin had every right to harangue Seidler for his prior "apathetic attitude," the Foreign Ministry and the Austrian government were able to cooperate closely in securing an immediate food shipment from Germany, forcing the reluctant Hungarians to get their house in order and carry out requisitions, and negotiating a larger percentage of the Romanian harvest. Furthermore, the possible peace with Ukraine promised additional grain supplies in the spring. This was no mean achievement, especially bearing in mind that the principal statesmen already had their hands full negotiating in Brest-Litovsk and trying to contain the spread of social disturbances in the hinterland. Whatever its institutional faults, the Habsburg establishment played an active role in confronting a crisis whose potential implications cannot be underestimated.

Growth and Spread of the Strike II

While Czernin and the Austrian government were frantically scrambling to address the food shortage, the strike movement continued to broaden. By 17 January, the strike had spread to Styria, as 20 000 metallurgists in Graz and 5 000 workers in nearby Bruck an der Mur put down their tools and took to the streets. The authorities reported that the movement was largely peaceful,[81] although by this point they were clearly beginning to lose track of the numbers. According to one police report, by the evening of 17 January there were 93 000 strikers in Vienna, 100 000 in Lower Austria, and 25 000 in Styria. The resolutions of the various worker assemblies had emphasized that the movement was mostly about a swift conclusion of peace. The workers also asked the government to send labour representatives to Brest-Litovsk. Although a mass movement was afloat, the report continued, there had been no major disturbances so far, with the exception of a few incidents involving younger people. The strike had not yet spread to Bohemia; however, according to a recent telegraph missive, the workers of Prague had declared themselves in solidarity with the workers of Vienna. In expectation of further disturbances, the authorities strengthened the garrison in Laxenburg (Emperor Karl's residence) with an additional battalion. The AOK also decided to increase the Vienna garrison by two regiments, which were scheduled to arrive from the Eastern Front in the following two days.[82]

A different police report suggested that there were in fact 100 700 strikers in Vienna by the evening of 17 January. Numerous demonstrations took place in several districts over the course of the afternoon. The speakers demanded improvement of the provisioning situation and the dispatch of labour delegates to Brest-Litovsk. They also asked the workers to follow the directives of the party leadership in the next day's issue of the *Arbeiter Zeitung* and to gather for renewed demonstrations. In Rudolfsheim-Fünfhaus (XV. *Bezirk*), 1 000 assembled workers proceeded to block the path of several street cars and ordered the passengers to depart, smashing the windows and bringing all traffic to a halt.[83]

As the situation appeared to be spinning out of control on 17 January, Czernin instructed the Foreign Ministry to arrange a meeting with the SDAPÖ leadership, preferably the reasonable Adler, Ellenbogen, Renner, and Seitz, and inform them in the utmost secrecy that he was determined to achieve peace in the east. Ukraine's claim to East Galicia presented the main obstacle, the foreign minister elaborated; thankfully, the Ukrainians had dropped this demand the previous day, which cleared the path to a quick resolution. The German position had not prevented an understanding with Petrograd, Czernin added; in fact, he had a very specific [*ganz bestimmten*] plan to bring about peace and was merely asking for a few days' vote of confidence.[84]

The social-democratic party executive accepted the Foreign Ministry's offer of *pourparler*. It was an arduous, four-hour long discussion that was nevertheless "carried out in the most polite manner," Flotow reported to Czernin. Adler refused to extend the vote of confidence [*Vorschluss an Vertrauen*] the foreign minister had asked for, as this was unnecessary; Czernin was already more popular than any other Austrian minister, Adler explained. He only wished that "Count Czernin would remain true to himself and not abandon the guidelines we have agreed on." He further criticized the Central Powers' refusal note of the Ioffe Program from 5 January. It would not suffice for the SDAPÖ leadership to simply tell the people to behave calmly; messages from Brest-Litovsk had to arrive, specifying that the Habsburg delegation was doing everything possible to implement the workers' demands. Furthermore, the Imperial and Royal Government had to assure the protesters that the negotiations would not break down over Poland (i.e., insistence on the Austro-Polish Solution). Seitz explained that the popular movement could be restrained for no more than four to five days. After that, news of positive developments had to appear, specifically that the four-point manifesto published in the *Arbeiter Zeitung* had been taken into consideration. The situation was critical. "If this time is lost, we will all end up facing the same danger!" Seitz warned. The use of the pronoun "we," which implied that the Imperial and Royal Government and the SDAPÖ executive were in it together, is deeply symbolic of the transformation Central European social-democracy had undergone immediately prior to and during the Great War – from a revolutionary party *par excellence* to a party of the social status quo, promoting limited political change through parliamentary means.

A slightly longer discussion on the question of evacuation and self-determination in the former Russian western borderlands ensued. Adler stated that Trotsky would not renounce his stance on self-determination; therefore, it should be accepted. In any event, Adler suggested, Poland would adhere to Austria of its own free will, a view which demonstrates that the Austro-Polish Solution and the consequent structural reorganization of the Habsburg Monarchy were not the sole preserve of the governing circles in Vienna. He cautioned, however, that the current Polish government had nothing in common with the people and thus had no right to represent them. Flotow replied that a revolutionary movement of the type currently taking place in Austria weakened the Habsburg delegation's bargaining position at the negotiating table in Brest-Litovsk, insisting that such peace demonstrations had in fact the opposite effect of delaying the peace still further. Adler insisted that the party executive had had nothing to do with the actual outbreak of disturbances.

Other social-democratic MPs explained that the workers were following the peace negotiations in Brest-Litovsk with the utmost attention and that they were perfectly well aware that Austria's food supplies would only last until 1 March (as demonstrated, the supply situation was actually far worse than that). From that point on, everyone would starve to death, should a peace treaty not facilitate Russian imports. Adler stressed that the Austrian government should consider itself lucky that the movement had been largely confined to Lower Austria and the Alpine region and had not spread to Bohemia and Moravia. He also asked Flotow to inform Czernin that the social-democratic parliamentary club had done everything possible to calm the workers; however, only good news from Brest-Litovsk could resolve the situation.[85]

Criticism of the way the peace conference was being handled was rife in all forums of political expression. During the budget committee discussions in the House of Representatives of the *Reichsrat* on 17 January, social-democrats demanded dutiful reports from the government on the course of negotiations in Brest-Litovsk and criticized the recent behaviour of the diplomats of the Central Powers, particularly "the unbelievable speech of the unbelievable General Hoffmann" from 12 January.[86]

Later the same day, the SDAPÖ leadership convened to determine their course of action. Wiener Neustadt's Schönfeld explained that the party leadership had not anticipated the movement and had therefore not made any preparations. This was perhaps slightly disingenuous, given his earlier subversive activities which had elicited interest from the War Ministry. Schönfeld also suggested that the party leadership not propose a separate Habsburg peace in Brest-Litovsk. Instead, he hoped the Austrian strike might be able to compel the German generals to renounce territorial aggrandizement. After a heated discussion, the conference decided to follow this advice. The decision was to implore the strikers not to disturb food and transport enterprises. A workers' council of Vienna, made up of executives from all districts, had to be set up. Lastly, the meeting decided to organize a permanent committee consisting of representatives of the party leadership, labour unions, and the Viennese party organization, in order to successfully tackle future exigencies at short notice.[87]

Viennese workers, following the example of their counterparts in Wiener Neustadt, had already begun setting up organizational committees on their own initiative in several districts, starting in Meidling (XII. *Bezirk*) and Margareten (V. *Bezirk*) on the morning of 16 January. That afternoon, the workers of Favoriten chose a thirteen-man delegation and the following morning established a district workers' council [*Arbeiterrat des Bezirkes*]. In this manner, over the course of 17 January, all Viennese districts proceeded to organize themselves without any directions from the central party executive. In the afternoon, they held demonstrations that accepted the four demands the party leadership had issued earlier in the *Arbeiter Zeitung*. However, more radical meetings insisted on the eight-hour workday and the release of Fritz Adler from prison. In some places, anarchists called for a "fight to the end."[88]

On 18 January, the *Arbeiter Zeitung* announced that the representatives of the district committees would meet that evening at 6 p.m. in the opening session of the Viennese workers' council.[89] The party leadership, in a second article aimed no doubt at the Austrian government and the Foreign Ministry, explained that a democratic peace with Russia would eventually lead to the coveted general peace. The article further claimed that the people were convinced that the obstacles to peace were not coming from the Bolshevik government, which had repeatedly enunciated its amicable intentions. Hence, the workers had taken it upon themselves to force the guilty parties – the German and Austro-Hungarian governments – to stop making difficulties. They did not understand why Germany continued to insist on maintaining its military occupation of Russia's western borderlands or why the Central Powers were engaging in diplomatic games instead of pursuing the paramount task of coming to terms with Russia.

"The people want peace, only peace," the article emphasized, "and they wish our representatives in Brest-Litovsk to pursue nothing but peace."[90]

By 18 January then, everyone had become utterly convinced that the subsequent course of the strike was closely linked to the prospects for peace. The widely-held perception of a close correlation between the outcome of the Brest-Litovsk negotiations and the outbreak of revolution in East Central Europe was expressed most eloquently by Austrian Prime Minister Seidler in a conversation with the German ambassador in Vienna, Count Botho von Wedel, that very same day. "The future depends on Brest-Litovsk," Seidler explained. "A successful settlement will eliminate all [domestic] dangers. Although I am always optimistic, in my opinion it would be impossible to contain the situation here if the negotiations go on without any result. Austria cannot bear to see the peace negotiations fail."[91]

The military were in complete agreement with the civilian authorities' assessment. "The true reasons [behind the Great January Strike], it seems to me – and this is also the opinion of the central authorities in the hinterland – are political, as the workers want to force an immediate peace," wrote the chief of general staff, General Arthur Arz von Straußenburg, to Czernin. The cause of the entire movement lay in the sluggish course of the Brest-Litovsk negotiations. General Hoffmann's speech from 12 January in particular had caused considerable excitement. The consequences of the movement for the army and for the entire war effort could be most dangerous, Arz warned, asking the foreign minister to adjust the reports coming from Brest-Litovsk accordingly in order to calm tempers.[92] In a further missive, the general added that the state of morale of the troops in the hinterland and on the Italian Front made it highly desirable to move Austro-Hungarian forces from the Eastern Front to the affected areas. Since the majority of Habsburg troops in the east were located on the Ukrainian section of the front, Arz suggested that Czernin try to come to terms with the Ukrainians first.[93]

Last but certainly not least, Emperor Karl himself became convinced of the close correlation between peacemaking and domestic disturbances. The current unrest in Austria and Hungary was not due to food scarcity, he told Count Demblin on 17 January. The workers' movement was focused on influencing the OHL, and it was agitating for peace. He asked Demblin to inform Czernin that "I must once again assure you that the entire fate of the Monarchy and of the dynasty depends on the quick conclusion of peace in Brest-Litovsk." The authorities could not allow the domestic situation to spin out of control for the sake of Courland, Lithuania, and Polish "dreams of grandeur [*Träumereien*]." "If we don't sign peace in Brest, there will be revolution here regardless of how much we have to eat," the emperor warned. Demblin remarked that "the food and peace questions go hand in hand," which was also the view held by Czernin. When the Austrian government attributed the unrest solely to the course of the peace negotiations, it created a vicious circle, as the successful conclusion of peace in Brest-Litovsk depended on the preservation of stability in the hinterland.[94] The emperor was correct in highlighting the political nature of the workers' demands, but he failed to grasp the extent to which peace and food were interrelated. The Bolsheviks would be unwilling to conclude a peace agreement if they saw that their revolutionizing tactics were about to bear fruit, which would undoubtedly happen if the principal Austrian industrial centres were allowed to completely run out of food. The Habsburg authorities would therefore have to repair the provisioning system *and* work for peace at Brest-Litovsk simultaneously.

While Habsburg statesmen blamed each other for the revolutionary situation explicitly and implicitly, the strike continued to grow and spread. The police estimated that there were 103 500 strikers in Vienna by the evening of 18 January. At an assembly of arsenal workers in Favoriten, a social-democratic MP stated that Germany had declared itself willing to renounce the annexation of occupied Russian territories in an attempt to calm the mood. Nevertheless, five hundred demonstrators endeavoured to march towards the headquarters of the semi-official *Reichspost* newspaper, raining a barrage of snowballs and stones on the security forces dispatched to secure the building. In the ensuing fracas, one policeman was slightly injured, and the helmet of another was broken. As the commander of the military detachment came under attack, he drew his sabre; several officers hastened to his defence and also drew their sabres without, however, injuring anyone. Eventually, the police arrested ten demonstrators, dispersing the rest.[95]

In the evening hours, a 1 000-man strong demonstration took place in Landstraße to demand the quickest possible conclusion to the peace negotiations in Brest-Litovsk. A similar gathering of roughly the same size in Brigittenau debated the authorities' explanation that rations must remain cut for the time being and stated the workers would hold the government responsible. Speakers announced that the strike would go on until it compelled the governments in Berlin and Vienna to conclude peace with Russia.[96]

In an attempt to appease the workers, Seidler decided to confer with the Foreign Ministry about releasing an official government response to the four demands. He proposed to accept unconditionally point two (reorganization of the Food Ministry), offer a vague explanation on point three (democratization of local elections), and agree to discuss point four (end to the militarization of industry) with the military authorities; since point one (successful outcome of the Brest-Litovsk Conference) was a matter of foreign policy, he asked Czernin for guidelines. He also promised to continue negotiating with the SDAPÖ leadership.[97]

The first session of the Viennese workers' council took place as planned late on 18 January. The party executive delivered a report on the movement up to that point. Some radical delegates raised additional demands, such as the eight-hour workday, an end to censorship, and the release of Fritz Adler. Others blamed the party leadership for formulating the four demands on its own, without conferring with the workers. The printing press workers, who had decided to join the strike on the following morning, brought up the question of how best to keep the masses informed, since the *Arbeiter Zeitung* would also be affected by the walkout. The council authorized the daily publication and distribution of a brochure entitled *Mitteilungen an die Arbeiter*. In addition, a 140-member committee was chosen to continue the negotiations with the government on 19 January[98] This meeting completed the coordination and organization of the movement, with parliamentary and street action seemingly working towards the same goal of compelling the authorities to provide bread and peace. The SDAPÖ leadership, which dominated the Viennese workers' council, appeared to be regaining control of the grassroots movement, stirring it towards moderation.

Why did the party leadership refuse to adopt some of the more radical demands and/or contemplate a potential revolutionary seizure of power? Two articles published in *Der Kampf*, the party's main theoretical journal, between January and March help explain the leaders' rejection of further radicalization. In the key article, entitled "The Tactical Dispute," Karl Renner argued that "you do not temper steel with the same tools you chisel stone, and in the same way you change the means of the class struggle" depending on the prevailing circumstances. In a state like Austria which already had universal male franchise, the workers could achieve much – though admittedly not everything – through the ballot. In an absolutist state like the defunct Russian Empire, they could not. In the former case, parliamentary action was preferable, whereas direct or revolutionary action worked best in the latter. "These examples show that the tactical situation differs from country to country and from time to time. The means are different, the contact points [*Angriffspunkte*] plentiful, but the goal is one [i.e., socialism]," Renner opined.

Renner went on to accuse the Austrian left radicals of falsely believing that capitalism and the state had exactly the same shape in every country and at all times, and that the class struggle must therefore take the same form and go through identical phases. It was clear that the Bolshevik tactic of a revolutionary seizure of power could only bring success if several factors were in play. First, the peasantry had to be revolutionary, with the land question dominant. In the Dual Monarchy, this was mostly true for Galician and Slovak peasants but not for the Czechs. Second, the state apparatus and army had to be completely destroyed, which was entirely not the case in Germany and only partly true in Austria. Third, the enemy at the gates had to be willing to make peace, which did not apply to the Western Front, where Germany still faced a mighty, determined coalition.[99]

Julius Deutsch expressed a similar sentiment in the theoretical overview of the history of radicalism he provided in "Radical Currents." Deutsch accused the radicals of being unable or unwilling to comprehend the complexity of the situation and of placing emotion [*Gefühl*] above understanding [*Verstand*]. The more radical a party or a movement was, he explained, the easier it would be for its simple and straightforward message to appeal to the immature masses. The newly converted worker already had plenty of emotion, but he needed to learn understanding in order to become a true socialist. Those who had not yet become genuine socialists were especially prone to radicalism. "Radical movements are to a great extent injurious to the general labor movement," Deutsch warned, as they imperilled the achievements the proletariat had already accomplished. The radicals were counting on the complete victory of the masses in the mistaken belief that they could achieve everything in one giant leap.[100]

While these theoretical deliberations of the SDAPÖ leaders help explain their view of what the main objectives of the Great January Strike should be, the situation on the ground remained fully charged. Outside the Imperial capital, a general strike was in effect in Linz on 18 January. That day, the workers of the machine factory in Brünn joined the strike. In Cracow, which had been one of the first industrial centers in Austria to experience social disturbances at the beginning of that week, street demonstrations continued to take place virtually uninterrupted. Women were particularly active during the protests in front of government buildings, especially City Council. By 17 January, workers had begun to walk out of the major industrial enterprises.[101]

The fact that the protests began to affect Hungary by 18 January was, arguably, of even greater consequence. Around eleven o'clock that morning, street car workers in Budapest went on strike. The workers were enraged by the authorities' decision of the previous day to forbid the publication of any reports of the Austrian events; by noon, work in all industrial enterprises had ceased. Fifteen demonstrations involving 40 000 protesters took place in different parts of Budapest in the early afternoon. Some groups of protesters marched towards the city centre, where the police checked their progress and successfully dispersed them.[102]

The motives of the Hungarian strikers were largely the same as those of workers in Vienna, so reported *Mitteilungen an die Arbeiter*. The Hungarian Social-Democratic Party, accordingly, declared a general strike. Since workers had no parliamentary representation, they were compelled to resort to direct grassroots action in order to protest against the unnecessary prolongation of the war and the annexationist policy of the government. The domestic situation, exacerbated in part by the unhappy prospect of the return to power of the archconservative Count István Tisza, had also contributed to the rise of the workers' movement. Austrian workers were already striking in their hundreds of thousands; the workers of Hungary now followed their example and laid down their tools in an act of solidarity.[103]

By the next day, 20 January, the strike had affected most major Hungarian cities, with workers' councils forming in Nagykanizsa, Szeged, and elsewhere.[104] Large crowds of women and children took to the streets in Preßburg.[105] The German consul general in Budapest reported that the popular movement was beginning to acquire revolutionary colours.[106] According to an anonymous Budapest merchant, "our present situation is extremely critical. Stock rooms are entirely empty. Owing to the lack of raw materials, our factories do not work. So it is impossible to replace the stock." By 26 January, even the workers of Szabadka, a town located in a rich, wheat growing region of southern Hungary, were protesting against the reduction of flour rations.[107] In the words of one Hungarian historian, "[t]he January strike marked a turning point in Hungary's labour movement towards the revolution."[108]

Meanwhile, back in Vienna, the grassroots movement had affected three hundred and thirty enterprises by the evening of 19 January, with the number of strikers peaking at 113 000. In the railway depot in Margareten, a meeting of workers' delegates discussed the ongoing negotiations with the government and decided to urge the workers of Austria to resume work immediately. However, another workers' gathering of several thousand people in the *Arbeiterheim* in Favoriten issued a protest against the party executive and decided not to resume work. The number of strikers in Lower Austria increased to 155 500 in total. The workers in the Neunkirchen and Ternitz districts in particular were showing very radical tendencies, the police warned. This was clearly evident from the circulated brochures, which called for the continuation of the strike. Simultaneously, the movement also affected Bohemia. The workers of the Škoda Works in Pilsen (around 50,000) conferred with a deputation of railway workers and subsequently sent a train with demonstrators through the city to spread their message. In several speeches, the workers' leaders called for solidarity with the striking workers of Vienna and Lower Austria. Some 7 000 workers also walked out in Kladno. Work in all large industrial enterprises in the Moravian capital of Brünn ceased for the day. In many other Moravian industrial centres, assemblies issued manifestoes affirming their solidarity with the workers of Vienna and Lower Austria. However, an actual joining in the general strike did not occur. According to the latest messages, the authorities could expect the resumption of work the next day. In Upper Austria, the workers' movement affected the Austrian Weapons Factory and other industrial enterprises in Steyr and the surrounding area. In Linz, the workers of the tobacco factory walked out, bringing the total number of strikers in that city to around 15 000 in total. Lastly, the movement spread also to Styria, affecting some 35 000 railway and metallurgical workers altogether.[109]

The eagerly anticipated crucial second phase of the negotiations between the SDAPÖ and the Austrian government took place on 19 January, as Prime Minister Seidler, the food minister, General Höfer, the minister of the interior, Count Toggenburg, and the minister of territorial defence, Lieutenant Field-Marshal von Czapp, received the workers' delegation led by Adler, Seitz, Renner, Domes, and Hanusch. Seitz began with a speech about the horrors of three and a half years of war leading up to the armistice and the Brest-Litovsk peace conference. The negotiations had raised people's hopes, but subsequent news of delays had stirred fears of breakdown. Combined with the precarious food situation and the militarization of industry, this had resulted in a grassroots movement that sought to bring about peace.

Seidler replied that the government was prepared to accept the workers' demands in an attempt to come to an understanding. If, at the present time only a separate peace with Russia was feasible, this was entirely the fault of the Entente, which had refused the Central Powers' repeated peace offers. The authorities had made clear on several occasions that the Brest-Litovsk negotiations would not break down on account of annexationist demands. The government considered Poland to be an independent state that would freely choose its future constitutional arrangement; the best way to do so would be to convene a constituent assembly. However, the Imperial and Royal Government had to refuse the Russian demand for immediate evacuation of Poland, not because the Habsburgs wanted to use the occupation to influence the Polish decision, but because the ongoing war on other fronts and the uncertain internal relations in Russia meant that the Central Powers could not do so without endangering their military position. Negotiations with Ukraine were going well, and an understanding was imminent, the prime minister promised. He also acknowledged the people's desire to receive abundant information about the peace conference and agreed to keep their elected representatives in the *Reichsrat* apprised of the latest developments. Seidler concluded by reading a note from Czernin, in which the foreign minister assured the social-democrats he was doing everything possible to conclude peace in the east; this explanation was immediately published on page one of *Mitteilungen an die Arbeiter*, in effect the only widely circulated publication in Vienna on 19 January.

After Seidler had finished, Food Minister Höfer elaborated on the food situation and declared himself ready to undertake the desired reorganization of the Food Ministry, while also explaining that the Austrian government was negotiating with Hungary for additional supplies. The minister of the interior, Toggenburg, also acknowledged the need for democratic reforms in municipal elections. Finally, the minister of territorial defence, Czapp, promised to introduce a new law that would see the transition of militarized industrial enterprises to civilian leadership. In conclusion, Seidler expressed his desire for the workers to remain calm and resume work. It was necessary for everyone to work together in order to bring the war to a swift end, he emphasized. On behalf of the workers' delegation, Adler thanked the Austrian government and added that the delegates would report the outcome of the meeting to the masses; however, it was too early to say what would happen then.[110]

3. The Ukrainian delegation in Brest-Litovsk, from left to right: Mykola Liubynskyi, Vsevolod Holubovych, Mykola Levytskyi, Lussentyi, Mykhailo Polosov, Oleksandr Sevriuk. F. Bruckmann, *Grosser Bilderatlas des Weltkrieges*. Wikimedia Commons.

Ending the Strike

Ending the Great January Strike proved much more difficult than starting it, the earnest efforts of the SDAPÖ central leadership notwithstanding. This, in turn, is demonstrative of the level of radicalization of the popular movement. The second session of the Viennese workers' council, which lasted from 10 p.m. on 19 January until 3:30 a.m. on 20 January, debated the party's response to the government's offer to acquiesce to the workers' demands. Seitz reported on the talks between the social-democratic delegation and the government, which were prolonged due to the need to communicate with Czernin in Brest-Litovsk. Seitz further outlined the government's replies to the four demands, declared that they were, on the whole, satisfactory, and urged the council to accept them and bring the strike to an end. The subsequent discussion featured several speeches, including two by representatives from the Wiener Neustadt workers' council. One of them doubted whether the Viennese workers' council had the authority to make a decision to end the strike on behalf of the entire Austrian labour movement. The Wiener Neustadt workforce put great value on the eight-hour workday and the release of Fritz Adler from prison, both of which Vienna had refused to countenance. Another radical delegate argued that the workers would not be satisfied until they knew for sure that the blood spilling had ended definitively on all fronts. Voices doubting the truthfulness of Czernin's promises and his ability "to break with the Junkers" were also heard. Finally, there was a suggestion to continue the struggle for another few weeks in order to compel the government to deliver on its promises.

Renner thanked the *Wiener Neustädter* for their role in spurring the movement but argued that Czernin's statement in effect meant that an Austro-Hungarian foreign minister had been held accountable by Parliament, let alone the workers, for the first time. Consequently, when Czernin returned to Brest-Litovsk (after his expected sojourn in Vienna), things would proceed much more swiftly. The proletariat must shepherd its forces, in case an additional crisis that required direct action were to arise in the immediate future. However, the delegates from Wiener Neustadt proved relentless, arguing that the movement "must go all the way," presumably even to a revolutionary seizure of power. They categorically refused to go along with the abrupt change of course Vienna proposed and accused the party leadership of making decisions over the head of Wiener Neustadt. As a counterproposal, they suggested holding a joint conference of Viennese and crownland social-democrats.

In contrast, several moderate speakers pointed out that there would be anarchy if the strike lasted for another week or longer and questioned who would bear the responsibility for such an outcome. Adler added that the movement had already achieved everything that was possible to achieve in three days. By prolonging the strike unnecessarily, the workers risked losing something, not least confidence in their own judgment and sense of respectability. In the closing speech before the vote, Seitz suggested that the Russian example was not applicable to Austria, since the Austrian peasantry and middle class were not nearly as revolutionary as their Russian counterparts. The proletariat remained the only bona fide revolutionary force in Austria; as such, it had to be used sparingly. To overextend it would be foolish. After much wrangling, the Viennese workers' council voted overwhelmingly, by a count of three hundred and eight votes to two, to call for an end to the strike, the two against being cast by the representatives from Wiener Neustadt.[111]

In accordance with the council's decision, on the morning of 20 January, *Mitteilungen an die Arbeiter* published an explanation of the government's reply and urged all Austrian workers to resume work the following day.[112] Over the course of 20 January, the vast majority of the 113 000 strikers in Vienna gathered throughout the various districts to discuss the council's resolution. In Ottakring (XVI. *Bezirk*), a meeting of 300 representatives took place at 9 a.m., with the majority of speakers in favour of the resumption of work. Moderate orators also assured the gathering that the Viennese workers' and district councils would remain in existence after the end of the strike. Radical delegates, however, accused the party leadership of being in league with the government. Subsequently, the decision was made to hold another meeting at 3 p.m. on Monday in order to decide whether to resume work on Tuesday, 22 January. Similar meetings in Margareten and Meidling decided to resume work on Monday afternoon rather than Monday morning, as the party had requested. The moderate social-democrats who presided over these assemblies had to overcome substantial opposition to the council's resolution. The deliberations in Favoriten, where the workers denounced the speakers as traitors and robbers, were especially heated. Radicals emphasized the need to continue the strike in order to aid their Hungarian comrades.[113] As this excitement demonstrates, the grassroots movement had gathered tremendous momentum, and the transition to normal working relations proved to be a drawn out, messy affair.

The Viennese police authorities estimated that only about 60 per cent of workers had resumed work during the day of 21 January, the rest disregarding the SDAPÖ central leadership's repeated urges to do so. The remaining strikers attended stormy conferences in several districts, which led to serious confrontations between radical elements and moderate party representatives, who were accused of betraying the workers. In one not untypical incident, as a gathering of some 2 000 in Landstraße was about to adopt a resolution on the resumption of work on 22 January, a young man by the name of Rudolf Beer took to the platform and delivered a fiery speech, in which he dismissed the promises of the government as a worthless piece of paper and insisted that young people would continue the strike. Beer, who was later arrested, was an unmarried, twenty-one year-old jurist from Brünn, who worked as a low ranking civil servant in the Austrian Food Ministry (vegetables division). This is probably as accurate a description of the typical Austrian male radical at this time as any, and it might also help explain the limitation of radicalism's appeal. Older workers, who did not share Beer's sentiment probably because they had much more to lose, decided to resume work. In the meantime, the police had to break up a radical demonstration involving around 1 400 young men and women in Favoriten, which appeared to be getting out of hand.[114]

In an attempt to clarify the situation and facilitate the orderly resumption of work, the *Arbeiter Zeitung* published a front page editorial on the strike on 22 January, which reminded the workers that their struggle had been above all about peace. "Peace, Freedom, and [rule of] Law – this was the goal of the struggle, and it has been achieved." The workers' representatives had become convinced that the only way to procure bread was through peace. "Peace policy is the only available food policy [*Friedenspolitik ist die einzige offene Ernährungspolitik*]," the editorial concluded.[115] The implication was that the radicals were endangering the swift conclusion of peace by prolonging the strike, thereby exacerbating the food crisis.

This line of reasoning appeared to resonate with the masses, and radicals in Vienna and Lower Austria began to lose their influence. The police estimated that the number of strikers in the Imperial capital decreased from 56 000 on the morning of 22 January to 14 700 by the evening. Most of these had also been content to go back to work, but the radicals had somehow managed to dissuade them.[116] On 23 January, the authorities reported that work had resumed throughout Vienna and in most affected industrial centers in Bohemia and Moravia. The situation in Lower Austria had improved markedly since the previous day, and work had already resumed or was scheduled to do so in Wiener Neustadt, Baden, and Wilhelmsburg.[117] The formal meeting of the Viennese workers' council which took place at 6 p.m. on 24 January, with representatives from several Lower Austrian workers' council in attendance, declared the Great January Strike officially at an end.[118]

However, the situation was not nearly as straightforward as the social-democratic party executive wished to have it appear. Even as the Great January Strike was winding down in Vienna and Lower Austria, its powerful reverberations continued to be felt elsewhere in the Austrian half of the Dual Monarchy. On 23 January, striking miners in Mährisch-Ostrau in Moravia and Orlau in Silesia adopted a resolution that called for a work boycott to push for bread, freedom, and the achievement of democratic peace in Brest-Litovsk.[119] A week later, most of the coal mines in Moravia and Silesia, which were vital for the Habsburg war effort, remained either fully or partially shut down. In Silesia, 8 200 miners out of a total of just over 11 600 had laid down their tools, while only 100 of the 2 300 miners in Moravia were at work.[120]

On 2 and 3 February, angry student crowds threw stones at the German Consulate in Lemberg, the provincial capital of Galicia and a contested Polish-Ukrainian space; the military had to intervene in order to disperse them.[121]

The situation in the Küstenland also remained critical. Although things were fairly quiet in Pola, disturbances in Trieste, which along with Wiener Neustadt and Cracow had been one of the focal points of social unrest early on, continued as late as 29 January. On that day, the number of strikers was approximately 4 000. A crowd of working women, men, and children proceeded to march to the Piazza Grande and protest in front of the governor's office, demanding bread and peace. The police were able to break up the demonstration without further incident. The *Lavoratore* (local social-democratic organ) published the resolution the gathering had passed, which called for a quick peace and the improvement of provisioning. The censors blacked out certain parts of the resolution, especially those referring to an immediate peace, in an attempt to prevent further agitation.

By 31 January, however, there were as many as 15 000 workers on strike in the port city. That evening, a workers' delegation visited the governor to demand an immediate peace, an improvement in the provisioning of food and coal in Trieste and the Küstenland, and the restoration of the city's municipal autonomy. The governor emphasized Emperor Karl's well-known desire for peace, referred to Czernin's remarks on the subject, and stressed that the duties of the Habsburg delegation in Brest-Litovsk would be easier if the population demonstrated support by remaining calm. He admitted to problems in the provisioning of food and coal; however, the Food Ministry had assured him that the government was doing everything possible to address these issues. Lastly, the governor referred to the promise made by the minister of the interior, Count Toggenburg, to introduce municipal election reform, insisting that the authorities would soon implement changes to ensure the participation of all social classes in the municipal government of Trieste. He concluded with an appeal to the workers to resume work as soon as possible. After a lengthy debate, the protesters agreed to do so the following day on the basis of the governor's explanation.[122]

"Everything is calm [*Es herrscht Ruhe*]," Seidler informed Czernin on 1 February.[123] As these individual cases demonstrate, however, dissent continued to simmer below the surface throughout Austria, producing occasional violent outbursts. Between 1 February and 3 February, 4 000 sailors from the Austro-Hungarian Fifth Fleet stationed in the Gulf of Cattaro in the Adriatic raised the red flag and mutinied in what one contemporary socialist author described as "the answer of the comrades in arms to the call for struggle by the comrades in the work place [i.e., the January strike.]"[124] The authorities feared a repetition of the January strike in late March, and a second wave of major strikes swept through Austria in June, after the already meager food ration had to be reduced yet again. In effect, the Dual Monarchy never again experienced a complete return to normalcy in wartime social and economic relations.

Conclusion: The Dog in the Night-time

Austria-Hungary had had its fair share of social unrest before January 1918, due to a combination of government repression, diminishing harvests, and the clear inability of Dualism to deal with the pressures of total war. As the Austrian government was forced to reduce the daily food ration in mid-January 1918, the workers of Wiener Neustadt spontaneously walked out of the factories, demanding bread and the swift conclusion of a non-annexationist peace in Brest-Litovsk as a prelude to general peace. In a matter of days, the strike movement spread like wildfire throughout Vienna and most Austrian crownlands, involving over 700 000 workers from Mährisch-Ostrau in the north to Trieste in the south, and from Salzburg in the west to Lemberg in the east. Regardless of their ultimate goal or political affiliation, statesmen ranging from social-democratic leaders to the emperor, the foreign minister, and the chief of general staff were unanimous that a genuine revolutionary situation had engulfed Austria. Given the gravity of the food crisis and the deadlock in Brest-Litovsk, the moment seemed opportune for a revolutionary seizure of power by the proletariat of Habsburg Central Europe.

What factors helped stem the tide of revolution in January 1918? Sociologist Theda Skocpol has emphasized the importance of military dissolution caused by international crises for the successful outcome of revolutionary situations.[125] In January 1918, the Habsburg army and government apparatus did not disintegrate amidst the revolutionary chaos. In fact, they were unusually active in attempting everything possible to prevent the looming collapse. The Austrian government and the Foreign Ministry successfully negotiated food shipments from Germany, Poland, and Romania, and food requisitions in Hungary.

They also entered into negotiations with the social-democratic leadership and proved willing to entertain their main demands. The Habsburg delegation in Brest-Litovsk moved closer towards peace with Ukraine. Acting in close cooperation with the civilian authorities, the AOK dispatched additional troops from the Eastern Front to the hinterland, which prevented revolutionary upheavals while being careful not to provoke an even more violent backlash by employing excessive force. In addition, the moderate social-democratic leadership, which had renounced violent revolutionary transformation in favour of a gradual parliamentary transition towards democratic socialism, was able to outflank the radical minority that pushed for a revolutionary seizure of power on the Bolshevik model, and then to guide the grassroots movement towards moderation. The moderate leadership also helped formulate reasonable demands the Habsburg establishment might be willing to countenance without a complete loss of prestige in an attempt to bring about a negotiated end to the strike.

Despite the successful prevention of a revolutionary seizure of power in Habsburg Central Europe, however, nothing was ever the same after January 1918. Austrian social-democracy grew in confidence, having retained the organizational structure it had created during the strike. The workers' councils in particular continued to operate virtually undisturbed by the authorities. The Great January Strike was akin to the curious incident of the dog in the night-time, to which Sherlock Holmes once drew Inspector Gregory's attention ("But the dog did nothing in the night-time," protested Inspector Gregory. "That was the curious incident," remarked Holmes) in that its implications were just as important as its failure to "bark." "The January strike could not lead to revolution immediately," observed Otto Bauer with the benefit of hindsight. "But it was a revolutionary demonstration of great historical impact, whose foremost contribution was as a prerequisite to the October and November Revolution."[126] Seen from this perspective, the Great January Strike emerges as the opening act of the Central European revolutions of 1918–19, which swept away the imposing Hohenzollern and Habsburg establishment and smashed the seemingly impregnable Imperial-dynastic edifice in the region. The Bolsheviks turned out to be correct in their conjecture that Brest-Litovsk would facilitate revolution in East Central Europe. Where they were in error was in the *timing* and *type* of revolution.

Chapter Four

The Brest-Litovsk System and Modern Ukrainian Statehood

Against the background, in mid-January 1918, of a revolutionary crisis unfolding in East Central Europe, and given the unavoidable conculsion that the Bolsheviks were not particularly interested in the conclusion of peace, the diplomats of the Central Powers in Brest-Litovsk during the second phase of the negotiations decided to turn to the recently arrived Ukrainian delegation in an attempt to break the deadlock and at the same time secure much needed food supplies. This fateful decision set in motion a sequence of events, which resulted in the signing of the first peace treaty of the Great War, between the Quadruple Alliance and the newly established Ukrainian People's Republic, necessitating an Austro-German military intervention which affected the course of both the Ukrainian and Russian revolutions. Ultimately, it fostered the dual process of Imperial collapse and nation-state formation in East Central Europe while playing an important role in the origins and early stages of modern Ukrainian statehood.

The large corpus of literature on the Ukrainian Revolution has mushroomed in the twenty-five years following Ukraine's re-emergence as an independent state. Valerii Soldatenko and Vladislav Verstiuk have investigated various aspects of Ukrainian statehood in its multiple incarnations between 1917 and 1920, paying special attention to the increasingly complicated relationship between Ukraine and Bolshevik Russia throughout this period.[1] Recent German-language studies of the Central Powers' intervention in Ukraine and of its relations to Ukrainian state-building have raised important questions about the periodization of the Great War in the east, about the course of Soviet history between 1917 and 1922, and about the international implications of Ukrainian statehood.[2]

The Brest-Litovsk System and Modern Ukrainian Statehood 121

This chapter aims to build on these works by proposing a connection between Brest-Litovsk and the origins of modern Ukrainian statehood. It is less concerned with the Ukrainian Revolution at large or with the war aims of the Central Powers in Ukraine. Instead, it argues that the diplomatic, political, and economic arrangements established by the peace conference (I refer to these arrangements collectively as "the Brest-Litovsk system") in the southwestern parts of the former Russian Empire provided the framework for the Ukrainization policies carried out by a succession of actual and would-be Ukrainian governments between the spring and winter of 1918. The Brest-Litovsk system both enabled and constrained these policies but did not singlehandedly determine them. Ukrainian elites, Imperial legacies, and revolutionary developments combined to shape multiple, at times competing, Ukrainization policies and their limitations. These policies involved Imperial professionals and Ukrainian functionaries from both sides of the old Habsburg-Romanov border, a Habsburg prince and a former tsarist general, and a socialist republic and a conservative monarchy in fluid relationships which highlighted the complexity of the nexus between national and Imperial at a time of total war and revolution. In spite of their substantial differences, the Ukrainization policies that emerged while the Brest-Litovsk system held sway shared a common organizational approach that emphasized bureaucratic efficiency, linguistic policy, and cultural nationalization. They also used a concept of nationality tied to ideological and economic factors. In these vital aspects, they anticipated certain elementss of early Soviet indigenization [*korenizatsiia*] policy.

Historians looking at Ukrainization in this period have often focused on the Central Rada's efforts during 1917, prior to the establishment of the Brest-Litovsk system. Pavlo Khrystiuk, prominent revolutionary statesman and author of one of the most influential accounts of the Ukrainian Revolution by a Ukrainian émigré, was among the first to address the policy. He dated its origins to April 1917 and explained that Ukrainization often began in earnest in the most Russified parts of Ukraine such as the Kharkiv *gubernia*, where the focus lay on introducing the use of the Ukrainian language in the school system by training sufficient numbers of teachers and procuring Ukrainian-language textbooks.[3] Subsequent Ukrainian émigré scholars often criticized the Rada's failure to carry out comprehensive Ukrainization of the army in particular. Recently, Vladislav Verstiuk has argued that "the general crisis conditions in the country and the army" were responsible for the failure of the policy rather than lack of endeavour on the part of the Central Rada.⁴ By drawing on Austrian archival records, this chapter will highlight some of the larger implications of the Brest-Litovsk Peace Conference for East Central Europe by seeking to demonstrate that Ukrainization policies continued under the auspices of the Brest-Litovsk system, and thus helped to shape the Ukrainian revolutionary experience.

Laying the Groundwork for the Brest-Litovsk System

The Central Powers, in the pursuit of an overall strategy aimed at sabotaging the Russian war effort, had shown interest in fomenting revolutionary unrest in Ukraine from the beginning of the war. To this effect, they sponsored the Galician-run Union for the Liberation of Ukraine (*Soiuz vyzvolennia Ukrainy*), which briefly operated in Lemberg before moving to Vienna and, eventually, to Berlin, as well as the émigré-run, Stockholm-based League of Russia's Foreign Peoples (*Liga der Fremdvölker Russlands*).⁵ Attempts during the period 1914–1916, however, were largely ineffective.

The situation changed dramatically with the February Revolution of 1917, as the end of Romanov rule in Russia jeopardized the dominant system of Imperial dynasticism in East Central Europe and ushered in an extended period of Imperial collapse and nation-state formation. The collapse of the Imperial centre in Petrograd had an immediate effect on nationalist activists in the borderlands, who began to clamour for greater national autonomy and cultural rights within the framework of a decentralized Russian federation. On 18 March, the Russian-language daily *Kievskaia mysl'* reported a large gathering the previous day of various Ukrainian national organizations in Kiev, which duly created a Central Rada aiming to serve as a local governing body. While recognizing the authority of the Provisional Government in Petrograd, the Rada immediately set about securing its own power base by arranging the return of exiled members of the Ukrainian intelligentsia, re-opening the cultural society Prosvita (enlightenment), and setting-up an official newspaper, *Rada*.⁶ As the connection between the centre and the periphery of the former empire became increasingly tenuous over the following months and the Bolsheviks overthrew the Provisional Government, the Central Rada proclaimed the existence of a sovereign Ukrainian People's Republic within a reorganized All-Russian Federation it wished to see created in the so-called Third Universal of 20 November.⁷

The Central Powers paid close attention to the course of events in Ukraine, hoping to benefit from the growing estrangement between Kiev and Petrograd. A not untypical Austrian report from the summer of 1917 highlighted the emergence within the former Russian Empire of a clearly defined Ukrainian national space, distinguished from its Great Russian counterpart by a different approach to the border and agrarian questions.[8] Given the uncertainty of the overall situation and the potentially dangerous repercussions provoked by Imperial collapse, however, Berlin and Vienna remained ambivalent about Ukrainian independence. The German Foreign Office cautioned against full-blown support for national revolution during what appeared to be a fluid, transitional phase [*Zwischenstadium*] of the "new order of relations on the Russian western border [*Neuordnung der Verhältnisse an der russische Westgrenze*]."[9] Indeed, as late as mid-December 1917, the Wilhelmstraße maintained that a premature recognition of Ukrainian independence would bring few benefits.[10]

Consequently, the representatives of the Central Powers did not arrive in Brest-Litovsk in early December 1917 expecting to negotiate with an independent Ukraine. Their eyes were firmly fixed on events in Petrograd and the goal of taking Russia out of the war, which would allow them to concentrate their military efforts elsewhere. In fact, Ukraine was not even mentioned in the early-December conferences on policy in Berlin, Kreuznach, and Vienna. As Jerry Hoffman and Oleh S. Fedyshyn have argued persuasively, the negotiations with the Ukrainians highlight the extent to which the Central Powers' entire *Ospolitik* in 1917–18 was an improvised and reactive affair.[11] By initiating the negotiations and early cooperation that led to the creation of the Brest-Litovsk system, the initiative lay firmly with Kiev, not with Berlin or Vienna.

At first, there was some disagreement among the Ukrainian leadership on the question of sending delegates to the peace conference; after all, the Third Universal had proclaimed the new Ukrainian People's Republic as part of an All-Russian Federation. However, the quickly escalating conflict with the Bolshevik Government in Petrograd persuaded the Socialist Revolutionary-dominated Rada to consider independent action. On 17 December, the General Secretariat of the Rada announced that it was combining the hitherto separate Southwestern and Romanian fronts along its borders into a single Ukrainian Front, and that it intended to conduct separate armistice negotiations "in the most decisive manner, bearing in mind the interests of the working people as well as the honor and dignity of the revolutionary army – Ukrainian and All-Russian." The last clarification and the promise to communicate with General Headquarters in Mogilev (provided the latter agreed to respect the wishes of the General Secretariat) left the door open for a possible reconciliation between Kiev and Petrograd, even if the prospects for such an eventuality remained remote.[12]

By the time the small Ukrainian delegation arrived in Brest-Litovsk, however, the representatives of the Central Powers and the Bolsheviks had already signed the armistice. According to the report the delegates Levytskyi and Hassenko delivered upon their return to Kiev, the Bolsheviks had given them a decidedly cold reception and refused to discuss any provisions of the armistice text. Since they did not in fact have a mandate to conduct separate peace negotiations (as opposed to armistice ones) with the Central Powers at this time, the two Ukrainian delegates decided to return to Kiev for fresh instructions, leaving a third delegate, Liubynskyi, as liaison. In contrast to the hostile attitude of the Bolsheviks, the report continued, the representatives of the Central Powers had welcomed them in a friendly manner. General Hoffmann had enquired about the state of the Ukrainian army and promised not to discuss strictly Ukrainian matters with the Bolsheviks once Berlin and Vienna received official communication about the Rada's intention to conduct separate peace negotiations.[13] The shrewd general had been quick to recognize the potential benefits of a separate Ukrainian delegation. According to his own admission, he "received the Ukrainians with pleasure, as their appearance offered a possibility of playing them off against the Petrograd delegation."[14] Czernin expressed a similar sentiment at the beginning of January.[15]

The growing estrangement between Ukraine and Soviet Russia in December 1917 further paved the way for cooperation between Kiev and the Central Powers. The continued insistence of the Ukrainian People's Republic on the establishment of an All-Russian Federation by the existing governments of the former empire's regions ran counter to Petrograd's determination to eliminate all centers of counter-revolutionary activity, starting with Ataman Alexei Kaledin's Don Cossack White forces. The Rada's decision to block the path of advancing Soviet troops through Eastern Ukraine while allowing retreating Don Cossacks safe passage further exacerbated the situation. This rise in tensions and mutual recriminations coincided with the proclamation by the First All-Ukrainian Congress of Soviets of a Central Executive Committee in Kharkiv on 24 December, which in effect meant the creation of a Ukrainian Soviet Republic in opposition to the Kiev-based Ukrainian People's Republic. In the circumstances, wrote high-ranking Bolshevik Vladimir Antonov-Ovseenko, whom Petrograd had instructed to pursue military actions against Kaledin, "conflict with the Rada was absolutely inevitable [*sovershenno neizbezhnym*]"[16] Having arrived in Kharkiv as early as 19 December, Antonov-Ovseenko aided local Bolsheviks in their successful attempts to push back the Rada's forces from Eastern Ukraine.

The outbreak of hostilities between the Central Rada and the *Sovnarkom* remains the subject of heated debates in Ukrainian historiography. At one end of the spectrum, Soldatenko argues it was a conflict between two different revolutions – national-democratic and social (socialist) – which marked the beginning of civil war in Ukraine.[17] At the other end, Pavlo Hai-Nyzhnyk and others describe it as "the first Ukrainian-Bolshevik war,"[18] laying the blame firmly at Petrograd's door and implying that Bolshevism in Ukraine was an alien, Russian imposition. While one cannot deny the fact that Bolshevism did in fact enjoy some measure of support in the more industrialized Donbass in particular, with its large population of Russian-speaking coal miners, it is questionable whether Ukrainian Bolsheviks would have enjoyed the success they did without considerable military and financial assistance from Petrograd. The person in charge of dispensing this assistance, Antonov-Ovseenko, held them in utter contempt, dismissing Kharkiv and Ekaterinoslav Bolsheviks as rubbish [*rukhliad'*] and disparagingly referring to them as "Bolsheviks" in a telegram to the Sovnarkom on 25 December.[19] Even Ukrainian historian Soldatenko, the foremost proponent of the civil war interpretation, points out that "the participation of the Petrograd revolutionary center on the side of the latter [social revolution, as represented by Ukrainian Bolsheviks] played a very important role in the course of the conflict."[20] At the same time, the course of the conflict impacted the Brest-Litovsk negotiations by providing the Central Powers with a clear opening.

Negotiations between the Central Powers and Ukraine and the Emergence of the Brest-Litovsk System

The dispatch of a small delegation to the armistice negotiations was the first act of Ukraine's new foreign policy. Its priorities were as yet uncertain, due to the fact that the Ukrainian People's Republic did not share the geopolitical prerogatives of the former Russian Empire or the revolutionary agenda of its Bolshevik successor. In light of the need to clarify Ukrainian foreign policy and the by now open hostilities between Kiev and Petrograd, on 24 December the General Secretariat of the Central Rada resolved to send a delegation to Brest-Litovsk, which would negotiate with the Central Powers independently of the Bolshevik delegation, and to release an official note to all belligerent and neutral countries to that effect.[21] The four-man strong delegation arrived in Brest-Litovsk precisely at 8:28 p.m. on 1 January 1918.[22] Initially, the Ukrainian delegates intended to steer a middle course between the delegations of the Central Powers and the Russian delegation, holding preliminary meetings with both sides. This proved futile, as fighting between Bolshevik troops and the Rada's forces intensified, and the goals of Petrograd and Kiev (world revolution versus national statehood) proved impossible to reconcile. This incompatibility was also evident to (reasonably) neutral observers at the time; as noted by Colonel Fokke: "The conflict between the Ukrainian Rada and the Soviet delegation in Brest was inevitable by the very nature of things."[23]

Ukrainian foreign policy quickly began defining itself in opposition to Bolshevik Russian foreign policy. Volodymyr Vynnychenko, prime minister of the Ukrainian People's Republic throughout most of the negotiations, recorded in his memoirs the contrast between the behavior of the Ukrainian delegation – "proper, peaceful, and even friendly at times" – and the hostile attitude of the Russians. Unlike Bolshevik Russia, Ukraine did not believe in world revolution; in fact, it actively sought the support of the Great Powers, viewed as necessary to bolster its fledgling statehood.[24] This is especially significant, since Vynnychenko was not universally hostile to the Bolsheviks – even as an émigré, for instance, he chose not to blame them for the outbreak of the conflict between the two sides in December 1917.[25] A second important tenet of Ukrainian foreign policy was the call for the incorporation of all territories inhabited by Ukrainian speakers into the Ukrainian People's Republic. Vynnychenko would have preferred the support of Britain and France, but the Entente's lukewarm reaction to Ukrainian independence left them dependent upon the Central Powers. Frank Golczewski has pointed out that Ukrainian foreign policy thereby "overlooked the dangers an all too tight relationship with the Great Powers could bring,"[26] but Ukraine's fledgling statehood did not realistically stand a chance against the far greater resources of Soviet Russia without outside support.

The Central Powers' diplomats, albeit sceptical at first, quickly recognized the advantages of separate negotiations with the Ukrainians, especially in the context of the endless propagandizing, dilatory tactics, and general irreverence of the Bolshevik delegates. The first preliminary meeting between the two sides took place on the morning of 4 January, when the most senior German diplomat present was Ambassador Rosenberg. The Ukrainians announced they were prepared to negotiate in Brest-Litovsk even if the Russians refused to return after the ten day interval (which they had threatened to do in the Ioffe Note of the same day), and generally appeared quite reasonable and courteous. They reiterated their desire to be part of an All-Russian delegation which included delegates from all successor states of the former Russian Empire (Don, Kuban, Belarus, Siberia, etc); however, due to Bolshevik hostility and their unreasonable claims to represent Russia as a whole, this seemed unlikely.[27]

Sensing an opportunity, Czernin and Kühlmann decided to attend the next meeting, which took place in the afternoon. The two leading diplomats queried the Ukrainians about the political and military situation in Ukraine, its relations with Russia, its legal claim to sovereignty, and its willingness to conclude peace on the basis of non-interference in the Central Powers' internal affairs. This was a particularly sensitive point for Czernin, who wanted to avoid the potentially tricky question of the Dual Monarchy's Ukrainian population.[28]

After a promising start and a second preliminary meeting on the following day, the first formal session between the delegates of the Quadruple Alliance and the Ukrainian People's Republic duly took place on 6 January. Given the anticipated return of the Russians the following day, the most important item on the agenda was the question of Ukraine's juridical status. This may seem a trivial matter, in light of the revolutionary chaos in the former Russian Empire, but the importance of sovereignty was one thing cabinet diplomats like Czernin and Kühlmann and proponents of national self-determination like Vynnychenko could agree on, even if they favoured different *types* of sovereignty (state versus national); in fact, the two were not necessarily mutually exclusive. Upon being asked whether the Central Powers were willing to recognize full Ukrainian independence from Russia, Kühlmann presented a list of three conditions. First, the negotiations should continue without interruption until the final signing of the treaty which, in order not to offend Russia, could take place in a Russian border town (Pskov was occasionally mooted). Second, the two sides should not become involved in one another's internal affairs. Third, the Ukrainians must recognize all agreements concluded at the peace conference up to this moment. The Ukrainian delegates acknowledged these conditions and somewhat abruptly withdrew to debate their answer, seemingly taken aback.[29]

After the Ukrainians had left, Kühlmann invited the chief diplomats, military experts, and legal advisers, including Hoffmann and Rosenberg, to a special conference, which discussed whether the Quadruple Alliance should accept Ukrainian independence *purement et simplement* or impose certain conditions (presumably in addition to the three already presented).[30] Should Ukraine be treated as a confederate state of Russia or as an independent political entity? The Ottoman foreign minister, Nessimi Bey, was in favour of the former, in order not to offend the Russians, and even then only on the condition that Ukraine accept the legal ramifications of all previous negotiations with Petrograd. The Bulgarian minister of justice, Popov, disagreed, arguing that under no circumstances should the Central Powers treat Russia and Ukraine as a federation, since one did not exist from a legal point of view. As for the independence of the Ukrainian republic, he added, they had already recognized it *de facto* by accepting the Rada's delegates in Brest-Litovsk. Nessimi Bey pointed out that Ukraine wanted *de jure* recognition, which required certain conditions. A genuine difference of opinion seemed to exist on this subject, as Kühlmann endorsed Popov's suggestion of recognizing Ukrainian independence *purement et simplement*, whereas Czernin, Hoffman, and Rosenberg adhered to Nessimi Bey's proposal to treat Ukraine as a confederate state of Russia. This was a curious reversal of the normal order of things in the alliance. It was the usually quiet and subordinate Ottomans and Bulgarians who framed the discussion, rather than the dominant Germans and Austrians. In addition, Czernin and Kühlmann found themselves in a rare situation of disagreement. While neither the Ottoman Empire nor Bulgaria had any direct interest in the status of Ukraine, both countries wanted to ensure that the issue would not delay or prevent the end of the war in the east. In contrast, Austria-Hungary was eager to impose conditions that would prevent the Ukrainian People's Republic from raising the issue of its "unredeemed brothers" in East Galicia.

A second session took place in the afternoon to resolve the outstanding differences within the alliance. The outcome was a compromise of sorts. The Central Powers would extend *purement et simplement* recognition and prepare a joint declaration to that effect. However, the declaration would be kept secret from the Ukrainians until Rosenberg persuaded them in private to accept the original list of three conditions.

At dinner, Liubynskyi and Sevriuk told the delegates of the Central Powers they were offended by this. Popov, seemingly buoyed by his untypically influential role during the earlier discussions, told the Ukrainians the conditions were mere "trifles [*melochi*]," which would not preclude an understanding between the two sides. Liubynskyi appeared to see the Bulgarian's point, but Sevriuk implied the Ukrainian delegation might choose to return to Kiev and leave it to the Ukrainian people to secure statehood through the sword. This veiled threat suggests that the Ukrainians were beginning to realize that perhaps the Central Powers needed them just as much as they needed the Central Powers, if either side were to get what it wanted in the face of the Bolsheviks' intransigence and revolutionary antics. The Rada's delegates were not quite the puppets of Austro-German imperialism Soviet historiography has traditionally portrayed them as nor the foolish dilettantes hopelessly out of their depth one finds on the pages of a recent study of the subject by a Russian historian.[31]

With the Russian delegation back in Brest-Litovsk, the first joint plenary session after the interval took place on 10 January. Given the escalating conflict between Petrograd and Kiev, Trotsky was understandably displeased at the sight of the Rada's delegates who, he wrote in his memoirs, "represented the Ukrainian variety of Kerenskyism [i.e., parliamentary social-democracy], and differed from their Great Russian prototype only in that they were even more provincial."[32] His irritation only increased when the Ukrainian state secretary for commerce and industry, Vsevolod Holubovych, read a lengthy note from the General Secretariat of the Central Rada which proclaimed the Ukrainian People's Republic a fully independent country.[33] Pressed hard by Kühlmann on the question of whether Ukraine should be accepted as a legitimate negotiating party at the proceedings, Trotsky reluctantly conceded that "in full accord with the fundamental recognition of the right of self-determination of every nation, even to complete severance, [the Russian delegation] sees no obstacle to the participation of the Ukrainian Delegation in the peace negotiations."[34] However, his adroit use of the phrase "the Ukrainian delegation" instead of "the delegation of the Ukrainian People's Republic/Central Rada" left the door open for the Bolsheviks to recruit their own Ukrainian delegation in due course.

Trotsky's statement seemed to settle the matter of Ukraine's status for the time being, although the Ukrainian delegates were apparently unhappy that the representatives of the Central Powers did not immediately reply to their proclamation with an official note of recognition. "They did not want to tie recognition to the conditions we gave them," Colonel Ganchev informed Prime Minister Radoslavov, "not because they think the conditions are unfair, but because they consider this connection between the two an insult." Over lunch, they had once again hinted to the Bulgarian military representative at the possibility of departing for Kiev. This produced the desired effect, as Ganchev promptly arranged a private meeting between the Ukrainians, Rosenberg, and Hoffmann. After debating the matter for two hours, the two sides reached a mutually acceptable compromise. The Central Powers would recognize the Ukrainian People's Republic as a fully-independent state *de facto*, but *de jure* recognition would "remain contingent on the peace treaty [*bleibt dem Friedensvertrag vorbehalten*]."[35] With the resolution of the thorny question of Ukraine's juridical status, the road to a quick understanding seemed clear.

In spite of the mutual willingness to come to an agreement, however, the Central Powers and Ukraine still had to overcome significant difficulties. Most of these stemmed from the Rada's desire to incorporate all Ukrainian-inhabited territories into the new Ukrainian state. There were around four million Ukrainians (also called Ruthenians) in the Habsburg Empire, mostly in East Galicia and North Bukovina; consequently, the delegation from Kiev wanted to annex these territories. Citing the principle of national self-determination, allegedly the guiding principle of the entire peace conference, Holubovych first broached the subject during a secret meeting with the German delegation on 13 January, when he asked for the outright annexation of East Galicia and the Kholm (Polish: Chełm, German: Cholm) *gubernia*, part of Congress Poland before 1912 and presently under Austro-Hungarian military administration, with a mixed Polish-Ukrainian population. Perhaps, he added as an afterthought that echoed Trotsky's proposal regarding the occupied territories, East Galicia could be "evacuated," so that its inhabitants could decide freely which state to join, if any. Kühlmann was aghast at such effrontery and refused to discuss the subject.[36]

Suffering from a nervous breakdown most likely caused by the bad news coming from the Habsburg home front, Czernin was loath to negotiate directly with the young Ukrainian delegates, even if this seemed to be the only way out of the impasse. Luckily for him, Hoffmann came to the rescue. In another example of smooth cooperation across the military-civilian divide, the general suggested that the Austro-Hungarian foreign minister authorize him to sound out the Ukrainians privately. Hoffmann spoke Russian – though not Ukrainian – and had considerable experience in dealing with Imperial Russian matters going back to the 1890s, when he had spent some time in St. Petersburg. At the ensuing meeting, Hoffmann agreed to the transfer of Kholm but brusquely rebuffed any Ukrainian claim to East Galicia. "I looked upon the demand for Austrian-Hungarian [sic] territory as a piece of impudence and I gave the two men to understand as much, in a somewhat rough manner," he wrote in his memoirs. Liubynskyi and Sevriuk promised to consider this proposal.[37]

It is difficult to ascertain whether the Ukrainians genuinely believed they could successfully persuade the Habsburgs to give up East Galicia. There is no doubt that Ukrainian statesmen felt strongly about the region, which was often seen as the birthplace of modern Ukrainian culture, and desired to see it incorporated into the Ukrainian People's Republic. However, given their extensive domestic difficulties, they may have been prepared to drop the demand for outright annexation from the very beginning, provided the Austrians also offered concessions. "It apparently had dawned upon the rulers in Kiev that the defeated side could not demand the cession of territory from the other party," Hoffmann remarked glibly.[38] By 16 January, they professed themselves content with a guarantee of free national, cultural, and political development of their Galician compatriots in Austria. In effect, this amounted to the creation of an autonomous Habsburg crownland comprising the Ukrainian majority-populated regions of East Galicia and North Bukovina.[39] It also offered to bridge the gap between the two opposing views of self-determination, as it provided for Ukrainian national self-determination *within* the Habsburg Empire, whose territorial integrity would remain uncompromised. Admittedly, neither side was entirely satisfied with this compromise solution and the Austrians would subsequently refuse to implement it.

The Ukrainian obsession with borders might seem ill-advised given the extremely shaky situation in which the Central Rada found itself in the second half of January, when the victorious advance of Bolshevik forces from the north and east under the deft guidance of Antonov-Ovseenko put the very existence of the Ukrainian People's Republic in serious peril. However, this was a key tenet of Ukrainian foreign policy. Political and linguistic borders are vital to successful nation-state building, as they serve to define the often nebulous boundaries of the imaginary national community, which had a tendency to blur and fluctuate in the multi-ethnic, multi-confessional borderlands of East Central Europe.[40] Habsburg Ukrainian leaders, whose constant clashes with Polish nationalists in Galicia had made them fully aware of this reality, had been campaigning for the creation of a separate Ukrainian political entity within Austria for some time, fearing that they might be subjected to Polonization if Galicia were to be united with Congress Poland by way of the Austro-Polish Solution. In late December 1917, the Ukrainian Parliamentary Club in the *Reichsrat* submitted for publication in the Swedish newspaper *Svenska Dagbladet* a statement which outlined the case for the recreation of the medieval Kingdom of Halych-Volhynia within the Dual Monarchy.[41] The secret Habsburg pledge – which quickly became common knowledge – to do just that in the treaty, even though never implemented, legitimized Ukrainian national claims in the area. Austrian Prime Minister Seidler rationalized the question of Ukraine's western borders in a speech in the *Reichsrat*: "the Ukrainians have the same right as other peoples, when it comes to choosing which state they should be a part of."[42] Ultimately, this attitude contributed to the creation of a second Ukrainian nation-state, the so-called West Ukrainian People's Republic, in the autumn of 1918.[43] The emphasis on border-making in the Kholm and East Galician regions thus necessitated the delineation of a Ukrainian national space that was clearly separate from its more powerful and potentially dangerous Polish and Russian neighbours.[44]

However, even the reduced Ukrainian demands for East Galician autonomy and Kholm put Czernin in an extremely difficult position. The transfer of the Kholm *gubernia*, with its substantial Polish population, to a Ukrainian People's Republic whose very existence was an affront to the Polish political and economic elite, would erode Polish support for the Habsburg cause, thereby making any future implementation of the Austro-Polish Solution extremely problematic. But the foreign minister had little room for manoeuvre, as the Ukrainian negotiations between 15 January and 20 January coincided with the worst phase of the Great January Strike in Austria, the main goals of which were the swift conclusion of peace in Brest-Litovsk and the relief of the food crisis. Only peace with Ukraine, the breadbasket of the Russian Empire, could potentially satisfy both conditions. On 17 January Czernin explained in a telegram to the Foreign Ministry, intended for the emperor, that the Central Powers were pursuing simultaneous negotiations with the Russians and the Ukrainians, both of which would ideally bear fruit. But whereas the former had nothing to export but revolution, the latter apparently had plentiful supplies of food, which they were willing to sell. Therefore, peace with Ukraine was more important than peace with Russia, in case the Central Powers were unable to achieve both.[45]

As Czernin prepared to travel to Vienna during the second adjournment of the conference in late January, he informed the Ballhausplatz that an Imperial Council would have to be convened to consider the possibility of creating an autonomous Ukrainian crownland.[46] "The question of East Galicia I will leave to the Austrian Ministry; it must be decided in Vienna," Czernin wrote in his diary. "I cannot, and dare not, look on and see hundreds of thousands starve for the sake of retaining the sympathy of the Poles, so long as there is a possibility of help."[47] Besides, he may well have added, the pro-Habsburg sentiment of the Poles was entirely a matter of calculation – they did not so much admire Austria as they disliked Prussia and Russia with a passion. In case the Central Powers won the war, the Poles would still prefer the accommodating Austrians to the unflinching Prussians. If they lost, none of the above considerations would be relevant, as the Poles would demand nothing less than outright independence within the historical borders of the Polish-Lithuanian Commonwealth – which is exactly what happened in 1919–21. With such deliberations in mind, Czernin returned to Vienna on 21 January.

The subsequent Polish reaction to the actual treaty confirmed the strategic nature of Polish sympathies for Austria. When Stephan von Ugron, the Ballhausplatz representative in Warsaw, explained the details of the Ukrainian treaty to the members of the Polish Regency Council in confidence on 10 February, Prince Zdzisław Lubomirski shook violently and barely found words to express his rage. He spoke of a Fourth Partition of Poland and accused the Dual Monarchy of selling Poland for a few wagons of grain. Józef Ostrowski categorically stated the treaty could not last, since the Polish people would protest to the entire world.[48] All three members of the Regency resigned within a matter of days. Von Ugron found Prime Minister Kucharzewski, whom he met on 11 February, considerably calmer and more composed but "very depressed" at such an egregious violation of the principle of self-determination, given that Ukrainians made up only seven per cent of Kholm's population (or so he claimed).[49] Popular demonstrations against the treaty took place in Cracow and across Congress Poland over the following weeks.[50]

At the Imperial Council of 22 January, Czernin urged acceptance of the Ukrainian conditions and reiterated his desire to conduct a separate peace with the Russians, should German obstinacy threaten to derail the negotiations. Austrian Prime Minister Seidler promised to obtain the two-thirds parliamentary majority required to implement the necessary constitutional changes, even in the face of opposition from the Polish Club. However, the Hungarian prime minister, Wekerle, and the joint finance minister, István Burián, protested against such a measure, emphasizing that "no interference in the affairs of the Monarchy from without could be tolerated," lest this set a dangerous precedent. Czernin angrily confronted Wekerle, maintaining that only Ukrainian grain could avert the imminent Austrian catastrophe in the absence of Hungarian wheat. The foreign minister preferred "the risk of death to the certainty of the same." In the end, the Imperial Council decided in favour of Czernin's proposal, persistent Hungarian opposition notwithstanding.[51] By the time the foreign minister returned to Brest-Litovsk on 28 January, he was fully authorized to accept the Ukrainian conditions in order to conclude a swift peace.

Was Czernin's strategy of accommodating the Ukrainians justified? Clifford F. Wargelin has argued that Habsburg policy in Brest-Litovsk "precipitated the collapse of ... authority over the nationalities, as the price of peace was exchanges of territory offensive to its own nationalities and subservience to the ambitions of the German High Command."[52] While the Ukrainian treaty ultimately destabilized Austria-Hungary by antagonizing the Poles, it is worth considering the alternative. Czernin warned on multiple occasions that the Ukrainian delegation had repeatedly urged the Germans to come to a separate accommodation at the expense of the Habsburgs. Negotiating privately with the Bolsheviks was no good either; as the foreign minister explained, "the Germans are in a position to play the Ukrainian card against us if we leave them alone with the Petersburgers [sic]."[53] Germany might sign a separate peace with Ukraine, leaving Vienna in the lurch and seriously compromising the integrity of the Quadruple Alliance at a time when overall victory in the war did not seem beyond the realm of possibility (the German offensive in the west was scheduled to commence on 21 March). In the circumstances, Austrian refusal to accommodate the Ukrainians would have amounted to an empty gesture that would merely have exacerbated an already critical domestic situation. Bismarck had once stated that the entire Balkans were not worth the healthy bones of a single Pomeranian grenadier. Similarly, Count Czernin and Emperor Karl now decided that Polish dreams were not worth the life of a single starving Viennese worker – even if she was striking in protest against the government.

The Austrians were not alone in experiencing domestic difficulties at this time, with conditions in Ukraine growing worse by the day as a result of ongoing fighting between Russian and Ukrainian Bolsheviks on one side and the Central Rada on the other. Khrystiuk described "the war with Russia as the tragedy of the Ukrainian Revolution."[54] Petrograd's forceful support of Ukrainian Bolshevism quickly threatened the Rada's shaky hold on the country. In late January, Kiev intercepted a message from People's Commissar for Nationalities Joseph Stalin to the leaders of the Ukrainian Soviet Government in Kharkiv, which promised the immediate transfer of a considerable sum of money. "In case the bank refuses to honor it, arrest the staff," the former Georgian bank robber instructed. "Now is not the time to whine, now is the time to act in a revolutionary manner!"[55] Trotsky had not been idle either, instructing his Red Guards along the Romanian front to subvert the Rada by any means possible.[56] As the Rada suffered a series of devastating defeats and fled to the western town of Zhitomir with as few as 2 000 reliable troops left, Trotsky recruited two Ukrainian Bolsheviks – "voiceless and unimportant pawns," as Colonel Fokke described them – and sent Kühlmann a note informing him that the Rada had fallen and the Ukrainian Soviets were now in charge. Their representatives would henceforth act as members of the Russian delegation.[57]

Unperturbed, Czernin reiterated the Quadruple Alliance's recognition of the Rada as the only legitimate governing body of Ukraine. Neither side had any illusions about the true motives of the Central Powers. As Vynnychenko put it, "the Germans were not doing this on account of the young peasant girl's [*khutorianka*, a traditional metaphor for Ukraine] beautiful eyes, but on account of her bread, sugar, coal, and other wonderful goods of this kind."[58] At 2:00 a.m. on 10 February 1918, the first peace treaty of the Great War was duly signed between the Central Powers and the Ukrainian People's Republic. The Ukrainians promised to provide the Central Powers with one million tons of foodstuffs by 31 July. In exchange, they succeeded in obtaining a secret pledge from the reluctant Austrians to create an autonomous Habsburg crownland comprising all Ukrainian-speaking territories in Austria (but not in Hungary). Ukraine also secured the incorporation of the disputed region of Kholm. These were notable advantages for Ukrainian foreign policy, and it is not entirely correct to claim, as Wlodzimierz Medrzecki does, that "the Ukrainian delegation that returned to the

> Der Friede mit der Ukraine.
> Die Schlußsitzung in der Nacht vom 9. zum 10. Februar,
> in der das Friedensprotokoll unterzeichnet wurde.

4. The peace with Ukraine. The closing session in the night of 9 to 10 February, when the peace treaty was signed. German postcard published in 1918. Wikimedia Commons.

second round of negotiations came no longer in the guise of a partner but more as a petitioner to Germany,"[59] since the Ukrainians held their ground remarkably well, to the dismay of the Austrians in particular.

The treaty was rather better than its reputation. Had Ukraine been able to enforce it, it would have been a decent peace, wrote Vynnychenko, and one specialist on the subject concurs.[60] Therein lay the problem, however, as the task of enforcing the treaty ultimately proved to be beyond the fledgling country's limited capabilities. Khrystiuk's evaluation of the treaty as "probably the only non-imperialistic treaty among the numerous treaties concluded at the end of the imperialist world war under the Dictat [*pid diktovku*] of the bourgeois Entente" is a bit of an overstatement, but it sums up perfectly the overwhelmingly positive attitude of Ukrainian émigrés; the fact that "the wheel of history crushed it does not lessen the importance of this treaty in the history of the Ukrainian people's struggle for national liberation and nation building," Khrystiuk concluded.[61] This positive view is in stark contrast to the universal condemnation of the treaty in Soviet (both Russian and Ukrainian) and post-1991 Russian studies. As Frank Golczewski observes, "the [Ukrainian] Brest Peace is an excellent example of a controversial historical event, which one can evaluate as one wishes."[62]

The treaty between the Central Powers and Ukraine provided the legal basis for the Brest-Litovsk system. First, it bolstered the Ukrainian People's Republic's juridical claim to independent statehood by providing official recognition of the new state by the countries of the Quadruple Alliance. Second, it established close relations between Ukraine and the Central Powers, by specifying that Ukraine was obliged to deliver at least one million tons of foodstuffs to the alliance. In exchange, the Central Powers pledged to transport the equivalent value in manufactured goods to Ukraine. Ratification of the treaty by Germany and Austria-Hungary was contingent upon Ukrainian deliveries. The Ukrainian delegation agreed with this proviso but asked that it not be made public, as it would be impossible to carry through the Rada.[63] The amount of grain Ukraine had promised to deliver to the Central Powers (one million tons or 60 million poods) might seem excessive, but the Ukrainians had already estimated somewhat optimistically that they would be able to send nearly four times as much grain (220 million poods) to European Russia and the front.[64] The breakdown of relations with Petrograd meant that Kiev was no longer bound by this obligation and could dispense of the grain as it saw fit.

The close economic and political relationship stipulated by the treaty required Austro-German military intervention on behalf of the Central Rada, which lacked the military power to counter the advancing Bolshevik forces. This materialized after the leaders of the Rada issued identical appeals "to the people of Germany" and "to the peoples of Austria-Hungary" on 17 February.[65] The OHL and the AOK instructed their troops not to treat Ukraine as occupied territory.[66] By late March, Bolshevik troops had been completely driven out of the territories claimed by the Ukrainian People's Republic, and the two High Commands divided the vast territory into two operational zones. The Austrian zone in South Ukraine included the southwestern part of Volhynia, as well as the entire Podolia, Kherson, and Ekaterinoslav *gubernias*, with Odessa as headquarters. The larger German zone extended over North and East Ukraine and the Crimea, including the capital Kiev.

In spite of having separate zones, Germany and Austria-Hungary agreed to cooperate in the procurement and transportation of foodstuffs.[67]

From March to November 1918, the Brest-Litovsk system created an independent Ukrainian nation-state, which was guaranteed by the presence of Austro-German troops, and was economically and politically linked with Central Europe rather than the rest of the former Russian Empire for the first time since the Khmelnytsky Uprising in the mid-seventeenth century. The sequence of Ukrainization policies which took place under the aegis of the system provides another outstanding example of the diverse implications of Brest-Litovsk across East Central Europe.

National in Form, Agrarian-Socialist in Content: Ukrainization under the Rada

In an analysis of Soviet indigenization policy in the 1920s and early 1930s, Terry Martin expanded Miroslav Hroch's three-phase model of the development of nationalist movements among small, stateless peoples in East Central Europe by adding an additional phase, D, in which the Soviet state imposed from above formal institutions of nationhood and a new state language.[68] During this phase, Soviet authorities remained vigilant against what they referred to as "bourgeois nationalist deviations," promoting cultures that were "national in form, socialist in content."

The Ukrainization policy of the Central Rada anticipated this approach in several ways. First, it pursued the introduction of the Ukrainian language in government and education in place of Russian. Russian was both the language of Imperial state administration and the language of the national group that appeared to pose the biggest threat to independent Ukrainian statehood, which made it doubly oppressive.

Second, the policy attempted to create Ukrainian state institutions in place of those remaining from the Imperial era, now partially destroyed, and no longer adequate. As the Rada leadership saw it, Ukrainian national statehood [*natsional'no-ukrains'ka derzhavnist'*] meant that all organs of state rule should henceforth be created in Ukraine.[69] Unlike the Grand Duchy of Finland, Ukraine had never constituted a single administrative entity within the Russian Empire and did not possess ready-made administrative organs which could smooth the path to full statehood. Ukrainian national statehood, therefore, entailed not merely the introduction of new civil servants or the reform of existing state structures, but the creation of entirely new ones. In that respect, the Ukrainian experience bears certain similarities to that of the aspiring nation states of Latvia and Estonia, which had also been divided along geographic and historic lines.[70]

Third, the SR-dominated Rada pursued the creation of not just *any* national culture, but one that was specifically agrarian-socialist. This was partly due to the change in demographics which late nineteenth and early twentieth century industrialization had brought to Ukraine. The influx of workers from the north meant that ethnic Russians and Jews comprised the bulk of the population in the main industrial urban centers. The majority of ethnic Ukrainians were peasants who led an often difficult existence alongside Polish and Russian landlords. This created a situation in which, as Steven L. Guthier has asserted, "class and ethnic cleavages were closely related ...."[71] The situation also led many leftist Ukrainian intellectuals to develop an anti-colonial nationalist discourse criticizing what they perceived to be Ukraine's position of colonial dependency with respect to the Imperial Russian metropolis.[72] Consequently, the Rada's Ukrainization policy aimed to strengthen the rural, ethnic Ukrainian element at the expense of the urban, industrial element deemed suspicious on the basis of its alien nationality or cosmopolitan tendencies. Unlike the Soviet state of the 1920s and 1930s, however, the Ukrainian People's Republic of 1918 did not possess a reliable police force, a standing army, or an experienced bureaucracy, severely limiting its ability to exercise power and almost institutionalizing its reliance on the military support of the Central Powers. If we apply the Hroch-Martin model, we would have to place it at an intermediate stage between phase C and phase D.

Linguistic Ukrainization of the bureaucracy and administration, "a pretty radical decision," according to Pavlo Hai-Nyzhnyk, due to the enormity of the challenge it posed, was the Rada's first order of business.[73] This meant that the old Imperial bureaucracy, which was Russian-speaking, conservative, and in favour of the re-unification of Ukraine and Russia, had to go. This was a very different scenario from the one in the Habsburg Empire, which had allowed linguistic particularism at the crownland and local level. The fact that official administrative business in Bohemia was carried out in Czech as well as in German, for instance, meant that at the time of the empire's collapse there already existed a large body of Czech-speaking, trained civil servants who had no trouble transferring their loyalties to the new Czechoslovak state. In contrast, Imperial Russian authorities had expressly forbidden the official use of Ukrainian, a language they considered to be an uneducated dialect of Russian at best and an insidious creation of Austrian professors at worst.

Who would replace the professional civil servants, then, was far from clear. The Rada's supporters were overwhelmingly students and intellectuals who had little experience in the day-to-day workings of bureaucratic machinery and were ill-suited for the job. Before the war, there had been plenty of Ukrainian civil servants employed in the central bureaucracy in St. Petersburg and Moscow and, as one Ukrainian informant working for Austrian intelligence pointed out, they might have been willing to return to Ukraine and become engaged in Ukrainization efforts. However, the Central Rada prevented the return of the expatriate Ukrainian intelligentsia in the mistaken belief that they were "counter-revolutionary bourgeois."[74] The cosmopolitan atmosphere of the two capitals might also have led to accusations that they were nationally suspect. Unable or unwilling to utilize this valuable asset, the Rada had no other option but to rely on the youthful socialist intelligentsia, whose inexperience meant that lack of coordination and confusion were typically the order of the day. However, the extent of revolutionary chaos in the former Russian Empire in 1917–18 would have rendered the return of Ukrainian civil servants from Petrograd extremely problematic if not virtually impossible, even if the Rada had welcomed them with open arms.

An additional hindrance to linguistic Ukrainization was the lack of popular understanding of the importance of this measure. Prominent scientist Vladimir Vernadsky – himself of Ukrainian origin – highlighted the lack of "ideological sympathy [*ideinogo sochuvstviia*]" the primarily Russian-speaking urban population of Poltava felt with the policy.[75] A decree to rewrite all public signs and carry out all clerical work in Ukrainian even led to popular "hatred [*nenavist'*] for the language" in the city.[76] The peasant masses, which were the main pillar of the Rada, also failed to recognize the need for linguistic Ukrainization. Amid revolutionary chaos, foreign invasions, and the dissolution of state authority, it made little sense to some to focus on what appeared to be a perfunctory matter. Why spend all this effort to enforce the use of Ukrainian in the public sphere when Russian was perfectly adequate? One Ukrainian journalist captured the popular attitude to linguistic Ukrainization in an article published in the *Nova Rada* on 26 March:

> How can one think of such stupidities as etiquette at such a catastrophic time, when one is standing on such shaky ground? Nobody's language

should be taken away in a free, democratic country; everybody should speak whatever he fancies. These actions of the Ukrainian Government will not win it any friends. Or has the government already established internal order? Have the political, economic, and financial relations all been settled, so that only Ukrainian etiquette is missing?[77]

Faced with such opposition, the Rada was eventually forced to take a step back and allow the use of Russian in internal office work.[78] In spite of concerted efforts, concludes Hai-Nyzhnyk, the Rada was unable to achieve the complete Ukrainization of clerical work.[79]

The pursuit of agrarian-socialist Ukrainian national statehood was arguably even more important to the Rada's fortunes than the imposition of language and the creation of an administrative apparatus. The agricultural revolution, which began throughout the former Russian Empire in the summer of 1917, was in many ways the most important aspect of what one scholar has described as "revolutions in collision."[80] By the spring of 1918, it had already gathered tremendous momentum, with peasants throughout Ukraine seizing large agricultural estates and driving landlords off their land.[81] This process had an additional national aspect, since most landlords were of Polish and Russian ancestry. Poles fleeing Ukraine described the situation as a state of open war between Polish landlords and armed peasants, with the local authorities favouring the latter.[82] As representatives of a peasant party, the Ukrainian SRs who dominated the Rada endorsed the socialization of land. They had little choice but to do so, in light of the importance of the agrarian question to the peasantry. As the German publicist Colin Ross, who travelled with the advancing German troops in March, wrote in a report for the chief of staff of *Ober Ost*:

> The peasants are mainly interested in the question of dividing the land; they will follow the Rada if it does not shy away from distributing the landlords' estates among them. But if the Rada alters anything in the Third and Fourth Universals, which promised the expropriation of [landlords'] land in favor of the peasantry, the peasants will support the Bolsheviks.[83]

In spite of its ideological commitment, however, the Rada did little to further the socialization of land apart from legislating on the matter. More often than not, the peasants seized the landlords' land on their own initiative. Since many peasants still practiced outdated methods of land cultivation, this had the predictable outcome of diminishing gross agricultural output. Whatever supplies of grain the peasants had they refused to sell on the market, as the scarcity of manufactured goods meant they had nothing to spend their money on. Instead, they preferred to make spirits and keep the remaining grain as a kind of insurance against future adversity. All this put the Rada in an awkward position. Curtailing the move towards the socialization of the land would have amounted to political suicide. Going along with it meant antagonizing the Central Powers, whose primary reason for being in Ukraine was the collection of foodstuffs. The Rada chose to do nothing and observed passively from the sidelines. Meanwhile, local commissars began to offer passive resistance by holding up the goods Austro-German military authorities had purchased and delaying their transportation across the border.[84]

The Rada's passivity had the effect of alienating both the peasantry and the Austro-German military authorities. Pavlo Khrystiuk recorded a curious "everyday episode [*stsenku z natury*]" in the village of Bukhny, Kiev *gubernia*, from the early spring of 1918, which confirmed Colin Ross's observation. "The [members of the] Central Rada are all bourgeois. They have deceived us. Hrushevskyi, an Austrian bourgeois, is in charge there," said one peasant. "We need to chase away this Central Rada," another agreed. "It will bring back the landlords, who will tear the skin from our backs." "We need to listen to the Bolsheviks," a third added. "They will give us everything. They will kick out the landlords and give the people what they need." Admittedly, this demonstrated not so much a rise in support for Bolshevism as a typically peasant distrust of city folk. "'Devil knows what's going on," yet another peasant exclaimed. "This one's a Bolshevik, this one's a *haidamak* [irregular troops supporting the Central Rada; it can also mean 'brigand']. Maybe they're all *haidamaks*, may epilepsy strike their mothers [*triastsia ikh materi*] ...."[85] While not necessarily representative of the Ukrainian peasantry as a whole, this episode demonstrates the shifting popular loyalties in the countryside at the time and the pre-eminence of the land question.

Prompted by the influential Baron Mykola Vasyl'ko (also known by the German version of his name, Nikolaus von Wassilko), an Austrian-Ukrainian statesman and member of the *Reichsrat* in Vienna who intermittently advised Czernin during the Brest-Litovsk negotiations, the Austrians began to contemplate a regime change in Kiev as early as late March. "Wassilko is of the opinion that we will not go far with the current government," the Austro-Hungarian ambassador in Kiev, Count

Johann Forgách von Ghymes und Gács, informed the Foreign Ministry on 28 March, "as it will obstruct the shipment of foodstuffs. He thinks we should remove it and install a government that can steady the ship, provided the Germans are not against this." The ambassador endorsed this course of action.[86]

The Austrians were not alone in their frustration with the Rada. Having had enough, the exasperated German military began to look for a replacement for the unruly Rada beginning in early April. On the evening of 24 April, the chief of staff of the German Army in Ukraine, General Wilhelm Groener, convened a secret meeting to discuss the situation, attended by the German ambassador, Baron Philip Alfons Mumm von Schwarzenstein, the Austro-Hungarian ambassador, Forgách, the German military attaché, Colonel von Stolzenberg, and the Austro-Hungarian military attaché, Major Fleischmann. The meeting decided that it was impossible to continue working with the Rada or to create a fully functioning occupation regime in the form of a General Government. Consequently, a new Ukrainian government would have to be formed as soon as possible, although no names were mentioned at this point. This government would have to remain dependent on the military support of the Central Powers, in order not to interfere with the collection and transportation of foodstuffs. To that effect, no independent Ukrainian army ought to be created as long as German and Austrian troops remained present in the country.[87]

The so-called Dobryi Affair, which broke out the day after the meeting at General Groener's, was the last straw. On the evening of 25 April, the director of the Russian Bank in Kiev Abram Dobryi was kidnapped from his home by three individuals who claimed to be members of the Committee for the Salvation of Ukraine, an anti-German secret organization. The Ukrainian city police units, dispatched to help, behaved passively. The Habsburg embassy informed the Foreign Ministry in Vienna that this incident appeared to be the result of terrorist action by revolutionary elements, which might have very serious repercussions. The Germans asked for the strongest military measures to be taken, and together with the Austrians sent a démarche to Prime Minister Holubovych, insisting that the Central Powers would under no circumstances tolerate terrorist acts. The German ambassador also demanded the release of Dobryi and the apprehension of the three kidnappers.[88]

As the Rada proved unable or unwilling to bring about the immediate release of Dobryi, the commander-in-chief of German forces in Ukraine, Fieldmarshal Hermann von Eichhorn, issued an order, effective immediately, whereby anyone found guilty of a breach of public order or of crimes against German and Habsburg troops would be prosecuted in German military courts rather than Ukrainian civil courts. The situation in Kiev remained calm, with German troops patrolling the streets.[89] On 28 April, a German military court examined the Dobryi case and the activities of the Society for the Salvation of Ukraine and found that high-ranking Ukrainian statesmen were implicated in both. Consequently, the judge issued arrest warrants for chief of city police, Bohatskyi, the minister of war, Shukovskyi, the minister of the interior, Tkachenko, and the director from the ministry of the interior, Danreskyi. As leading members of the Union who were guilty of involvement in the kidnapping of Dobryi, these statesmen were promptly arrested. Simultaneously, the foreign minister, Liubynskyi, was also arrested for giving a speech lambasting the German military. From that point on, the situation quickly neared its denouement. The Rada appealed directly to Berlin and issued an order countermanding that of Eichhorn. In retaliation, German troops broke up the meeting of the Rada and arrested everyone present.[90]

Two days later, a former general in the Imperial Russian Army, Pavlo Skoropadskyi, overthrew the government on 30 April in a nearly bloodless coup, as the German military authorities in Kiev looked on approvingly. The Germans did not help replace the Rada because it was weak or inefficient. They did so primarily because it "conducted an independent internal policy which was very often contradictory to the expectations of the Central Powers," as one scholar has suggested.[91] Agrarian socialism of the Ukrainian variety was a completely alien concept to the conservative Habsburg and Hohenzollern monarchies, as one contemporary anonymous Austrian writer pointed out.[92] It made much more sense to back a conservative regime, and Pavlo Skoropadskyi and his Hetmanate seemed to be the perfect fit.

In addition to the twin difficulty of conducting a policy of Ukrainization with limited resources while trying to fulfil its economic obligations to the Central Powers, the Rada also had to confront a volatile political climate in large urban centers. Cities like Kiev and Odessa were microcosms of Imperial Russian society. By 1914, they had become large, cosmopolitan, bustling, commercial centers with a growing middle class, a developing public sphere, and a nascent civil society.[93] Their diverse, multi-ethnic populations were primarily interested in promoting the rule of law and their commercial interests, which were often at odds with the policies of economic Ukrainization that the Rada favoured.

The case of Odessa is particularly instructive. Out of a population that had increased from 800 000 to one million during the war, only about 10 per cent were Ukrainian speakers.[94] There was a single Ukrainian-language daily newspaper, compared to twenty in various other languages. The City Duma, dominated by Social Democrats (SDs), Jewish entrepreneurs, and industrialists, was the most important political factor. It refused to recognize the Rada, pursuing a policy that aimed to transform Odessa into a Free City; this was especially popular in industrial circles. In addition to the largely Jewish middle class and the largely Jewish and Russian working class, there were small but well organized Polish, Georgian, Tatar, and German communities. The disintegration of the old Imperial Russian army combined with general revolutionary upheaval led to the unregulated proliferation of arms in Odessa, to the point where there were tens of thousands of rifles, several pieces of artillery and tons of ammunition up for grabs. Consequently, all ethnic groups had well-equipped military detachments which enabled them to oppose both the Rada and the City Duma with impunity. Ukrainization by force was out of the question.

The powerlessness of the Rada's functionaries, who often risked their lives by remaining in Odessa, underlined the central government's hopeless situation. Only five members of the original twelve man strong commissariat sent to the city by Kiev the previous autumn were among the living by the spring of 1918, the other seven having been assassinated. General Commissar O. Komornyi, who had been given virtually dictatorial powers in order to restore the rule of law and normal, everyday life throughout the country, arrived in Odessa with big words and even bigger intentions. Once there, he met determined opposition and eventually left for Kiev at the end of March, not planning to return. Prime Minister Vsevolod Holubovych eventually persuaded him to go back to Odessa, promising him the substantial sum of 70 million rubles, currently printed in Leipzig, for administrative purposes.[95] However, no money appeared to be forthcoming, and a desperate Komornyi told Austro-Hungarian military authorities he considered his position untenable and would tender his resignation once again. This was hardly surprising; as Hai-Nyzhnyk has pointed out, one could not realistically expect a single person lacking sufficient manpower and bureaucratic support to successfully take on a task which the Ministry of the Interior had failed to carry out.[96] In private conversations with Habsburg officers, Komornyi stated repeatedly that only full occupation by the Central Powers and the taking up of administration by the higher military authorities could restore order and normal economic life.⁹⁷ The Central Powers, with their hands full elsewhere, had neither the military nor the financial capability to institute a formal occupation regime like the ones they had in Poland, Romania, and Serbia. Hence, they turned to Skoropadskyi.

The Conservative Turn: Skoropadskyi and the Hetmanate

Between May and October 1918, two competing views of Ukrainization, one embodied by the new ruler of Ukraine, Hetman Pavlo Skoropadskyi, and the other by the Habsburg prince Wilhelm (alias Vasyl Vyshyvanyi) who aspired to replace him, dominated the political landscape. The change of government in Kiev at the end of April 1918 did not alter the fundamental bases of the Brest-Litovsk system, as Skoropadskyi's ascent to power was conditional on his assuming all responsibilities laid out in the peace treaty. In fact, the Central Powers deliberately withheld official recognition of the new government for over a month, waiting to see whether this experiment was worthwhile. Upon finally receiving official notes of recognition from the German and Austro-Hungarian ambassadors in Kiev on 2 June, a euphoric Skoropadskyi was quick to assure Berlin and Vienna that the Ukrainian State (*Ukrains'ka Derzhava*, the official name of the Hetmanate) would work closely with the Central Powers.⁹⁸ This was largely borne out by his subsequent track record, leading to descriptions both contemporary (by the Austro-Hungarian ambassador, Count Forgách) and subsequent (by historians like Irina Mikhutina) of Skoropadskyi as a tool of German policy. Skoropadskyi's memoirs paint a more complicated portrait of a man aware of his limitations, who tried to conduct an independent internal policy but was ultimately thwarted by prevailing circumstances. The Hetman claimed to have opposed both ardent Ukrainophiles and Great Russians, pursuing the creation of a Ukrainian identity that was distinct yet closely related and friendly to that of Russia, with a possible view to creating an All-Russian confederation.⁹⁹ Oleh S. Fedyshyn provides a more balanced account, suggesting that the Hetman's control gradually increased over time, while Taras Hunczak emphasizes that it would be erroneous to believe that "during Skoropadskyi's rule no constructive contribution was made to Ukrainian statehood."¹⁰⁰ Contemporary Ukrainian scholarship often views the Hetmanate as an ultimately unpopular alternative model of social and national development which curtailed many of the progressive, national-democratic achievements of the Ukrainian Revolution.[101]

With the approval of the Central Powers, the Hetman's domestic policy heralded a sharp turn to the right. The first measure to this effect was the replacement of the radical Ukrainian youth which, as Skoropadskyi saw it, had demonstrated its administrative incapability during the previous government, with the old Imperial civil servants. This brought on accusations of Russification, not all of which were unjustified. While the Hetman and his ministers publicly proclaimed their adherence to the independent existence of the Ukrainian State, many of their functionaries made no secret of the fact that their allegiances lay elsewhere. In a particularly revealing case, the newly appointed *starosta* (provincial governor) of Kharkiv, a former general in the Imperial army, wasted no time in explaining to the local civil servants that they should not forget they were servants of a united Russia. To the embarrassment of the government, his remarks made their way to the local dailies. Queried by the Austro-Hungarian ambassador on the subject, the Hetman explained there would be an investigation of the *starosta*, who would be removed from his post if the allegations were true.[102]

However, not all former Imperial servants were opponents of independent Ukrainian statehood. The aforementioned Vernadsky was actively involved in the creation of a Ukrainian Academy of Sciences.[103] The memoirs of Aleksei Tatishchev, a Russian-born civil servant who worked as a secretary in the Ukrainian State's Council of Ministers from the end of May 1918 until the fall of the Hetmanate in mid-December, describe a rather complex dynamic. Although the foreign minister, Dmytro Doroshenko, was the only ardent [*iaryi*] Ukrainian in the first cabinet of the Hetmanate, the Russian ministers tried to act like Ukrainian nationalists in working on the consolidation of the state.[104] In an outstanding example, the minister of labour, a Russified German, decreed the compulsory use of Ukrainian in the ministry.[105] The main problem, as Tatishchev saw it, was precisely this language policy. Tatishchev himself spoke some Ukrainian, which he had learned in his childhood, and he considered administrative Ukrainian to be a perfectly acceptable chancellery language developed from local dialects. However, he thought it a mistake to make Ukrainian the only official state language, since many bureaucrats did not actually understand it (the Hetman was also more comfortable speaking Russian, and he wrote his memoirs in Russian rather than Ukrainian). Such people would often write in Russian, adding Ukrainian endings.[106] The ensuing confusion considerably slowed down the pace of government work.

The Hetman was convinced that the efficient, experienced, Imperial civil servants were indispensable to his Ukrainization policy, as he told the Austro-Hungarian ambassador repeatedly. The government had proved its credentials by decreeing the obligatory use of Ukrainian in all schools, in the bureaucracy, and in the justice system. There were plans to establish a Ukrainian university, a Ukrainian Academy of Arts and Sciences, and other institutes of higher education which would help swell the ranks of the Ukrainian national intelligentsia.[107] Skoropadskyi also compared his Ukrainization efforts favourably to those of the Rada, arguing that the latter had done virtually nothing to promote Ukrainian culture institutionally:

> The Central Rada did not open any educational institutions, except for the most outrageous [*bezobrazneishee*] establishment that was the People's Ukrainian University, where people demonstrated more than they studied. Why, in fact, it was called Ukrainian, I do not know, as almost all lectures were read in Russian. All Ukrainian culture consisted of was various sorts of confused young people running around Kiev in hats with tassels, sporting an *oseledets'* [traditional Ukrainian Cossack haircut].[108]

In contrast, the argument went, the Hetman's institutional policy would enable the government to replace the Russian-speaking Imperial bureaucrats with fully capable Ukrainian ones in due course. In the short term, however, the presence of so many Russian-speaking government officials in high places (though not in the regions, where many local government officials remained in their positions after the fall of the Rada) helped spread pro-Russian attitudes favouring the eventual re-unification of Ukraine with a non-Bolshevik Russia. The Germans, who were aware of the threat such attitudes posed, pushed for further Ukrainization. On 27 June, Ambassador Mumm brought a hand-written note from Kaiser Wilhelm to the Hetman, demanding Ukrainization of the central government. The German councillor, von Berchen, had a long conversation with Doroshenko and others to that effect. The government was quickly reshuffled, and the new ministers were markedly more Ukrainophile.[109] In spite of the serious difficulties and frequent changes of personnel, there was slow but steady progress. "By autumn 1918 a bureaucracy had been established which was functioning reasonably well," Stephen Velychenko concludes.[110] Skoropadskyi was naturally keen to defend his contributions in his memoirs, insisting in a somewhat exaggerated manner that the main accomplishment of his regime was the emergence "in all aspects of popular life of a sense of statehood."[111] Whether the particular sense of statehood the Hetman promoted was popular beyond the upper classes of Ukrainian society is another matter.

Personnel problems also blighted the main Ukrainization project of the Skoropadskyi regime – the creation of a Ukrainian army. In choosing the title of Hetman, Skoropadskyi had made a conscious attempt to present himself as a successor to the Cossack Hetmans of the early modern era, whose authority rested on their endeavours as military leaders. By creating a modern Ukrainian army, he could claim to be re-establishing these military traditions and, through them, an ideological connection with the Cossack Hetmanate. Furthermore, while the Rada's lack of military support had made it easy to dispense with, Skoropadskyi was acutely aware of the importance of an army for the long term feasibility of his government. The Central Powers were initially opposed to the formation of a separate Ukrainian army, but the setbacks they suffered on the Western and Italian fronts and the general instability in the countryside convinced them to acquiesce in the matter.

As a former general in the Imperial Russian army, Skoropadskyi understandably turned to the old officer corps. The results did not bode well for Ukrainian statehood. As one Austrian report explained, regardless of what these officers might say in their professional capacity as Ukrainian administrators, they were in fact Russians and made no secret of it. The same was true of the staff officers in Kiev who were trying to organize the army. The majority did not consider themselves Ukrainian citizens at all. They were Russian officers who, as long as the Bolsheviks remained in charge, hoped to serve a future reunified White Russia as best they could in Ukraine. To make matters worse, many of them were members of Russian ultra-nationalist organizations like the infamous Black Hundreds; one Austrian informant witnessed a conversation involving seventeen "Ukrainian" officers, who seemed to agree that no such thing as a Ukrainian people or a Ukrainian state existed. To them, the Ukrainians were traitors to Russia, just like the Bolsheviks and the peasants. "I hate workers and peasants from the bottom of my heart," said one. "Both have betrayed the fatherland." It would be ludicrous to expect such people to organize a Ukrainian army capable of defending Ukraine against a non-Bolshevik Russia, concluded the report.[112] In contrast to the officer corps, the Ministry of Defence was allegedly the most "chauvinistic" of all government ministries, as its staff had remained virtually unchanged from the time of the Rada.[113] This ideological chasm made a concerted, joint effort impossible. The new military law, which decreed a first national draft to be carried out in the winter of 1918–19, proved too little too late. In the event, no Ukrainian army to speak of emerged, the government's endeavours notwithstanding.

If the Rada's vision of Ukrainian national statehood had revolved around agrarian-socialism, Skoropadskyi's was based on the restoration of private property, with a view towards winning the support of the propertied classes. "Our Ukrainian is an individualist," the Hetman argued in his memoirs without much supporting evidence, "who does not need any socialization. He is decidedly against it."[114] With Austro-German military backing, he made a concerted effort to curb the agrarian revolution and restore the landlords to their agricultural estates. This resulted in numerous peasant rebellions and general unrest throughout the countryside. Both the Ukrainian government and Austro-German military authorities responded with energetic actions against the agitation and riots breaking out in different parts of the country; the poor organization of both administrative and police services on the part of the Ukrainian authorities, however, and the passive or even active resistance offered by some personnel left over from the previous regime meant that the brunt of the pacification campaign fell to German and Habsburg forces.[115] By early June, they faced full-scale rebellions in Zvenihorod and Elizavethrad, which required the transportation of additional troops to the affected areas.[116]

With the bulk of the peasantry firmly against the Hetman and engaged in sabotage activities and brigandage, the situation deteriorated quickly. On 30 July, a young Russian Left-SR assassin called Boris Dontsov (or Donskoi) threw a hand grenade at Eichhorn as the field marshal was crossing the street on the way back to his flat after lunch; Eichhorn died from his wounds that evening. The authorities believed that terrorist acts against the German ambassador and the Hetman were also planned.[117] By early August, an increasingly nervous Skoropadskyi had decided to send his family to Germany and was making succession plans in case he were assassinated, citing insecurity in Kiev and the political uncertainty of the two Brest-Litovsk treaties, which constituted the basis of the Ukrainian State. The German ambassador told his Austro-Hungarian colleague that he, too, was planning to go on extended leave and hoped never to return to Ukraine.[118]

The Hetman continued to harbor thoughts of Ukrainization of his government, now conveniently paired with democratization, throughout the autumn. He reshuffled his cabinet for the fourth and final time at the end of October in an ultimately fruitless attempt to solicit American support for Ukrainian national statehood.[119] The withdrawal of the Central Powers from Ukraine in late October–early November precipitated the dissolution of the Brest-Litovsk system. Bereft of popular support, the Hetmanate followed soon after. Ironically, Skoropadskyi's most cherished reform – the establishment of a Ukrainian army – played an important part in his downfall. Resentful of their Russian officers and of the draft, rank and file troops deserted in droves to the Directory, after it staged an uprising on 16 November in Bila Tserkva, Berdychiv, and Kharkiv. On 14 December, the Directory's troops entered Kiev, marking the formal end of the Hetmanate and restoring the Ukrainian People's Republic.[120]

Habsburg Ukrainization?: Wilhelm von Habsburg/Vasyl Vyshyvanyi

There was a fundamental contradiction at the centre of the Brest-Litovsk system. On the one hand, the system condemned Imperial dynasticism in much of East Central Europe by supporting the creation of nation states like Ukraine. On the other hand, it sought to preserve Imperial dynasticism further west. The Ukrainization policy of Wilhelm von Habsburg sought to address this contradiction and reconcile Imperial rule and the nation state. Although ultimately unsuccessful, it represents an important chapter of early Ukrainian statehood, pointing out the possibilities the Brest-Litovsk system offered as well as the blurring of the lines it engendered between Imperial and national.

Groomed from an early age to become a future king of Poland by his ambitious father Archduke Stefan, Wilhelm came from a generation of Habsburg leaders who seriously engaged nationalism for the first time. As historian Timothy Snyder has put it in his recent political biography of Wilhelm, they did so "not with a sense of historical inevitability, with the premonition that nations had to come and to conquer, that empires had to shudder and fall. They thought that freedom for Poland and Ukraine could be reconciled to the expansion of Habsburg rule in Europe."[121] Wilhelm eventually rebelled against his father's Polish orientation and decided to throw in his lot with the Ukrainians. After graduating from the military academy in Vienna in January 1915, he asked for and received a command post of a Ukrainian detachment in the Habsburg army. It was at this time that he acquired his nickname, "the red prince," as a result of his close relationship with his Ukrainian troops, whom the higher military authorities considered politically suspect.[122] Also around this time, Wilhelm's penchant for wearing an embroidered blue and yellow shirt gave him his Ukrainian alias, Vyshyvanyi (embroidered). His Ukrainophile tendencies quickly became known in important political circles. The young prince was particularly active during the course of the Brest-Litovsk negotiations. He met Count Czernin in a nearby village and tried to influence him to favour the Ukrainian cause. He was also in touch with Ukrainian delegates, informing them about the attitude of the Austrians towards them.[123]

Wilhelm got his big chance soon after Brest-Litovsk. In March 1918, Emperor Karl, whose tendency to pursue informal policy with the help of family members is perhaps best known through the so-called Sixtus Affair, sent Wilhelm to Ukraine at the head of an eponymous battle group. The archduke was to become the emperor's "eyes and ears" in Ukraine.[124] Most of the troops serving in Battle Group Archduke Wilhelm were Galician Ukrainians, including the famous Ukrainian Sich Sharpshooters [*Ukrains'ki Sichovi Stril'tsi*, USS], an all-Ukrainian auxiliary corps created in the autumn of 1914 in Galicia to combat the Russians. Wilhelm would rely heavily on these loyal troops in the implementation of his Ukrainization policy.

Battle Group Archduke Wilhelm carried out a fighting advance to the city of Oleksandrivsk, not far from the celebrated Cossack fortress of Sich, where it established its headquarters and quickly became engaged in nation-building activities. The USS took the lead, often acting in concert with the local administrators the Rada had appointed. Everywhere they went in the spring of 1918, wrote one Sich Sharpshooter, they brought the Ukrainian national idea – "their advance was a mobile propaganda machine for Ukrainian statehood."[125] They opened a national theatre in Oleksandrivsk and staged daily plays. They performed music numbers in the town park, where the local intelligentsia used to gather. They helped start a periodical, *Sich*. In an attempt to spread their influence, they organized joint trips to the countryside with local Cossack forces.[126] They read the journal *Prosvita* with the locals and offered classes in Ukrainian language and studies, while also helping organize local armed battalions.[127] Archduke Wilhelm considered the policy of cultural Ukrainization indispensable to the independent existence of the fledgling state. "There are only two possibilities: either an opponent would be able to send me away and russify, or I will be able to remain and ukrainize," he is reputed to have said on the subject.[128] Frank Golczewski agrees that these activities "played a very important role in the [spreading of Ukrainian] national education myths."[129]

The Hetman coup presented difficulties, as local Ukrainian administrators were replaced, often by Russians who tried to clamp down on Ukrainian nationalist activities. However, it also presented opportunities, as Wilhelm's headquarters in Oleksandrivsk quickly became the focal point of opposition to Skoropadskyi's regime. Unhappy with Skoropadskyi's policies, Zaporozhians allegedly wanted to carry out a coup with the aid of the USS and proclaim Wilhelm Hetman.[130]

Following the attempt by the Hetman authorities, the German, and the Habsburg troops to curb the agrarian revolution and return the land to the landlords, the peasants started arming themselves and resisting. The USS were sent to pacify a certain district but refused to shoot at the peasants. This was tantamount to high treason and punishable by death, but Wilhelm used his authority to protect them. The incident became widely known in the countryside, leading to the steady growth of Wilhelm's popularity.[131] On another occasion, the USS arrived at the central square in the village of Dobrovelychkivtsi and proceeded to sing Ukrainian songs to the accompaniment of their military orchestra. The initially apprehensive locals began to mingle and quickly joined them in song and dance. Soon, they were offering bread and salt to the Sharpshooters as a sign of hospitality and appreciation.[132] This method of pacification was typical of Wilhelm's view of Ukrainization, which focused on the peasantry and the socialization of land. He was a red prince indeed. "My troops and I tried to protect the local population from some of the excesses of the Austrian military occupation," wrote Wilhelm of his actions. "Many Ukrainian nationalist activists came to us, as they knew we would protect them."[133]

As news of the archduke's Ukrainophile actions spread, rumors of a possible Habsburg regency under Wilhelm began to circulate.[134] The Austro-Hungarian general chief of staff brought up the presence of Archduke Wilhelm in Ukraine in conversation with the representative of the Foreign Office, adding that apparently the archduke was a contender for the Ukrainian throne. The OHL also made inquiries about Wilhelm's activities.[135] Tentative plans for a coup did, in fact, exist, as certain socialist politicians in Odessa came up with the idea to proclaim

Wilhelm Hetman in opposition to Skoropadskyi. One of the atamans of the USS took this proposal to the archduke in Oleksandrivsk. Wilhelm thought it over and replied that he would not decline the post if that was the will of the Ukrainian people. At a conference in Kiev, however, the leaders of the Ukrainian SDs and SRs voted down the proposal as too dangerous.[136] Although this plan came to nothing, it is demonstrative of Wilhelm's growing popularity in Ukrainian political circles, where his candidacy was seriously considered. Apparently, there were at least two subsequent occasions when Cossack troops "crowned" Wilhelm King of Ukraine.[137]

Skoropadskyi also became concerned with Wilhelm's perceived aspirations and spoke several times with the Austro-Hungarian ambassador, Count Forgách, about the situation in Oleksandrivsk. He emphasized that, thanks to Wilhelm's actions, Oleksandrivsk had become the destination of all dissatisfied elements in Ukraine. Equally concerned, Forgách suggested recalling the archduke in a letter to the Austro-Hungarian foreign minister, Count István Burián, Czernin's successor after April 1918.[138] Habsburg civilian and military authorities became convinced that Wilhelm should be recalled from Ukraine, but as long as he had the emperor's ear, he was untouchable. The commander of the Habsburg Eastern Army stationed in Ukraine, General Alfred Krauss, told Ambassador Forgách he might reassign the archduke without asking the emperor.[139] Eventually, he succeeded in relocating Wilhelm and his troops to Elizavethrad, after about a month and a half in Oleksandrivsk.[140]

However, the archduke continued his Ukrainization efforts in Elizavethrad unperturbed. Under his guidance, USS members opened a small theatre in a nearby village, which offered performances twice a week. These were often accompanied by dances, at which the USS lads would dance with the local girls, thereby establishing connections with the local population. Wilhelm also sent many USS members to different parts of Ukraine, especially Podolia and Kherson, to open Ukrainian schools and spread literacy.[141] Recognizing the need for more functionaries, he began recruiting local Ukrainians into the USS, which roughly doubled in size.[142]

Habsburg and especially German military authorities in Ukraine opposed Wilhelm's Ukrainization policy, primarily because it favoured the socialist-leaning peasantry and undermined the authority of Skoropadskyi's regime. The matter eventually reached Kaiser Wilhelm, who demanded an explanation. Emperor Karl decided that a personal visit from the archduke might be the best way to set the record straight and wrote a letter to the Kaiser to that effect.¹⁴³ Wilhelm decided to use the opportunity to solicit the Kaiser's support for his candidacy to the Ukrainian throne. Having arrived at General Headquarters in Spa at the beginning of August, he raised the subject with the representative of the German Foreign Ministry, von Lersner. The diplomat told the archduke not to mention his wish to the Kaiser, as the Kaiser could not answer in the affirmative, whereupon the archduke dropped the matter. Neither Emperor Karl nor Kaiser Wilhelm appeared to be aware of the archduke's plans; Karl even dismissed the whole thing as a malicious rumor. However, the German government claimed to be in possession of a letter from the archduke, in which he allegedly put himself forward as the most adequate candidate for the Ukrainian throne. He did not want to force himself, but if the people were to choose him, he would be ready to comply.¹⁴⁴ The reception itself was friendly, and Wilhelm assured the Kaiser he had no political aspirations. The Kaiser took to the young archduke and awarded him the Iron Cross.

After his visit to Spa, Wilhelm returned to Ukraine and resumed his Ukrainization policy. The AOK continued to receive reports, which accused Wilhelm and his troops of supporting the peasants in their opposition to current socio-economic conditions in Ukraine, of spreading Bolshevik ideas among the population, and of conducting activities against landlords and Jews, including open propaganda for partitioning the land.¹⁴⁵ More importantly, Wilhelm's increasingly independent behaviour began to alarm Emperor Karl, who wrote a cautionary letter to the archduke. It was currently impossible to see how events in Ukraine would unfold and whether the Hetmanate would last, stated the emperor. If Skoropadskyi's regime were to fall, it would be of no consequence to the Dual Monarchy. The situation would be completely different if a Habsburg prince were proclaimed Hetman with the emperor's consent. In this case, the Monarchy would undoubtedly support such a regime. However, the candidacy of a Habsburg archduke for the post presented great difficulties in Austria-Hungary's relations with Germany, which in turn could threaten the collection and transportation of foodstuffs. Although professing himself happy with the friendly relations with various Ukrainian groups which Wilhelm had promoted, the emperor asked him to cease any further activities in that direction for the time being.¹⁴⁶ By early September, Karl had agreed to have Wilhelm and his Ukrainian troops recalled from Ukraine under the pretext of guaranteeing their security.¹⁴⁷ On 9 October, they left for Bukovina.

By the end of the month, the USS had become actively involved in the creation of the West Ukrainian People's Republic, which took place amidst bitter clashes with local Polish forces in the formerly Habsburg town of Lemberg (Ukrainian: Lviv, Polish: Lwów) in East Galicia.[148]

Archduke Wilhelm's Ukrainization policy represents an important stage of early Ukrainian statehood. A product typical of the Brest-Litovsk program, it tried to reconcile the nation state with continued Habsburg rule in Europe by creating a populist monarchy under a Habsburg "red prince." Wilhelm promoted cultural Ukrainization as well as the socialization of land, which was the main issue for the majority of Ukrainian peasants throughout the revolutionary period of 1917–18. Wilhelm's Ukrainization policy offered a more inclusive and tolerant version of Ukrainian nationalism. In a way, the archduke embodied successful Ukrainization. His early career demonstrated that Wilhelm von Habsburg, an Austrian prince who had only learned to speak Ukrainian in his adolescence, could become Vasyl Vyshyvanyi, prospective leader of the Ukrainian national movement. Ukrainian nationalism could adapt to changing circumstances and meet the demands of war and revolution.

Conclusion

In his examination of the emergence of the notion of ethnicity in late-Imperial Bashkiria, Charles Steinwedel writes that "the Tsarist regime provided concepts and important precedents for the ethnic organization of educational, spiritual, and political institutions. With the destruction of the Tsarist regime ... the new Soviet regime systematized the language of ethnicity and built upon the foundations laid by its predecessor."[149] While a similar connection also existed in Ukraine, the Ukrainian experience with nationalization policies in 1918 provided an even more important context of "concepts and important precedents" for subsequent Soviet nationality policy.

This significance was due to the fact that, in the eight months following the Brest-Litovsk Peace Conference – where the diplomats of the Ukrainian People's Republic and the Central Powers cooperated to sign the first peace treaty of the Great War – a new system regulated the state of affairs in what had been the southwestern part of the Russian Empire. Both parties were indispensable to its establishment. Without Ukraine's involvement in Brest-Litovsk, the peace conference might have taken a very different course. Similarly, without the Central Power's military involvement in Ukraine after the conference, modern Ukrainian statehood might have developed along different lines. Between March and November 1918, the Brest-Litovsk system promoted the existence of an ostensibly independent Ukrainian state, supported by Austro-German troops, which was nevertheless economically and politically closely oriented towards East Central Europe. By attempting to reconcile the emergence of nation states with continued Imperial rule, the system thus highlighted the complexity of the relationship between national and Imperial at the time.

The Brest-Litovsk system also provided the setting for several Ukrainization efforts by actual and prospective Ukrainian governments, which were meant to bolster Ukrainian statehood. The Austro-German military presence obviously influenced policy, but it was by no means the sole determining factor. Ukrainian agency, revolutionary conditions, and Imperial legacies were all important factors in the shaping of Ukrainization policies. The policies of the Rada, Hetman Pavlo Skoropadskyi, and the "red prince" Wilhelm von Habsburg/Vasyl Vyshyvanyi differed in important facets, such as the political form of government and the nature of socio-economic relations in the state, but they had two things in common: they were nationality policies which shared a common operational approach and which also had a very specific socio-economic and ideological program tied to the notion of nationality. For the Rada, it was agrarian-socialist Ukrainization under a revolutionary republican government. For Hetman Pavlo Skoropadskyi, it was a conservative monarchy based on the restoration of private property and the support of a Ukrainian army. For Archduke Wilhelm, it was a populist monarchy under Habsburg suzerainty which prioritized the cultural Ukrainization of the peasantry as well as the socialization of the land economy. It is perhaps impossible for *any* nationality policy to be completely devoid of an ideological factor, but in establishing a clear relationship between the two, the various Ukrainization efforts of the Brest-Litovsk system anticipated certain aspects of early Soviet indigenization policy.

Chapter Five

Brest-Litovsk and the Elusive Bulgarian "Dream of Byzantium"

National statehood in the northern zone of East Central Europe was a relatively novel concept (Poland excepted), since the Russian Empire had begun to disintegrate only in the wake of the February Revolution. In contrast, in the southern zone of East Central Europe there was already a turbulent history of several decades, dating back to the time when Lord Byron sacrificed himself in a romantic gesture for the cause of Greek independence. Whereas Imperial collapse in the north only began in 1917, it was more or less an accomplished fact in the south by 1913, as the Ottoman Empire, the erstwhile Imperial overlord, had been reduced to a mere foothold in Eastern Thrace protecting the capital of Constantinople. This meant that consecutive stages of national statehood existed in the two regions at the time of the Brest-Litovsk Peace Conference – nation-state *formation* in the northern zone of East Central Europe and nation-state *consolidation* in the southern zone of East Central Europe. The main difference between these two stages was the primary focus of government policy. In Ukraine it was on domestic policy, aimed at the nationalization of diverse populations and the state economy under Great Power protection. In Bulgaria, it was on foreign policy, a key aspect of which was seeking international recognition of the annexation of newly-conquered territories at a major peace conference. A side-by-side examination of these two cases can shed significant light on the nature of national statehood as well as on the diverse implications of the Brest-Litovsk Peace Conference in the various regions of East Central Europe affected by it.

As one French scholar has pointed out, the Great War has been a painful and hence relatively neglected topic in Bulgarian public memory and historiography, becoming, in effect, "an invisible war" largely conspicuous by its absence.¹ The same is equally true of Bulgaria's involvement in the Brest-Litovsk Peace Conference. The few existing studies – two journal articles and two chapters in recent monographs – show a remarkable continuity in methodology and argumentation. With minor differences in emphasis, they focus on the alleged perfidious reluctance of Bulgaria's ungrateful allies (the other three members of the Central Powers alliance) to either honour their territorial promises or recognize the country's rightful national aspirations.² The continuity across the 1989 ideological divide may appear surprising at first glance. However, substitution of the teleological narrative of Marxist-Leninist historiography (the victory of communism as the endpoint of historical progress) with the equally teleological narrative of the nation-state is not uncommon in Eastern European historiography. In a recent overview of post-Soviet Ukrainian historiography, Serhy Yekelchyk has noted that "the Marxist methodological ghosts of the past ritualistically denounced in present-day Ukrainian historical works have much in common with the equally reductionist nation-centric theories of the present."³ Thus, the legacy of Marxist-Leninist methodology and the dominant national-history paradigm have so far prevented many Bulgarian scholars (and many of their Eastern European colleagues trained in the same fashion) from looking at their subject of inquiry from a different perspective. This is especially true of nationally sensitive topics, such as Bulgaria's involvement in the Brest-Litovsk Peace Conference.

This chapter views Bulgarian policy in Brest-Litovsk as a crucial focal point in a long, elusive, and ultimately disastrous "dream of Byzantium."⁴ I do not use the term Byzantium here in reference to Constantinople, as the conquest of the one-time Byzantine capital had been on the Bulgarian political agenda only briefly during the First Balkan War. Instead, I use it as shorthand for its geopolitical implications – regional hegemony in the Balkans and Great Power status. The continuity of Bulgarian foreign policy between 1878 and 1918 demonstrates that this was a widely-shared vision of Bulgarian society rather than the work of a small, Coburg-led *camarilla*, as Marxist-Leninist historians have occasionally argued. Bulgarian diplomacy in Brest-Litovsk pursued the juridical-legal, international recognition of this "dream of Byzantium" under the guise of national unification [*natsionalno obedinenie*], thereby invoking and contributing to the discourse on national self-determination at the conference. Its failure to achieve this goal led to the considerable worsening of the domestic situation in Bulgaria, contributing to the fall of the Radoslavov government in June 1918 and the abdication of King Ferdinand in October. Ultimately, the failure of Bulgarian policy in Brest-Litovsk demonstrated the futility of the quest for regional hegemony in the southern zone of East Central Europe. This quest represents a particularly virulent form of the process of nation-state consolidation that is not unique to Bulgaria. As Mark Mazower has argued persuasively, "[t]he sense of mission in Balkan politics was driven by the dream of territorial expansion."[5] The *megali idea* championed by the Greek prime minister, Eleftherios Venizelos, at the Paris Peace Conference in 1919–20 bore a striking similarity to the Bulgarian "dream of Byzantium" and used much of the same imagery.[6] Furthermore, as already discussed, Fritz Fischer and his school essentially accused Wilhelmine Germany of pursuing the same goal, except on a much larger, worldwide scale.

Bulgaria's War Aims

Most primary and secondary accounts of Bulgaria's involvement in the Great War begin with the Treaty of San Stefano in 1878.[7] Given the Bulgarian obsession with this treaty and its vital importance in Sofia's subsequent foreign policy, it is necessary to outline its implications briefly in order to highlight the continuity of Bulgarian foreign policy. Having soundly defeated their Ottoman adversaries in the 1877–78 war, the victorious Russians forced them to sign a punitive peace in the Constantinople suburb of San Stefano on 3 March 1878 (the birthday of Emperor Alexander II). This treaty created a sprawling independent Bulgarian state, through which the Russians hoped to exercise decisive influence in the Balkans and, most importantly from their point of view, control the Black Sea straits. In light of the firm British and Austro-Hungarian opposition to these Russian aims, however, San Stefano was meant to be a preliminary treaty pending a final settlement arbitrated jointly by the Great Powers. At the subsequent Congress of Berlin (June–July 1878) – where Bismarck famously professed to play the role of honest broker – the British and the Austrians compelled the Russians to limit their gains. The revised settlement created a reduced Principality of Bulgaria, which was nominally vassal to the Sublime Porte but independent for all intents and purposes, and the autonomous province of Eastern Rumelia within the Ottoman Empire, which nevertheless united with Bulgaria soon after in 1885. Macedonia reverted to direct rule from Constantinople.[8]

There was a popular outcry in Bulgaria against the perceived grave injustice of the Congress of Berlin. Bulgarian politicians conveniently forgot the provisory nature of the San Stefano treaty and remained obsessed with the recreation of San Stefano's Bulgaria in the following decades, as a stepping-stone towards even greater objectives. The memoirs of Vasil Radoslavov demonstrate this perspective. "Thus, future Bulgaria inherited a clearly defined policy of struggle – struggle for the unification of the divided nation [*razpokusaniia narod*]," so wrote the former prime minister regarding the implications of San Stefano from his exile in Germany in the early 1920s.[9] Governments, princes, and means might change, but the ultimate goal of securing a dominant position in the Balkans remained constant.

By the outbreak of the Great War in August 1914, Bulgaria's blind pursuit of maximalist foreign policy goals and its inability to compromise had left it defeated and isolated in the wake of the Second Balkan War.[10] Disillusioned with its erstwhile protector Russia, and deeply resentful of its former ally turned bitter enemy, Serbia, Bulgaria slowly gravitated towards the Central Powers under the new Austrophile government of the German-educated Radoslavov. This move had nothing to do with any particularly deep sympathies and everything to do with the belief that it would be the best course for the realization of Bulgaria's foreign policy objectives. In the final analysis, writes Anne Christine Holden, "Bulgaria's alliance with the Central Powers in 1915 represents a typical attempt by a small power to gain advantages by choosing the winning side in a major conflict whose chief issues are of little concern to her."[11]

The secret military convention between Germany, Austria-Hungary, and Bulgaria, signed on 6 September 1915, outlined Bulgaria's official war aims. These included not only the acquisition of Serbian-held Macedonia but also a considerable chunk of Old Serbia itself along the Morava River (Serbian: Pomoravlje, Bulgarian: Pomoravie or Moravsko). Additional clauses stipulated that Bulgaria would regain Southern Dobrudja (lost in 1913) and secure a favourable border rectification in the area in case Romania joined the Entente, and would occupy the Aegean coastal cities of Drama, Serres, and Kavala in case Greece did the same.[12] In the lead-up to the Brest-Litovsk Peace Conference, Radoslavov reiterated these aims, now including all of the Dobrudja, in the *Narodno Subranie* (Parliament) on 1 December 1917: "Bulgaria cannot refuse this offer [of peace from the Bolsheviks]. She has achieved everything she entered this war for – her unification within her historical, ethnographic boundaries – Macedonia, Moravsko, and the Dobrudja. This is the first principle of our program for negotiations for a separate or a general peace."[13]

These official war aims went beyond the borders proposed at San Stefano or national unification. A sixty-one page study by the German Foreign Office from November 1917 explored the subject thoroughly, establishing that Sofia's unofficial objectives included Greek Salonica, Ottoman Eastern Thrace, and a protectorate over Albania. Ultimately, the study concluded, these aims pursued the establishment of Balkan hegemony and a Bulgarian Monroe Doctrine in the area [*Balkanhegemonie und Monroe-Doktrin*].[14] The preponderance of power in a strategically vital region of Europe and a direct connection to Central Europe via a shared border with Hungary would have amounted, in effect, to minor Great Power status. Bulgarian diplomats virtually admitted as much. In early March 1918, the Bulgarian consul general in Hamburg engaged in a political campaign against the existing balance of power on the Balkan Peninsula, arguing that it would never result in durable peace. On the contrary, he claimed, the existing balance of power only stirred new conflicts that threatened Central Europe's economic interests in the area. An enlarged, militarily, politically, and economically strengthened Bulgaria was the best guarantor of peace in the Balkans. Far from cautioning these indiscreet remarks, the Foreign Ministry in Sofia approved the actions of its representative.[15] The rhetoric of national unification was a convenient excuse for regional hegemony.

The "dream of Byzantium" was not limited to the Radoslavov government. Both the king and educated society fully endorsed it. The ruler's official title after 1908 was tsar, and even though it had lost much of its Imperial connotations by the early twentieth century (Bulgarian diplomatic missions routinely translated it as *roi* and the name of the state as *Royaume de Bulgarie*), Ferdinand fancied himself as more than an ordinary monarch, occasionally appearing in the ceremonial garb of a Byzantine emperor.[16] When it appeared that Russia might be willing to make peace, he endeavoured to use a visit to the Italian Front in early November 1917 to elevate his status. With Emperor Karl present and Kaiser Wilhelm expected to arrive from Germany, Ferdinand suggested that the three monarchs inspect the troops at the front jointly, in order to demonstrate to the entire world the strengthening of their new Triple Alliance. The Ottoman Sultan was conveniently left out of the equation, even though his claim to an Imperial title, unlike Ferdinand's, was widely recognized in European capitals. When he got news of

Ferdinand's intentions, Kaiser Wilhelm was not amused in the least. He pointed out that the king had planned this "theatrical coup" in order to present himself as an equal sovereign of a Great Power alongside the two Central European emperors. In any event, he added, Ferdinand had no right to be present at the inspection of the troops, since no Bulgarian soldier was anywhere near the Italian Front. It turned out that Emperor Karl was not particularly enthusiastic about this plan either, and Ferdinand's clever schemes came to naught.[17] He would have to find another way to boost his status.

It is possible to discover the attitudes of the Bulgarian intelligentsia towards the policy of regional hegemony thanks to an initiative of the Bulgarian General Staff. In the expectation of a peace conference in the foreseeable future, in June 1916 the military authorities decided to commission leading university professors from a variety of disciplines (history, linguistics, economics, ethnography, sociology) to travel to the newly-conquered territories from Serbia and compile reports on local socio-economic conditions. Thirteen academics – the *crème de la crème* of Bulgarian educated society – were contacted, and all agreed to participate. The purpose of this enterprise was made explicit in the letter of invitation: "It is precisely in scholarly studies that one finds the data required to set the state life of the new territories on the right track and defend the country's interests at the future international [peace] negotiations."[18] The project, dubbed A Scientific Expedition in Macedonia and the Pomoravie, provides important insight into the intelligentsia's views of Bulgaria's war aims. As Liliana Vladeva points out, scholarly support for the country's "national unification" played an important role in the formation of policy in the lead up to and during Brest-Litovsk.[19]

The scholars' reports aimed to legitimize Bulgaria's claim to all territories conquered from Serbia (Macedonia, Kosovo, and the Morava region), some of which went far beyond Bulgaria's San Stefano borders and encompassed diverse non-Slavic populations, including Albanians, Turks, and Aromanians (also called Vlachs). There was a consensus on the need to create an active military and civilian administration engaged in Bulgarianizing the Serbian and nationally-indifferent populations, although this was not nearly as urgent or as central as was the case in Ukraine. Policy suggestions did not end there – one academic advocated spreading Bulgaria's influence to Albania proper, with a view towards establishing a secure outlet on the Adriatic.[20] Another summarized the nationalist intelligentsia's uncompromising attitude towards Bulgaria's war aims with the following words:

A strictly military regime not just for the Pomoravie but also for the whole of Macedonia, especially for Macedonia, for at least twenty years – this is the only way to go. Perhaps such a regime would not be popular with our leftist circles, but the untainted sons of the fatherland will defend it by any means and at any cost. All preferences and favors must disappear, as we are laying the ground for a *Great Bulgaria!*[21]

So much for national unification and national self-determination, both of which were repeatedly invoked in Bulgaria's official war aims. And while Bulgarian academics ardently advocated the imposition of harsh administrative measures in areas allegedly populated by genuine Bulgarians, in an ironic twist the war-weary locals along the Morava River were telling the visitors in their Serbian dialect with a Bulgarian inflexion: "Let there be peace, we don't care who rules us [*Da bude mir, pa da vlada koj hoće*]."[22]

Bulgarian Policy in Brest-Litovsk I: Opposing the Ioffe Program

Valentin Aleksandrov has described Bulgaria's participation in the Brest-Litovsk Peace Conference and the signing of the peace treaties as "one of the greatest moments in Bulgarian diplomatic and military history," as the country emerged among the victors on the Eastern Front.[23] This is an extremely idealized view of what was in effect a hollow victory that hardly obscured the inability of Bulgarian diplomacy to secure the international recognition of the country's new borders at the peace conference and place the final realization of the "dream of Byzantium" on a more solid footing. Bulgarian diplomats probably suspected that this would be a difficult task to accomplish even in the best of circumstances, but especially so given Bolshevik rhetoric and insistence on "no annexations and indemnities." Hence, they were in no particular hurry to endorse Petrograd's proposal to engage in immediate peace negotiations. Writing to Prime Minister Radoslavov in mid-November 1917, the ministers plenipotentiary in Berlin and Vienna, Dimitur Rizov and Andrei Toshev respectively, contrasted the praiseworthy, "cool and detached" German approach to the Bolshevik Decree on Peace with the Austrians' "histrionics," and even made disparaging remarks about Czernin.[24] At the same time, Toshev objected to the term annexations in a private conversation with Czernin, who somewhat reluctantly conceded that the Central Powers might possibly state that it did not refer to national unification.[25]

In spite of the Ballhausplatz's reassurance, the Bulgarians remained markedly unenthusiastic about negotiating with the Bolsheviks. "From what I have heard over the last few days," Kajetan Mérey telegraphed the Foreign Ministry from Brest-Litovsk on 15 December, "I gather people in Sofia want an armistice but are not too keen on an actual peace [treaty]." He could not say whether this was due to concerns over the stability of the Radoslavov government or additional reasons.[26] However, it seems that Sofia simply underestimated the importance of the forthcoming negotiations at first. Radoslavov told the Austro-Hungarian minister plenipotentiary in Sofia, Otto Czernin, on 18 December that he did not intend to travel to Brest-Litovsk because Bulgaria's interest in the peace talks with Russia was only secondary. He could rely on the Russian-educated justice minister, Popov, for an adequate view of Russian internal conditions. Radoslavov even questioned the presence of Czernin and Kühlmann, in light of the absence of Trotsky and Lenin. The Bulgarian prime minister would attend personally any future negotiations with the Western Powers, of course.[27] Alternatively, Georgi Markov claims that Radoslavov refused to travel to Brest-Litovsk in order to check domestic challenges to his Liberal government,[28] which was subject to growing criticism both from the left and right of the political spectrum.

In any event, in the prime minister's absence, Popov's dubious leadership style and obduracy involved the Bulgarian delegation in several quarrels with its allies during the first two phases of the peace conference (22 December 1917 – 18 January 1918), while at the same time contributing little to the joint policy of the Quadruple Alliance or to the conference as a whole. "The Bulgarians did not open their mouths [at the plenary sessions]," Trotsky wrote dismissively in the introduction to the official Bolshevik publication of the proceedings.[29] On the other hand, they were quite loquacious behind closed doors.

The first confrontation between the Bulgarian delegation and its allies occurred over the Central Powers' reply to the Ioffe Program from 22 December. Ioffe's insistence on a peace of "no annexations and indemnities" set all sorts of Bulgarian alarm bells ringing. Colonel Ganchev immediately wired Radoslavov for instructions on whether to accept the Ioffe Program or raise the Dobrudja Question.[30] The prime minister replied that the Russian proposal was completely unacceptable [*nepriemliva*]. In objecting, the colonel should emphasize Bulgaria's war aims, as outlined in the manifestoes of 1 October 1915 (declaration of war on Serbia) and 1 September 1916 (declaration of war on Romania), which stated that Sofia was fighting a war of national unification. This project involved the liberation of Bulgarians from the "Serbian yoke" in Macedonia and from Romanian rule in the Dobrudja (both northern and southern). However, he instructed Ganchev not to mention the Dobrudja Question unless Romanian delegates arrived at Brest-Litovsk, as this would presumably lead to trouble with the Ottomans.[31]

As already discussed in chapter two, Czernin and Kühlmann quickly agreed on a common course of action, which they presented to the Ottoman and Bulgarian delegates at 5:00 p.m. on 23 December. After a brief discussion, they successfully persuaded the somewhat reluctant Ottomans to go along. However, Popov strenuously objected to the "no annexations and indemnities" clause. Kühlmann retorted "through clenched teeth" that the clause was not dangerous to Bulgaria, as it had special treaties with the Central European empires which guaranteed its territorial acquisitions, and it was only unifying anyway. The suspicious Popov interpreted this remark as a clever ploy on the German state secretary's part, allegedly intended to leave the Dobrudja Question out of the negotiations and put the Bulgarians in an even worse bargaining position later on. Popov wished to bring it up and insist on including a proviso to the main clause, specifying the borders within which the Bulgarian nation had clearly "self-determined itself."[32] In fact, nothing could have been further from Kühlmann's mind. As the state secretary informed Imperial Chancellor Hertling, the regrettable delay in the negotiations was due to the fact that the Bulgarians had made their expected objection, which the alliance could not accept. Hence, they were burning the wires between Brest-Litovsk and Sofia but would hopefully come round in the end.[33]

Radoslavov did not wish to go as far as Popov, but he nevertheless instructed the Bulgarian delegates to accept the clause – "the delegations of the Quadruple Alliance agree to an immediate general peace without annexations and indemnities" – only on the condition that it be qualified with the phrase, "but this does not apply to Bulgaria, which has been fighting for its unification [*Selbsteinigung*]."[34] Accordingly, Popov showed Kühlmann the proposed amendment on the morning of 24 December. The state secretary declared himself categorically against it but agreed to consult with Czernin and the Ottomans, who also flatly refused. At lunch, one of the legal experts of the German Foreign Ministry, von Kriege, endeavoured to convince the Bulgarian minister of justice that he had nothing to fear, as the secret agreements between Berlin, Vienna, and Sofia were still binding. Besides, Kriege added in a reassuring echo of Popov's own phraseology, everyone knew that the Bulgarians were liberating, not annexing. This was perhaps a reference to the 1912 Serbian-Bulgarian secret agreement to divide Ottoman Macedonia into two separate zones – an uncontested one, which would go to Bulgaria, and a contested one, whose ownership would be decided courtesy of arbitration by the Russian emperor. Since there was never a referendum in the area, it is unclear which state the Macedonian Slavs would have preferred to join – if any.[35]

As an added incentive, General Hoffmann produced a telegram from the Dobrudja in which the population expressed a wish to see the province join Bulgaria. All was in vain. Popov declared that his government's domestic situation would grow considerably worse if it accepted the no annexations clause, since the Bulgarian people would interpret it as relinquishing already occupied territories. A second meeting between Popov, Kühlmann, and Czernin took place in the afternoon. "We argued until 5 o'clock," Popov explained to Radoslavov in his report, stressing his commitment to the Bulgarian cause. Czernin and Kühlmann reiterated that the qualification desired by the Bulgarian delegation would be gravely injurious to the interests of the Central Powers, not least Bulgaria itself, as it would draw unnecessary world attention to Bulgaria's territorial aims. Looking for a way out of the impasse, Kühlmann suggested the Bulgarian delegation send a separate note to the Russians expressing its reservations, as he personally would never agree to any alterations of the joint statement. The Bulgarian minister of justice flatly refused, presumably because he realized such an isolated gesture could easily be dismissed. In order to enjoy genuine international recognition, the "dream of Byzantium" required the formal approval of friend and foe alike. An irritated Czernin said in a loud voice that such an amendment would set a dangerous precedent, which Italy could use to Austria's detriment in the future. He also brought up his German colleague's repeated assurances that the secret treaties would remain in force. Popov refused to budge but promised to telegraph Sofia for further instructions.[36] The entire affair infuriated Czernin, who privately told another Bulgarian delegate, Todor Anastasov (who just so happened to be Radoslavov's son-in-law), that he was extremely angry with the whole delegation because some of its members, particularly Popov, were incredibly obstinate.[37]

The proviso the Bulgarians wanted to incorporate was unacceptable to Czernin and Kühlmann not because they were devising some devious scheme to deprive Bulgaria of territories already promised it, as Bulgarian historians have suggested, but because singling out *any* country for special treatment would have set a dangerous precedent for the later stages of the negotiations, as Czernin pointed out. It was also unnecessary, since the Central Powers' acceptance of the entire Ioffe Program was to be made conditional on the acceptance of the Western Entente Powers, which was not forthcoming. In any event, Sofia had the secret treaties to fall back on. The whole thing amounted to a tempest in a teapot.

If you live in a teapot, however, a tempest may be a very uncomfortable thing, as Jane Austen pointed out. It most certainly was for the Bulgarian delegates, who turned a blind eye to reason and continued to persist stubbornly with their objections. "To emphasize in whatever form in the allies' [i.e., Central Powers'] reply that [they] accept, even in the case of a general peace, a peace without annexations, would mean unconditional surrender and the end of Bulgaria's participation in the war," Radoslavov explained in his memoirs.[38] To avoid such an eventuality, after the stormy second meeting on 24 December, Popov decided to ignore his allied diplomats altogether and sound out Ioffe on the subject of Bulgaria's borders. After all, he had been made leader of the Bulgarian delegation precisely owing to his earlier Russian connections. Unsurprisingly, the leader of the Russian delegation replied that the Bolsheviks would make no exceptions for any country. He added that if Bulgarians really comprised a majority in Macedonia and the Dobrudja, the no annexations clause would actually help Bulgaria. The people would elect to join it in a free and open referendum, thereby bolstering Sofia's claim to these disputed territories.

As Popov knew full well, however, referenda could cause complications, especially in territories which until fairly recently had been multi-ethnic Imperial borderlands. When a Bulgarian nationalist activist in pre-1912 Ottoman Macedonia had objected to the fact that the local Slavs had religious services in Greek, he had received an unenthusiastic response: "[T]hey bolted raw cabbage and washed it down with mastic and only said it did not matter; many of them spoke Greek. The priest took a suck at the bottle and was of the same opinion. He spoke the local Slavic dialect himself for ordinary purposes, but he had learned all the services in Greek. It was a good service and what did it matter?"[39] Popov therefore enquired whether the urban or peasant population in a given area should be given self-determination if a town were Greek but the surrounding countryside Bulgarian. Ioffe, who probably had not expected such a specific question at this point, replied somewhat confusedly that the countryside should receive preferable treatment because it feeds the city (a highly questionable assertion from a strictly Marxist point of view, even bearing in mind Lenin's concept of the *smychka* – alliance – between workers and poor peasants).⁴⁰ Since the Bolsheviks would subsequently insist on referenda conditions unacceptable to the Central Powers, Ioffe's answer to Popov's inquiry was hardly a ringing endorsement of Bulgarian policy in Brest-Litovsk.

Initially, Radoslavov continued to insist on amending the by now notorious clause on the morning of 25 December. "Tell Kühlmann and Czernin that if the [joint] declaration has a special proviso that referenda do not apply to Germany's colonies [point six], it would make no difference if they added our note," the prime minister instructed Colonel Ganchev. If they still refused, he added in a more conciliatory manner, Ganchev ought to insist on adding to the minutes of the proceedings that Bulgaria was fighting for its national unification. In any event, the Bulgarian delegates should explain that they objected only to the term "annexations"; everything else was acceptable.⁴¹ This was a sensible remark by the Bulgarian prime minister in that it implied that territories in Europe should be treated in the same manner as overseas colonies. However, no one but the Bolsheviks (for their own ideological reasons) would consider this notion seriously either at Brest-Litovsk or at Paris. On a more positive note, Radoslavov's further clarification seemed to offer a way out of the deadlock.

The prime minister's sudden willingness to offer concessions was in part due to the repeated warnings, now also coming from members of the Bulgarian delegation, that obstinacy may have dangerous repercussions for Sofia. "If we refuse to accept, the others will go ahead and endorse it [the declaration] without us anyway, which would leave us isolated," wrote Anastasov. Kühlmann and Czernin had repeatedly assured the Bulgarian delegates that they had nothing to fear, since they were liberating rather than conquering. "They promise to support us to the end, and since it was only through their help that we liberated these territories, we should be content," reasoned Anastasov. Besides, he elaborated, the clause would stand only if it were unanimously accepted by all belligerent states, which was unthinkable. It had been added only out of courtesy to the Russians. Kühlmann was angry that the Bulgarians had been delaying the conference for two days, while Czernin had told Anastasov that Minister Popov had failed to grasp the delicate nature of the wording of the Central Powers' statement. The Bulgarian delegate pleaded for immediate instructions, warning the prime minister: "If we refuse, there would be grave political and practical consequences, and we might make a huge and possibly irreparable mistake."[42]

In the end, the Bulgarians consented to endorse the joint declaration unamended. Following General Hoffmann's memoirs, Wheeler-Bennett claims that this was due to a personal letter from King Ferdinand to Colonel Ganchev.[43] There is little evidence elsewhere of an actual letter, but the king probably did use his considerable influence with the prime minister – who was already beginning to come round anyway – to secure Bulgarian acquiescence. Radoslavov wrote defensively in his memoirs, no doubt in part to refute subsequent allegations that he was a tool of the unpopular Ferdinand, that Bulgaria's decision to drop its earlier objections "did not result from pressure from above, or from a personal intervention of the Bulgarian king. It resulted from a unanimous decision of the Council of Ministers, only after Kühlmann and Czernin gave Mr Popov a signed declaration stating that all treaties and conventions between Bulgaria, Austria-Hungary, and Germany remained in force, and the respective governments were required to work for their fulfillment."[44] In the final analysis, the Bulgarian king, prime minister, and certain members of the delegation in Brest-Litovsk probably arrived at the same conclusion – to carry out a dignified retreat – more or less independently.

Interlude: Domestic Concerns and the Dobrudja Question

For the purposes of Bulgarian policy in Brest-Litovsk, the Austro-German pledge to honour the secret treaties was not as good as an outright amendment to Czernin's Christmas Speech, but it was infinitely better than coming out entirely empty-handed. Doubts remained nonetheless. The commander-in-chief, Major General Nikola Zhekov, was at first unpleasantly surprised at the unexpected turn of events. Evidently unaware of the existence of the pledge, on 26 December he complained to Radoslavov that the Central Powers' declaration did not go far enough in guaranteeing Bulgaria's control of the occupied territories. He also found the reference to the free will of populations with respect to their state affiliation "improper and dangerous [*neumestna i opasna*]," a tacit admission that the "dream of Byzantium" went beyond national unification. "While we can be sure a majority in Macedonia and the Dobrudja would vote for union with Bulgaria," the general explained, "this would not be the case in other territories [i.e., the Morava region and Kosovo]."[45] Zhekov felt reassured when the prime minister informed him of the note Kühlmann and Czernin had presented to Popov.[46] However, he suggested that the government look into the possibility of issuing an additional Bulgarian note, stipulating that while the Bulgarian delegation agreed wholeheartedly with the joint note of the Quadruple Alliance, it wanted to emphasize that the Bulgarian state had never pursued an expansionist foreign policy – it had merely striven to achieve national unification. While certain Bulgarian populations had been forcibly deported and others assimilated, Bulgaria possessed all the proper documents to defend its rightful desire for full national unification. Sofia had joined the Great War only in order to right the wrongs it had suffered at the Congress of Berlin in 1878 and the Treaty of Bucharest in 1913, which concluded the Second Balkan War.[47] Radoslavov seems to have decided against this measure, as neither Popov nor Ganchev presented such a note to the Russian delegation.

Like General Headquarters in Kiustendil, the Royal Palace in Sofia was apprehensive with respect to the latest developments in Brest-Litovsk. The head of Ferdinand's Secret Chancery, Dobrovich, told the Austro-Hungarian minister plenipotentiary, Otto Czernin, that the king was very concerned about the course of negotiations and feared that the acceptance of the principle of no annexations by the Central Powers might allow Russia to bring the Western Entente Powers to the peace conference. Domestic conditions might also take a turn for the worse, as the opposition would doubtless hold Ferdinand personally responsible for any failure to achieve Bulgaria's war aims.[48] Admittedly, only the fringe Narrow Socialists, precursors to the Bulgarian Communist Party, were openly opposed to the policy of regional hegemony, with all other parties in favour. As the vice-speaker of the *Narodno Subranie* told Otto Czernin in confidence, however, the opposition blamed the Radoslavov government and the king for not securing the entire Dobrudja (rather than just Southern Dobrudja and a border rectification) as compensation for the country's participation in the war in the secret treaties with Germany and Austria-Hungary. The Russophobe, Vienna-born Ferdinand did not wish to press the matter in 1915–16, the argument went, because he feared a common border with Imperial Russia on personal grounds. As Radoslavov had put the private interests of the monarch before those of the nation, he was also culpable. To corroborate this information, Otto Czernin explained to the Foreign Ministry in Vienna that he had already heard plenty about the Dobrudja Question and how dangerous it could be for the government and, indeed, for the crown.[49]

The relentless pressure of the opposition and the dubious loyalty of about a dozen of his own Liberal MPs left Radoslavov and his minority government little room for manoeuvre. The government had jumped on the nationalist bandwagon and could no longer restrain nationalist sentiment. Hence, the prime minister's days in power would be numbered if he appeared insufficiently invested in the "dream of Byzantium." And if Radoslavov went, Ferdinand's position on the throne might well become untenable.

Without a doubt, the Central Powers' answer to the Ioffe Program would have a negative effect on public opinion at home, since many people had no knowledge of the fact that this was merely a ruse to conclude a separate peace with Russia, concurred Colonel Ganchev in a telegram to the prime minister. It might therefore be a good idea to show party leaders in Sofia the text of the promissory note Czernin and Kühlmann had provided, as well as official telegrams outlining Bulgarian protestations. It might also be useful to inform concerned individuals that the German delegates had promised to make an official declaration in the Reichstag or in the semi-official *Norddeutsche Allgemeine Zeitung* immediately after the conclusion of peace with Russia, explaining that they would fulfil their obligations "in all circumstances." Kühlmann had even asked one of the Bulgarian delegates to tell King Ferdinand that he had not stopped considering Bulgarian interests for a minute and that they were one of his biggest concerns.[50] The main problem was not so much the absence of any specific guarantees from Germany and Austria-Hungary of Bulgaria's aspirations, as the government's appalling inability to make full use of the guarantees it did have.

In the virtual absence of any thorough studies of the Bulgarian home front during the Great War, it is difficult to ascertain how and why exactly the Dobrudja Question became so important for Bulgarian public opinion and consequently for the delegation in Brest-Litovsk. It was no longer a case of national self-determination *per se*, since even the most rabid nationalist had to admit that ethnic Bulgarians were a minority in Northern Dobrudja (probably not even the largest minority, although reliable figures are impossible to come by). Nor was this a case of restoring the San Stefano borders, the alleged goal of national unification, since these had also left out most of Northern Dobrudja. Naturally, unfavourable demographic figures rarely stopped any statesman from pursuing self-determination, either at Brest-Litovsk or at Paris. The Bulgarians maintained that the region constituted an historic whole that should not be artificially divided along demographic lines. Kühlmann's approach to the Baltic provinces in his debates with Trotsky was similar in that respect, as was the Hungarian insistence at Paris on the historic unity of the lands of the Apostolic Crown of St. Stephen. Ironically, the Romanians made the same argument when they took over Southern Dobrudja from the Bulgarians after the Second Balkan War and again in 1919. When the numbers were not in their favour, the Bulgarian authorities invoked *historic* self-determination, unveiling medieval maps from the reign of Tsar Simeon in the tenth century and Tsar Ivan-Assen II in the thirteenth century, when Bulgaria spread across much of the Balkans. It mattered little that the Serbs and the Greeks could (and did) point to the similar extent of their respective medieval empires during the reigns of Tsar Stefan Dušan in the fourteenth century and Emperor Basil II in the eleventh. As Winston Churchill observed wryly, the Balkans produce more history than they can consume.

Another explanation for the sensitivity of the Dobrudja Question is the prevailing sense of victimization, an essential part of Bulgarian national identity at the time. The long centuries of "Turkish yoke" cast a long shadow over the nation-building endeavours of the Balkan peoples, which routinely blamed the erstwhile Imperial overlord for everything that was wrong with their societies. "For most Balkan nations," elaborates Tomislav Z. Longinović, "the process of writing down the nation as a permanent trace of collective imaginary is permeated by the ambiguous relationship to imperial rule by an alien power. As the new nations emerged in the course of the nineteenth century, the submission was culturally coded as part of a shameful legacy that had to be left behind, yet it was never relegated to complete forgetfulness."[51] In addition to this difficult relationship with their Ottoman past, the widespread notions of having been wronged by the Great Powers at the Congress of Berlin and by their treacherous Balkan allies in 1912–13, and finally betrayed by their one-time liberator, Russia, in 1913, further strengthened the Bulgarians' view of themselves as innocent victims surrounded by rapacious wolves. Even the unprecedented military victories and occupation of large parts of Serbia and Romania in 1915–16 could not bring about a complete reversal in mindset. If anything, they made matters worse, rationalizing the pursuit of regional hegemony as the only secure form possible of nation state consolidation.[52]

Consequently, the refusal of Germany and Austria-Hungary to simply hand over Northern Dobrudja to Sofia, even though they were not contractually obligated to do so, raised the by now familiar cries of victimization. It hardly occurred to Bulgarian statesmen that Vienna and Berlin might have their own interests in what was after all a key strategic area. With Bulgaria all but set to dominate the Balkans in the pursuit of regional hegemony and, hence, nearly all direct routes between Central Europe and the Eastern Mediterranean, the Austrians wanted to reconcile with Romania, while the Germans wanted to leave the last remaining land route to the Black Sea – the Cernavodă-Constanța railroad – and the important port of Constanța out of Bulgarian hands. "To allow Bulgaria to absorb the whole Dobrudja, as the Bulgarians wished, was unfavorable to Germany's future. I should have preferred northern Dobrudja to remain Romanian," Ludendorff wrote in his memoirs, emphasizing the importance of the railway connection and his preference for Constanța as a free city under German administration.[53] At the time of the negotiations, however, his views were less definitive. On 18 December 1917, he told Imperial Chancellor Hertling that he would agree to Bulgarian rule of the whole Dobrudja if the German government considered such a solution of the question necessary.[54] Even the OHL's willingness to compromise on this issue was not enough to resolve it to everyone's satisfaction, however, since the cohesion of the Central Powers alliance was already quite low.

To complicate matters still further, the Ottomans demanded territorial compensation from Bulgaria in Thrace in case the Bulgarians took over all of the Dobrudja. Grand Vizier Talaat Pasha explained the Ottoman point of view to the Austro-Hungarian ambassador, Pallavicini, on 22 December 1917. He wished the Dobrudja Question to be resolved at a later time, in conjunction with a resolution of the situation in Western Thrace, where 400 000 Muslims resided (a great overestimation, Pallavicini noted), in a favourable way for the Sublime Porte. He pointed out the need to improve the Ottoman European border, as it would strengthen the defences of the capital. In addition, the resolution of the Thracian Question would eliminate future tensions between the Ottoman Empire and Bulgaria of the type that had plagued Austro-Italian relations before the war. Pallavicini also sought the opinion of the Bulgarian minister plenipotentiary in Constantinople, Kolushev, who quite sensibly agreed that Bulgaria should not be unreasonable in the Dobrudja Question, as its interests required good relations with Romania after the war. He promised to present this point in a future audience with King Ferdinand but explained that the king did not share his views and wanted to annex the entire province.[55] Kolushev was indeed a solitary voice of dissent, drowned out by the choir of Bulgarian statesmen in pursuit of the "dream of Byzantium" and the *idée fixe* of Northern Dobrudja.

If Sofia was hesitant to compromise on the Dobrudja Question, it would not even dream of doing so on the Thracian Question. In fact, as Otto Czernin explained in a telegram to his older brother, in Bulgaria there was no such thing as a "Thracian Question." "The Bulgarians are obsessed with the idea of extending their borders in all directions as much as possible, and nothing could be further from their perception of reality than the relinquishment of a region which they have already contractually annexed," wrote the generally pro-Bulgarian minister plenipotentiary. Consequently, Sofia would not be persuaded by the Ottoman arguments, as it had never relinquished anything willingly, especially to the Turks. In order not to endanger future friendly relations between the two states, Otto Czernin added, Vienna would have to tread carefully. It would be in the interest of the Quadruple Alliance to delay the resolution of these interrelated questions as long as possible.[56] This is exactly what the already preoccupied Kühlmann and Czernin proceeded to do in Brest-Litovsk, promising their increasingly restless Ottoman and Bulgarian allies to help resolve all outstanding issues at some point in the future, perhaps at the end of the war. No one was satisfied, least of all the two leading diplomats of the Central Powers, who had their hands full dealing with Bolsheviks, Ukrainians, and domestic unrest.

Bulgarian Policy in Brest-Litovsk II: Rapprochement with Russia and Ukraine?

Contrary to what Valentin Aleksandrov has asserted, Bulgarian involvement in Brest-Litovsk did not end with the Christmas incident over the Central Powers' reply to the Ioffe Program.[57] Disillusioned with their allies' reluctance to endorse their foreign policy objectives in public, the Bulgarians distanced themselves slightly from Germany and Austria-Hungary and decided to negotiate with the Russians privately in the hope of coming to an arrangement about Bulgaria's extended borders on the basis of self-determination. To this end, Popov asked Radoslavov to dispatch to Brest-Litovsk at least three well-known experts on self-determination. They should gather different types of documents bolstering Bulgaria's claim to the newly conquered areas, including but not limited to historical and archaeological sources (including notes on historical monuments), documents on rebellions against Ottoman rule, state documents such as records on the Bulgarian Exarchate, and international conventions such as the Constantinople Commission of 1876 and the San Stefano Treaty of 1878. The academics would have to translate everything into Russian and prepare multiple copies for circulation in Brest-Litovsk and elsewhere. It was paramount to include a very clear and detailed map demonstrating the extent to which Bulgarians had "determined themselves" on the Balkan peninsula on the basis of demographic composition, historical records, and international conventions. The academics should not be concerned about the fact that some of these claims were in the distant past (i.e., invoking historic rights rather than national self-determination), Popov concluded, in another tacit admission that self-determination was merely a means to a greater end. They should also bear in mind "that the countryside determines the city, not the other way around," a reference to his earlier conversation with Ioffe.[58] The prime minister agreed to arrange for four Bulgarian professors to join the delegation.[59] The use of academics was a novel approach at Brest-Litovsk, which would become increasingly common during the extended peacemaking process at the end of the Great War, especially at the Paris Peace Conference. However, nothing came of this initiative, as the Bulgarian academics travelled only as far as Berlin, where they remained for several weeks due to the scarcity of food provisions in Brest-Litovsk.[60]

These difficulties did not discourage Popov, who proceeded to talk to the Bolsheviks on his own on the morning of 27 December. It is unclear who said what exactly, but the two sides were evidently acting at cross purposes. According to Popov, the Russian delegation offered him a separate peace based on the *status quo ante*, including the full restoration of commercial treaties between the two countries and the addition of a Bulgarian representative to the Danube Commission which regulated sailing along the river.[61] On 29 December, the semi-official *L'Echo de Bulgarie* published an article entitled "The Peace between Bulgaria and Russia," which reported Radoslavov's speech in the *Naradno Subranie* from the previous day, in which the prime minister had allegedly declared that the peace between Bulgaria and Russia was a true sign of the firm decision of the negotiators to work towards peace in mutual agreement.[62]

Had Bulgaria really broken rank with the Central Powers and come to a private arrangement with Petrograd? It was a false alarm, as there was no separate peace between Bulgaria and Russia whatsoever. "I am very disturbed by Radoslavov's false statements," Czernin wrote angrily to his brother in Sofia on 30 December, instructing him to relay his displeasure to the prime minister. "They will only make the negotiations more difficult and give the entire world the impression that Russia and Bulgaria have signed a separate peace."[63] The whole affair was one big misunderstanding, Radoslavov explained to Otto Czernin. His speech in the *Narodno Subranie* was intended primarily for domestic consumption, with the *promise* of quick peace meant to counter the socialists. He had spoken solely of an understanding of *principles* between Bulgaria and Russia, but his cabinet ministers and the press had misquoted him. The minister of war had telegraphed Commander-in-Chief Zhekov about the alleged formal conclusion of peace between the two countries. However, the younger Czernin believed Radoslavov might have had ulterior motives, with the prime minister and/or the king planning to use this "agreement in principle" with the Russians in case the joint negotiations were to fall through. In such an eventuality, things might indeed come to a separate peace, which would be greeted positively by the entire Bulgarian population, he concluded.[64] There could have been such a thought at the back of Radoslavov's mind, but Georgi Markov is probably correct in ascribing the whole incident to Popov's extreme eagerness to play a leading role clearly disproportionate to his actual abilities.[65]

Over the course of January, Popov attempted to use his "agreement in principle" with Ioffe to establish closer relations with the Russians and the newly-arrived Ukrainians in order to secure the coveted legal recognition of Bulgaria's borders. He concluded from his private conversations with the Rada's delegates that Kiev would "gladly see the Dobrudja become part of Bulgaria." He had changed his mind on the subject and now believed that secret conventions would not be sufficient in and of themselves, and that the territorial questions should be settled openly then and there. He asked Radoslavov to prepare the German and Austrian governments to that effect and emphasized that the Brest-Litovsk conference provided the perfect opportunity to have Ukraine and Russia acknowledge Bulgaria's new borders, thereby initiating the process of international recognition.[66]

This policy would be made easier, the minister of justice told the prime minister in a telephone conversation on 12 January, if the latter attended the proceedings personally. "It is absolutely necessary that you come here," Popov stressed. Radoslavov appeared reluctant do so, replying evasively that he was "also fine here [in Sofia]," before demanding "a specific lead, so that my arrival might help achieve something concrete with the 'Russian brothers' [*bratushkite*; this term has a negative connotation in Bulgarian]." Popov reiterated his earlier insistence that now was the best time to convince not just the Russians but also the other members of the Quadruple Alliance to recognize Bulgaria's new borders. "One word from Kühlmann will suffice," he promised rather optimistically, before stressing that only in Brest-Litovsk could the prime minister fully grasp the importance of the situation. Popov complained that the Germans and Austrians did not want to hear anything about Bulgaria's borders. If the Russians signed a peace treaty that did not outline the territorial settlement in the Balkans, they would hardly be willing to accept the full extent of Bulgaria's acquisitions at a later date. Only now would they do so. Finally, Popov complained, Kühlmann had been discourteous to Bulgaria by assigning him (Popov) an "unbecoming" seat at the dinner table. In retaliation, Popov had deliberately avoided Kühlmann all evening and left without saying goodbye. This had evidently had the desired effect, since the following day Popov received an "appropriate" seat. "And Kühlmann even drank to my health," he concluded smugly. Radoslavov promised to consider travelling to Brest-Litovsk at some point but offered little specific advice other than that he approved of Popov's policy up to this point.[67]

In the meantime, Popov continued to hold private meetings with the Russian and Ukrainian delegates. For an alleged expert on Russian matters, his failure to distinguish between their respective goals (world revolution versus national-statehood) or grasp what by now was clear to every single member of the German and Austro-Hungarian delegations – that the Bolsheviks were not particularly interested in the conclusion of peace – is most astonishing. He had come to the conclusion that "these gentlemen" (the Russian and Ukrainian delegates), their stubbornness notwithstanding, were ready to make all sorts of concessions in order to achieve the peace they desperately needed, he informed the prime minister a week later. He was utterly convinced that if the Bulgarian delegation told the Russians and Ukrainians that Bulgaria required certain specified borders – because "the Bulgarian people have long since determined themselves within them" – they would not refuse, "even if we demand the entire Balkan Peninsula" (which was near enough the truth). Besides, Popov added gratuitously, Russia and Ukraine were completely disinterested in what went on in the Balkans. They were busy trying to establish an All-Russian Federation, and this question would preoccupy them exclusively for the next fifteen to twenty years! The minister of justice continued his masterful analysis of the latest geopolitical trends with the assertion that Austria-Hungary and Germany were obsessed with the Balkans because they planned to dominate the Mediterranean and Black Seas. This idea had gripped the imagination of Austro-Germany [sic] to such an extent that anyone who opposed it would be crushed by the "mighty German-Austrian fist." If Bulgaria refused to go along with this project, she would be smashed more easily than she could have been hitherto, Popov added, invoking the perennial Bulgarian sense of victimhood. It was important for Sofia to take a firm position on the border issue sooner rather than later, implying that regional hegemony was necessary to safeguard Bulgaria's security against its current allies as well as its enemies. Any hesitation could be fatal and lead to a catastrophe, he warned. The Bulgarian delegation should insist on resolving all outstanding questions during the Brest-Litovsk Peace Conference. The government should come up with a map clearly designating Bulgaria's maximum demands, which would be subject to debate and compromise in Berlin and Vienna until a final agreement was reached. Once the bargaining was over, Popov would ask Kühlmann to raise the question at the conference; two words from Kühlmann should resolve everything, he reiterated. After Bulgaria had secured such recognition, it would have the support of the Russian republics and the obvious obligation on the part of Germany and Austria-Hungary, sanctioned in international law, to support Sofia's foreign policy objectives. Public opinion would then calm down, especially if the Dobrudja were acquired.[68]

In the absence of any specific instructions from Radoslavov, Popov continued to raise the issue of Bulgaria's borders with tedious regularity with Kühlmann and Czernin, who had clearly had enough of the Bulgarian minister's antics. Over dinner on 20 January, Popov casually asked Kühlmann whether he would object to Russo-Ukrainian recognition of Bulgaria's borders. The German state secretary "turned scarlet" and replied he would ask Count Czernin. Popov suggested that this would be inconvenient at the dinner table (because Ottoman Grand Vizier Talaat Pasha would have overheard, he pointed out in his report). After dinner the exasperated Kühlmann left Popov to discuss the matter with Rosenberg and Hoffmann, who listened politely. They were concerned with Bulgaria's interests and would like to see them fulfilled, they explained. However, asking the Ukrainians and Russians to recognize Bulgaria's future borders would mean accepting them as factors in Balkan politics, which was against the interests of every single member of the Quadruple Alliance, Bulgaria included.

The relentless Popov replied that his main task at the conference was to assure the Bulgarian people that their future borders were recognized by all participants. This could be considered a triumph of Bulgarian policy, which would completely calm public opinion. The Russians would doubtless accept such a clause, as long as Kühlmann stated firmly that these conditions were necessary for the conclusion of peace. General Hoffmann suggested that the Bulgarian delegation sound out the Ukrainians privately and helped arrange a meeting on the following morning.[69] Hoffmann's ongoing close cooperation with the diplomats, even on this seemingly unimportant issue (from a German point of view), provides yet another example of the ability of individual actors to bridge the civilian-military divide.

Popov's meeting with the delegates from Kiev on 21 January was his last act as leader of the Bulgarian delegation. The minister of justice outlined Bulgaria's request to the Ukrainian minister of commerce, Holubovych, adding that, as fellow Slavs, the Bulgarians would be very grateful to Ukraine and possibly of good use in the future. Holubovych replied he would gladly give the Dobrudja to Bulgaria, thereby establishing a common border between the two countries, but he could not possibly comment on the other territories, as they had nothing to do with Ukraine. Because Popov's conversation with Holubovych had the nature of a "Ukrainian love affair [*silna liubov s Ukraina*]" accompanied by great disaffection with Germany and Austria-Hungary, Colonel Ganchev felt compelled to explain to the Ukrainians that this exchange of views was strictly private.[70]

When news of Popov's indiscretion nonetheless reached Berlin, the German Foreign Ministry summoned Bulgarian Minister Plenipotentiary Rizov and demanded that Radoslavov stop his delegate's bungling actions before he could do any serious harm. Imperial Chancellor Hertling had already instructed German Minister Plenipotentiary in Sofia Count Alfred von Oberndorff to talk to the prime minister personally. "In general," Rizov concluded with brutal honesty, "our delegates [in Brest-Litovsk] have compromised themselves so much with their internal quarrels and wrangling, that all other delegates see them as poor relatives who have come here on a long holiday."[71] On 25 January, he advised the prime minister to keep Popov in Sofia and travel to Brest-Litovsk himself in order to "repair the damage and mend fences with the allies."[72]

Consequently, Radoslavov decided to head the Bulgarian delegation personally after the second ten-day adjournment. He seems to have spent his time in Brest-Litovsk reconciling with Kühlmann and Czernin rather than meeting with the Russian or Ukrainian delegates. The recall of Popov signified the failure of the Bulgarian policy of pursuing legal recognition for their extended borders and, by implication, of the "dream of Byzantium." Like other outstanding questions (such as the Polish Question), the resolution of the Dobrudja Question was unceremoniously postponed until the peace negotiations with Romania in Bucharest, and then indefinitely until it became moot with the impending defeat of the Central Powers in the autumn. As a compromise, Romania relinquished the province to the Quadruple Alliance as a whole, which set-up a four-power condominium. Perhaps to demonstrate that there were no ill feelings among the allies during the final phase of the Brest-Litovsk negotiations, Prince Leopold of Bavaria organized a celebration of King Ferdinand's birthday on 27 February. A German military band performed the Bulgarian national anthem, and the prince, ever the perfect host, raised a toast to Ferdinand's health, expressing the wish that the king receive an honourable peace with Russia as a birthday present.[73]

Conclusion

Bulgarian policy in Brest-Litovsk was an important episode in the country's long term pursuit of a "dream of Byzantium" – a project that entailed regional hegemony in the southern zone of East Central Europe under the guise of national unification. The Bulgarian delegates sought to achieve their goal by persuading the participants in the conference to legally recognize new Bulgarian borders that went far beyond those of the Treaty of San Stefano in 1878, and beyond the alleged goal of national unification or any reasonable application of the right to national self-determination. When faced with opposition, they accused the Germans and Austrians of treachery, invoking the secret treaties between the three countries. They ignored Ottoman calls for compensation, refusing to negotiate a mutually acceptable settlement directly with Constantinople. By obstinately refusing to endorse the joint reply to the Ioffe Speech for two days, the Bulgarians threatened the integrity of the Central Powers' alliance and exposed its growing cracks under the pressures of total war and exhaustion. They tried to play the self-determination card to win the support of the Bolsheviks and invoked fraternal Slavic solidarity with the Ukrainian delegation, without much success. The recall at the end of January of chief delegate

Popov was a virtual admission of the bankruptcy of Bulgarian policy, which had alienated the country from its allies while failing to establish close ties with the Russians and the Ukrainians, and it had not achieved institutional recognition of regional hegemony.

The elusive Bulgarian "dream of Byzantium," as revealed by the priorities of the Bulgarian delegation at the Brest-Litovsk Peace Conference, represents a specific form of the consolidation stage of national statehood predicated on regional hegemony as the only source of long term state security. It is by no means unique to Bulgaria or to the Balkans. Rather, it is demonstrative of the inherent contradictions within the concept of the nation state, and indicative of the dangers plaguing the pursuit of maximalist nationalist goals under the guise of self-determination in the context of Imperial collapse during the final phase of the Great War – as the Poles and Greeks would also learn in 1919–21. At Brest-Litovsk, Bulgarian obsession with such goals merely precipitated what Bulgarian public memory still sees as a second national catastrophe within six years – military defeat, near-revolutionary domestic turmoil, and the loss of additional territories at the final conclusion of peace.

Chapter Six

The Second Treaty of Brest-Litovsk and After

Ukraine and Bulgaria played a not inconsiderable role in Bolshevik considerations during the Brest-Litovsk Peace Conference. Ukraine's plentiful deposits of raw materials and food resources could have strengthened the revolution in Russia, while Bulgaria could have served as a convenient staging ground for the further spread of revolution across the members of the Central Powers alliance. However, the main concern of Bolshevik policy was Central Europe, Germany in particular. As Europe's most industrialized state, Germany held the key to the long term prospects of world revolution. Depending on the circumstances, it could become a bastion of the counter-revolution or the main pillar of the new communist world order, spreading Bolshevik propaganda and proletarian revolution to Britain and France. How to proceed vis-à-vis Germany once it became clear that a peace without annexations and indemnities was unlikely to materialize at Brest-Litovsk, then, was at the top of the Bolshevik leaders' list of priorities in the second half of January 1918. Previously, the Bolsheviks had sought to exploit the considerable differences between the members of the Central Powers alliance and between the German civilian and military factions. Now, for the first time since the successful seizure of power in October, they had to overcome the growing discord in their own ranks. The Central Powers, on their part, needed to find out whether they could compel the Russians to actually sign the treaty in conjunction with their successful negotiations with Ukraine. These concerns of the two sides informed the latter stages of the peace conference between late January and early March.

Bolshevik Dilemmas during the Second Adjournment: 18 January – 30 January 1918

While the authorities in Vienna, Budapest, and Berlin were busy dealing with the Great January Strike, Bolshevik leaders in Petrograd tried to re-evaluate the immediate prospects of revolution in East Central Europe and their own policy at Brest-Litovsk. Trotsky felt the revolutionary upheaval in Austria fully justified his dilatory approach to the negotiations and believed a definitive revolutionary demonstration – in the form of what he termed a "no war, no peace" formula – would deliver the final blow to the Hohenzollern and Habsburg establishments. In addition, he was adamant that it was absolutely necessary to deny the rumors, rife in the Western Entente countries and even in certain German and Austrian circles, that the Bolsheviks were agents of the German Foreign Ministry. "It was these considerations," wrote Trotsky in his memoirs, "that gave me the idea of a political demonstration at Brest-Litovsk expressing the slogan: 'We end the war, we demobilize the army, but we do not sign the peace.'"[1] He doubted the ability of the German army to renew its offensive against the proponents of a democratic peace; in any event, the Petrograd government could always sign the treaty at a later date.

The *Narkomindel* elaborated this policy at a speech given at the Third All-Russian Congress of Soviets on 26 January. The German attempt to set up a *cordon sanitaire* in the occupied western borderlands of the former Russian Empire had failed conspicuously, he explained, as evidenced by the events in Vienna and Budapest (i.e., the Great January Strike), which demonstrated that civil war was well under way in Austria. The impending collapse of the Central Rada in Ukraine would further enhance the position of the Russian delegation at Brest-Litovsk, which would continue to fight for a just democratic peace. In the meantime, the Russian army would be demobilized. "And if German imperialism attempts to break us on the wheel of its military machine," Trotsky concluded, referencing Nikolai Gogol's *Taras Bulba*, "we will address our older brothers in the West, as Ostap addressed his father, with the words: 'Do you hear?' And the international proletariat will answer – we firmly believe this: 'I hear!'"[2] In essence, this was a continuation of the original Bolshevik policy of using the negotiating table in Brest-Litovsk as a platform from which to spread world revolution. As one of the chief theoreticians and proponents of the concept of permanent revolution, Trotsky was keen to pursue this policy which was not, as Irina Mikhutina has written dismissively, the result of his "diplomatic helplessness."[3] He appears to have genuinely believed that the Great January Strike in Austria was a prelude to proletarian revolution in East Central Europe, describing its outbreak in the *History of the History of the Russian Revolution to Brest-Litovsk*, written during the negotiations in February 1918, as "the first act of recognition of our methods of conducting the peace negotiations."[4] Nor did he make this remark in a vacuum. The *Narkomindel* had regular access to German and Austrian newspapers in Brest-Litovsk and was well informed of the political situation in the two leading countries in the Central Powers alliance, at one point referring to certain social-democratic publications in a telegram to Lenin on 31 January.[5]

Events at the end of January 1918 seemed to vindicate Trotsky's position. Even though the worst part of the Great January Strike had passed, the situation in Austria-Hungary remained precarious, and the workers' councils – notably those in Vienna and in more radical Wiener Neustadt – continued to meet on a regular basis. Between 28 January and 1 February, the strike movement spread from Austria-Hungary to Germany, where it displayed the by now familiar combination of political and economic demands, centred on the quick conclusion of a peace without annexations and indemnities on the basis of the principle of national self-determination, as defined by the Russian delegation in Brest-Litovsk. On 30 January, 350 000 workers were on strike in Berlin, and the movement was even more widespread in provincial centers like Hamburg and Nuremberg.[6] Trotsky had every right to believe his policy of "no war, no peace" would deliver the *coup de grâce*.

In contrast to Trotsky and his optimistic overview of the international situation, Lenin, who had earlier been every bit as firm a believer in the immediate outbreak of world revolution, began to have serious doubts about its successful short term prospects. The Bolshevik leader expressed these doubts in his famous twenty-one "Theses on the Question of the Immediate Conclusion of a Separate and Annexationist Peace," which he penned on 20 January and read at a meeting of around sixty leading party functionaries in Petrograd the following day. The first five theses discussed the nature of the impending civil war in Russia, a successful outcome of which required the undivided attention of the revolutionary government. During this transitional period, Soviet foreign policy must be predicated first and foremost on the survival of the revolution *in Russia* rather than on the outbreak of the revolution *in Europe* (as Trotsky's policy implied). "It would be a mistake ... to base the tactics of the Russian socialist government on attempts to determine whether or not the European, and especially the German, socialist revolution will take place in the next six months. ... [A]ll such attempts, objectively speaking, would be nothing but a blind gamble."[7]

With the Brest-Litovsk negotiations heading for a showdown, further delays would be impossible, and the Soviet government would be faced with the difficult choice of signing an annexationist peace or waging a revolutionary war. In theses nine through eighteen, Lenin addressed and refuted the arguments in favour of revolutionary war. Signing an annexationist peace would be a tactical necessity rather than a deal with the imperialists, as the proponents of revolutionary war suggested. If anything, an immediate revolutionary war in unfavourable circumstances would make the Bolsheviks dependent on and thus agents of Anglo-French imperialism and, even worse, endanger the survival of the Russian Revolution. The army was in a state of complete disintegration and in no condition to fight. The party had never promised to wage revolutionary war before coming to power; it had merely stated that a socialist government *"had to 'prepare for and wage'* a revolutionary war," Lenin added in a fine example of Bolshevik sophistry, which tried to hide the fact that the party had in fact promised all things to all men before October. In conclusion, asserted thesis eighteen, "it would be absolutely impermissible tactics to stake the fate of the socialist revolution, which has already begun in Russia, merely on the chance that the German revolution may begin in the immediate future, within a matter of weeks. Such tactics would be a reckless gamble." With revolutionary war unfeasible, the only solution was to sign an immediate separate peace with the Central Powers, which would be the only way to extricate the Russian Revolution from the ongoing imperialist war. Lenin expected the war in the west to continue for some time, which would give the Bolsheviks sufficient time to construct a socialist republic in Russia, "a living example to the peoples of all countries."[8]

Here were the theoretical origins of Stalin's subsequent policy of socialism in one country, which would replace Trotsky's permanent revolution. What factors made Lenin seemingly turn away from the immediate pursuit of world revolution so abruptly, at the very moment when it seemed that revolution was about to materialize in East Central Europe? "It was an eminently reasonable policy synthesizing Bolshevik aspirations and harsh reality, preserving and strengthening a centre of revolutionary socialism ...," writes Richard K. Debo in his study of early Soviet foreign policy.[9] One could (and did) presumably argue with a straight face that the preservation of socialist revolution in one country – *any* country – fostered the eventual realization of world revolution and did not constitute a betrayal of proletarian internationalism. At this point, Lenin was still thinking in terms of months rather than decades, so it would be a mistake to fully equate his policy with Stalin's socialism in one country.

Alternatively, Irina Mikhutina suggests that hiding behind Lenin's revolutionary rhetoric was the natural objective of any state power, the international recognition of a state's sovereignty.[10] Lenin was beginning to think and act like the head of a state rather than the leader of a revolutionary movement. This is an important observation, which emphasizes Lenin's leading role in the gradual transformation of the Bolshevik Party from an underground organization of professional revolutionaries to a party-state machine. In *The Immediate Tasks of the Soviet Government*, written soon after in March–April 1918, Lenin already argued that the task of organization was "the most important and most difficult aspect of the socialist revolution" and outlined the need to create a "new, Soviet type of state," thereby focusing on state-building and statehood.[11] At the same time, Lenin's commitment to world revolution remained unflinching, and it cannot be dismissed as mere rhetoric. Lenin was above all an ideologue, who took his long-term ideological goals very seriously. It is precisely this unshakeable belief that enabled him to make what to others might appear to be opportunistic, short-term decisions.

Last but certainly not least, Iurii Felshtinskii suggests that the evolution of Lenin's ideas was driven primarily by the desire to "carry out world revolution under his direct guidance and preserve for himself the leadership of the International," which meant that he was in no great hurry to foster a German revolution that would shift the emphasis of the proletarian revolution away from less-industrialized, relatively backward Russia to the heart of industrial Europe.[12] Given Lenin's thirst for power, there is certainly some truth in this assessment.

While bearing in mind these different explanations offered by historians of Lenin's new policy, it is important to note that the Bolshevik leader did not fully abandon the hope of imminent world revolution. As early as 21 January, the day after he had composed his twenty-one theses, he added a twenty-second, which read:

> The mass strikes in Austria and in Germany, and, subsequently, the formation of the Soviets of Workers' deputies [i.e., workers' councils] in Berlin and Vienna, armed clashes and street fighting in Berlin – all this should be regarded as evidence of the fact that *the revolution in Germany has begun*. This fact offers us the opportunity, for the time being, of further delaying and dragging out the peace negotiations.[13]

Similarly, he wrapped up his concluding speech at the Third All-Russian Congress of Soviets on 31 January to stormy applause with the words: "We close this historic Congress of Soviets under the sign of the mounting world revolution, and the time is not far off when the working people of all countries will unite into a single world-wide state ..."[14] Clearly, Lenin had not broken completely with Trotsky and the concept of permanent revolution. His twenty-one theses had been aimed primarily at the proponents of immediate revolutionary war, which he considered the greatest danger. Lenin's critique of Trotsky's "no war, no peace" policy in the theses had been indirect, and his admission to the possibility of delaying the Brest-Litovsk negotiations still further made a renewed alliance a distinct possibility between the two Bolshevik leaders against the so-called Left Communist – a diverse group including notable high-ranking Bolsheviks like Nikolai Bukharin and Karl Radek, and the entire Moscow Regional Bureau.

Looking back at the French Revolution for revolutionary precedents and a clue as to the eventual unfolding of events was a common exercise for revolutionaries and non-revolutionaries alike at the time. (As we have seen, Czernin, too, spent his free time reading memoirs from the time of the French Revolution.) When the Left Communists did so, they saw the example of the *levée en masse*, which had enabled the French Revolution to defeat a vastly superior coalition of conservative powers in the early 1790s. By proclaiming its Russian equivalent in January 1918, the Bolsheviks would inspire Russian workers and peasants to lead a victorious revolutionary war against the Central Powers, which would have the added benefit of spreading the revolution westwards. When Lenin objected that the Russian revolutionaries must finish off their own bourgeoisie before they could deal with the German bourgeoisie, Radek declared: "The muzhik must carry on the war." "But don't you see the muzhik voted against the war?" Lenin retorted in desperation. "Excuse me, when and how did he vote against it?" insisted Radek. "He voted with his feet, he is running away from the front," was Lenin's eminently sensible answer.[15]

Such exchanges were quite common during the second adjournment; and since Lenin's authority was not yet unquestionable, he could not simply force his way over the heads of his opponents. Besides, the policy of revolutionary war was extremely popular with party members at the time, as he had to admit himself. About half of high-ranking party functionaries favoured this approach, whereas Trotsky and Lenin received around a quarter of votes each.[16] During the extended meeting of the Party Central Committee on 21 January, "Ilych felt the hostile glances of his comrades upon him," his wife Nadezhda Krupskaia remembered. "I can almost hear the unutterably weary and bitter tone in which he said to me, when his speech was over: 'Ah, well, let's go!'"[17] However, Lenin was not given to prolonged bouts of despair and resignation, and he began to envision a tactical rapprochement with Trotsky, which would defeat the proponents of revolutionary war. After all, Trotsky, too, was convinced that it would be impossible to renew the war. "On this point, there was not even a shadow of disagreement between Lenin and me," he wrote. "We were both equally bewildered at Bukharin and the other apostles of a 'revolutionary war.'"[18] In the circumstances, Trotsky's "no war, no peace" policy could become a bridge between the opposing views of Lenin and the Left Communists, preserving unity within the party.

Consequently, an extremely important private meeting between the two Bolshevik leaders took place around this time in the Smolny. Since Lenin left no notes, Trotsky's account in *My Life* and *Lenin* is the only available source; as such, it should be viewed with caution. Accordingly, Trotsky argued that the Germans would be unable to renew their offensive and probably acquiesce quietly with a *de facto* end to the war in the east. "All this is very attractive and one could only wish for nothing better," Lenin mused, but General Hoffmann would "find hand-picked regiments of rich Bavarian peasants" and invade. What would the Bolsheviks do then? "Then we shall be forced to sign the peace, but it will become clear to all that we have no other way out," Trotsky replied, emphasizing that this demonstration would dispel the rumors of a collusion between the Bolsheviks and the Imperial German Government once and for all. "To be sure, there are advantages ..." Lenin admitted. "And yet there are too many risks. There is nothing more important in the world than our revolution; the revolution has to be safeguarded no matter what the price." With this in mind, he queried Trotsky on his position in case the Germans did resume their advance. "We sign the peace at the points of their bayonets," came the reply. "The moral of the scene is obvious to the working class of the whole world." "And then will you not support the slogan of a revolutionary war?" Lenin persisted. "Under no circumstances," the *Narkomindel* promised. Having heard this, Trotsky adds, Lenin allegedly decided that the "no war, no peace" policy should be given a chance, even though it would probably lead to additional territorial losses in the Baltic in case of a successful German offensive. "We will only risk losing Esthonia [sic] and Livonia," he concluded, adding with a wry smile: "For the sake of a good peace with Trotsky, Latvia and Esthonia are worth losing."[19]

What can we make of this discussion? The agreement between the two Bolshevik leaders was "tenuous at best," as Debo asserts.[20] Since nothing was put down on paper, both Lenin and Trotsky could and probably did subsequently modify their accounts so as to reflect their personal views and deflect blame. In a speech at the Seventh Party Congress on 7 March, Lenin criticized the policy of "no war, no peace," describing it as a "gamble [*avantiura*], which has borne its [poisoned] fruit" – although he reserved his most vehement negative remarks for Bukharin and the Left Communists rather than Trotsky.[21] Part of this subsequent criticism is undoubtedly due to the lack of clarity on when exactly the Bolsheviks would sign the peace if the Central Powers simply refused to countenance Trotsky's statement and issued an ultimatum. Would the Petrograd government wait until the German army was actually on the march, as Trotsky wanted, or would it sign on the dotted line right away, which was Lenin's preference? These were questions which would become extremely important in the next few weeks. In the meantime, Lenin supported Trotsky's policy at the Central Committee meeting on 24 January, as did Bukharin and enough Left Communists for the motion to pass. However, this temporary truce did not end the serious disagreements within the Bolshevik leadership.

The final resolution, passed by the Third All-Russian Congress of Soviets on 27 January, was worded in a particularly vague manner in order to conceal the new policy from the Central Powers. "Proclaiming once again in front of the entire world the striving of the Russian people for an immediate end to the war," the proclamation read, "the All-Russian Congress authorizes its delegation to stand fast by the principles of peace on the basis of the program of the Russian Revolution [i.e., the Ioffe Program]."[22] In effect, this amounted to little more than a further delay in negotiations, leaving room for scholarly disagreements. Following the official Stalinist party line, Soviet historians routinely argued that Trotsky disobeyed a directive to sign the peace by pursuing his treacherous "no war, no peace" policy, which put the existence of the revolution at stake. This interpretation was largely derived from a passing remark by Lenin in a second speech at the Seventh Party Congress on 8 March, which stated that Trotsky's tactic of delaying the negotiations "became incorrect when the state of war was declared at an end and the peace was not signed. I absolutely definitively suggested signing the peace."[23] Felshtinskii was one of the first historians to question this stance on the basis of a lack of specific evidence that such a directive in fact existed. He claimed that Lenin had "slandered [oklevetal]" Trotsky in order to put the blame for the German February advance squarely on the shoulders of the Narkomindel.[24] Arguing specifically against Felshtinskii on this point, Mikhutina dismissed the rapprochement between Lenin and Trotsky with the words: "It is well known that Trotsky acted on his own initiative," without, however, specifying to whom it is well known.[25]

Characteristically, neither scholar substantiated his or her claim with any new documents; the fragmentary and incomplete nature of the existing sources means that this difference of opinion is unlikely to be resolved definitively. The most recent Russian-language study of the subject, by Pavel Makarenko, simply recounts the differences between Soviet historiography and Felshtinskii (it does not refer to Mikhutina), without taking a stance either way.[26] In the absence of any supporting evidence, this episode is perhaps most important in highlighting the serious, ongoing rifts in Bolshevik ranks, which made pursuit of a coherent, single-minded policy in Brest-Litovsk extremely difficult over the following weeks.

The Third Phase of Negotiations: 30 January – 10 February 1918

The Central Powers were surprisingly well informed of the deliberations going on in Petrograd during the second adjournment. On 28 January the Bulgarian minister plenipotentiary, Stefan Chaprashikov, wrote to Sofia that, following Trotsky's return to the capital, there had been endless debates about the stance the Russian government should adopt at the resumption of the peace negotiations. He outlined the two main options – Trotsky's "no war, no peace" policy and the Left Communists' policy of revolutionary war (Lenin's twenty-one theses were kept secret at the time) – and explained that the former had seemingly prevailed. The Bulgarian representative claimed to have had information about a private statement by Trotsky, according to which the

Narkomindel would delay the negotiations as much as possible until either the Germans broke them off (he would not take the initiative) or the long-awaited revolution in Germany and Austria-Hungary materialized. Trotsky had also expressed the opinion that the Germans would gain little from renewed hostilities. Even if they were to take Petrograd, they would only acquire a starving city, which was a hotbed of revolutionary activity. Chaprashikov concluded that the Bolsheviks would continue treating the Brest-Litovsk negotiations merely as a forum from which to preach revolution to the peoples of East Central Europe.[27] On the same day, the Austro-Hungarian consul general in Petrograd, Hempel, informed Vienna that the formula "no war, no peace" had been accepted at a meeting of Bolsheviks and Left SRs. In the meantime, the Russians would delay the negotiations in the hope that the unrest in Germany and Austria-Hungary would lead to revolution.[28]

Such reports from Petrograd only seemed to strengthen Czernin's and Kühlmann's conviction to push through the negotiations with the Ukrainians to a successful conclusion before deciding what to do with Trotsky. In light of the need to clarify the situation in the east prior to launching the Spring Offensive in the west, the OHL was firmly in favour of an ultimatum, having already urged Kühlmann to issue one as early as mid-January. On that occasion, the state secretary had been able to evade such a course of action, thanks in part to General Hoffmann's support (see chapter 2). However, this temporary setback did nothing to alter the opinions of the generals in Kreuznach. "The Russian negotiators, especially Trotsky, degraded the conference table, at which the reconciliation of two mighty opponents was to be affected, to the level of a muddle-headed tub-thumper's street corner. ... The representatives of our government indulged in a good deal of false optimism in their dealing with the peace question," explained Hindenburg in his memoirs.[29] By the end of January 1918, however, the belief that the delegations of the Central Powers would have to put Trotsky on the spot and force him to make a definitive decision was no longer the sole preserve of the OHL. The German minister plenipotentiary in Sofia, Count Oberndorff, informed the German Foreign Ministry that the Bulgarian government was firmly in favour of an ultimatum; Undersecretary von dem Bussche immediately forwarded this information to the German delegation in Brest-Litovsk.[30] The Ottoman government was just as dissatisfied with the impasse, judging by its decision to unilaterally violate the armistice by having its forces in the Caucasus move into Russian territory on 6 February; the Ottoman advance met little opposition.[31]

Even Czernin, whose cautious approach to the negotiations sought to avoid open confrontation with the Russian delegation, was beginning to come round. Buoyed by the promising developments in the negotiations with the Ukrainians, he began to consider the possibility of breaking with Trotsky for the first time. The Petrograd delegation continued to behave stubbornly after its return to Brest-Litovsk, Czernin wrote in a telegram to Emperor Karl on 30 January. There was no doubt that the Bolsheviks had no intention of coming to an understanding with the Central Powers. However, the growing conflict between Petrograd and Kiev, which had escalated to a state of war, provided an opening. "The question is whether or not a change of tactics is necessary in these new circumstances," Czernin explained, "and whether it is possible to fight alongside the Ukrainian troops against the Bolsheviks." Given the necessity to acquire Ukrainian supplies, public opinion in Austria-Hungary might accept the resumption of war. The foreign minister believed the Ukrainians had an alliance with Romania, in which case Berlin and Vienna must also win the Romanians for the enterprise. The Romanians were willing to make peace, and they ought to be treated kindly. "With a certain amount of effort I can persuade Kühlmann that my plan is sound," promised Czernin, "after which he will attempt to win over the Kaiser." If Emperor Karl also agreed with this course of action, he should discreetly inform the King of Romania that he would be able to retain his throne if he proved willing to conclude an alliance with the Central Powers. Naturally, such an alliance necessitated the sacking of the pro-Entente Brătianu Cabinet, as well as certain border corrections in favour of Hungary in the Carpathians and the sending of food supplies to Austria. In exchange for these concessions, the Central Powers would assist Romania in acquiring Bessarabia. In the meantime, Emperor Karl should intimate that the alliance would be used to fight world revolution, which threatened all monarchies in the world equally.[32] The emperor gave his principal approval of the foreign minister's proposal but insisted, among other things, that the odium of the collapse of the negotiations in Brest-Litovsk be put on Trotsky and his revolutionary antics, especially his direct appeals to the Austrian press over the heads of the Austro-Hungarian delegation.[33]

This was a complete *volte-face* on the part of the Habsburg leadership. Whereas in late December 1917 Czernin had threatened Kühlmann and Hoffmann with a separate peace between Austria-Hungary and Russia, he now proposed that the Central Powers lead an anti-Bolshevik crusade with the help of Ukraine and Romania. As we will see, he had not abandoned all hope of reaching some sort of an agreement with Trotsky altogether, but the imminent peace with Ukraine, accompanied by the subsequent arrival of Ukrainian foodstuffs, made Czernin – and Emperor Karl – contemplate if not exactly welcome a breakdown of negotiations in Brest-Litovsk. There was a growing realization in Habsburg circles that it would be impossible to reason with Lenin and Trotsky in the long run. Liberal Hungarian politician Gyula Andrássy the Younger, the last foreign minister of the Dual Monarchy, expressed a similar view after the war: "It was impossible to come to an agreement with the Bolsheviks. ... They should only have been approached with a sword in one's hand and with orders and an ultimatum."[34]

In his study of Austria-Hungary's involvement in the Brest-Litovsk Peace Conference, Wolfdieter Bihl suggests that "the foreign minister did not appear to be entirely convinced by his own plan" of using the Ukrainians against the Russians.[35] Bihl mentions Czernin's telegram in passing and only in reference to the latter's belief that the Bolsheviks would not sign the peace. In fact, the telegram exchange of 30 January between the foreign minister and the emperor provides concrete evidence of the ongoing evolution of Habsburg policy in Brest-Litovsk away from the initial position of peace at any price. In the event, Czernin's plan was never put to the test, the Central Powers electing to pursue an indecisive middle course between fighting Bolshevism and putting up with it. The plan would have been difficult to implement in any case, since it would have necessitated the commitment of a considerable number of Austro-German troops which were badly needed elsewhere. It is also arguable whether the Central Rada would have been willing to send its meagre forces beyond the territories it claimed for the Ukrainian People's Republic. In the circumstances, the importance of Czernin's plan lies primarily in demonstrating that the Austro-Hungarian delegation in Brest-Litovsk was not simply, in the words of Arthur J. May, "an unbrilliant second to the Germans."[36] Nor did the OHL have a monopoly on agency in the Central Powers alliance.

Upon his return to Brest-Litovsk, Trotsky quickly became aware that the delegations of the Central Powers had certain knowledge of his "no war, no peace" policy; worse still, he found several references to it in the German press. He deemed it best to deny these reports in the interest of further delaying the negotiations, as per the resolution of the Third All-Russian Congress of Soviets. To this end, the *Narkomindel* composed a draft declaration he intended to deliver at the first plenary session after the adjournment, in which he would admit to the Bolsheviks' desire to spread the revolution to Europe but flatly deny that he was not interested in signing the peace. On the contrary, the argument went, world revolution and peace went hand in hand, since the demobilized soldiers returning from the trenches would hold their erstwhile bourgeois masters fully responsible for the bloodshed they had unleashed.[37]

Upon further consideration, however, Trotsky decided that the Germans and Austrians would find this refutation far more plausible if they happened to "accidentally" discover it for themselves. Suspecting the *Ober Ost* staff was reading his correspondence with Petrograd over the direct wire, he wrote a lengthy telegram to Lenin on 31 January, "not so much to warn Lenin that the secret of our decision had been blabbed abroad, but to try to put the Germans off the track."[38] The telegram referred specifically to the *Politiken*, a left-wing German newspaper, which had published a report on the Bolshevik decision to refuse to sign the treaty. Since the press in Germany and Austria-Hungary was full of all sorts of reports of "horrors in Petrograd, Moscow, and all over Russia, of hundreds and thousands of murdered people, of the rattle of guns," it might be helpful if the Petrograd Telegraph Agency and Bolshevik circles in neutral Stockholm were to set the record straight. To make his willingness to conclude peace in Brest-Litovsk more believable, Trotsky went on to accuse the German delegation of delaying the negotiations and the German press of deliberately spreading misinformation. "These asses [*osly*]," he added, in reference to the German press, "cannot comprehend that it is precisely from the perspective of the development of the European revolution that peace at the earliest possible time is of the utmost importance to us."[39]

It is unclear whether *Ober Ost* intercepted this telegram, but the entire subsequent exchange between Brest-Litovsk and Petrograd clearly shows that the Bolshevik leaders assumed the Germans had access to their correspondence, which makes their true intentions during this period difficult to ascertain. Two days later, Trotsky dispatched another telegram *en clair*, in which he complained that the Hughes telegraph had stopped working altogether. He also explained that the delegates of the Central Powers were leading separate negotiations with the Central Rada in order to present the Russians with the *fait accompli* of a Ukrainian treaty.[40] Lenin responded with two open radio messages on 3 and 4 February, which elaborated that the Rada had been deposed and power in Ukraine had passed to the Soviet government in Kharkiv, that the revolution was spreading to Finland, that Cossack regiments were fighting the conservative government of Ataman Kaledin in the Don region, and that the Petrograd Soviet intended to dispatch a message to the Berlin and Vienna workers' councils.[41] The implied assumption was that, having lost their Ukrainian "trump," the imperialist governments of the Central Powers might be forced to reconsider their uncompromising stance on the occupied borderlands or risk full-scale revolution in East Central Europe.

In reality, however, this amounted to little more than an elaborate exercise in wishful thinking. The representatives of the Central Powers viewed these difficulties merely as transitory. "[They] were transitory in so far as at any time we could support the [Central Rada] government with arms and establish it again," as Hoffmann put it pithily.[42] If the Bolsheviks refused to play by the established rules of diplomacy, why should the Central Powers not do the same? Besides, Trotsky himself had recognized the Central Rada as the legitimate government of Ukraine at the beginning of January; his withdrawal of recognition at the end of the month was hardly in accordance with international law.

Very little of substance took place during the official proceedings in late January–early February. Czernin and Kühlmann had prioritized peace with Ukraine and would try to confront Trotsky only after it was concluded. For his part, Trotsky welcomed the additional delay and the opportunity to berate what he believed to be his adversaries' hypocritical negotiations with a Central Rada delegation which had little support outside Brest-Litovsk. This involved a spectacular verbal clash with Liubynskyi, one of the Rada's chief delegates, on 1 February. In the pursuit of his policy of using the Ukrainians against the Russians, Czernin had "tried to get the Ukrainians to talk over things openly with the Russians, and succeeded almost too well."[43] In his speech, Liubynskyi accused the Soviet government of being no different from its Provisional and Imperial predecessors in attempting to stifle national revolution in Russia. "[I]nstead of the principle of the right of self-determination, the Bolshevik Government carried out the principles of anarchy and destruction to create everything anew …," he declared. The Ukrainian people had devoted themselves to peaceful state construction, whereas the Bolsheviks insisted on interfering in their internal affairs by setting up Soviets and sponsoring the illegitimate government in Kharkiv. "Our future, our history, our descendants, and broad masses of working people on both sides of the front will themselves decide which of us is right and which is guilty, which is Socialist and which is counter-revolutionist, which creates and which destroys what has been created," Liubynskyi concluded on a combative note.[44]

Even as seasoned an orator as Trotsky seemed taken aback by this verbal assault, which was a devastating critique of Bolshevik policy. "Perfectly pale, he stared fixedly before him, drawing nervously on his blotting paper," noted Czernin in his diary. "Heavy drops of sweat trickled down his forehead."[45] Without a doubt, Czernin was well pleased with the way things were going. In case of a definitive break with Trotsky, he could point to Liubynskyi's speech as evidence that Bolshevik political and diplomatic methods rather than the Central Powers' annexationist demands had caused the rupture – just as Emperor Karl had instructed him to do. Trotsky played down his reaction to the speech in his memoirs, dismissing Czernin's description as exaggerated. The *Narkomindel* had found the scene distressing indeed, but only because of "the frantic self-humiliation of what was after all a representative body of the revolution [the Central Rada] before vain aristocrats who only despised them."[46] However, this explanation seems to have been a belated attempt to save face, as Colonel Fokke's description of the scene is almost exactly the same as Czernin's.[47]

Following the showdown with the Rada's delegates, the Russian delegation was running out of subjects to pontificate on, and the delegations of the Central Powers (not to mention the OHL) were running out of patience. After the session of the Territorial Committee on 3 February discussed the question of Polish representation at the peace conference in almost exactly the same terms as those employed in mid-January, Trotsky decided to travel to German-occupied Warsaw on 5 February, ostensibly for "shopping [*Einkaufe*]." In all probability, his actual aim was to get in touch with local Bolsheviks and possibly engage in agitation work, as a member of the Austrian delegation surmised.[48] The *Narkomindel*'s visit proved uneventful, although local Jews and socialists apparently tried to arrange a small and utterly inconsequential welcoming demonstration. On the whole, ordinary Poles viewed Trotsky "with curiosity," reported the representative of the Austro-Hungarian Foreign Ministry.[49] No major disturbances took place.

While Trotsky was in Warsaw, Czernin and Kühlmann attended a conference with the Imperial German Government and the OHL in Berlin on 5 February, which discussed peace with Ukraine, peace with Romania, and the possibility of peace with Russia. There were few differences on the first two points, with incoming foodstuffs a major incentive to conclude treaties with Ukraine and Romania as quickly as possible. Thereupon, things took a turn for the worse, as Czernin produced a memorandum on German and Austro-Hungarian war aims he had drawn up with Imperial Chancellor Bethmann-Hollweg in the spring of 1917. According to the minimum program and the terms of the Dual Alliance outlined in this document, Austria-Hungary was obliged to fight only to maintain Germany's territorial integrity. Ludendorff, who seemed to be unaware of the existence of this document, objected vehemently on the grounds that "a peace guaranteeing only the territorial status quo would mean we have lost the war." (This sentence appears in Czernin's diary slightly differently, as: "If Germany makes peace without profit, then Germany has lost the war"). Ludendorff elaborated in one of his books that he "opposed an 'agreement with negative war aims only'; we needed safety zones for our industrial centres in Germany [i.e., the Polish border strip], and therefore must have positive war aims ...." It was the same old argument, derived from the principles of their pervasive military culture, which the generals had been making since the December conferences. "The controversy was growing more and more heated," noted Czernin in his diary, "when Hertling nudged me and whispered: 'Leave him alone, we two will manage it together without him.'" Thus, the morning session of the conference concluded with the typical postponement of a definitive settlement. Kühlmann and Czernin were authorized to examine the matter and come up with a mutually acceptable clarification of the terms of the alliance between Germany and Austria-Hungary.[50]

With the thorny issue of war aims temporarily settled (albeit to no one's satisfaction), the afternoon session of the conference looked into the possibility of peace with Bolshevik Russia. Hertling insisted that the Central Powers must break with the Bolsheviks after the conclusion of peace with Ukraine if Trotsky continued to prove obdurate. Czernin suggested that the Ukrainian treaty might induce the Russians to compromise. If not, he added, "our hands will be untied," enquiring what the military authorities intended to do in this case. Ludendorff replied he would welcome the termination of the armistice and the resumption of military actions, as this would clarify the military situation in the east and thereby help the imminent offensive in the west. The first quartermaster-general favoured advancing into the Baltic littoral, in order to protect the property of the wealthy German minority in Livonia and Estonia. Kühlmann concurred but emphasized that "the chief value of these military operations lies in strengthening the Russians' desire for peace." The moral effect of a peace with Trotsky would be considerable, he concluded.[51]

Apart from the not untypical confrontation between Ludendorff and Czernin during the morning session, the conference of 5 February demonstrated an almost unprecedented unity of purpose between the OHL, the German Government, and the Austrians. Everyone agreed that the ongoing shenanigans in Brest-Litovsk must come to an end one way or another. Ludendorff was naturally in favour of an immediate break with Trotsky, but he did not oppose the diplomats' insistence on one last approach. Similarly, Kühlmann and Czernin did not object to a limited military offensive in the Baltic. Given the level of discord between Kreuznach, Berlin, Vienna, Constantinople, and Sofia on almost every other policy concerning the Central Powers alliance – from the future status of Northern Dobrudja to the feasibility and exact terms of the *Mitteleuropa* project – this rare moment of unanimity could only be attributed to Bolshevik revolutionary policy at Brest-Litovsk. In a month and a half, the Bolsheviks had succeeded in bringing about what Bethmann-Hollweg, Burián, Czernin, Hertling, Kühlmann, Conrad von Hötzendorff, Ludendorff, Kaiser Wilhelm II, Emperor Franz Joseph, and Emperor Karl had all failed to achieve in three and a half years of ceaseless toil – a (temporarily) united Central Powers alliance.

With the principal negotiators back in Brest-Litovsk after their respective trips to Berlin and Warsaw, the Austrian delegation embarked on one last attempt to persuade Trotsky to listen to reason. On 6 February, Richard Schüller of the Austrian Ministry of Commerce and *Sektionschef* of the Austro-Hungarian Foreign Ministry Gustav Gratz approached Trotsky on the possibility of reaching a compromise. The seemingly insuperable differences between the German and Russian positions on the status of the occupied territories were merely a matter of phrasing, they insisted. Trotsky blamed Kühlmann, who wanted to recognize the right to self-determination in one sentence and annex everything in the next. Schüller stressed the need to find solutions to practical issues rather than get bogged down in theoretical deliberations. "These too are important to us, for we are convinced that the conditions now being created will be but temporary and will be dissolved by the universal revolution," was Trotsky's predictable reply. He might find it possible to sign an annexationist peace, the *Narkomindel* added, as long as the Central Powers did away with the holier-than-thou attitude and openly acknowledged it as such. Schüller declared that this clarification might suggest a way out of the impasse and promised to relay the contents of the conversation to Czernin. The foreign minister would consider the matter and intervene personally.[52]

Having overcome considerable opposition from Hoffmann, who had clearly had enough of the interminable delays, Czernin and Gratz visited Trotsky in his lodgings the following day, 7 February. The foreign minister warned that a breach in the negotiations was imminent and enquired what peace conditions the Russians would be willing to entertain. Trotsky reiterated his position from the previous day and insisted that Germany must clearly state that it intended to pursue annexations. When Gratz suggested that the two opposing sides might agree to disagree in view of their diametrically opposed definitions of annexations, however, Trotsky appeared to suddenly change his mind. "It is not necessary that Germany should acknowledge in the treaty that she is making annexations, but I must reserve the right to describe Germany's activities as annexations," he declared. Czernin proposed that the final treaty simply refer to "territorial changes," which would leave things open to interpretation. "I believe this way can be followed," concurred Trotsky. He further demanded the return of the Moonsound Islands and Riga to Russia and a slight revision of the Lithuanian border. Most importantly, however, the Central Powers must stop all negotiations with the Central Rada, which, he claimed, no longer possessed any real power in Ukraine. The Austrians promised to confer with their allies and continue negotiating on the basis of at least some of these conditions.[53]

Was this unexpected turnaround merely a tactical ploy on Trotsky's part, or did he genuinely begin to have second doubts about the feasibility of his "no war, no peace" policy? Debo suggests that it was a little bit of both, adding that "his [Trotsky's] mind was too supple and his imagination too fertile to plod myopically toward that objective heedless of all other considerations."[54] We could also view this episode as one final attempt by the *Narkomindel* to unsettle the leading powers of the Central Powers by playing off the more accommodating Austrians against the more uncompromising Germans. The flamboyant Trotsky is unusually quiet on this matter in his memoirs and did not leave any notes in his personal archives; nor did he attempt to contact Lenin in Petrograd, probably because he suspected the Germans were reading his correspondence. All of this means that it is impossible to ascertain his true motives with any degree of certainty. In any event, Hoffmann refused to consider the territorial alterations Trotsky required, and the Austrian and German delegations delivered a joint statement to the effect that the negotiations with the Central Rada had gone too far to be discontinued at this point. Kühlmann alone did not lose hope of reaching some sort of an agreement with Trotsky on the basis of avoiding the question of annexations altogether.[55]

Two events forced the issue – the signing of the treaty between the Central Powers and the Ukrainian People's Republic in the early hours of 9 February and an egregious incident instigated by Bolshevik propaganda. "[D]espite my protest and notwithstanding all Trotsky's assurances," wrote Hoffmann, "the propaganda appeals 'to all' and more especially to the troops were despatched as usual. It was at this time that an appeal was addressed to the troops in which they were summoned to murder their officers."[56] Following this Bolshevik provocation, on 9 February the Kaiser telegraphed Kühlmann to present the Russian delegation with the following ultimatum: "Trotsky has until 8:00 p.m. tomorrow, 10 [February], to sign *the peace straight away* on *our* conditions, with immediate handover of the Baltic littoral up to and including the Narva-Pskov-Dvinsk line, without self-determination ...."[57] The Kaiser had actually decided to answer the Baltic barons' incessant pleas for help three days previously, and on 7 February Hindenburg had ordered Hoffmann to demand the evacuation of Livonia and Estonia or break with Trotsky.[58] The interception of the Bolshevik telegram provided an additional impetus.

Kühlmann, however, had other plans. The state secretary showed the ultimatum to Czernin, who explained that his instructions from Emperor Karl were to continue negotiating with the Russians for the time being. Since it would not be possible to obtain new instructions by the evening, once the German delegation delivered the ultimatum the Austro-Hungarian foreign minister would officially declare that he now had a free hand to conduct separate talks with Petrograd. Kühlmann was seemingly impressed enough to tell his Austrian colleague he would ask the Kaiser to rescind the order.[59] The Austro-Hungarian delegation was actually able to telephone the Imperial Court at Laxenburg and receive the following verbal telegram from Emperor Karl: "It goes without saying that I condemn the actions of the Bolsheviks, but my instructions remain the same. Please continue negotiating with Trotsky until you are absolutely convinced he does not want to sign the treaty. In this case, I expect a note about the breakdown [of negotiations]."[60]

Kühlmann was reluctant to threaten the integrity of the Central Powers alliance and felt it might still be possible to avoid a definitive break with Petrograd. Consequently, he telegraphed the Kaiser that this was an inopportune moment for an ultimatum; he would resign rather than go through with such rash policy. The state secretary would wait until 4:30 p.m. on 10 February and move on with the scheduled plenary session if he did not receive any further missives. "Nothing occurred until four-thirty and Kühlmann kept the order for an Ultimatum in in his pocket," observed Hoffmann. In the meantime, the state secretary dispatched Rosenberg to Trotsky with a request for a written statement outlining the Russian position on Riga and the Moonsound Islands. Trotsky, however, refused to comply.[61]

In the circumstances, Kühlmann's last-ditch attempt to prevent the looming break seemed to matter little and change even less. Nonetheless, it is demonstrative of the continuing ability of the German civilian government to challenge the generals – and the Kaiser – on important policy issues. Imperial Chancellor Hertling supported the state secretary in this endeavour, telegraphing the Kaiser that he fully agreed with Kühlmann's position.[62] On this occasion, Wilhelm accepted that it would be wiser not to present the demand for the evacuation of Livonia and Estonia as an ultimatum.[63] However, he still favoured a police action in the two provinces, which would serve the dual purpose of defending the Baltic Germans from the Bolshevik marauders and, bizarrely enough, preventing the British from establishing a foothold in the Baltic.[64] Trotsky's dramatic gesture rendered this exchange of views purely academic.

At the end of the session of 10 February, Trotsky finally delivered his cherished *coup de théâtre* with considerable oratorical flair and pomp. "The peoples are awaiting with impatience the result of the peace negotiations at Brest-Litovsk," his speech began. They were clearly tired of this war of extermination and longed for the conclusion of peace. When the British had occupied African colonies, Baghdad, and Jerusalem, and the Germans had taken over Belgium, Serbia, Romania, Poland, and Lithuania, the principal imperialist powers of the two opposing alliances had revealed their true colours and exploded the defensive war myth. "That is a struggle for the partition of the globe," emphasized the *Narkomindel*, echoing Lenin's *Imperialism: The Highest State of Capitalism*. The Russian Revolution refused to participate in this imperialist war and shed the blood of its peasant soldiers, who must return to their homes and begin the creation of a socialist state. Following this lengthy preamble, Trotsky finally came to the point:

> We are going out of the war. We inform all peoples and Governments of this fact. We are giving the order for a general demobilization of all

armies opposed at the present to the troops of Germany, Austria-Hungary, Turkey, and Bulgaria .... At the same time we declare that the conditions as submitted to us by the Governments of Germany and Austria-Hungary are opposed in principle to the interests of all peoples. These conditions are refused by the working masses of all countries, amongst them by those of Austria-Hungary and Germany.

If the Central European empires intended to annex territories, Trotsky continued, they must do so openly. "We are going out of the war, but we feel ourselves compelled to refuse to sign the peace," he concluded. Thereupon, the *Narkomindel* produced an official note, signed by all members of the Russian delegation, which briefly outlined this policy.[65]

Trotsky must have thoroughly enjoyed the impact of his speech. "The impression was of a bomb that had just exploded," wrote Fokke in his memoirs. "The declaration struck like lightning from a clear sky. The Germans expected nothing of the sort." General Hoffmann was heard to exclaim *"Unerhört!"* (unheard of) in disbelief. Kühlmann was the first to regain his composure and ask Trotsky for an adjournment of the session until the following day, in order to allow the delegations of the Central Powers to discuss their reply to the Russian statement, which was without precedent in the history of international relations. Trotsky replied that the Russian delegation had no further instructions and must return to Petrograd forthwith. At this, the Bolsheviks rose from their chairs, bid everyone present farewell, and took leave of the conference. At 6:50 p.m., Kühlmann, visibly shaken, closed the session. The Russian delegation left for Petrograd the same evening, with Kamenev mimicking Hoffman's reaction and shouting *"Unerhört!"* as the other Bolsheviks chuckled in delight. Seeing them off at the train platform was a German major, who asked Colonel Fokke: "What now? Are we going to have to fight you once again?" Fokke shrugged. The train departed.[66]

Resumption of Hostilities and the Final Phase of Negotiations: 11 February – 3 March 1918

The Central Powers' reaction to Trotsky's *coup de théâtre* was not unanimous. Later that evening, the German and Austro-Hungarian delegations convened to determine the best course of action. The two main options were to tacitly accept Trotsky's *fait accompli* or end the armistice and resume military operations. Czernin, who had earlier advocated waging war on the Bolsheviks in association with Ukraine and Romania, now suddenly changed his mind and, along with Kühlmann, came out in favour of the former option, arguing that Germany and Austria-Hungary could not attack owing to domestic concerns. Hoffmann was the sole proponent of the second course of action, emphasizing the need to fight Bolshevism. In his report to Emperor Karl, Czernin expressed the opinion that the current state of affairs in Russia did not leave Berlin and Vienna much hope for a definitive peace. "We must, in any case, prepare ourselves for the possibility to resume the war against Russia," he concluded, "especially if the situation in Ukraine merits it and we are forced to intervene in order to protect the new state from Bolshevik terrorism."[67] The foreign minister was convinced the Dual Monarchy would have to intervene in Ukraine, as a potential Bolshevik takeover of that country would threaten the importation of much needed food supplies. The Habsburgs had compromised their relationship with the Poles for the sake of Ukrainian grain by agreeing to a Ukrainian annexation of Kholm and the creation of a Ukrainian crownland in East Galicia in the face of unrelenting Polish opposition. Now they would have to back their Ukrainian policy militarily in order to make sure all their previous efforts had not been in vain. However, this issue need only be addressed once the Central Rada submitted a formal request for help, which it did in due course (see chapter 4). The situation further north was of less concern to Austria-Hungary, since after the peace with Ukraine the Dual Monarchy had ceased to share borders with Russia and there were no Habsburg troops in that section of the front. Germany would have to take care of that mess on its own.

Kühlmann, who was aware that the Austrians would not join Germany in a renewed offensive against Russia in the Baltic, believed the Central Powers must accept the new status quo in order to extricate themselves from the revolutionary quagmire in the east once and for all. The most important thing from his perspective was that "Russia could no longer hurt us," as he put it in his memoirs.[68] This was not just a retrospective rationalization. The state secretary outlined his point of view in a lengthy telegram to Hertling on 10 February. "According to the well-known dictum of Clausewitz," his report began, "war is the prosecution of policy [by other means], and we must ask ourselves: what policy will this war prosecute?" One could answer that the resumption of hostilities would seek to bring about Bolshevik acceptance of German demands "in black and white," but Kühlmann was extremely doubtful whether war was the best way to achieve this objective in the prevailing circumstances. The Bolshevik Government would most probably withdraw from Petrograd to another city, perhaps as far east as Siberia, in which case the war would go on indefinitely. A renewed offensive against Russia would also have serious domestic repercussions, as the patience of the masses was coming to an end. The situation was completely different with respect to Finland and Ukraine, Kühlmann added reassuringly; since these two were independent states, the Central Powers had a free hand and could dispatch military forces to defend their interests (especially the transportation of foodstuffs from Ukraine) if necessary. As far as Russia was concerned, however, the best course of action would be to do nothing.[69] The Russians must be left alone "to continue stewing in their own juice," Kühlmann told Imperial Chancellor Hertling's son over breakfast on 12 February.[70]

A conference between Kaiser Wilhelm, the German Government, and the OHL convened at Bad Homburg on 13 February to determine the German response to Trotsky's declaration. Kühlmann insisted that a renewed German offensive would probably have the adverse effect of strengthening the revolution and national cohesion in Russia, as had happened with the French Revolution. It would also be wrong to renew the war for the sake of the German elites in Livonia and Estonia. Ludendorff argued that the war in the east must be concluded definitively, which could be achieved through military operations alone. The Kaiser was also in favour of intervening in Russia before Britain, his perennial bugbear, had done so. "The Bolsheviks must disappear," he emphasized. "Once we reach Narva [on the border between Estonia and Russia], we will negotiate with Petrograd .... A police action, not war." Crucially, Hertling and Vice Chancellor Payer, who had earlier supported the state secretary's position, dropped their objection to the termination of the armistice in favour of a limited offensive. According to Payer's memoirs, they were doubtful the peace negotiations could come to a formal end without renewed military action. A German offensive in the Baltic would conceivably force the Bolsheviks to return to Brest-Litovsk and sign the peace, thereby settling the matter once and for all. Kühlmann alone "remained obdurate," as Ludendorff put it, but the state secretary offered the sole voice of dissent. The council authorized the resumption of hostilities, effective 17 February.[71] This was another halfway measure, which seemed to satisfy no one for long. On the one hand, the OHL did not achieve its maximum demand of effecting a regime change in Russia, although this notion would continue to be entertained intermittently. On the other hand, Kühlmann had been unable to persuade the generals to acquiesce with Trotsky's *fait accompli*.

In the meantime, Trotsky defended his declaration in a report to the Petrograd Soviet on 17 February. Having outlined briefly the first two phases of the peace conference, he enquired: "Why did Kühlmann and Hohenzollern negotiate with us at the green table for two whole months? They needed our signature …. Let Kühlmann go back to Germany, show his peace to the workers, and explain why our signature is not there." The *Narkomindel* was confident the Germans would not resume the war against Russia, stressing that there was only a ten per cent chance of their doing so. In case they succeeded, however, the Russian Revolution would hold German social-democracy responsible for its failure to carry out a revolutionary seizure of power.[72]

Unlike Trotsky, Lenin was far more concerned with the possibility of a renewed German offensive. In the circumstances, he had every reason to be. On 17 February, Hoffmann gave General Samoilo, who had remained in Brest-Litovsk, a note from the German Government on the resumption of a state of war between the two countries at noon on the following day. This missive confirmed Lenin's worst fears. "In spite of everything, they cheated us. They gained five days," he allegedly told Trotsky, in reference to the provisions of the armistice, which required a seven-day period between the formal termination of the armistice and the resumption of hostilities. "This beast will not let a thing go. That means that now there is nothing but to sign the old conditions, if only the Germans will stick to them." Trotsky insisted that they should wait and see whether the German army was actually capable of advancing into Russian territory, but Lenin was adamant that the time for experiments was over.[73] The *Narkomindel* had had a chance to try his "no war, no peace" policy, and it had failed. The Bolsheviks would now have to try to salvage whatever they could from its wreckage. In accordance, Trotsky immediately wired a telegram to Brest-Litovsk, enquiring about the German note, which, he suspected, was probably a provocation.[74] Hoffmann confirmed the veracity of the note, explaining that Trotsky's declaration on 10 February had terminated the armistice.[75]

The renewal of hostilities between Germany and Russia did not affect Austria-Hungary. Trotsky wrote to Czernin on 18 February to ascertain whether the Dual Monarchy considered itself at war with Russia. Before replying, Czernin informed Ambassador Hohenlohe in Berlin that, as Prime Minister Seidler had stated in the *Reichsrat* on 19 February, the state of war between the two countries had ended. Since

His Majesty had no intention of resuming hostilities with Russia, the Dual Monarchy could not join in the German ultimatum which, after all, could be rejected. The ambassador should discreetly inform the German Government that the Austrians found the renewal of hostilities and the occupation of Estonia and Livonia regretful. Czernin would send a formal response to Trotsky's enquiry in due course.[76] Judging by Undersecretary von dem Bussche's response, however, the Germans had expected Vienna to take such a stance and did not insist on Habsburg participation in the military operation.[77]

In contrast to the Habsburg civilian authorities, the AOK was much more reluctant to stand by idly while the Germans advanced in the north. The chief of the General Staff, General Arz, informed Czernin on 20 February that he could "under no circumstances agree with Seidler's [aforementioned] speech," adding that, "regardless of whether it actually comes to fighting or not, the state of war is effective for Austro-Hungarian forces, due to the fact that the armistice has been terminated." He insisted that Habsburg troops must join their German allies, lest the proposed policy of passivity unsettle the Central Powers alliance and thereby only serve to prolong the war.[78] Neither Czernin nor Emperor Karl was swayed by Arz's arguments, and the Dual Monarchy limited its subsequent military operations in the east to Ukraine, where it dispatched the quarter-million strong *Ostarmee* within a week. Given the Habsburg army's patchy track record in the war, it was far easier for the Austro-Hungarian Government to reign in the compromised AOK than it was for the German Government to limit the ambitions of the seemingly successful OHL.

Over the next few days, German forces swept through Livonia and Estonia mostly unopposed, capturing a large number of abandoned guns and war materiel. "It is the most comical war I have ever known – it is almost entirely carried on by rail and motor-car," noted Hoffmann in his diary. "We put a handful of infantrymen with machine guns and one gun onto a train and push them off to the next station; they take it, make prisoners of the Bolsheviks, pick up a few more troops and go on."[79] The rapidity of the German advance worried Lenin greatly, lest the Germans decide to march on Petrograd and do away with the Soviet Government altogether. At the evening meeting of the Central Committee on 18 February, he argued vehemently in favour of the immediate conclusion of peace. "This thing has gone so far that continued sitting on the fence will inevitably ruin the revolution," Lenin warned. Revolutionary war was unfeasible, and the Bolsheviks should be prepared to give up Ukraine, Finland, Livonia, and Estonia for the sake of the revolution.[80]

There was strong opposition to this course of action, primarily from Bukharin and the Left Communists, and Lenin had to use his considerable skills of persuasion to the utmost effect in order to prevail. To this effect, he published in *Pravda* during the last week of February and the first week of March a series of articles expanding on his earlier twenty-one theses on peace. The proponents of revolutionary war had engaged in revolutionary phrasemaking, a particularly dangerous kind of wishful thinking. Drawing on the lessons of the French Revolution, Lenin argued that Russia lacked the economic base necessary for the successful prosecution of revolutionary war, which France had had in 1792–3. The revolution in Germany could not bring miraculous belief, as it was not yet mature enough. The peace terms the German imperialists had offered, while admittedly harsh, were not unprecedented in the history of international relations. They amounted to a new Peace of Tilsit, Lenin suggested, referencing the conditions Napoleon had imposed on the defeated Prussians in 1807. In fact, the Tilsit terms were far more severe and humiliating than the ones the Central Powers were offering now. "Yet after a few years Prussia recovered and in a war of liberation, not without the aid of robber states that waged against Napoleon by no means a war of liberation but an imperialist war, threw off the Napoleonic yoke." The Bolsheviks must therefore accept a temporary new Tilsit, as even an "unfortunate peace" would provide the Russian Revolution with a much needed respite, which would allow it to consolidate its domestic hold on power and organize a new army. As history was now moving forward at an even greater pace, Lenin reasoned, Soviet Russia would be able to overthrow the foreign yoke even faster than Prussia had done at the end of the Napoleonic Wars.[81]

There was undeniable logic in Lenin's argumentation based on a correct comparison of the relative strength of the opposing forces of revolution and counter-revolution. Bukharin's revolutionary war may have appeared a far more attractive option based on revolutionary precedent; however, its successful outcome depended on too many imponderables. Most Bolshevik leaders – Trotsky included – seem to have grasped this, and the momentum inexorably swung away from revolutionary war towards the immediate conclusion of peace. As Debo has argued persuasively, the events of these frantic days demonstrate Lenin's "political genius" and remarkable ability to "find some political profit in *every* situation."[82] One might prefer to substitute for "political genius" a "remarkable ability to combine ideological imperatives with a keen sense of *Realpolitik*," but without Lenin at the helm, the Russian Revolution may not have survived beyond the early spring of 1918.

On the evening of 18 February, Lenin dispatched a telegram to Berlin, which outlined in no uncertain terms the Bolsheviks' willingness "formally to conclude peace on the terms the German Government demanded at Brest-Litovsk."[83] It was unconditional surrender. The Germans, however, were in no hurry to reply to the Russian overture, as they simply went ahead with their military operations. Hoffmann acknowledged receipt of the wireless communication but declared it did not constitute an official document; the Russians must deliver a written note "to the German commander at Dünaburg [Dvinsk]." "Last night a reply came in at once that a courier was on the way with the document," Hoffmann wrote in his diary on 20 February. "He [Trotsky] seems to be in a devil of a hurry – we are not."[84] Upon receipt of the written note, Kühlmann transmitted the new peace terms to *Ober Ost*, which the German Government and the OHL had already agreed on. In addition to renouncing Poland, Courland, and Lithuania, Russia would have to evacuate Livonia and Estonia forthwith and conclude peace with Finland and Ukraine. The Russians had forty-eight hours to signal their approval.[85] Hoffmann handed the terms to the Soviet courier on 22 February.

The All-Russian Central Executive Committee (VTsIK) convened on the evening of 23 February to consider the Russian reply in a stormy session that lasted until the early hours of the morning. Lenin reiterated his reasons for accepting the new, harsher German terms, in view of the extremely difficult situation in which the Russian Revolution had found itself. This would be merely a temporary, strategic retreat, he insisted, before concluding his speech to rippling applause with this promise: "This revolutionary movement which at present has no possibility of offering armed resistance to the enemy, is rising and it will offer resistance later, but offer it it will."[86] At 4:30 a.m. on 24 February, just two and a half hours before the German ultimatum was set to expire, the gathering accepted the peace conditions by 126 votes in favour to 85 against, with 26 abstentions. A telegram – *en clair* – to this effect, signed by Lenin and Trotsky, was dispatched immediately to Berlin, Vienna, Constantinople, and Sofia.[87] The Russian delegation, now headed by Grigorii Sokolnikov (Trotsky had decided to resign as *Narkomindel*), set off for Brest-Litovsk the following day.

Most of the votes against acceptance of the peace conditions were cast by Left SRs, the Bolsheviks' junior partners in the *Sovnarkom* who had split from the main Socialist Revolutionary Party in October 1917 and endorsed the Bolshevik seizure of power. They had been in favour of a peace without annexations and indemnities but believed the final treaty would "turn us into slaves of the German plutocrats" who nevertheless continued their advance towards Petrograd and Moscow, "demanding the last piece of bread and requisitioning grain and iron," as Left SR leader Maria Spiridonova explained in a telegram to local Soviets in Tula in March.[88] The Left SRs would subsequently vote against ratification of the Brest-Litovsk Treaty, dismissing it as "renunciation of the international program inaugurated by the social revolution in Russia and [as] capitulation before international imperialism," and would therefore resign from the *Sovnarkom* in protest on 16 March.[89] The Left SRs, explained the secretary of the Central Committee of the party, Leontiev-Nechaev, in his "Outline of the Emergence of the Party of Left Socialist-Revolutionaries," published in May 1918, understood clearly that the world's bourgeoisie intended not simply to stifle the Russian Soviet Republic economically and cripple it territorially but to destroy it altogether.[90] The growing estrangement between the former coalition partners in the first *Sovnarkom* would soon culminate in the Left SRs July 1918 uprising.

The fourth and final phase of negotiations, which lasted a mere three days between 1 March and 3 March, involved little actual negotiating. Having witnessed the ongoing capability of the German army to take to the offensive, the Bolsheviks had no alternative but to sign on the dotted line, and the Central Powers knew it. Kühlmann and Czernin had already gone to Bucharest to negotiate peace with Romania and decided against returning to Brest-Litovsk. Ambassador Rosenberg, who had earlier ably represented the Wilhelmstraße during the armistice negotiations, would be able to take care of things in their absence.[91] As Rosenberg told Bulgarian representative Toshev privately, he would insist on signing the treaty within three days of the opening session, as Germany was eager to transfer all free divisions away from the Eastern Front.[92]

Prior to the arrival of the Russians, the German and Austro-Hungarian delegations held a preliminary meeting with their Ottoman allies on the afternoon of 26 February, at which the Ottoman representatives raised the question of Kars, Batum, and Ardahan. Since the future status of these provinces which the Russians had seized in 1878, was very important to the government in Constantinople, the Ottomans insisted, the Sublime Porte could not be seen to back down on the matter, even though it had not been mentioned in the German note from 22 February. Perhaps it might be possible to specify in the treaty that the Ottoman Empire would determine the future status of these territories, Hakki Pasha suggested.[93] Rosenberg was receptive to including this amendment in the final text, and the two diplomats persuaded the Austrians and Bulgarians to agree. The latter were probably thinking that the Ottomans would drop their demands for territorial compensation in Western Thrace if they gained territory in the Caucasus. This last-minute addendum was, in the words of Michael Reynolds, "a triumph of Ottoman diplomacy." It would enable the Ottomans to seek compensation for the territorial losses in Palestine and Mesopotamia by advancing further into the Muslim-populated territories of the Caucasus and perhaps even linking up with the Turkic populations of Russian Central Asia (Turan).[94]

At the opening plenary session on 1 March, Sokolnikov declared his willingness to "accept the conditions Germany had dictated to the Russian Government at the barrel of a gun." However, he refused to form special committees, preferring all discussions to take place during the joint proceedings. Rosenberg replied that there could be no talk of a dictated peace, since the Russian delegation was free to refuse to sign. He then read out the terms, which now included the cession of Kars, Ardahan, and Batum. After a clarification of certain technical matters, the session was adjourned, with Sokolnikov barely opening his mouth.[95] During the final session on 3 March, he lodged an official protest against the terms of the peace, which was in no way a peace of understanding, but reiterated the Russian delegation's willingness to sign the document:

> The negotiations between Russia on the one hand and Germany and its allies on the other have clearly demonstrated that the so-called "peace of understanding" is in actuality an annexationist and imperialist peace. The peace currently being concluded in Brest-Litovsk is not a peace based on the free understanding of the peoples of Russia, Germany, Austria-Hungary, Bulgaria, and Turkey. It is a peace dictated at the barrel of a gun. This is a peace that revolutionary Russia is forced to accept through clenched teeth.[96]

This was one last rhetorical salvo on the part of the Bolsheviks. Since the proceedings of the peace conference continued to be sent out to the world press, Sokolnikov was aware that painting the peace in the darkest possible hues provided additional ammunition for the Russian

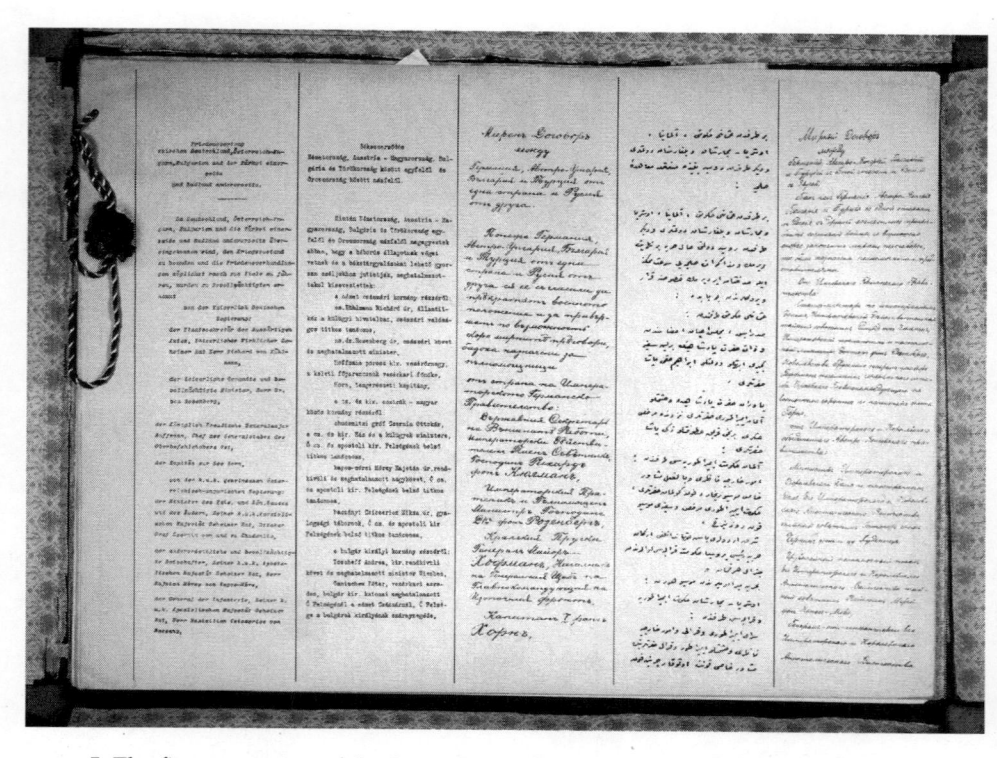

5. The first two pages of the Second Treaty of Brest-Litovsk, signed on 3 March 1918, in German, Hungarian, Bulgarian, Ottoman Turkish, and Russian. Wikimedia Commons.

Revolution in its ongoing struggle with world imperialism. The representatives of the Central Powers raised half-hearted objections but ultimately allowed the matter to rest, thankful that the long ordeal had finally come to an end. The official signing of the second peace Treaty of Brest-Litovsk took place between 4:34 pm and 5:50 pm on 3 March 1918 – exactly forty years after the signing of another short-lived treaty which proposed to remake East Central Europe at San Stefano.

The Provisions of the Peace and Its Aftermath

Few treaties in the history of international relations have been vilified as much as the second Treaty of Brest-Litovsk. Wheeler-Bennett set the tone in the West in the 1930s, when he asserted that "the political clauses of the treaty could scarcely be excelled in Draconian severity."[97] The Fischer School elaborated this view in the 1960s and 1970s, in relation to Germany's war aims and its alleged quest for domination in Europe. Lenin's description of the treaty as a new Tilsit Peace formed the basis of Soviet historiography. Karl Radek, the erstwhile proponent of revolutionary war, summarized this view eloquently in a report he gave at the Moscow Soviet Theater on 2 October 1918: "We, comrades, did not conclude the Brest peace; the Brest peace was forced upon us at gunpoint. We, comrades, were victims of German imperialism at the time. Soviet foreign policy was a policy of retreat, which sought to protect central Russia, the heart of world revolution."[98] Since the *glasnost* era in the late 1980s, Soviet and Russian historians have been able to debate the implications of the treaty freely. While some have questioned Lenin's assertion that it provided much needed breathing space and a respite for the Russian Revolution, they have by and large continued to adhere to the central premise of Brest-Litovsk as a dictated peace.[99] Gerhard Ritter remains the sole proponent of the view that Brest-Litovsk was not a peace of force, even if it was not a peace of reconciliation either.[100]

What were the main provisions of this allegedly draconian peace, which suffers from an almost universal opprobrium? As far as territorial changes were concerned, Russia was obliged to relinquish Congress Poland, Courland, Lithuania, the Moonsound Islands, and Riga, with the proviso that "Germany and Austria-Hungary purpose to determine the future status of these territories in agreement with their populations" (Article III). It would likewise have to evacuate the districts of Kars, Ardahan, and Batum, whose populations would determine the territories' future status "in agreement with the neighboring states, especially with Turkey" (Article IV). Livonia and Estonia west of the Narva and Dvina rivers would also have to be evacuated by Russian regular forces and Red Guards, although there was no mention of the future international status of the two provinces (Article VI). Last but not least, Russia was obliged to recognize Ukraine and Finland as independent states and conclude peace treaties with their respective governments forthwith (Article VI).[101] Appendices to the main treaty regulated the largely reciprocal, bilateral economic relations between Russia and each member of the Quadruple Alliance, pending the ratification of new commercial treaties. Lastly, legal-political supplemental treaties included articles on the mutual reimbursement for POW costs, which amounted to hidden indemnities for Germany and (quite possibly, depending on the method of calculation) for Austria-Hungary.[102]

These conditions were definitely harsh from the perspective of the former Russian Empire; in fact, they amounted to its partial dissolution. However, the Bolsheviks could have secured far more lenient terms at Brest-Litovsk, had they refrained from at least some of their revolutionary antics and exhibited a genuine desire to make the best of a bad situation. This was never on the agenda, however, as their main objective during this period was fostering world revolution rather than securing a favourable territorial settlement for a Russia they considered merely the weakest link in the chain of world imperialism. "Had we really wanted to obtain the most favorable peace, we would have agreed to it as early as November," wrote Trotsky. "But no one ... raised his voice to do it. We were all in favor of agitation, of revolutionizing the working classes of Germany, Austria-Hungary, and all of Europe."[103] They had gambled on world revolution and lost, at least for the time being. In the process, they had driven Ukraine and Finland straight into the willing arms of the Central Powers and forfeited Estonia and Livonia.

According to the provisions of the treaty, the old empire lost 780 000 square kilometres of territory populated by 56 million people, which included 27% of its arable land, 26% of its railways, 33% of its textile industry, 73% of its iron and steel production, 89% of its coal deposits, and 90% of its sugar production.[104] As the *Arbeiter Zeitung* noted in an editorial on 5 March, Imperial collapse on this scale was almost wholly unprecedented. It marked the reversal of the work of centuries and Russia's withdrawal from European affairs, with the country reduced to its pre-Petrine borders. "Where formerly the tsar suppressed a dozen peoples," the editorial concluded, highlighting the explosive consequences of Imperial collapse, "a group of new states has risen which will be a source of continuous disturbances and fermentation in Europe."[105]

The new states that emerged from the wreckage of the Russian Empire – whose populations, while ethnically diverse, were by and large non-Russian – were not simply reduced to the status of Hohenzollern and Habsburg colonies. Although all existed in complex interdependence with Central Europe over the next eight months, some were never under Austro-German occupation (Finland), others grew increasingly independent over time (Skoropadskyi's Ukrainian Hetmanate), while still others were being prepared for eventual association with one of the two empires (Congress Poland under the Austro-Polish Solution). "[T]he Treaty of Brest-Litovsk institutionally identified the

Bolsheviks with the thirty provinces of ethnic or Great Russia," writes Stephen Velychenko in relation to this aspect of the peace, "making them, despite their internationalist rhetoric, into the creators of the first modern Russian national state."[106] Thus, the treaty concluded the first phase of the extended process of Imperial collapse in the former Russian Empire, which had begun with the February Revolution in 1917. If one compares this process of dissolution of the dynastic empires of East Central Europe with the decolonization of the British, French, Dutch, and Portuguese overseas empires after the Second World War, as Joshua Sanborn has done,[107] one can conclude that the treaty was a peace of decolonization.

Seen from the perspective of Imperial collapse and decolonization, the second Treaty of Brest-Litovsk is not as severe as it might appear at first glance. Although it is typically compared to Versailles, the Russian Treaty of Brest-Litovsk actually has much more in common with the Treaty of Trianon, which the Entente imposed on Hungary in 1920. The pre-Trianon Kingdom of Hungary was an integral part of the Habsburg Empire, although it occasionally resembled and could easily be mistaken for a nation state, not unlike the Russian Empire. According to the provisions of the treaty, Hungary lost 72% of its pre-war territory along with 64% of its pre-war population of close to 21 million, which also left over three million or one-third of ethnic Magyars under foreign rule. Like Germany (but unlike Austria and, later, Bulgaria and Turkey), Hungary was required to pay substantial reparations. The Hungarian army was reduced to a police force of 35 000 men with no General Staff. Adding insult to injury, the Entente forbade newly-landlocked Hungary to have a surface navy or build any submarines. Seen as the "dismantling of historic Hungary," Trianon was met with unanimous opposition and resentment throughout the country, whose leading statesmen continued to harbor revisionist thoughts until the end of the Second World War.[108]

More importantly, however, the two treaties marked the transformation of two Imperial states (or sub-Imperial, in Hungary's case) into nation states for the first time in their history. In both cases, the transformation was an incredibly painful one, but to describe the terms of the treaty as draconian is perhaps a bit of an overstatement. The victorious Entente may have condemned the second treaty of Brest-Litovsk, but it did little or nothing to restore Russia's lost territories in Eastern Europe, although important differences in attitude existed, with France in favour of the re-emergence of a strong White Russia (minus Poland) as a counterweight to Germany, and Britain content to live with a weakened Red Russia. In the aftermath of the second phase of the extended continuum of violence, between November 1918 and 1923, the western borderlands of the former Russian Empire emerged as a convenient *cordon sanitaire* against the westward spread of Bolshevism. The Bolsheviks were obliged to cede very little territory they actually controlled at Brest-Litovsk – Poland, Lithuania, and most of Latvia were long gone, and Finland and Ukraine had been *de facto* independent for almost a year; Estonia was the only region where strong support for Bolshevism existed. In general, treaties that confirm the existing military status quo are not draconian by default.

A more important if less frequently asked question is why the Brest-Litovsk settlement failed to establish a stable peace during its existence. (The question becomes moot for the period following the collapse of the Central Powers in late October–early November 1918). Whatever its merits or lack thereof, the treaty was a fairly accurate reflection of the huge disparity of forces between the Central Powers and Bolshevik Russia in 1918. This alone should have guaranteed its existence at least in the short run, as was the case with Versailles. However, the situation on the ground in Eastern Europe in the months after March 1918 resembled Trotsky's "no war, no peace" policy more than anything else, as the two sides continued to engage in numerous skirmishes, border conflicts, and provocations of all sorts. The German civilian and military authorities soon became convinced that the Bolsheviks were not to be trusted. They therefore supported various anti-Bolshevik groups in European Russia, such as the Don and Kuban Cossacks.[109]

At the same time, the Central Powers shied away from a complete break with the Bolsheviks, pursuing what was in effect a series of halfway measures that further destabilized the already volatile situation engendered by Imperial collapse in Eastern Europe. "[A] real state of peace did not exist in the East," observed Hoffmann in his memoirs, "we still had a weak, but consecutive line of troops along the front facing the Bolshevik bands; there was shooting almost every day; we did not know what was really going on in Russia ..." By spring 1918, the general had become a firm proponent of an anti-Bolshevik crusade that echoed Czernin's thoughts at the end of January: "I supported the opinion that it would be best to clear the situation in the East, that is, to denounce the peace, to march on Moscow, to form another Russian Government, to grant them better conditions of peace than the Brest-Litovsk

Treaty had given them – for instance, at first Poland might be returned to them – and to conclude an alliance with the new Government."[110] This plan met with little enthusiasm elsewhere. The OHL had its hands full with the Spring Offensive in the west, and the Austrians seemed unwilling to tamper with the status quo in the east, however unsatisfactory it might be. "The Soviet government, which is the only one willing to stand by the Brest treaty while simultaneously fighting the Entente, cannot and must not be deposed," wrote the Austro-Hungarian ambassador in Kiev, Count Forgách, to the Ballhausplatz in mid-July.[111]

Contrary to the views of Soviet historiography, the Bolsheviks, too, had no intention of observing the provisions of the peace faithfully, even though it was supposedly meant to provide them with a respite.[112] Lenin himself admitted as much publicly in the aforementioned speech at the Seventh Party Congress on 7 March: "Yes, of course, we are violating the treaty; we have violated it thirty or forty times. Only children can fail to understand that in an epoch like the present, when a long, painful period of emancipation is setting in ... there must be a strong, circumspect struggle." The formal conclusion of peace could mean only one thing – an intensification of ideological and guerilla warfare against the Central Powers and their client states like Ukraine. Lenin went on to cite his favourite example of the Peace of Tilsit, which the Prussians had also violated: "The Hoffmann of those days – Napoleon – time and again caught the Germans violating the peace treaty, and the present Hoffmann will catch us at it. Only we shall take care that he does not catch us soon." [113] The cat-and-mouse game the two opposing sides had played at the Brest-Litovsk Peace Conference continued to be the order of the day in its aftermath.

In the event, the Germans very nearly did "catch" the Bolsheviks in the early summer of 1918. Following one violation too many, on 12 June Kühlmann presented a thinly-veiled ultimatum to the Soviet ambassador in Berlin, Ioffe. Unless Russian forces stopped all attacks on German troops along the demarcation lines in Taganrog and elsewhere, and the Russian Black Sea Fleet returned to its ports as per the provisions of the treaty by 15 June, it read, "the German command will be forced to take further measures."[114] On 13 June, Ioffe telephoned Moscow – the Bolsheviks had transferred the seat of government from Petrograd to Moscow on 12 March – to explain the gravity of the situation and ask for further instructions. "Any continuous, even slight, provocation on our part will be used immediately from the [German] military perspective," he warned. "It is necessary to avoid this under all circumstances." Newly minted People's Commissar for War Trotsky insisted that the continued existence of the peace treaty would be unfeasible unless both sides observed the demarcation line conscientiously. So far, the Germans had been the ones to violate it at will through a number of "wicked provocations." It was imperative to have reciprocity on this issue, Trotsky concluded. Unlike his fiery colleague, Lenin was willing to accept the German ultimatum unconditionally and instructed Ioffe to that effect.[115] Russian acceptance avoided a complete breakdown of relations. Characteristically, however, there was a glaring difference between what the Bolsheviks promised to do and what they actually did, as the crews of the Russian Black Sea Fleet, which was supposed to return from Novorosiisk to Sevastopol, blew up the ships in order to prevent their falling into German hands. A single battle cruiser arrived at Sevastopol intact.[116]

Another major incident that threatened the continued existence of the second Treaty of Brest-Litovsk occurred in early July, this time at the instigation of the Left SRs, the Bolsheviks' former allies and partners in the first *Sovnarkom* who continued to oppose the treaty. In preparation for a planned uprising against the Bolsheviks, on 6 July two Left SR assassins were able to gain admission to the German Embassy in Moscow by presenting falsified Cheka documents and claiming they had to speak to Ambassador Mirbach urgently. They were led into an anteroom, where Count Mirbach greeted them. One of the assassins fired a shot at the ambassador but missed. Mirbach attempted to make a run for the door, at which point the second assassin shot him in the back of the head. In the ensuing confusion, the two terrorists threw a bomb into the room, jumped out of the window, ran to a car waiting for them around the corner, and sped away.[117]

Mirbach's assassination was the signal for the Left SR uprising. Although it enjoyed a brief success – the rebels succeeding in capturing "Iron" Feliks Dzerzhinskii, head of the Cheka – the Bolsheviks were quickly able to regain the initiative and suppress the revolt.[118] The Germans sought to exploit the situation by demanding that a German garrison be admitted to Moscow for the protection of the embassy. With German power ebbing steadily after a series of successful Entente counteroffensives in the west, however, the Bolsheviks steadfastly refused. "Lenin reasons the Germans will back down," Stalin wrote to his close associate Sergo Ordjonikidze.[119] He was correct. Mirbach's replacement, Karl Hellferich, ventured outside the embassy building only once for fear of his life and departed from Moscow after a brief stay. On 9 August the German authorities informed the People's Commissariat for Foreign Affairs that the German Embassy would be relocated from Moscow to Pskov, which was under German occupation.[120] The Austro-Hungarian, Ottoman, and Bulgarian embassies moved to Petrograd three days later.

Germany made one final, half-hearted attempt to set its relations with Soviet Russia on a more solid basis by pushing through an additional bilateral treaty on 27 August. The fact that the treaty did not include the other three members of the Central Powers alliance was merely a temporary measure in the interest of expediency, the Germans reassured their Habsburg allies. This proved to be too little too late. The Bolsheviks grew more confident with each news dispatch of the deteriorating military situation of the Central Powers and less willing to accommodate Berlin and Vienna. Commenting on an article by Karl Radek in *Izvestiia* from 10 October entitled "The Entente and Brest," the Austrian minister in Russia, Georg de Pottere, remarked that, whereas earlier the Bolsheviks had been proponents of the idea of national self-determination, "now we find clear traces of Bolshevik imperialism," evidenced by the pursuit of reunification of the former Russian Empire under the Bolshevik sceptre.[121] The experience of Ukrainian statehood and Lenin's vehement opposition to Great Russian chauvinism, however, meant that this "Bolshevik imperialism" was qualitatively different from its Romanov predecessor, resulting in the emergence of the Soviet Union as the world's first affirmative action empire, in Terry Martin's apt phrase. The Soviet government officially renounced the Treaty of Brest-Litovsk on 13 November 1918.

The ideological gulf between the conservative, monarchical Central Powers and the utopian-revolutionary Bolsheviks rendered a stable peace in East Central Europe impossible during the Brest-Litovsk period. The two sides' respective goals of preserving Imperial dynasticism and spreading world revolution proved entirely incompatible. In the prevailing atmosphere of intense mutual distrust, the Brest-Litovsk peace became, in a reversal of Clausewitz's famous dictum invoked by Kühlmann in February, a means of prosecuting war by other means. As political scientist Charles Kupchan sensibly remarks, "[i]t is not simply the absence of conflict that makes a zone of stable peace a unique and intriguing phenomenon. Rather, it is the emergence of a deeper and more durable peace, one in which the absence of war stems not from deterrence, neutrality, or apathy, but from a level of interstate comity that effectively eliminates the prospect of armed conflict."[122] At the Brest-Litovsk Peace Conference, this interstate comity was conspicuous by its absence, as *Ostpolitik* and world revolution proved impossible to reconcile.

Conclusion: Brest-Litovsk and Europe's Twentieth Century

The struggle is mercilessly cruel.
The struggle, as they say, is epic.

Nikola Vaptsarov

Historians often view Europe's "short twentieth century," the years between 1914 and 1989 (a concept popularized by Eric Hobsbawm in *The Age of Extremes*), as an ideological clash between liberal democracy, communism, and fascism.[1] "The unremitting struggle between them to define modern Europe lasted most of this century," writes Mark Mazower.[2] This clash culminated in the 1930s and 1940s, when all three ideologies sought to remake Europe in their own image, often with the use of extreme levels of coercion and violence. While Europe's dynastic empires were long gone by then, they had played a vital role in the early stages of the age of ideological warfare, at Brest-Litovsk. This is not to say that ideology had no impact on the Great War prior to the conference, Woodrow Wilson's liberal internationalism being the most prominent example. However, it was at Brest-Litovsk, the twilight of empire, where following the collapse of the Romanov Empire the three remaining proponents of Imperial dynasticism engaged the representatives of the first communist state in a three-month verbal duel open to the scrutiny of world public opinion, that the clash of ideologies which was to dominate the twentieth century truly emerged. It was precisely in relation to Brest-Litovsk that the American president, Wilson, and the British prime minister, David Lloyd George, enunciated their ideas of a world made safe for democracy and came out in favour of national self-determination.

Two vastly different worlds met at the half-burnt Russian fortress of Brest-Litovsk in December 1917. Flush with success in the wake of their recent revolutionary seizure of power in Petrograd, the Bolshevik professional revolutionaries sought to use the first ever open peace negotiations in the history of international relations to spread proletarian revolution on the world stage. In contrast, the traditional cabinet diplomats of the Central Powers sought to accommodate Imperial collapse in the former Russian Empire and contain its westward spread. In light of these mutually exclusive objectives, the conference soon became the setting for a wide-ranging polemic, with the application of the new concept of self-determination in the western borderlands of the former Russian Empire as the bone of contention. The discourse on self-determination in Brest-Litovsk ensured that this new principle became a staple of international relations long before it was the subject of discussion at the Paris Peace Conference. Brest-Litovsk's focus on East Central Europe also meant that self-determination's immediate resonance was felt most strongly in this crisis zone of Europe, contributing to the collapse of the previously dominant framework of Imperial dynasticism throughout the region.

As the Brest-Litovsk negotiations stalled in mid-January, a mass strike broke out in the Austrian half of the Habsburg Monarchy, spreading to Hungary and Germany. Across East Central Europe demands were the same as those which provoked the strike – the immediate conclusion of a non-annexationist peace at Brest-Litovsk and the improvement of the provisioning situation. A great revolutionary demonstration, the Great January Strike served as a prelude to revolution in East Central Europe. In an attempt to contain the domestic unrest and provide bread and peace, the Habsburg establishment started a dialogue with the moderate social-democratic leadership while the Austrian and German delegations in Brest-Litovsk turned to the newly arrived Ukrainians, who sought to bolster their claim to independence. The negotiations between the Central Powers and Ukraine proceeded fairly smoothly, some disagreements over the Polish-Ukrainian contested district of Kholm and the status of the Ukrainian population in Austrian Galicia notwithstanding. These negotiations and the subsequent Austro-German military intervention on behalf of the weak Ukrainian Central Rada, along with Bulgaria's failed attempt to secure regional hegemony in the Balkans under the guise of national self-determination, affected the development of national statehood in East Central Europe, demonstrating the blurring of lines between Imperial and national engendered by the Great War.

Conclusion: Brest-Litovsk and Europe's Twentieth Century

The final stages of the Brest-Litovsk Peace Conference between late January and early March 1918 were decisive in clarifying the nature of relations between the Central Powers and Soviet Russia. As negotiations with Ukraine were about to bear fruit in the imminent conclusion of a treaty, the Central Powers needed to find out definitively whether the Bolsheviks could be induced to come round and sign the peace. For their part, the Bolsheviks had to deal with growing dissent in their own ranks for the first time since the October Revolution. Three major factions emerged at the end of January – the proponents of Trotsky's "no war, no peace" policy, the proponents of Lenin's immediate conclusion of peace, and the proponents of Bukharin's revolutionary war. Although they disagreed among themselves, Trotsky and Lenin were forced to conclude a temporary alliance in order to defeat the supporters of the third, most popular option. Consequently, Trotsky received the green light to go ahead with his cherished theatrical declaration, which he duly delivered at the plenary session of 10 February.

Although the Austrians and the German civilian faction wanted to agree with the Bolsheviks' *de facto* end to hostilities, the OHL gained the upper hand and launched a military offensive in Estonia and Livonia. Fully convinced that the Germans meant business, the Bolsheviks requested and received new terms, which were understandably harsher than the ones originally proposed. The Russian delegation returned to Brest-Litovsk and signed the treaty without so much as looking at it on 3 March. However, the formal conclusion of negotiations did not result in durable peace between the Central Powers and Soviet Russia, as mutual distrust, provocations, and border skirmishes remained the order of the day. This uneasy equilibrium lasted until early November, when the victorious Entente Powers made the Germans renounce the treaty as a prerequisite for granting them an armistice in the west.

Its short duration notwithstanding, the Brest-Litovsk settlement became an important hallmark in Europe's short twentieth century. The Ukrainian treaty of 10 February facilitated the emergence of modern Ukrainian statehood, and the subsequent Russian treaty of 3 March played an important role in what Joshua Sanborn has aptly described as Russia's "war of decolonization" by formalizing the end of colonial relationships between imperial society and the peoples of much of East Central Europe.[3] Further west, hundreds of thousands of repatriated Austro-Hungarian POWs, as per the provisions of the second treaty, contributed to the radicalization of the Habsburg home front and the dissolution of the Dual Monarchy. "In their deplorable condition," reported Lieutenant Second Grade Adalbert Balogh upon his return from a mission in Russia, "they have become a willing band of agitators, who travel from camp to camp preaching the Bolshevik gospel."[4] Béla Kun, the leader of the short-lived Hungarian Soviet Republic in 1919, was one such radicalized Habsburg POW in Russia who brought his Russian revolutionary experience to East Central Europe in the wake of Brest-Litovsk. A young Mátyás Rákosi, Hungary's future Stalinist dictator, was another.[5] Taken as a whole, the two treaties initiated a transformation of East Central Europe from an Imperial to a post-Imperial space which is, in many ways, still ongoing.

The Central Powers' collapse in late-October–early-November 1918 seemed to vindicate Lenin's claim that the Brest-Litovsk settlement was a masterful, temporary retreat, a breathing spell [*peredyshka*] for Soviet Russia, rather than a necessity forced by the huge disparity of forces and the failure of the Great January Strike in Austria to spark proletarian revolution in East Central Europe. It also had the effect of further cementing Lenin's unquestionable authority in the party by promoting the view of the peace negotiations and their outcome as a necessary if painful lesson the Bolsheviks had to learn in their maturation as a party of government. "In the period of the Brest-Litovsk Peace," stated the 1938 *Short Course in the History of the All-Union Communist Party (Bolsheviks)*, "Lenin taught the Party how to retreat in good order when the forces of the enemy are obviously superior to our own, in order to prepare with the utmost energy for a new offensive. History has fully proved the correctness of Lenin's line."[6]

Consequently, Soviet foreign policy continued to use the tried and tested method of dual policy, first devised and implemented at Brest-Litovsk, over the following seven decades. Mikhail Gorbachev's reforms of *glasnost* and *perestroika* marked the formal end of the Brest-Litovsk period of Soviet foreign relations; in his famous speech at the United Nations in December 1988, Gorbachev asserted that "de-ideologization of interstate relations has become a demand of the new stage [of international relations]."[7] As communist regimes across East Central Europe tumbled and the Berlin Wall came crashing down in November 1989, the mercilessly cruel ideological struggle that defined Europe's short twentieth century, which Brest-Litovsk had helped usher in, finally came to an end.

Notes

Introduction: A Forgotten Peace

1 My definition of East Central Europe, usually described as the lands between Germany and Russia, comes from Paul Robert Magocsi, *Historical Atlas of East Central Europe: 1 (A History of East Central Europe)* (Seattle: University of Washington Press, 1995); Oscar Halecki, *Borderlands of Western Civilization: A History of East Central Europe* (New York: The Ronald Press, 1952). As the borders of Germany and Russia have fluctuated considerably since the early 19th century, I find it more useful to have more specific geographic delimitations - hence the reference to the Elbe and Dnieper rivers. This extended definition therefore includes most of historic Prussia as well as right-bank Ukraine.
2 Peter Holquist, *Making War, Forging Revolution: Russia's Continuum of Crisis, 1914–1921* (Cambridge: Harvard University Press, 2002), 2–7.
3 Mark Von Hagen, "The Entangled Eastern Front in the First World War," in *The Empire and Nationalism at War*, ed. Eric Lohr et al., Russia's Great War and Revolution, 1914–1922: 2 (Bloomington: Slavica Publishers, 2014), 11.
4 Iván T. Berend, *The Crisis Zone of Europe: An Interpretation of East-Central European History in the First Half of the Twentieth Century* (Cambridge and New York: Cambridge University Press, 1986). Berend proposes an extended continuum of upheaval and crisis, which lasted from the *fin-de-siècle* to the Second World War. His analysis focuses on the interrelationship between economic, social, political, and ideological developments in the area, especially on the wide range of socio-political and ideological reactions to failed or semi-successful economic modernization.
5 Patricia A. Weitsman, *Dangerous Alliances: Proponents of Peace, Weapons of War* (Stanford: Stanford University Press, 2004), 166.

6 The literature on the Paris Peace Conference is enormous. Some of the more important recent works, which considerably broaden the topic beyond the earlier, more narrow focus, are Norman A. Graebner and Edward M. Bennett, *The Versailles Treaty and Its Legacy: The Failure of the Wilsonian Vision* (Cambridge: Cambridge University Press, 2011); Alan Sharp, *Consequences of Peace: The Versailles Settlement, Aftermath and Legacy* (London: Haus Publishing, 2010); Margaret MacMillan, *Paris 1919: Six Months That Changed the World* (New York: Random House, 2002); Manfred F. Boemeke, Gerald D. Feldman, and Elisabeth Gläser, eds., *The Treaty of Versailles: A Reassessment After 75 Years* (Cambridge, U.K: Cambridge University Press, 1998); among older works, Arno J. Mayer, *Politics and Diplomacy of Peacemaking: Containment and Counterrevolution at Versailles, 1918–1919* (New York: Vintage, 1969) saw the conference as a flawed Allied attempt to deal with the Russian Revolution; most influentially, John Maynard Keynes, *The Economic Consequences of the Peace* (New York: Harcourt, Brace and Howe, 1920) condemned the Treaty of Versailles, arguing that reparations crippled the Germany economy and hampered general European economic recovery. His view became especially influential in Britain during the 1930s, contributing to the policy of appeasement.
7 John Wheeler Wheeler-Bennett, *The Forgotten Peace: Brest-Litovsk, March 1918* (New York: Morrow, 1939); this theme is also present in the documentary collection Z.A.B Zeman, ed., *Germany and the Revolution in Russia, 1915–1918: Documents from the Archives of the German Foreign Ministry* (London: Oxford University Press, 1958); Sydney D. Bailey, "Brest-Litovsk: A Study in Soviet Diplomacy," *History Today* 6, no. 8 (1956):511–21 largely followed Wheeler-Bennett's pioneering study.
8 Werner Hahlweg, *Der Diktatfrieden von Brest-Litowsk 1918 und die bolschewistische Weltrevolution* (Münster: Aschendorff, 1960).
9 Fritz Fischer, *Germany's Aims in the First World War* (New York: W.W. Norton, 1967); Peter Borowsky, *Deutsche Ukrainepolitik 1918 unter besonderer Berücksichtigung der Wirtschaftsfragen* (Lübeck and Hamburg: Mathiesen Verlag, 1970) refined Fischer's analysis, distinguishing between the old-fashioned imperialism of territorial annexations which the German High Command pursued at Brest-Litovsk and the economic imperialism the German Foreign Office allegedly favoured.
10 Wolfgang Steglich, *Die Friedenspolitik der Mittelmächte, 1917/18* (Wiesbaden: F. Steiner, 1964).
11 Gerhard Ritter, *The Sword and the Scepter: The Problem of Militarism in Germany*, vol. 4: *The Reign of German Militarism and the Disaster of 1918* (Coral Gables: University of Miami Press, 1969), 114–15.

12 Winfried Baumgart, *Deutsche Ostpolitik 1918: Von Brest-Litowsk bis zum Ende des Ersten Weltkrieges* (Vienna: Oldenbourg, 1966), 370; Winfried Baumgart, "Brest-Litowsk und Versailles. Ein Vergleich zweier Friedensschlüsse," *Historische Zeitschrift* 210, no. 3 (June 1970):583–619; for a summary of the main issues involved in the Fischer Controversy from the period, see Wolfgang J. Mommsen, "The Debate on German War Aims," in *German Imperialism, 1914–1918: The Development of a Historical Debate* (New York: John Wiley & Sons, 1972), 195–218.

13 The most important work is Wolfdieter Bihl, *Österreich-Ungarn und die Friedensschlüsse von Brest-Litovsk* (Vienna: Böhlau, 1970); see also Clifford F. Wargelin, "Bread, Peace, and Poland: The Economic, Political, and Diplomatic Origins of Habsburg Policy at Brest-Litovsk, 1914–1918." (PhD diss., University of Wisconsin at Madison, 1994); Clifford F. Wargelin, "A High Price for Bread: The First Treaty of Brest-Litovsk and the Break-up of Austria-Hungary, 1917–1918," *The International History Review* 19, no. 4 (November 1997):757–88.

14 The most important émigré-Ukrainian studies are Oleh S. Fedyshyn, *Germany's Drive to the East and the Ukrainian Revolution, 1917–1918* (New Brunswick: Rutgers University Press, 1971); Stephan M. Horak, *The First Treaty of World War I: Ukraine's Treaty with the Central Powers of February 9, 1918* (Boulder: East European Monographs, 1988); for the Soviet Ukrainian perspective, see I.I. Chervinkiv-Koroliov, "Pro zmovu nimets'koho imperializmu z Tsentral'noiu Radoiu u Brest-Lytovsku v 1918 r.," *Ukrains'kyi Istorychnyi Zhurnal*, no. 5 (May 1983):17–28.

15 Irina V. Mikhutina, *Ukrainskii Brestskii mir: Put' vykhoda Rossii iz Pervoi mirovoi voiny i anatomiia konflikta mezhdu Sovnarkomom RSFSR i pravitel'stvom ukrainskoi Tsentral'noi Rady* (Moscow: Izdatel'stvo Evropa, 2007).

16 The best English-language overview of the formative period of Soviet foreign policy, including the Brest-Litovsk negotiations, is Richard K. Debo, *Revolution and Survival: The Foreign Policy of Soviet Russia, 1917–18* (Toronto: University of Toronto Press, 1979); Richard K. Debo, *Survival and Consolidation: The Foreign Policy of Soviet Russia, 1918–1921* (Montreal: McGill-Queen's University Press, 1992).

17 A.O. Chubarian, *Brestskii mir* (Moscow: Gospolitizdat, 1964); Abdulkhan A. Akhtamzian, "O Brest-Litovskikh peregovorakh 1918 goda," *Voprosy Istorii* no. 11 (November 1966):32–46; V.I. Tkachev, "Bor'ba s levymi kommunistami v period Brest-Litovskikh peregovorov (Na materialakh partiinykh organizatsii Povol'zhia)," *Voprosy Istorii KPSS* no. 6 (June 1986):56–69; R. G. Simonenko, *Brest: Dvobii viini i miru* (Kiev: Politvydav Ukrainy, 1988).

18 Branko Polic, "Brestlitovski mir: Prijelomni trenutak Oktobarske revolucije," *Politička Misao* 14, no. 3 (June 1977):467–92.
19 Igor' Nikolaevich Ksenofontov, *Mir, kotorogo khoteli i kotoryi nenavideli: Dokumental'nyi reportazh* (Moscow: Izd-vo polit. lit-ry, 1991); Iurii Felshtinskii, *Krushenie mirovoi revoliutsii. Brestskii mir. Okriabr' 1917 – noiabr' 1918* (London: Overseas Publications Interchange, 1991).
20 These interpretations are, respectively, Iaroslav Butakov, *Brestskii mir: Lovushka Lenina dlia kaizerovskoi Germanii* (Moscow: Veche, 2012); Pavel Vasil'evich Makarenko, "Bolsheviki i Brestskii mir," *Voprosy Istorii*, no. 3 (March 2010):3–21; Anatolii Utkin, *Unizhenie Rossii: Brest, Versal', Miunkhen* (Moscow: Eksmo Algoritm, 2004).
21 S.A. Tratstsiak, *Brėstski mir i hramadska-palitychnyia pratsėsy ŭ Belarusi : listapad 1917 – studzen' 1919 h.* (Minsk: Belaruskaia navuka, 2009); Valentin Aleksandrov, *Brest-Litovskiiat miren dogovor 1918 g.: Voennostrategicheski prichini i mezhdunarodnopravni posleditsi* (Sofia: Voenno izdatelstvo, 2009).

1 Ospolitik Meets World Revolution

1 For an overview of the military campaigns, see Norman Stone, *The Eastern Front, 1914–1917* (New York: Penguin Books, 1998); Graydon A. Tunstall, *Blood on the Snow: The Carpathian Winter War of 1915* (Lawrence: University Press of Kansas, 2010); R.L. DiNardo, *Breakthrough: The Gorlice-Tarnów Campaign, 1915* (Santa Barbara: Praeger, 2010); Timothy C. Dowling, *The Brusilov Offensive* (Bloomington: Indiana University Press, 2008).
2 Sergei P. Melgunov, *Legenda o separatnom mire (kanun revoliutsii)* (Paris, 1957), 10; see also L.L. Farrar, "Carrot and Stick: German Efforts to Conclude a Separate Peace with Russia, November 1914–December 1915," *East European Quarterly* 10, no. 2 (1976):153–79; Janusz Pajewski, "Friedensaktionen in den Anfängen des I. Weltkriegs," *Acta Poloniae Historica*, no. 70 (1994):111–26.
3 Penfield to the State Department, unnumbered, 31 March 1917. National Archives and Records Administration, Record Group 84: Records of Foreign Service Posts. Diplomatic Posts. Austria, vol.449.
4 Ottokar Czernin, *In the World War* (New York: Harper & brothers, 1920), 166.
5 Hahlweg, *Der Diktatfrieden von Brest-Litowsk*, 17–18.
6 Storck to Czernin, Bericht nr. 19587, 16 May 1917, Beilage 2: Waffenstillstands Vertrag. Haus-, Hof-, und Staatsarchiv, Politisches Archiv I:

Allgemeines, Karton 956-2 t) Friedensverhandlungen mit Rußland/ Russland (1917.11–1918).
7. "Nam nuzhen mir," in Leon Trotsky, *Sochineniia*, vol. 3: Istoricheskoe podgotovlenie Oktiabria, part 2: Ot Oktiabria do Bresta (Moscow and Leningrad: Gosudarstvennoe Izdatel'stvo, 1925), http://magister.msk.ru/library/trotsky/trotl333.htm.
8. "Imperialism, the Highest Stage of Capitalism," in V.I. Lenin, *Collected Works*, vol. 22 (Moscow: Progress Publishers, 1964), 189–190.
9. "The non-economic superstructure which grows up on the basis of finance capital, its politics and its ideology, stimulates the striving for colonial conquest." Ibid., 22:262.
10. Jane Tabrisky Degras, ed., *Soviet Documents on Foreign Policy*, vol. 1 (London: Oxford University Press, 1951), 1–3, quotation on 1.
11. Among the most important studies, Hahlweg, *Der Diktatfrieden von Brest-Litowsk*, 18–20 reviews cursorily Czernin's exchanges with the Imperial German Government but makes no mention of the other two allies; Bihl, *Österreich-Ungarn und die Friedensschlüsse von Brest-Litovsk* completely ignores the subject.
12. Hew Strachan, *The First World War* (New York: Viking, 2004), 156.
13. Demblin to the Foreign Ministry, no. 5, 9 November 1918. HHStA, PA I, K 956-2.
14. The Austro-Hungarian Foreign Minister to the Chancellor. Vienna, 10 November 1917. In Zeman, *Germany and the Revolution in Russia, 1915–1918*, 76–7.
15. Albeit a constituent state of the German Empire, the Kingdom of Bavaria retained its own army and diplomatic corps. The Imperial chancellor was also visiting Munich at the time.
16. Czernin to Hohenlohe (no. 664), Pallavicini (no. 473), Otto Czernin (no. 398), Demblin (no. 13), Thurn (no. 49), 11 November 1917. HHStA, PA I, K 956-2.
17. Czernin to Hohenlohe, no. 670, 12 November 1917. HHStA, PA I, K 956-2.
18. "Russland bietet den Frieden an!" *Arbeiter Zeitung*, 11 November 1917.
19. "Die große Friedenskundgebung." *Arbeiter Zeitung*, 12 November 1917.
20. Czernin to Hohenlohe, no. 670, 12 November 1917. HHStA, PA I, K 956-2.
21. Thurn to the Foreign Ministry, no. 40, 12 November 1917. HHStA, PA I, K 956-2.
22. See Thomas Rhodes, *The Real von Kühlmann* (London: N. Douglas, 1925).
23. The State Secretary to the Minister in Munich. Berlin, 13 November 1917. In Zeman, *Germany and the Revolution in Russia*, 84.
24. Hohenlohe to the Foreign Ministry, no. 721, 13 November 1917. HHStA, PA I, K 956-2. The claim that the Bolsheviks were German agents, quite widespread at the time and in some early academic works, was based on

the assistance (financial and transportation) the German Foreign Ministry extended to Lenin, which enabled him to return from neutral Switzerland to Russia in April 1917. The most recent study on the subject based on Russian and Western sources concludes that German money was not the primary factor behind the Bolsheviks' ascent to power in 1917–1918 and in no way subordinated them to the wishes of Germany. See Genadii Sobolev, *Taina "nemetskogo zolota"* (St. Petersburg: Izdatel'skii Dom Neva, 2002).

25 Quoted in Karl Friedrich Nowak, *The Collapse of Central Europe* (London: K. Paul, Trench, Trubner, 1924), 2.
26 Pallavicini to Czernin, no. 92, 13 Nov 1917. "Principielle Zustimmung der Pforte zum Antwortvorschlage der k.u.k. Regierung an Russland." HHStA, PA I, K 956-2.
27 On the importance of the German alliance to Ottoman strategic thinking, see Mustafa Aksakal, *The Ottoman Road to War in 1914: The Ottoman Empire and the First World War* (Cambridge: Cambridge University Press, 2008).
28 Toshev to Radoslavov, no. 2831, 13 November 1917. Tsentralen Durzhaven Arkhiv, fond 176k: Ministerstvo na vunshnite raboti i izpovedaniiata, opis 3, arkhivna edinitsa 602, list 16.
29 Otto Czernin to the Foreign Ministry, no. 648, 11 November 1917. HHStA, PA I, K 956-2.
30 Degras, *Soviet Documents on Foreign Policy*, 1:3–4.
31 Czernin to Demblin (for His Majesty), unnumbered, 21 November 1917. HHStA, PA I, K 956-2.
32 Obrashchenie Sovetskogo pravitel'stva k polkovym, divizionnym, korpusnym i armeiskim komitetam, Sovetam rabochikh, soldatskikh i krest'ianskikh deputatov. Vsem, vsem, vsem. 24 November 1917. *Sovetsko-germanskie otnosheniia ot peregovorov v Brest-Litovske do podpisaniia rapall'skogo dogovora* (Moscow: Izdatel'stvo politicheskoi literatury, 1968), 4–5.
33 Rosenberg to the Foreign Office, no. 3, 23 November 1917; Rosenberg to the Foreign Office, no. 7, 24 November 1917. NARA, RG 242: Foreign Records Seized Collection, microcopy no. T 120: Records of the German Foreign Office Received by the Department of State, roll 1797, D 822972; D 822977.
34 On the Christmas Truce, see Malcolm Brown and Shirley Seaton, *The Christmas Truce: The Western Front December 1914* (New York: Hippocrene Books, 1984); the most comprehensive overview of the local armistices on the Eastern Front in November 1917 can be found in Allan K. Wildman, *The End of the Russian Imperial Army* (Princeton: Princeton University Press, 1980), 379–94.

35 The Royal Legation in Constantinople (Kolushev) to Prime Minister Radoslavov, no. 514, 20 December 1917. TsDA, f. 176k, op. 3, a.e. 602, l. 70.
36 *Sovetsko-germanskie otnosheniia*, 7–9. Csáky to the Foreign Ministry, no. 2, 28 November 1917. HHStA, PA I, K 956-2.
37 Storck to Czernin, no. 24549, 24 November 1917. HHStA, PA I, K 956-2. The AOK raised this objection first.
38 Ganchev to Radoslavov, no. 2177, 2 Dec 1917. TsDA, fond 313k: Vasil Radoslavov, op. 1, a.e. 2460, l. 12.
39 Quoted in MacMillan, *Paris 1919*, 211.
40 Rosenberg to the Foreign Office, no. 18, 30 November 1917. NARA, RG 242, T 120, roll 1797, D 822999-D 823000.
41 Csáky to the Foreign Ministry, no. 5, 30 November 1917. HHStA, PA I, K 956-2.
42 Arz to Czernin, no. 455, 29 November 1917. HHStA, PA I, K 956-2.
43 D. G. Fokke, "Na stsene i za kulisami Brestskoi tragikomedii: Memuary uchastnika Brest-Litovskikh mirnykh peregovorov," *Arkhiv Russkoi Revoliutsii* 20 (1930):12.
44 Ibid., 13. Emphasis added.
45 Mikhutina, *Ukrainskii Brestskii mir*, 16.
46 Fokke tells the following amusing story about the recruitment of the peasant, one R. Stashkov. Even if possibly embellished, it illustrates perfectly the unorthodox approach of the Russian delegation during the negotiations. While driving to Petrograd's Warsaw Station to catch the train to Dvinsk, the Bolshevik delegates suddenly realized that the delegation did not have a representative of the Russian peasantry. As luck would have it, they happened to overtake a peasant walking down the street. "Where are you heading?" the delegates asked. "To the railway station, comrades," came the answer. "Get in, we'll give you a lift." The peasant agreed, but soon realized the car was going in the wrong direction. "I have to go to Nikolaevskii Station. I'm travelling to Moscow," he protested. The delegates queried him about his political affiliation. "I'm an SR, comrades. Where I come from, everyone is an SR." "Left or Right?" the delegates persisted. "Left, comrades. The most leftist [*samyi leveiushchii*] of them all." At this point, the delegates decided to recruit the peasant. "Don't bother going to your village. Come with us to Brest; we are going to make peace with the Germans." Fokke, "Na stsene i za kulisami," 16–17.
47 Rosenberg to the Foreign Office, no. 30, 3 December 1917. NARA, RG 242, T 120, roll 1797, unnumbered.
48 Fokke, "Na stsene i za kulisami," 21.

49 *Proceedings of the Brest-Litovsk Peace Conference: The Peace Negotiations between Russia and the Central Powers 21 November, 1917–3 March, 1918* (Washington, D.C.: Government Printing Office, 1918), 14.
50 Wheeler-Bennett, *The Forgotten Peace*, xii.
51 *Proceedings of the Brest-Litovsk Peace Conference*, 14–16.
52 Fokke, "Na stsene i za kulisami," 33–4.
53 Ibid., 43–5.
54 *Proceedings of the Brest-Litovsk Peace Conference*, 17–18.
55 Fokke, "Na stsene i za kulisami," 46.
56 *Proceedings of the Brest-Litovsk Peace Conference*, 19–32, quotation on 29.
57 Max Hoffmann, *The War of Lost Opportunities* (New York: International publishers, 1925), 200–1.
58 Fokke, "Na stsene i za kulisami," 57–8.
59 Bülow to the Foreign Office, no. 52, 9 December 1918. NARA, RG 242, T 120, roll 1798, D 823218–823219.
60 Hoffmann, *The War of Lost Opportunities*, 202.
61 Czernin to Demblin (for His Majesty), no. 10, 9 December 1917. HHStA, PA I, K 1052-2 Krieg 70: Friedensverhandlungen mit Russland, Ukraine, Rumänien, (1917–18).
62 Demblin (from His Majesty) to Czernin, no. 24, 9 December 1917. HHStA, PA I, K 1052-2.
63 Obrashchenie narodnogo komissara inostrannykh del k poslam Velikobritanii, Frantsii, SShA, Italii, Kitaia, Iaponii, Rumynii, Bel'gii i Serbii po voprosu o peremirii. 6 December 1917. *Sovetsko-germanskie otnosheniia*, 27–8.
64 Fokke, "Na stsene i za kulisami," 64–7.
65 Ibid., 70–2, quotation on 72.
66 Meckling, *Die Aussenpolitik des Grafen Czernin*, 266–7; Gary W. Shanafelt, *The Secret Enemy: Austria-Hungary and the German Alliance, 1914–1918* (Boulder: East European Monographs, 1985), 162–3.
67 Czernin, *In the World War*, 19–33, quotation on 27.
68 On the Austro-Polish Solution, see Clifford F. Wargelin, "The Austro-Polish Solution: Diplomacy, Politics, and State Building in Wartime Austria-Hungary 1914–1918," *East European Quarterly* 42, no. 3 (Fall 2008):253–73; Joachim Lilla, "Innen- und aussenpolitische Aspekte der Austropolnischen Lösung 1914–1916," *Mitteilungen des Österreichischen Staatsarchivs* 30 (January 1977):221–50.
69 Czernin to Mérey, no. 24, 14 December 1917. HHStA, PA I, K 1052-2.
70 Czernin to Müller (for His Majesty), no. 91, 24 December 1917. HHStA, PA I, K 1078: Brester Kanzlei. Czernin suggested the following course of

action to that effect: "1. A new economic arrangement between Austria and Hungary must precede the work regarding an economic union with Germany. 2. The military arrangement must be fully worked out. Once these two matters are completed, we will not sign on the dotted line until the Germans categorically promise to leave Poland to us – otherwise, we are withdrawing our propositions. The Germans are employing the following tactic: they want to delay the economic and military questions in order to secure Courland and Lithuania and then, when Your Majesty has come to difficulties and the entire world can see that we might come out empty-handed, we would be forced to buy Poland expensively. Speed is of the essence, if we are not to find ourselves in a laughable situation."

71 Besprechungen zwischen Reichsleitung und Oberster Heeresleitung (Berlin), 6/7 December 1917. Werner Hahlweg, ed., *Der Friede von Erest-Litowsk: Ein unveröffentlichter Band aus dem Werk des Untersuchungsausschusses der deutschen verfassunggebenden Nationalversammlung und des Deutschen Reichstages* (Düsseldorf: Droste, 1971), 81–3.

72 Olavi Arens, "The Estonian Question at Brest-Litovsk," *Journal of Baltic Studies* 25, no. 4 (1994):305–31.

73 Ergebnis der Besprechung im Gr. H. Qu. am 18 Dezember 1917. NARA, T 120, roll 1499, D 814700-D 814703.

74 Imanuel Geiss, *Der polnische Grenzstreifen 1914–1918: Ein Beitrag zur deutschen Kriegszielpolitik im Ersten Weltkrieg* (Hamburg and Lübeck: Moll-Winter, 1960).

75 Ergebnis der Besprechung im Gr. H. Qu. am 18 Dezember 1917. NARA, T 120, roll 1499, D 814700-D 814703.

76 Isabel V. Hull, *Absolute Destruction: Military Culture and the Practices of War in Imperial Germany* (Ithaca: Cornell University Press, 2005), 2–4.

77 In a later essay on the permanent bases of German foreign policy, Kühlmann described his view of state security thus: "Judging by our past experience, the goal of all German efforts in the domain of foreign policy must be security .... M. Jules Cambon has given a masterly definition of the security of a state: "Security! The term signifies more indeed than the maintenance of a people's homeland, or even of their territories beyond the seas. It also means the maintenance of the world's respect for them, the maintenance of their economic interest, everything, in a word, which goes to make up grandeur, the life itself, of the nation." Jules Cambon et al., *The Permanent Bases of Foreign Policy: France, Great Britain, Germany and the United States* (New York: Council on Foreign Relations, 1931), 70–1.

78 In a subsequent speech he gave in the Reichstag, which precipitated his dismissal, he stated that "[w]ithout any exchange of opinions in this

coalition war of such enormous dimensions, and in consideration also of the number of oversea powers taking part, an absolute finish of the war can scarcely be expected by mere military decisions alone and without any kind of diplomatic discussions." Extract from the Statement of Foreign Minister von Kühlmann in the Reichstag on Peace Proposals, 27 June 1918. Ralph Haswell Lutz, ed., *Fall of the German Empire, 1914–1918*, vol. 2 (Stanford: Stanford University Press, 1932), 353.

79 Nowak, *The Collapse of Central Europe*, 4–5.
80 Shelley Baranowski, *Nazi Empire: German Colonialism and Imperialism from Bismarck to Hitler* (Cambridge: Cambridge University Press, 2011), 4.
81 On the Pan-German League in general and its views of Russia and eastern expansion in particular, see Roger Chickering, *We Men Who Feel Most German: A Cultural Study of the Pan-German League, 1886–1914* (Boston: Allen & Unwin, 1984); Jerry Hans Hoffman, "The Ukrainian Adventure of the Central Powers, 1914–1918" (PhD diss., University of Pittsburgh, 1967), 3–11.
82 Diary entry for 5 February 1918. Czernin, *In the World War*, 247.
83 See Osmo Jussila, Seppo Hentilä, and Jukka Nevakivi, *From Grand Duchy to Modern State: A Political History of Finland since 1809* (London: Hurst & Co, 1999).
84 Arens, "The Estonian Question at Brest-Litovsk," 305.
85 Pallavicini to Czernin, no. 717, 13 December 1917. HHStA, PA I, K 1052-2.
86 Pallavicini to Czernin, no. 726, 17 December 1917. HHStA, PA I, K 1053: Liasse Krieg 70/1, 2 Friedensverhandlungen.
87 Michael A. Reynolds, *Shattering Empires: The Clash and Collapse of the Ottoman and Russian Empires, 1908–1918* (Cambridge: Cambridge University Press, 2011), 171–2.
88 Leon Trotsky, *The Permanent Revolution; Results and Prospects* (London: New Park, 1962), 279.
89 See V.I. Lenin, *What Is To Be Done?: Burning Questions of Our Movement* (New York: International Publishers, 1969), esp. 108–31; for a revisionist analysis of the work's importance in the development of Bolshevik theory and practice, see Lars T. Lih, *Lenin Rediscovered: 'What Is to Be Done?' in Context* (Leiden: Brill, 2006).
90 Leon Trotsky, *My Life: An Attempt at an Autobiography* (Mineola: Dover Publications, 2007), 334. Emphasis added.
91 Ibid., 341. In his memoirs, published in 1929, Trotsky claimed that he "intentionally exaggerated," which is probably an attempt to save face – the original remark is quite in character.
92 On the differences between Lenin and Trotsky, see Debo, *Revolution and Survival*, 11–20.

93 B.J. Field, "Permanent Revolution and Temporary Reaction," 9. Houghton Library, MS Rus 13.1: Leon Trotsky Exile Papers, roll 31, 15965.
94 Diary entry for 20 December 1917. Czernin, *In the World War*, 221.
95 Czernin to the Foreign Ministry (for His Majesty and the two Prime Ministers), no. 76, 21 December 1917. HHStA, PA I, K 1052-2.
96 In his memoirs, Trotsky claimed that he had conducted the exchange with Csáky and Czernin. See Trotsky, *My Life*, 375–6. Citing Russian archival sources, including a telegram exchange between Trotsky and Ioffe on the subject, Irina Mikhutina accuses Trotsky of deliberate dishonesty and artifice. See Mikhutina, *Ukrainskii Brestskii mir*, 191–2. She is correct in pointing out that Ioffe, not Trotsky, was the driving force on the Russian side – the German-language versions of the two telegrams present in the Austrian State Archives bear Ioffe's signature. Count Csáky also discussed the matter verbally with Ioffe (Trotsky was in Petrograd at the time). See Csáky to Czernin, no. 193, 24 January 1918. HHStA, PA I, K 1077: Brester Kanzlei, for Csáky's summary and a copy of the first telegram. See also Czernin to Csáky, no. 184, 24 January 1918; and Csáky to Czernin, no. 198, 27 January 1918. HHStA, PA I, K 1053. However, Ioffe and Trotsky may very well have composed the second telegram jointly, which would explain why it eventually found its way into Trotsky's private archive (see below). For the German description of these events, see Kühlmann to the Foreign Office, no. 218, 25 January 1918. NARA, RG 242, T 120, roll 1787, D 815238.
97 Ioffe to Czernin, unnumbered, 26 January 1918. HHStA, PA I, K1077. This is an exact German translation of The Chairman of the Russian Peace Delegation to Czernin, unnumbered, January 1918. Houghton Library, MS Rus 13: Leon Trotsky Soviet Papers, box 1, T 3. It is worth noting that there is no typed name or handwritten signature in the Russian-language copy present in Trotsky's archive.
98 "Outline Programme for Peace Negotiations," in V.I. Lenin, *Collected Works*, vol. 26 (Moscow: Progress Publishers, 1977), 349–50. Emphasis added.

2 Peacemaking and Self-Determination at Brest-Litovsk

1 Mérey to Czernin, no. 57, 16 December 1918. HHStA, PA I, K 1052.
2 Diary entry for 26 December 1917. Czernin, *In the World War*, 251.
3 Czernin to Hohenlohe, no. 751, 14 December 1917. HHStA, PA I, K 1052-2. That Czernin valued Kühlmann extremely highly is evident from a conversation with the Bulgarian minister plenipotentiary in Vienna,

Andrei Toshev, on 18 October 1917, in which Czernin had suggested he wished to see Kühlmann appointed Imperial chancellor, as his long diplomatic career and distinguished work as state secretary for foreign affairs had singled him out as an extremely promising if still relatively young statesman. Czernin even joked that he would decree a special religious service of thanksgiving on the day this appointment became fact. Toshev to Radoslavov, no. 2617, 18 October 1917. TsDA, f. 176k, op. 3, a.e. 655, l. 221–2.

4 Richard von Kühlmann, *Erinnerungen* (Heidelberg: Verlag Lambert Schneider, 1948), 515.

5 Arno J. Mayer, *Political Origins of the New Diplomacy, 1917–1918* (New Haven: Yale University Press, 1959), 293–312; Alfred Cobban, *National Self-Determination* (New York: Oxford University Press, 1945).

6 Erez Manela, *The Wilsonian Moment: Self-Determination and the International Origins of Anticolonial Nationalism* (Oxford: Oxford University Press, 2007), 5.

7 See, among others, ibid., 22–4; Lloyd E. Ambrosius, *Wilsonianism: Woodrow Wilson and His Legacy in American Foreign Relations* (New York: Palgrave Macmillan, 2002), 2–4.

8 Allen Lynch, "Woodrow Wilson and the Principle of 'National Self-Determination': A Reconsideration," *Review of International Studies* 28, no. 2 (April 2002):419–36; Arthur Walworth, *Wilson and His Peacemakers: American Diplomacy at the Paris Peace Conference, 1919* (New York: Norton, 1986); Theodore P. Greene, *Wilson at Versailles* (Boston: Heath, 1957).

9 Trygve Throntveit, "The Fable of the Fourteen Points: Woodrow Wilson and National Self-Determination," *Diplomatic History* 35 (2011):445–81.

10 Eric D. Weitz, "From the Vienna to the Paris System: International Politics and the Entangled Histories of Human Rights, Forced Deportations, and Civilizing Missions," *The American Historical Review* 113, no. 5 (December 2008):1328.

11 "The Revolutionary Proletariat and the Right of Nations to Self-Determination," in V.I. Lenin, *Collected Works*, vol. 21 (Moscow: Progress Publishers, 1964), 408. Emphasis in the original.

12 "The Socialist Revolution and the Rights of Nations to Self-Determination," in V.I. Lenin, *Collected Works*, vol. 22 (Moscow: Progress Publishers, 1964), 146. Emphasis added.

13 Ibid., 22:147–8. This dialectic reasoning is comparable to the idea of the dictatorship of the proletariat preceding the disappearance of class antagonisms and classes in general.

14 Ibid., 22:150–2; Arno J. Mayer, *Political Origins of the New Diplomacy, 1917–1918* (New Haven: Yale University Press, 1959), 298–303.
15 "The Discussion on Self-Determination Summed Up," in Lenin, *Collected Works*, 22: 328. Emphasis in the original.
16 Ibid., 22:338.
17 Ibid., 22:343.
18 Quoted in Weitz, "From the Vienna to the Paris System," 75. Emphasis added. Wilson had expressed a similar sentiment in his "Peace without Victory" speech from 22 January 1917 without, however, referring to self-determination as such.
19 For more on this issue, see David Stevenson, "The Failure of Peace by Negotiation in 1917," *The Historical Journal* 34, no. 1 (March 1991):65–86.
20 *Mirnye peregovory v Brest-Litovske s 22/9 dekabria do 3 marta (18 fevralia) 1918 g.*, vol. 1: Plenarnye zasedaniia, zasedaniia politicheskoi komissii (Moscow: Izdanie Narodnogo komissariata inostrannykh del, 1920), 5–6. Hakki Pasha also asked for French, the traditional language of European diplomacy, to be accepted as an official language at the conference, alongside the languages of the attending delegations. No one raised any objections to this proposal, although Hakki Pasha was possibly the only delegate to actually speak in French during the proceedings. French was the language of one of the main adversaries of the Central Powers; besides, most of the Russian delegates were fluent in German (especially Trotsky and Ioffe), due to their previous experience as covert revolutionary agents in Central Europe. In addition, General Hoffmann spoke Russian fluently.
21 *Proceedings of the Brest-Litovsk Peace Conference*, 38–9.
22 David Lloyd George, *Memoirs of the Peace Conference*, vol. 2 (New York: H. Fertig, 1972), 497.
23 Lloyd E. Ambrosius, *Wilsonian Statecraft: Theory and Practice of Liberal Internationalism During World War I* (Wilmington: SR Books, 1991), 1–34, quotation on 1; for a more positive assessment of Wilson's foreign policy, see Thomas J. Knock, *To End All Wars: Woodrow Wilson and the Quest for a New World Order* (New York: Oxford University Press, 1992); for a recent analysis of the inherent contradictions of Wilsonianism, see John A. Thompson, "Wilsonianism: The Dynamics of a Conflicted Concept," *International Affairs* 86, no. 1 (January 2010):27–47.
24 Debo, *Revolution and Survival*, 408.
25 Diary entry for 20 December 1917. Czernin, *In the World War*, 246.
26 Diary entry for 23 December 1917. Ibid., 247–8.
27 Fokke, "Na stsene i za kulisami," 102–3.

28 *Proceedings of the Brest-Litovsk Peace Conference*, 40.
29 Ibid., 41.
30 Ibid., 42.
31 Diary entry for December 26. Czernin, *In the World War*, 252.
32 Czernin to the Foreign Ministry, no. 98, 26 December 1917. HHStA, PA I, K 1052-2.
33 Hindenburg to Hoffmann, no. 25870, 26 December 1917. NARA, RG 242, T 120, roll 1787, D 814732-D 814733
34 Kühlmann to Hertling, no. 1, 27 December 1917. NARA, RG 242, T 120, roll 1787, D 814738-D 814739.
35 Erich Ludendorff, *Ludendorff's Own Story*, vol. 2 (New York and London: Harper & brothers, 1920), 168–9.
36 Hoffmann, *The War of Lost Opportunities*, 208–9.
37 Quoted in Nowak, *The Collapse of Central Europe*, 12.
38 Czernin to the Foreign Ministry (for His Majesty and the two Prime Ministers), no. 102, 27 December 1917. HHStA, PA I, K 1052-2.
39 Manfried Rauchensteiner, *The First World War and the End of the Habsburg Monarchy, 1914–1918* (Vienna, Cologne, and Weimar: Böhlau, 2014), 765.
40 Hoffmann, *The War of Lost Opportunities*, 209–11; Wheeler-Bennett, whose account is based primarily on the memoirs of Hoffmann, Czernin, and Fokke, shares this opinion. Wheeler-Bennett, *The Forgotten Peace*, 125–6; Bihl merely reports the incident, without offering any explanation of Czernin's actions. Bihl, *Österreich-Ungarn und die Friedensschlüsse von Brest-Litovsk*, 47–8.
41 Nowak, *The Collapse of Central Europe*, 12.
42 "On General Hoffmann's representation, Herr von Kühlmann now assumed a position in regard to Courland and Lithuania more in accord with the Kreuznach agreements [i.e. a tougher stance]; in this he, no doubt, placed himself in opposition to Count Czernin, who, in order to support Herr von Kühlmann, in the most incomprehensible manner threatened to conclude a separate peace on behalf of Austria-Hungary." Erich Ludendorff, *Ludendorff's Own Story*, 2:169.
43 Czernin, *In the World War*, 228.
44 Kühlmann to Hertling, no. 2, 29 December 1917. NARA, RG 242, T 120, roll 1787, D 814821.
45 Hoffmann, *The War of Lost Opportunities*, 211.
46 Bussche to Kühlmann, no. 120, 29 December 1917. NARA, RG 242, T 120, roll 1787, D 814893-D 814894.
47 Demblin to Czernin, no. 11, 27 December 1917. HHStA, PA I, K 1078.

48 Czernin to Müller (for Wekerle), no. 115, 28 December 1917. HHStA, PA I, K 1078.
49 Bussche to Kühlmann, no. 117, 28 December 1917. NARA, RG 242, T 120, roll 1791, D 816728.
50 On the evolving dynamics of the Austro-German alliance and Czernin's personal role in this process, see Shanafelt, *The Secret Enemy*; Robert F. Hopwood, "Interalliance Diplomacy: Count Czernin and Germany, 1916–1918" (PhD diss., Stanford University, 1965).
51 Martin C. Dean, *Austrian Policy during the French Revolutionary Wars, 1796–1799*, MHD-Sonderreihe Bd. 3 (Vienna: HGM/MHI, 1993), 33. Alliances also played a role in Prussian/German foreign policy, of course, Bismarck's systems in the 1870s and 1880s providing the outstanding example. However, alliances were more of a tactical necessity for Prussia/Germany as opposed to a *sine qua non* for Austria.
52 *Mirnye peregovory v Brest-Litovske*, 33–8.
53 Ibid., 38–40, quotation on 38.
54 On the Comintern, see Duncan Hallas, *The Comintern* (London: Bookmarks, 1985).
55 Mérey to Czernin, no. 45, 14 December 1917. HHStA, PA I, K 1078.
56 Chaprashikov to Radoslavov, no. 7, 17 January 1918. TsDA, f. 176k, op. 3, a.e. 1041, l. 9.
57 Count von Mirbach to His Excellency the Imperial Chancellor, no. 1, 30 December 1917. NARA, RG 242, T 120, roll 1787, D 815461-D 815467.
58 Demblin to Czernin, no. 5, 26 December 1917. HHStA, PA I, K 1080.
59 "Germans in Petrograd." *Berliner Lokal Anzeiger*, 19 February 1918. English translation in Garrett to the State Department, no. 874, 25 February 1918. NARA, RG 59: Records of the Department of State, microcopy M 367: Records of the Department of State Relating to World War I and Its Termination, 1914–1929, roll 82.
60 Hempel to the Foreign Ministry, no. 2, 6 January 1918. HHStA, PA I, K 1080.
61 Bussche to the Representative of the Foreign Office at *Ober Ost* (for Kühlmann), no. 234, 17 January 1918. NARA, RG 242, T 120, roll 1790, N/A.
62 Chaprashikov to Radoslavov, no. 26, 22 January 1918. TsDA, f. 176k, op. 3, a.e. 1039a, l. 1.
63 Panaiot Panaiotov, *Bulgaro-suvetski otnosheniia i vruzki, 1917–1923* (Sofia: Durzhavno izdatelstvo nauka i izkustvo, 1982), 59–63.
64 Chaprashikov to Radoslavov, no. 31, 23 January 1918. TsDA, f. 176k, op. 3, a.e. 1039a, l. 2.

65 Chaprashikov to the Foreign Ministry, no. 72, 1 February 1918. TsDA, f. 176k, op. 3, a.e. 1039a, l. 5.
66 Radoslavov to Chaprashikov, no. 235, not dated. TsDA, f. 176k, op. 3, a.e. 1039a, l. 4.
67 Chaprashikov to the Foreign Ministry, no. 88, 3 February 1918, TsDA, f. 176k, op. 3, a.e. 1039a, l. 6.
68 Chaprashikov to the Foreign Ministry, no. 133, 18 February 1918. TsDA, f. 176k, op. 3, a.e. 1039a, l. 9.
69 Chaprashikov to the Foreign Ministry, no. 134, 20 February 1918. TsDA, f. 176k, op. 3, a.e. 1039a, l. 10.
70 Panaiotov, *Bulgaro-suvetski otnosheniia i vruzki, 1917–1923*, 26.
71 Martin Kitchen, *The Silent Dictatorship: The Politics of the German High Command under Hindenburg and Ludendorff, 1916–1918* (New York: Holmes & Meier Publishers, 1976); Ritter, *The Sword and the Scepter*, 4. The two studies disagree on the qualitative value of OHL supremacy (Ritter is more apologetic, whereas Kitchen is rather accusatory), but neither study seriously questions it.
72 Hoffmann, *The War of Lost Opportunities*, 211.
73 Ibid.
74 "To add to Germany a broad strip of border-land with a population of about two million Poles, as the General Headquarters demanded would, in my opinion, only be a disadvantage to the Empire …. In my opinion, the new Polish frontier ought to be drawn in such a way that it should bring to the Empire the smallest possible number of Polish subjects and that there should be only a few unimportant corrections of the frontier …. The increase in Polish inhabitants, which would amount to about 100 000, would have to be taken into the bargain. But beyond that not a man." Ibid., 212–13.
75 Vejas G. Liulevicius, *War Land on the Eastern Front: Culture, National Identity and German Occupation in World War I* (Cambridge: Cambridge University Press, 2000).
76 Winfried Baumgart and Konrad Repgen, eds., *Brest-Litovsk* (Göttingen: Vandenhoeck & Ruprecht, 1969) also rely exclusively on memoirs and diaries (both published and unpublished); Hahlweg, *Der Friede von Brest-Litowsk*; and *Sovetsko-germanskie otnosheniia* barely touch the matter.
77 According to Chief of the Naval Cabinet von Müller, Kühlmann and Hoffmann had previously agreed on this border. If correct, this is demonstrative of even greater cooperation between the civilian government and the general. However, Kühlmann himself makes

no mention of this in his memoirs. *Aus dem Tagebuch des Chefs des Marinekabinetts von Müller.* Baumgart and Repgen, *Brest-Litovsk*, 22–3.
78 Kühlmann, *Erinnerungen*, 525–9; "General Ludendorff contradicted these objections in a somewhat vehement manner," writes Hofmann diplomatically. Hoffmann, *The War of Lost Opportunities*, 213–14; for Ludendorff's rather watered-down version of events, see Ludendorff, *Ludendorff's Own Story*, 2:170–4.
79 *Aus dem Tagebuch des Grafen Karl von Hertling.* Baumgart and Repgen, *Brest-Litovsk*, 24.
80 Diary entry for 4 January 1918. Czernin, *In the World War*, 225.
81 Hoffmann, *The War of Lost Opportunities*, 215.
82 Erich Ludendorff, *The General Staff and Its Problems: The History of the Relations between the High Command and the German Imperial Government as Revealed by Official Documents*, vol. 2 (London: Hutchinson & co, 1920), 524–45, quotation on 530.
83 Diary entry for 4 January 1918. Czernin, *In the World War*, 256.
84 Quoted in Wheeler-Bennett, *The Forgotten Peace*, 137.
85 David Lloyd George, *Memoirs of the Peace Conference*, vol. 2 (New York: H. Fertig, 1972), 497.
86 Manela, *The Wilsonian Moment*, 38–42; Mayer, *Political Origins of the New Diplomacy*, 313–67.
87 Nota predsedatelia rossiiskoi mirnoi delegatsii predstaviteliam tsentral'nykh derzhav, 2 January 1918. *Sovetsko-germanskie otnosheniia*, 173.
88 Judah L. Magnes, *Russia and Germany at Brest-Litovsk: A Documentary History of the Peace Negotiations* (New York: The Rand School of Social Science, 1919), 47.
89 Telegramm der russischen Delegation (St. Peterburg) an die Vorsitzenden der Delegationen des Vierbundes. 4 January 1918. Hahlweg, *Der Friede von Brest-Litowsk*, 142.
90 For the complete text of the telegram, see Rosenberg to the Foreign Ministry, no. 28, 5 January 1918. NARA, RG 242, T 120, roll 1787, D 814910-D 814912.
91 Kühlmann, *Erinnerungen*, 524.
92 Privatschreiben Seiner Exzellenz des Herrn Ministers an Prinzen Hohenlohe in Berlin, 2 January 1918. HHStA, PA I, K 1053. Czernin also refused to rule out holding referenda in the occupied territories at some future point. "Kühlmann and I are certain that, given careful preparation, the referenda will not result in the return of these territories [to Russia]," he explained.

93 Declarations of independence, however dubious and influenced by the German occupation authorities, did in fact exist. They were issued by the respective "national" or land assembly, emphasized that the country was exercising its justifiable right to self-determination, and typically requested close association with Prussia. See, for example, the full texts of the Courland and Lithuania declarations, *Oberbefehlshaber Ost Oberquartiermeister* to the Foreign Office, 23 September 1917. NARA, RG 242, T 120, roll 1792, D 818440-D818448; Lersner to the Foreign Office, 11 December 1917. NARA, RG 242, T 120, roll 1792, D 818449-D 818450.
94 Borowsky, *Deutsche Ukrainepolitik*, 298–9.
95 *Mirnye peregovory v Brest-Litovske*, 243.
96 Trotsky, *My Life*, 369.
97 Cobban, *National Self-Determination*, 12.
98 Liulevicius, *War Land on the Eastern Front*, 178.
99 *Ober Ost* Section Vp to *Ober Ost* Section Ic (for the attention of Secret Counsellor Nadolny), no. 1276, 16 January 1918. NARA, RG 242, T 120, roll 1792, D 818637-D 818638.
100 *Oberbefehlshaber Ost Oberquartiermeister* to the Foreign Ministry, 23 September 1917. NARA, RG 242, T 120, roll 1792, D 818440-D818448.
101 Von Keyserlingk to the OHL and the Admiralty Staff, no. 7, 3 January 1918. NARA, RG 242, T 120, roll 1792, D 818533.
102 *Proceedings of the Brest-Litovsk Peace Conference*, 67.
103 Ibid.
104 *Proceedings of the Brest-Litovsk Peace Conference*, 68–82.
105 Lloyd George, *Memoirs of the Peace Conference*, 2:595.
106 *Proceedings of the Brest-Litovsk Peace Conference*, 68–79; *Mirnye peregovory v Brest-Litovske*, 72–80.
107 Mark von Hagen, "The Great War and the Mobilization of Ethnicity in the Russian Empire," in *Post-Soviet Political Order: Conflict and State Building*, ed. Barnett R. Rubin and Jack Snyder (London and New York: Routledge, 1998), 34–57.
108 See Zdzisław Winnicki, *Rada regencyjna Królestwa Polskiego i jej organy (1917–1918)* (Wrocław: Wektory, 1991).
109 Kucharzewski to Hertling, no. 89, 18 December 1917. NARA, RG 242, T 120, roll 1796, D 822457-D 822458.
110 Kühlmann to the Foreign Office, no. 134, 21 December 1917. NARA, RG 242, T 120, roll 1796, D 822461-D 822462.
111 Bussche to Rosenberg, no. 12, 3 January 1918. NARA, RG 242, T 120, roll 1796, D 822480.

112 Radowitz to Kühlmann, unnumbered, 18 January 1918. NARA, RG 242, T 120, roll 1796, D 822504–822505.
113 Kühlmann to Kucharzewski, unnumbered, 20 January 1918. NARA, RG 242, T 120, roll 1796, D822508-D 822509.
114 *Mirnye peregovory v Brest-Litovske*, 85–7, quotation on 85.
115 Hoffmann, *The War of Lost Opportunities*, 218–20; Diary entry for 12 January 1918. Czernin, *In the World War*, 237; *Proceedings of the Brest-Litovsk Peace Conference*, 82–3. The last remark was a reference to the Bolsheviks' violent dispersal of the Belarusian *Hromada* (council), which had convened in Minsk on 30 December.
116 Trotsky, *My Life*, 373.
117 *Mirnye peregovory v Brest-Litovske*, 85.
118 Trotsky, *My Life*, 375.
119 Bussche to Rosenberg, no. 209, 16 January 1918. NARA, RG 242, T 120, roll 1787, D 815321.
120 Kühlmann to the Foreign Office, no. 137, 17 January 1918. NARA, RG 242, T 120, roll 1787, D 815324.
121 Gautsch to the Foreign Ministry, no. 117, 30 December 1917. HHStA, PA I, K 1052.
122 *Proceedings of the Brest-Litovsk Peace Conference*, 115.
123 Leon Trotsky, *The History of the Russian Revolution to Brest-Litovsk* (London: G. Allen & Unwin, 1919), 135.

3 The Great January Strike as a Prelude to Revolution in Austria

1 See Horst Haselsteiner, "The Habsburg Empire in World War I: Mobilization of Food Supplies," in *East Central European Society in World War I*, ed. N.F. Dreisziger, Béla K. Király, and Albert A. Nofi (Boulder: Social Science Monographs, 1985), 87–102. The Austrian Food Ministry was known as *Ernährungsamt*.
2 Clifford F. Wargelin, "The Economic Collapse of Austro-Hungarian Dualism, 1914–1918," *East European Quarterly* 34, no. 3 (Fall 2000):281.
3 Penfield to the State Department, no. 1596, 13 May 1916. NARA, RG 84, Diplomatic Posts. Austria, vol. 449.
4 Maureen Healy, *Vienna and the Fall of the Habsburg Empire: Total War and Everyday Life in World War I* (Cambridge: Cambridge University Press, 2004), 84.
5 Penfield to the State Department, no. 2110, 22 October 1916. NARA, RG 84, Diplomatic Posts. Austria, vol. 449.

6 Protokoll über die Gemeinsame Sitzung der Parteivertretung, der Gewerkschaftskommission und des Wiener Vorstandes am 1. Juni 1917. Verein für Geschichte der Arbeiterbewegung, Partei-Archiv vor 1934, Mappe 2: Sitzungsprotokolle Parteivorstand etc., 27.7.1916 – 15.11.1921, 542a.
7 Hans Hautmann, "Vienna: A City in the Years of Radical Change 1917–1920," in *Challenges of Labour: Central and Western Europe, 1917–1920*, ed. Chris Wrigley (London and New York: Routledge, 1993), 93.
8 Richard Georg Plaschka, Horst Haselsteiner, and Arnold Suppan, *Innere Front: Militrässistenz, Widerstand und Umsturz in der Donaumonarchie 1918*, vol. 1: *Zwischen Streik und Meuterei* (Vienna: Verlag für Geschichte und Politik, 1974), 59–106; Richard Georg Plaschka, "The Army and Internal Conflict in the Austro-Hungarian Empire, 1918," in *East Central European Society in World War I*, ed. N.F. Dreisziger, Béla K. Király, and Albert A. Nofi (Boulder: Social Science Monographs, 1985), 338–53. In his excellent account, Plaschka pays special attention to the military measures the Austrian government and the AOK took to contain the strike. However, he does not discuss the negotiations between the social-democratic leadership and the government, the government's attempts to procure food, or any effects the strike had on policy in Brest-Litovsk and vice versa.
9 Karl Flanner, *Nieder mit dem Krieg! Für sofortigen Frieden!: Der grosse Jännerstreik in Wiener Neustadt* (Wiener Neustadt: Verein Museum und Archiv für Arbeit und Industrie im Viertel unter dem Wienerwald, 1997); Ernst Winkler, *Der grosse Jänner-Streik 1918: Ein Kampf für Brot, Frieden und Freiheit.* (Wiener Neustadt: Druck- und Verlagsanstalt Gutenberg, 1968); Siegfried Höppner, "Der Januarstreik im Jahre 1918 in Wien und Niederösterreich und die Sozialdemokratische Partei Österreichs," *Wissenschaftliche Zeitschrift der Humboldt-Universität zu Berlin* 7, no. 1 (January 1957):61–68; "Revolution unerwünscht: Die abgewürgte sozialistische Revolution vor 70 Jahren." *Wochenend Panorama*, 17 January 1988; for a socialist interpretation, which attributes the failure of the Great January Strike to lead to proletarian revolution to the absence of a revolutionary mass organization of the Bolshevik type in Austria at the time, see "80 Jahre Jännerstreik: Die Oktoberrevolution, die Sozialdemokratie und die österreichische Arbeiterklasse. Eine Broschüre der SJ SozAk (St. Pölten)," 7. VGA, Chronologisches Archiv, Lade 15, Mappe 27: Jännerstreik 1918.
10 Wargelin, "Bread, Peace, and Poland," 289–330; Bihl, *Österreich-Ungarn und die Friedensschlüsse von Brest-Litovsk*, 87–92. Wargelin's account focuses on the government's views of the movement, especially as expressed in Czernin's correspondence and the negotiations with

social-democratic leaders, and how these affected the foreign minister's ongoing negotiations with Ukraine. Bihl provides a schematic overview of the course of the strikes, without taking a stance.
11 Rauchensteiner, *The First World War and the End of the Habsburg Monarchy, 1914–1918*, 871.
12 Healy, *Vienna and the Fall of the Habsburg Empire*, 33.
13 The corresponding figures for wheat, rye, and barley for Hungary in 1917 were 81, 80, and 46, and for Russia in 1916 (the last harvest before the revolution) 80, 103, 85. Leo Grebler and Wilhelm Winkler, *The Cost of the World War to Germany and to Austria-Hungary* (New Haven: Yale University Press, 1940), 151, 153; Peter Gatrell, *Russia's First World War: A Social and Economic History* (New York: Pearson/Longman, 2005), 159.
14 Czernin to Demblin (for His Majesty), no. 2, 20 December 1917. HHStA, PA I, K 1078.
15 "Eine Revolution für den Frieden." *Arbeiter Zeitung*, 9 November 1917.
16 Protokoll der Sitzung des deutschen Parteivorstandes gemeinsam mit dem Wiener Vorstand, 16 November 1917; Protokoll der Sitzung des deutschen Parteivorstandes am 22. November 1917. VGA, PA vor 1934, M 2, 572–572a and 573–4.
17 Untitled activity report for 1917. VGA, PA vor 1934, M 27: Entwurf Organisationsstatut Arbeiterwehr. Feldschutzdienst. Von Bernaschek an Fritz Adler gesandte Unterlagen Geschichte der Arbeiterräte in Ober-Österreich.
18 *Um Friede, Freiheit und Recht: Der Jännerausstand des niederösterreichischen Proletariats* (Vienna: Verlag der Wiener Volksbuchhandlung Ignaz Brand, 1918), 3.
19 Ibid., 3.
20 Protokoll der Sitzung des deutschen Parteivorstandes am 6. Dezember 1917. VGA, PA vor 1934, M 2, 574–6.
21 Protokoll der Sitzung des deutschen Parteivorstandes am 22. Dezember 1917. VGA, PA vor 1934, M 2, 576–8.
22 Protokoll der Sitzung des deutschen Parteivorstandes am 3. Jänner 1918. VGA, PA vor 1934, M 2, 579–81.
23 Fürstenberg to the Foreign Ministry, no. 8, 6 January 1918. NARA, RG 242, T 120, roll 1787, D 814954.
24 Czernin to Hohenlohe (no. 5) and Flotow (no. 57), 8 January 1918. HHStA, PA I, K 1077: Brester Kanzlei 1917–1918.
25 Stellvertretender Generalstab der Armee, Abteilung IIIb, Abwehr, Abschrift 1002, 6 January 1918. NARA, RG 242, T 120, roll 1788, D 815507.

26 The Secretariat of the Social-Democratic Party of Styria (Lindner) to the Central Party Executive, no. 522, 7 January 1918. VGA, Sozialdemokratische Parteistellen, K 149, M 1078: Steiermark, 351.
27 Czech to Lindner, unnumbered, 10 January 1918. VGA, SDP, K 149, M 1078, 352.
28 Note des Kriegsministerium an das Ministerium des Innern über die bedrohliche Situation in Wiener Neustadt, 12 January 1918; Note des Kriegsministerium an das Ministerium für Landesverteidigung über die Agitation in den Daimlerwerken in Wiener Neustadt, 12 January 1918. Rudolf Neck, *Arbeiterschaft und Staat im Ersten Weltkrieg 1914–1918 (A. Quellen)*, vol. I: *Der Staat (2. Vom Juni 1917 bis zum Ende der Donaumonarchie im November 1918*, Veröffentlichungen der Arbeitsgemeinschaft für Geschichte der Arbeiterbewegung in Österreich 3 (Vienna: Europa-Verlag, 1968), 189–91.
29 Sammelbericht der Polizeidirektion Wien an das Ministerium des Innern über die sozialdemokratische Versammlungswelle für den Frieden, 10–15 January 1918. Ibid., 186–9; "Der Friedensbeschluss der Wiener Arbeiter." *Arbeiter Zeitung*, 15 January 1918.
30 *Um Friede, Freiheit und Recht*, 4.
31 The following reconstruction of events in Wiener Neustadt on 14 January is based on Telegramm der Lokomotivfabrik in Wiener Neustadt an das Eisenbahnministerium über den Ausbruch eines großen Streikes, 14 January 1918; Sammelakt des Ministerium des Innern mit den einlaufenden (meist telefonischen) Meldungen über den großen Streik in Niederösterreich, 14–24 January 1918. Neck, *Arbeiterschaft und Staat im Ersten Weltkrieg 1914–1918 (A. Quellen)*, I:196–7; Flanner, *Nieder mit dem Krieg!*, 11–13, brochures on 12; "Protest der Wiener Neustädter Arbeiter wegen der gekürzten Mehlquote." *Arbeiter Zeitung*, 16 January 1918.
32 Flanner, *Nieder mit dem Krieg!*, 23–4.
33 David Mandel, *The Petrograd Workers and the Fall of the Old Regime: From the February Revolution to the July Days, 1917* (New York: St. Martin's Press, 1983), 49; on the role of the *Putilovtsy* in the February Revolution, see also S.A. Smith, *Red Petrograd: Revolution in the Factories, 1917–1918* (Cambridge and New York: Cambridge University Press, 1983).
34 Flotow to Czernin, no. 113, 16 January 1918. HHStA, PA I, K 1081: Brester Kanzlei 1917–1918; *Um Friede, Freiheit und Recht*, 8.
35 Sammelakt des Ministerium des Innern mit den einlaufenden (meist telefonischen) Meldungen über den großen Streik in Niederösterreich, 14–24 January 1918. Neck, *Arbeiterschaft und Staat im Ersten Weltkrieg 1914–1918 (A. Quellen)*, I:199–202.

36 Landwehr to Czernin, unnumbered, 16 January 1918. HHStA, PA I, K 818-1 o): Lebensmittelnot von Mitte Jänner 1918 und die damit zusammenhängende Ausstandsbewegung (1918.01–1918.02).
37 *Um Friede, Freiheit und Recht*, 9.
38 "Arbeiter und Arbeiterinnen!" *Arbeiter Zeitung*, 16 January 1918.
39 Plaschka, Haselsteiner, and Suppan, *Innere Front*, 1:62.
40 Otto Bauer, *Die Österreichische Revolution* (Vienna: Wiener Volksbuchhandlung, 1923), 63. After the January strike, Bauer began to distance himself from the left radicals in the party, moving closer towards the moderate majority. His brief account of the strike in his study of the Austrian Revolution reflects this political reorientation. At the time, the Bulgarian minister plenipotentiary in Vienna and future prime minister, Andrei Toshev, whose reports to the Foreign Ministry in Sofia reveal an insightful observer, identified Bauer as the leader of the general strike. The Minister Plenipotentiary in Vienna (Toshev) to the Prime Minister (Radoslavov), no. 148, 22 January 1918. TsDA, f. 176, op. 3, a.e. 889, l. 9.
41 Ernst Hanisch, *Der große Illusionist: Otto Bauer (1881–1938)* (Vienna, Cologne, and Weimar: Böhlau, 2011), 91. Hanisch does not broach the question of Bauer's authorship of the manifesto either.
42 O. B., "Würzburg und Wien," *Der Kampf: Sozialdemokratische Monatsschrift* 10, no.11–12 (November-December 1917):320–8.
43 Herbert Steiner, "Otto Bauer und der Kampf um den Frieden 1917–1918," *Zeitgeschichte* 15, no. 4 (January 1988):138.
44 "A Turn in World Politics," in V.I. Lenin, *Collected Works*, vol. 23 (Moscow: Progress Publishers, 1964), 267.
45 The Chairman of the Russian Peace Delegation to Czernin, unnumbered, January 1918. Houghton Library, MS Rus 13, box 1, T 3.
46 *Um Friede, Freiheit und Recht*, 6.
47 Ministerium des Innern. Staatspolizeiliches Bureau. Abschrift. Vienna, 16 January 1918. HHStA, PA I, K 818-1 o).
48 Streng vertrauliche Meldung der Polizeidirektion Wien an das Ministerium des Innern über militärische Vorkehrungen, 16 January 1918. Neck, *Arbeiterschaft und Staat im Ersten Weltkrieg 1914–1918 (A. Quellen)*, I:242.
49 Bericht der Polizeidirektion Wien an das Ministerium des Innern über die Zunahme des Streiks. 16 January 1918. Ibid., 240–1.
50 "Streik in Wien und Niederösterreich," *Arbeiter Zeitung*, 17 January 1918.
51 Bericht der Polizeidirektion Wien an das Ministerium des Innern über die Ausbreitung des Streiks. 16 January 1918. Neck, *Arbeiterschaft und Staat im Ersten Weltkrieg 1914–1918 (A. Quellen)*, I:242–6.

52 Protokoll der Sitzung des deutschen Parteivorstandes am 16. Jänner 1918. VGA, PA vor 1934, M 2, 584.
53 *Um Friede, Freiheit und Recht*, 9.
54 Sammelakt des Ministerium des Innern mit den einlaufenden (meist telefonischen) Meldungen über den großen Streik in Niederösterreich, 14–24 January 1918. Neck, *Arbeiterschaft und Staat im Ersten Weltkrieg 1914–1918 (A. Quellen)*, I:208.
55 "Der Ausstand: Erklärung des Parteivorstandes." *Arbeiter Zeitung*, 17 January 1918.
56 "Die Erregung der Massen." *Arbeiter Zeitung*, 17 January 1918.
57 Charles Tilly, *From Mobilization to Revolution* (Reading: Addison-Wesley Pub. Co, 1978), 204.
58 Gatrell, *Russia's First World War*, 154–72; see also the classic contemporary study of government food regulation policy and its shortcomings, N.D. Kondrat'ev, *Rynok khlebov i ego regulirovanie vo vremia voiny i revoliutsii* (Moscow: Nauka, 1991 [1922]).
59 Czernin to Flotow (for His Majesty), no. 108, 15 January 1918. HHStA, PA I, K 1077. Coudenhove's letter is attached at the end.
60 Demblin to Czernin, no. 21, 16 January 1918. HHStA, PA I, K 1079.
61 Landwehr to Czernin, no. 109, 16 January 1918. HHStA, PA I, K 1079.
62 Kühlmann to the Foreign Ministry, no. 126, 16 January 1918. NARA, RG 242, T 120, roll 1787, D 815503.
63 Czernin to Landwehr, no. 121, 16 January 1918. HHStA, PA I, K 818-1 o).
64 Czernin to Flotow (for Seidler), no. 140, 17 January. HHStA, PA I, K 1077.
65 Hönning to the Foreign Ministry, no. 15, 17 January 1918. HHStA, PA I, K 818-1 o).
66 Hönning to the Foreign Ministry, no. 16, 20 January 1918. HHStA, PA I, K 818-1 o).
67 Von Ugron to the Foreign Ministry, no. 75, 22 January 1918. HHStA, PA I, K 818-1 o).
68 Thurn to the Foreign Ministry, no. 1, 20 January 1918. HHStA, PA I, K 818-1 o).
69 Müller (from Seidler and Landwehr) to Czernin (for the OHL), no. 163, 19 January 1918. HHStA, PA I, K 1079.
70 Hohenlohe to the Foreign Ministry, no. 43, 18 January 1918. HHStA, PA I, K 1079.
71 Lajos von Windischgrätz, *My Memoirs* (Boston and New York: Houghton Mifflin Company, 1921), 141–9, quotation on 146.
72 Czernin to the Foreign Ministry, no. 162, 19 January 1918 (copy of no. 12 from 16 January 1918 to Otto Czernin in Sofia). HHStA, PA I, K 818-1 o).

73 Otto Czernin to the Foreign Ministry, no. 32, 16 January 1918. HHStA, PA I, K 818-1 o).
74 Otto Czernin to the Foreign Ministry, no. 31, 16 January 1918. HHStA, PA I, K 818-1 o).
75 Otto Czernin to the Foreign Ministry, no. 33, 17 January 1918. HHStA, PA I, K 818-1 o).
76 Otto Czernin to the Foreign Ministry, no. 37, 18 January 1918. HHStA, PA I, K 818-1 o).
77 Otto Czernin to the Foreign Ministry, no. 48, 21 January 1918. HHStA, PA I, K 818-1 o).
78 Otto Czernin to the Foreign Ministry, no. 49, 21 January 1918. HHStA, PA I, K 818-1 o).
79 Otto Czernin to the Foreign Ministry, no. 51, 22 January 1918. HHStA, PA I, K 818-1 o).
80 Von Sendler to the Foreign Ministry, no. 59, 23 January 1918. HHStA, PA I, K 818-1 o).
81 Sammelakt des Ministerium des Innern über die Streikbewegung in der Steiermark, 17–24 January 1918. Neck, *Arbeiterschaft und Staat im Ersten Weltkrieg 1914–1918 (A. Quellen)*, I:265.
82 Müller to Czernin, no. 136, 17 January 1918. HHStA, PA I, K 1081.
83 Bericht der Polizeidirektion Wien an das Ministerium des Innern über die Verschärfung des Streiks, 17 January 1918. Neck, *Arbeiterschaft und Staat im Ersten Weltkrieg 1914–1918 (A. Quellen)*, I:252–62.
84 Czernin to the Foreign Ministry (for Flotow), no. 34, 17 January 1918. HHStA, PA I, K 818-1 o).
85 Flotow and Müller to Czernin, no. 139, 18 January 1918. HHStA, PA I, K 818-1 o).
86 *Um Friede, Freiheit und Recht*, 17.
87 Protokoll der Sitzung des deutschen Parteivorstandes am 17. Jänner 1918. VGA, PA vor 1934, M 2, 584–5.
88 *Um Friede, Freiheit und Recht*, 13–15.
89 "Arbeiter und Arbeiterinnen." *Arbeiter Zeitung*, 18 January 1918.
90 "Eine verpflichtende Erklärung." *Arbeiter Zeitung*, 18 January 1918.
91 Bussche to Rosenberg, no. 267, 19 January 1918. NARA, RG 242, T 120, roll 1788, D815605-D815606.
92 Arz to Czernin, no. 840, undated but not later than 18 January 1918. HHStA, PA I, K 1079.
93 Arz to Czernin, no. 842, 18 January 1918. HHStA, PA I, K 1079.
94 Demblin to Czernin, no. 22 and no. 24, 17 January 1918. HHStA, PA I, K 1079.

95 Bericht der Polizeidirektion Wien an das Ministerium des Innern über die weitere Ausdehnung des großen Streiks, 18 January 1918. Neck, *Arbeiterschaft und Staat im Ersten Weltkrieg 1914–1918 (A. Quellen)*, I:269–71.
96 Bericht der Polizeidirektion Wien an das Ministerium des Innern über die verschärfte Streiklage, 18 January 1918. Ibid., 274–5.
97 Müller to Czernin, no. 145, 18 January 1918. HHStA, PA I, K 818-1 o).
98 *Um Friede, Freiheit und Recht*, 23–4.
99 Karl Renner, "Die taktische Streit," *Der Kampf: Sozialdemokratische Monatsschrift* 11, no. 1 (January 1918):18–30, quotations on 23–4.
100 Julius Deutsch, "Radikale Strömungen," *Der Kampf: Sozialdemokratische Monatsschrift* 11, no. 2 (February 1918):71–8, quotation on 74.
101 *Um Friede, Freiheit und Recht*, 18.
102 Müller to Czernin, no. 156, 19 January 1918. HHStA, PA I, K 1081.
103 "Die ungarischen Arbeiter schliessen sich an." *Mitteilungen an die Arbeiter*, 19 January 1918.
104 József Galántai, *Hungary in the First World War* (Budapest: Akadémiai Kiadó, 1989), 278.
105 Bericht des Militärkommandos Pozsony an das Kriegsministerium über die Streikbewegung im Gebiet von Preßburg, 24 January 1918. Neck, *Arbeiterschaft und Staat im Ersten Weltkrieg 1914–1918 (A. Quellen)*, I:304–5.
106 Bussche to Rosenberg, no. 265, 19 January 1918. NARA, RG 242, T 120, roll 1788, N/A.
107 Hugh Wilson to the State Department, no. 2424, "The Economic Situation in Hungary," 19 February 1918. NARA, RG 59, M 367, roll 81.
108 Galántai, *Hungary in the First World War*, 278.
109 K.k. Ministerium des Innern. Staatspolizeiliches Bureau. Dritte und vierte zusammenfassende Informationen über die Arbeiterbewegung, 19 January 1918. HHSrA, PA I, K 818-1 o).
110 K.k. Ministerrats-Präsidium. Pressedepartement. Vienna, 20 January 1918. VGA, ChA, L 15, M 27; "Graf Czernin haftet und bürgt!" *Mitteilungen an die Arbeiter*, 19 January 1918.
111 *Um Friede, Freiheit und Recht*, 35–43; "Die Versammlung der Vertrauensmänner." *Mitteilungen an die Arbeiter*, 20 January 1918.
112 "Arbeiter und Arbeiterinnen!" *Mitteilungen an die Arbeiter*, 20 January 1918.
113 Bericht der Polizeidirektion Wien an das Ministerium des Innern über Versammlungen der Streikenden und weitere Streiks, 20 January 1918. Neck, *Arbeiterschaft und Staat im Ersten Weltkrieg 1914–1918 (A. Quellen)*, I:290–1. "Die Vorgänge am Sonntag." *Arbeiter Zeitung*, 21 January 1918.
114 Bericht der Polizeidirektion Wien an das Ministerium des Innern über den Abbruch der Streiks, 21 January 1918. Ibid., 295–6.

115 "Friede, Freiheit und Recht!" *Arbeiter Zeitung*, 22 January 1918.
116 Bericht der Polizeidirektion Wien an das Ministerium des Innern über die Wiederaufnahme der Arbeit, 22 January 1918. Neck, *Arbeiterschaft und Staat im Ersten Weltkrieg 1914–1918 (A. Quellen)*, I:298–300.
117 K.k. Ministerium des Innern. Staatspolizeiliches Bureau. Siebente zusamenfassende Inforation über die Arbeiterbewegung, 23 January 1918. HHStA, PA I, K 818-1 o).
118 *Um Friede, Freiheit und Recht*, 48.
119 K.k. Ministerium des Innern. Staatspolizeiliches Bureau. Abschrift des Berichtes des Landespräsidiums in Troppau vom 24. Jänner 1918. HHStA, PA I, K 818-1 o).
120 K.k. Ministerium des Innern. Staatspolizeiliches Bureau. Troppau, 2 February 1918. HHStA, PA I, K 818-1 o).
121 The Representative of the Imperial and Royal Ministry of Foreign Affairs at the AOK to Czernin, no. 26615, 9 February 1918. HHStA, PA I, K 818-1 o).
122 K.k. Ministerium des Innern. Staatspolizeiliches Bureau. Telephone messages from Trieste from 29 January and 1 February 1918. HHStA, PA I, K 818-1 o).
123 Seidler to Czernin, unnumbered, 1 February 1918. HHStA, PA I, K 818-1 o).
124 Bruno Frei, *Die Roten Matrosen von Cattaro: Eine Episode aus dem Revolutionsjahre 1918* (Vienna: Verlag der Wiener Volsbuchhandlung, 1927), 21; the best scholarly analysis of the Cattaro Mutiny is Richard Georg Plaschka, *Cattaro-Prag, Revolte und Revolution: Kriegsmarine und Heer Österreich-Ungarns im Feuer der Aufstandsbewegungen vom 1. Februar und 28. Oktober 1918* (Graz and Cologne: Verlag Hermann BohlausNachf, 1963), 15–192.
125 Theda Skocpol, *States and Social Revolutions: A Comparative Analysis of France, Russia, and China* (Cambridge and New York: Cambridge University Press, 1979), 285.
126 Bauer, *Die Österreichische Revolution*, 65–6.

4 The Brest-Litovsk System and Modern Ukrainian Statehood

1 A comprehensive overview of the vast literature on the Ukrainian Revolution and the plethora of historiographical debates is beyond the scope of this chapter. Some of the most important recent works on the subject include V.F. Soldatenko, *Revoliutsiina doba v Ukraini (1917–1920 roky): Lohika piznannia, istorychni postati, kliuchovi episody* (Kiev: Parlament'ske vyd-vo, 2011); V.F. Soldatenko, *Ukraina v revoliutsiinu dobu: Istorychni ese-khroniky*, 4 vols (Kiev: Svitogliad, 2010); V.F. Soldatenko, *Ukrains'ka*

revoliutsia: Kontseptsiia ta istoriohrafiia (Kiev: Poshukovo-vydavnyche ahenstvo "Knyha pam'iati Ukrainy, 1997); V.A Smolii et al., *Narysy istorii ukrains'koï revoliutsii 1917–1921 rokiv*, 2 vols. (Kiev: Naukova dumka, 2011); the classic early Ukrainian émigré studies are Volodymyr Vynnychenko, *Vidrozhdennia Natsii*, 3 vols. (Kiev and Vienna: Dzvin, 1920); Pavlo Khrystiuk, *Zamitky i materialy do istorii Ukrains'koi revoliutsii*, 4 vols. (Vienna: Sotsiologichnyi ukrains'kyi instytut, 1921); the most notable subsequent Ukrainian émigré studies published in English are Fedyshyn, *Germany's Drive to the East and the Ukrainian Revolution, 1917–1918*; O.S. Pidhainy, *The Formation of the Ukrainian Republic* (Toronto and New York: New Review Books, 1966); John Stephen Reshetar, *The Ukrainian Revolution, 1917–1920: A Study in Nationalism* (Princeton: Princeton University Press, 1952).

2 Wolfram Dornik, ed., *Die Ukraine zwischen Selbstbestimmung und Fremdherrschaft 1917–1922* (Graz: Leykam, 2011); Wolfram Dornik and Stefan Karner, eds., *Die Besatzung der Ukraine 1918: Historischer Kontext, Forschungsstand, wirtschaftliche und soziale Folgen* (Graz, Vienna, and Klagenfurt: Verein zur Förderung der Forschung von Folgen nach Konflikten und Kriegen, 2008); Caroline Milow, *Die ukrainische Frage 1917–1923 im Spannungsfeld der europäischen Diplomatie* (Wiesbaden: Harrassowitz Verlag, 2002).

3 Pavlo Khrystiuk, *Zamitky i materialy do istorii Ukrains'koi revoliutsii*, vol. 1 (Vienna: Sotsiologichnyi ukrains'kyi instytut, 1921), 20.

4 V.F. Verstiuk, "Ukrains'ka Tsentral'na Rada i ukrainizatsiia viis'kovykh chastyn rossiis'koi armii," *Ukrainski Istorichni Zhurnal*, no. 3 (2012):27.

5 On Austro-German subversion in general and their relations with the Union for the Liberation of Ukraine in particular, see Fedyshyn, *Germany's Drive to the East and the Ukrainian Revolution, 1917–1918*, 30–41; Hoffman, "The Ukrainian Adventure of the Central Powers, 1914–1918," 12–84; on the League of Russia's Foreign Peoples, see Seppo Zetterberg, *Die Liga der Fremdvölker Russlands 1916–1918: Ein Beitrag zu Deutschlands antirussischem Propagandakrieg unter den Fremdvölkern Russlands im Ersten Weltkrieg* (Helsinki: Finnische Historische Gesellschaft, 1978).

6 "V ukrainskikh organizatsiiakh." *Kievskaia mysl'*, 5 (18) March 1917. In V.F. Verstiuk, ed., *Ukrains'ka Tsentral'na Rada: Dokumenty i materialy u dvokh tomakh*, vol. 1: *4 bereznia-9 hrudnia 1917 r.* (Kiev: Nauk. dumka, 1996).

7 Proclamation of the Ukrainian People's Republic. Rex A. Wade, ed., *Documents of Soviet Foreign Policy: The Triumph of Bolshevism, 1917–1919*, vol. 1, Documents of Soviet History (Gulf Breeze: Academic International Press, 1991), 38–40.

8 Szechenyi to Czernin. Übersendung eines Berichtes über die Bildungder ukrain. autonomen Republik im Rahmen eines russ. Föderativstaates, über die Machtbefugnisse der ukrain. Zentralrada und über die Agrarfrage. 21 August 1917. Theophil Hornykiewicz, ed., *Ereignisse in der Ukraine 1914–1922, deren bedeutung und historische Hintergründe*, vol. 1 (Philadelphia: W.K. Lypynsky East European Research Institute, 1966), 264–5.
9 Übersicht über die Russische Fremdbevölkerung. Stand vom 12 Dezember 1917. NARA, RG 242, T 120, roll 1792, D 818464-D 818471.
10 Rosenberg to the Foreign Ministry, no. 96, 16 December 1917. NARA, RG 242, T 120, roll 1792, D 818456-D818457.
11 Hoffman, "The Ukrainian Adventure of the Central Powers, 1914–1918"; Fedyshyn, *Germany's Drive to the East and the Ukrainian Revolution, 1917–1918*; for the opposite view, see Peter Borowsky, "Germany's Ukrainian Policy during World War I and the Revolution of 1918-19," in *German-Ukrainian Relations in Historical Perspective* (Edmonton and Toronto: Canadian Institute of Ukrainian Studies Press, 1994), 84–95.
12 Vidozva Heneral'noho sekretariatu do voiniv-ukraintsyv Pivdenno-Zakhidnoho ta Rumuns'koho frontiv i tylu. 4 (17) December 1917. Verstiuk, *Ukrains'ka Tsentral'na Rada*, 1:500–2, quotation on 501.
13 Protokoly zasidan' Heneral'noho sekretariatu. 6–8 (19–21) December 1917. Ibid., 521–3.
14 Hoffmann, *The War of Lost Opportunities*, 217.
15 Diary entry for 6 January 1918. Czernin, *In the World War*, 232.
16 V.A. Antonov-Ovseenko, *Zapiski o Grazhdanskoi voine*, vol. 1 (Moscow: Gosudarstvennoe Izdatel'stvo, 1924), 48.
17 V.F. Soldatenko, *Grazhdanskaia voina v Ukraine (1917–1920 gg.)* (Moscow: Novyi khronohraf, 2012), 96; V.F. Soldatenko, *Revoliutsüni al'ternatyvy 1917 roku i Ukraina* (Kiev: Naukova dumka, 2010), 292–303.
18 Pavlo Hai-Nyzhnyk, *UNR ta ZUNR: Stanovlennia orhaniv vlady i natsional'ne derzhavotvorennia: 1917–1920 rr.* (Kiev: Shchek, 2010), 275; see also V. Doroshkevich and N. Voloshyn, "Nezalezhnist' Ukrainy: Nova sproba. Zaglian'mo do radianskikh dzherel," *Literaturna Ukraina*, no. 3 (1991).
19 V.A. Antonov-Ovseenko – Sovnarkom, 25 December 1917. A.V. Kvashonkin, ed., *Bol'shevistskoe rukovodstvo: Perepiska 1912-1927*, Seriia "Dokumenty sovetskoi istorii" (Moscow: ROSSPEN, 1996), 30–2.
20 Soldatenko, *Grazhdanskaia voina v Ukraine (1917–1920 gg.)*, 96.
21 Protokoly zasidan' Heneral'noho sekretariatu. 24 December 1917. Verstiuk, ed., *Ukrains'ka Tsentral'na Rada*: 2, 13.
22 Gautsch to Wiesner, no. 1, 1 January 1918. HHStA, PA I, K 1077.
23 Fokke, "Na stsene i za kulisami," 162.

24 Volodymyr Vynnychenko, *Vidrozhdennia natsii*, vol. 2 (Kiev and Vienna: Dzvin, 1920), 202–3.
25 Vynnychenko, *Vidrozhdennia natsii*, 2:135–6.
26 Frank Golczewski, *Deutsche und Ukrainer 1914–1939* (Paderborn: Schöningh, 2010), 194.
27 Protokoll der ersten Vorbesprechung mit den ukrain. Delegierten. 4 January 1918. Hornykiewicz, ed., *Ereignisse in der Ukraine 1914–1922*, vol. 2: 49–52.
28 Protokoll der zweiten Vorbesprechung mit den ukrain. Delegierten. 4 January 1918. Ibid., 52–5.
29 Protokoll der gemeinsamen Sitzung der verbündeten Delegationen mit den ukrain. Delegierten. 6 January 1918. Ibid., 58–64.
30 The following reconstruction of events (the two meetings and dinner on 6 January) is based on Popov to Radoslavov, unnumbered, 6 January 1918. TsDA, f. 313k, op. 1, a.e. 2463, l. 185–7.
31 A good example of Soviet historiography on the subject is Chervinkiv-Koroliov, "Pro zmovu nimets'koho imperializmu z Tsentral'noiu Radoiu u Brest-Lytovsku v 1918 r."; the recent Russian-language study is Mikhutina, *Ukrainskii Brestskii mir*, esp. 143–212. For more on Mikhutina, see my review in *Ab Imperio: Studies of New Imperial History and Nationalism in the Post-Soviet Space* no. 4 (2012):470–6.
32 Trotsky, *My Life*, 376.
33 *Proceedings of the Brest-Litovsk Peace Conference*, 56–8.
34 Ibid., 59.
35 Ganchev to Radoslavov, no. 2300, 11 January 1918 and no. 2303, 13 January 1918. TsDA, f. 313k, op. 1, a.e. 2465, l. 34, 43.
36 Protokoll der allgemeinem vertraulichen Besprechung zwischen der deutschen und der ukrain. Delegation. 13 January 1918. Hornykiewicz, ed., *Ereignisse in der Ukraine 1914–1922*, 2:80–7.
37 Hoffmann, *The War of Lost Opportunities*, 220–1.
38 Ibid., 222.
39 Protokoll der Besprechung zwischen der deutschen, österr.-ung. und ukrain. Delegation. 16 January 1918. Hornykiewicz, *Ereignisse in der Ukraine 1914–1922*, 2:106–10.
40 See Pieter M. Judson, *Guardians of the Nation: Activists on the Language Frontiers of Imperial Austria* (Cambridge, MA: Harvard University Press, 2006).
41 Storck to Czernin, no. 26131, 22 Jan 1918. "Die österreichische Ukrainer und die Friedensverhandlungen." HHStA, PA I, K 1041–2 Krieg 58: Angelegenheiten der Ukraine (1918.01–1918.10).

42 Stenographische Protokolle über die Sitzungen des Hauses der Abgeordneten des österreichischen Reichsrates. XXII. Session, III. Band. 19 February 1918. Hornykiewicz, ed., *Ereignisse in der Ukraine 1914–1922*, 1:290.
43 On the West Ukrainian People's Republic, see Vasyl Kuchabsky, *Western Ukraine in Conflict with Poland and Bolshevism, 1918–1923* (Edmonton and Toronto: Canadian Institute of Ukrainian Studies, 2009); Vasyl Rasevych, "Die westukrainische Volksrepublik von 1918/19," in *Die Ukraine zwischen Selbstbestimmung und Fremdherrschaft 1917–1922*, ed. Wolfram Dornik (Graz: Leykam, 2011), 181–200.
44 On the role of political borders in the emergence of modern nation states, see Peter Sahlins, *Boundaries: The Making of France and Spain in the Pyrenees* (Berkeley: University of California Press, 1989); on the importance of borders and borderlands for foreign policy. see Emily S. Rosenberg, "Considering Borders," in *Explaining the History of American Foreign Relations*, ed. Michael J. Hogan and Thomas G. Paterson, 2nd ed. (Cambridge: Cambridge University Press, 2007).
45 Müller to Demblin (for His Majesty), no. 12, 18 January 1918. HHStA, PA XL: Interna, K 262: Telegramme an Grafen Demblin (1917–1918).
46 Czernin to Müller (for Demblin, resp. His Majesty), unnumbered, 19 January 1918. HHStA, PA I, K 1077.
47 Diary entry for 20 January 1918. Czernin, *In the World War*, 241.
48 Von Ugron to the Foreign Ministry, no. 62, 10 February 1918. HHStA, PA I, K 1080.
49 Von Ugron to the Foreign Ministry, no. 65, 11 February 1918. HHStA, PA I, K 1080.
50 Wargelin, "Bread, Peace, and Poland," 371–2.
51 Protokoll eines am 22. Jänner 1918 unter Seiner k.u.k. Apostolischen Majestät abgehaltenen Kronrates. Miklósné Komjáthy, ed., *Protokolle des Gemeinsamen Ministerrates der Österreichisch-Ungarischen Monarchie (1914–1918)* (Budapest, Akadémiai Kiadó, 1966), 627–33; a thorough if somewhat melodramatic account of the council is also available in Czernin's diary. See Diary entry for 22 January 1918. Czernin, *In the World War*, 241–5.
52 Wargelin, "A High Price for Bread," 758.
53 Müller to Demblin (for His Majesty), no. 12, 18 January 1918. HHStA, PA XL, K 262.
54 Pavlo Khrystiuk, *Zamitky i materialy do istorii Ukrains'koi revoliutsii*, vol. 2 (Vienna: Sotsiologichnyi ukrains'kyi instytut, 1921), 77.
55 The Royal Legation in Stockholm to the Ministry of Foreign Affairs and Confessions in Sofia, no. 169, 25 January 1918. TsDA, f. 176k, op. 3, a.e. 700, l. 106.

56 Karakhan to Kuzmin and Reizon, January 1918. Houghton Library, MS 13, box 1, T 5.
57 Fokke, "Na stsene i za kulisami," 128; Trotsky to Kühlmann, unnumbered, 3 February 1918. NARA, RG 242, T 120, roll 1787, D 815344.
58 Vynnychenko, *Vidrozhdennia natsii*, 2:284–5.
59 Wlodzimierz Medrzecki, "Germany and Ukraine between the Start of the Brest-Litovsk Peace Talks and Hetman Skoropadskyi's Coup," *Harvard Ukrainian Studies* 23, no. 1/2 (June 1999):49.
60 Vynnychenko, *Vidrozhdennia Natsii*, 2: 289; Horak, *The First Treaty of World War I*, 45.
61 Khrystiuk, *Zamitky i materialy do istorii Ukrains'koi revoliutsii*, 2:114–15.
62 Golczewski, *Deutsche und Ukrainer 1914–1939*, 322–3.
63 Protokoll der Sitzung der österreichisch-ungarisch-ukrainischen Komission die Abfassung des Kollektivfriedensvertrages zwischen Deutschland, Österreich-Ungarn, Bulgarien und der Tuerkei einerseitz und der Ukrainischen Volksrepublik anderseitz. 7 Feb 1918. HHStA, PA I, K 1082: Brester Kanzlei.
64 Medrzecki, "Germany and Ukraine," 58.
65 Riedl to the Foreign Ministry (for Wiesner), unnumbered, 17 Feb. HHStA, PA X: Rußland, K 152: Entwicklung des russischen Reiches zu einer Pluralität von Staaten (1917–1918).
66 Müller to Storck, no. 3196, 12 Mar 1918. HHStA, PA X, K 152.
67 Army High Command, Chief of the General Staff to the Foreign Ministry, no. 1326, 29 Mar 1918. HHStA, PA X, K 152.
68 Terry Martin, *The Affirmative Action Empire: Nations and Nationalism in the Soviet Union, 1923–1939* (Ithaca: Cornell University Press, 2001); the three phases of Hroch's original model are: non-political scholarly interest in language, folk customs, and traditions (Phase A); the formation of a nationalist elite (Phase B); the rise of a mass national movement (Phase C). Miroslav Hroch, *Social Preconditions of National Revival in Europe: A Comparative Analysis of the Social Composition of Patriotic Groups among the Smaller European Nations* (New York: Columbia University Press, 2000). Hroch originally developed the model in the late 1960s in Czech- and German-language publications.
69 Vynnychenko, *Vidrozhdennia natsii*, 1:255.
70 Recent scholarship on Latvia and Estonia has focused on the escalating levels of violence in the pursuit of competing alternatives of statehood during this period. See Taavo Minnik, "The Cycle of Terror in Estonia, 1917–1919: On Its Preconditions and Major Stages," *Journal of Baltic Studies* 46, no. 1 (2015):35–47; Aldis Minins, "Latvia, 1918–1920: A Civil War?," *Journal of Baltic Studies* 46, no. 1 (2015):49–63.

71 Steven L. Guthier, "The Popular Base of Ukrainian Nationalism in 1917," *Slavic Review* 38, no. 1 (Spring 1979):32.
72 Stephen Velychenko, "Ukrainian Anticolonialist Thought in Comparative Perspective. A Preliminary Overview," *Ab Imperio: Studies of New Imperial History and Nationalism in the Post-Soviet Space* no. 4 (2012):339–71.
73 Hai-Nyzhnyk, *UNR ta ZUNR*, 18.
74 K.k. Gendarmeriekommandant für Galizien und die Bukowina in Czernowitz to the Foreign Ministry, no. 435, 19 June 1918. "Bericht über die ukrainische Verhältnisse." HHStA, PA X, K 153: Entwicklung des russischen Reiches zu einer Pluralität von Staaten (1917–1918).
75 Diary entry for 19 March 1918. V.I. Vernadsky, *Dnevniki 1917–1921: Oktiabr' 1917 – ianvar' 1920* (Kiev: Naukova dumka, 1994), 60.
76 Diary entry for 12 April 1918. Ibid., 70.
77 K.k. Ministerium für Landesverteidigung, no. 12864/XX. 1 May 1918. "Politische und wirtschaftliche Zustände in den an Galizien und die Bukowina angrenzenden ukrainischen und bessarabischen Gebieten." HHStA, PA X, K 152.
78 Medrzecki, "Germany and Ukraine," 56.
79 Hai-Nyzhnyk, *UNR ta ZUNR*, 23.
80 Christopher Read, *From Tsar to Soviets: The Russian People and Their Revolution, 1917–1921* (New York: Oxford University Press, 1996).
81 See Arthur E. Adams, "The Great Ukrainian Jacquerie," in *The Ukraine, 1917–1921: A Study in Revolution*, ed. Taras Hunczak (Cambridge: Distributed by Harvard University Press for the Harvard Ukrainian Research Institute, 1977), 247–71.
82 Von Ugron to the Foreign Ministry, no. 355, 1 May 1918. HHStA, PA X, K 152.
83 "Doklad nachal'niku operatsionnogo otdeleniia germanskogo vostochnogo fronta o polozhenii del na Ukraine v marte 1918 goda." *Arkhiv Russkoi Revoliutsii* 20 (1930):288.
84 Trauttmansdorff to the Foreign Ministry, no. 28443, 5 Apr 1918. HHStA, PA X, K 152.
85 Khrystiuk, *Zamitky i materialy do istorii Ukrains'koi revoliutsii*, 2:136–7.
86 Forgách to the Foreign Ministry, no. 78, 28 March 1918. HHStA, PA X, K 152.
87 Princig an das k. u. k. Min. d. Äussern: Besprechung beim General Gröner über politisch und militärisch sich immer mehr zuspitzende Lage in der Ukraine. 25 April 1918. Hornykiewicz, *Ereignisse in der Ukraine 1914–1922*, 1:400–2.
88 Von Princig to the Foreign Ministry, no. 248/2537, 25 April 1918. HHStA, PA X, K 152.
89 Von Princig to the Ministry, no. 253/2561, 26 April 1918. HHStA, PA X, K 152.

90 Von Princig to the Foreign Ministry, no. 266/2620, 28 April 1918. HHStA, PA X, K 152. For more on the Dobryi Affair and the Committee for the Salvation of Ukraine, see Pavlo Hai-Nyzhnyk, "Vikradennia bankira A. Dobroho v kvitni 1918 roku (rekonstruktsiia ta analiz podii)," *Naukovi zapiski: Seriia pedahohichni ta istorychni nauky*, no. 120 (2014):212–28.
91 Medrzecki, "Germany and Ukraine," 59.
92 Äusserungen eines anonymen Verfassers über österreichische und deutsche Politik in der Ukraine. Hornykiewicz, *Ereignisse in der Ukraine 1914–1922*, 1:322–6.
93 See Wayne Dowler, *Russia in 1913* (DeKalb: Northern Illinois University Press, 2010), esp. 90–190.
94 The following discussion is based on two reports – one by the Austro-Hungarian military commander in Odessa, Count Kirchbach, and another by the Bulgarian representative in the General Staff of Army Group Mackensen, Lieutenant Colonel Popov. Arz to Czernin, no. 1329, 30 Apr 1918. HHStA, PA X, K 152; Shtab na Deistvuiushtata Armiia, Otdel operativen, Otdelenie vunshno-politichesko, Sektsiia adm-stopanska, no. 1604, 10 Apr 1918. "Prepis ot donesenieto na bulgarskiia predstavitel pri Shtaba na Grupata Makenzen po obshtoto politichesko polozhenie v iuzhna Rusiia sled idvaneto na germanskite voiski tam." TsDA, f. 176k, op. 3, a.e. 700, l. 227–34.
95 Unskilled labourers in Kiev in 1918 typically earned around 8 rubles per day, and lower level government clerks around 8–10.5 rubles. For a detailed discussion of prices and wages in revolutionary Ukraine, see Velychenko, *State Building in Revolutionary Ukraine*, 305–16.
96 Hai-Nyzhnyk, *UNR ta ZUNR*, 64.
97 Army High Command, Chief of General Staff to the Foreign Ministry, no. 1356, 1 Apr 1918. HHStA, PA X, K 152.
98 Forgách to the Foreign Ministry, no. 507, 2 Jun 1918. HHStA, PA X, K 152.
99 Pavlo Skoropadskyi, *Spohady: Kinets' 1917 – hruden' 1918*, ed. Jaroslav Pelenski (Kiev and Philadelphia: Institut ukrains'koi akheohrafii ta dzhereloznanstva im. M.S. Hrushevs'koho, 1995).
100 Fedyshyn, *Germany's Drive to the East and the Ukrainian Revolution, 1917–1918*, 133–84; Taras Hunczak, "The Ukraine under Hetman Pavlo Skoropadskyi," in *The Ukraine, 1917–1921: A Study in Revolution*, ed. Taras Hunczak (Cambridge, MA: Distributed by Harvard University Press for the Harvard Ukrainian Research Institute, 1977), 74.
101 See, for example, V.F. Soldatenko, *Ukraina v revoliutsiinu dobu: Istorychni ese-khroniky*, vol. 2: *Rik 1918* (Kiev: Svitogliad, 2010).
102 Forgách to the Foreign Ministry, no. 496, 31 May 1918. HHStA, PA X, K 152.

103 Vernadsky, *Dnevniki 1917–1921*, 85–123.
104 A.A Tatishchev, *Zemli i liudi: v gushche pereselencheskogo dvizheniia, 1906–1921* (Moscow: Russkii put', 2001), 301.
105 Velychenko, *State Building in Revolutionary Ukraine*, 109.
106 Tatishchev, *Zemli i liudi*, 304–6.
107 Forgách an Burián, no.61, 5 July 1918. "Bericht über die Bemühungen des Hetmans und seiner Regierung in der Frage der Ukrainisierung sowie über die sehr schwierige Lage des Hetmans in Anbetracht eines immer akuter werdenden Kampfes zwischen großrussischen und ukrainisch-nationalen Strömungen." Hornykiewicz, *Ereignisse in der Ukraine 1914–1922*, 3:141–7.
108 Skoropadsky, *Spohady*, 125–6.
109 Trauttmansdorff to Burián, no. 30,862, 30 June 1918. K. u. k. AOK, Operations Abteilung." Vertrauliche Nachrichte (no. 554a). HHStA, PA X, K 152.
110 Velychenko, *State Building in Revolutionary Ukraine*, 107.
111 Skoropadsky, *Spohady*, 267.
112 K.k. Gendarmeriekommandant für Galizien und die Bukowina in Czernowitz, no. 435, 19 June 1918. "Bericht über die ukrainische Verhältnisse." HHStA, PA X, K 153.
113 Tatishchev, *Zemli i liudi*, 312.
114 Skoropadsky, *Spohady*, 50.
115 Forgách to Burián, no. 30/Pol, 31 May 1918. "Repressivmassregeln gegen die Unruhen auf dem Lande und Proteste dagegen." HHStA, PA X, K 152.
116 Forgách to the Foreign Ministry, no. 542, 9 June 1918; Forgách to the Foreign Ministry, no.549, 11 June 1918. HHStA, PA X, K 152.
117 Fürstenberg to the Foreign Ministry, no. 739 and 741, 30 July 1918. HHStA, PA X, K 153.
118 Forgách to the Foreign Ministry, no. 802, 13 August 1918. HHStA, PA X, K 153.
119 Fürstenberg to Andrássy, no. 116/Pol, 25 October 1918. HHStA, PA X, K 153.
120 Soldatenko, *Grazhdanskaia voina v Ukraine (1917–1920 gg.)*, 234–52.
121 Timothy Snyder, *The Red Prince: The Secret Lives of a Habsburg Archduke* (New York: Basic Books, 2008), 5.
122 "Memuary Vilhelma Habsburha, Polkovnika USS: Avtobiografiia," 1919, <http://www.parafia.org.ua/biblioteka/istoriya-mova/ukrajinskyj-patriot-iz-dynastiji-habsburhiv/dokumenty-1-2-memuary-ertshertsoha-vilhelma-habsburha-lotrinhena/>.
123 Nikifor Hirniak, *Polkovnik Vasyl Vyshyvanyi* (Winnipeg: D. Mykytiuk, 1956), 13.

124 Snyder, *The Red Prince*, 101–2.
125 Bohdan Hnatevich, ed., *Ukrains'ki Sichovi Stril'tsi 1914–1920* (Lviv: Slovo, 1991), 97.
126 Vasyl Vyshyvanyi, "Ukrains'ki Sichovi Stril'tsi z vesni 1918 r. do perevorotu v Avstrii," in *Polkovnik Vasyl Vyshyvany*i (Winnipeg: D. Mykytiuk, 1956), 49.
127 Hnatevich, *Ukrains'ki Sichovi Stril'tsi 1914–1920*, 102.
128 Quoted in Snyder, *The Red Prince*, 104.
129 Frank Golczewski, *Deutsche und Ukrainer 1914–1939*, 273.
130 Hnatevich, *Ukrains'ki Sichovi Stril'tsi 1914–1920*, 98.
131 Hirniak, *Polkovnik Vasyl Vyshyvanyi*, 17.
132 Hnatevich, *Ukrains'ki Sichovi Stril'tsi 1914–1920*, 100–1.
133 Vyshyvanyi, "Ukrains'ki Sichovi Stril'tsi z vesni 1918 r. do perevorotu v Avstrii," 51.
134 Trauttmansdorff to Burián, no. 30,273, 9 Jun 1918. Beilage: K. u. k. Armeeoberkommando, Nachrichten Abteilung, no. 13,078, "Zukünftige Gestaltung in der Ukraina. Standort am 6.Juni 1918." HHStA, PA X, K 152.
135 Trauttmansdorff to Burián, no. 30,070, 1 Jun 1918. "Gerüchte in der Ukraina über eine Thronkandidatur Erzherzog Wilhelms." HHStA, PA X, K 154-1-2 8): Tätigkeit Erzherzog Wilhelms in der Ukraine und seine Abberufung, 1918.06–1918.10.
136 Hirniak, *Polkovnik Vasyl Vyshyvanyi*, 19–23.
137 Ibid., 27–8.
138 Forgách to Burián, no. 604, 24 Jun 1918. HHStA, PA X, K 154.
139 Forgách to Burián, no. 574, 16 Jun 1918. HHStA, PA X, K 154.
140 Vyshyvanyi, "Ukrains'ki Sichovi Stril'tsi z vesni 1918 r. do perevorotu v Avstrii," 51.
141 Ibid., 53.
142 "Memuary Vilhelma Habsburha, Polkovnika USS."
143 Entwurf eines an AH. Handschreibens an S.M. Kaiser Wilhelm den ... Juli 1918. HHStA, PA I, K 523: Liasse XLVII/12d, Beziehungen Erzherzog Wilhelms zu ukrainischen Notabilitäten (1918.05)
144 Von Marsovszky to Burián, no. 183, 21 Aug 1918; Forgách to Burián, no.851, 23 Aug 1918. HHStA, PA I, K 154.
145 Trauttmansdorff to Burián, no. 32,390, 30 Aug 1918. HHStA, PA I, K 154.
146 Entwurf eines Allerhöchsten Telegrammes an Seine k.u.k. Hoheit Erzherzog Wilhelm. HHStA, PA I, K 523.
147 Trauttmansdorff to Burián, no. 32,573, 7 Sep 1918. HHStA, PA X, K 154.
148 Hnatevich, *Ukrains'ki Sichovi Stril'tsi 1914–1920*, 129–33.
149 Steinwedel, "To Make a Difference," 81.

5 Brest-Litovsk and the Elusive Bulgarian "Dream of Byzantium"

1 Bernard Lory, "Une guerre invisible? La mémoire de la Première Guerre mondiale en Bulgarie," *Guerres mondiales et conflits contemporains* 57, no. 228 (October 2007):37–49; a good English-language introduction to Bulgaria's involvement in the war, which focuses mostly on military history, is Richard C. Hall, "Bulgaria in the First World War," *Historian* 73, no. 2 (2011):300–15.
2 Aleksandrov, *Brest-Litovskiiat miren dogovor 1918 g.*, 191–220; Georgi Markov, *Goliamata voina i bulgarskata strazha mezhdu sredna Evropa i Orienta, 1916–1919* (Sofia: Akademichno izdatelstvo "Prof. Marin Drinov," 2006), 143–86; Liliana V. Vladeva, "Brest-Litovskiiat mir i Bulgariia," *Izvestiia na durzhavnite arkhivi*, no. 72 (1996):47–61; Gencho Kamburov, "Raznoglasiia v Chetvorniia suiuz pri pregovorite v Brest-Litovsk i Bukuresht prez 1918 g.," *Istoricheski pregled* 27, no. 3 (June 1971):48–58.
3 Serhy Yekelchyk, "A Long Goodbye: The Legacy of Soviet Marxism in Post-Communist Ukrainian Historiography," *Ab Imperio: Studies of New Imperial History and Nationalism in the Post-Soviet Space* no. 4 (2012):401.
4 I have borrowed this phrase from Stephen Constant, a biographer of Bulgaria's King Ferdinand, who uses it in a narrow sense to explain Ferdinand's growing fascination with the seemingly imminent conquest of Constantinople in November – December 1912, during the First Balkan War. "Hitherto Byzantium had been a romantic fancy, a *fin-de-siècle* historical pose in which he could indulge by having his portrait painted as emperor of Byzantium, a means of impressing his guests, a harmless exercise in home theatricals. But now, with the applause of Europe ringing in his ears, the idea of Byzantium assumed what his French secretary, the poet Paul de Chèvremont, called 'a perilous consistency.' Fancy was becoming reality." Stephen Constant, *Foxy Ferdinand, Tsar of Bulgaria* (New York: Franklin Watts, 1980), 259.
5 Mark Mazower, *The Balkans: A Short History* (New York: Modern Library, 2000), 96.
6 See MacMillan, *Paris 1919*, 347–65, 427–58; Nicholas X. Rizopoulos, "Greece at the Paris Peace Conference, 1919: Venizelos and the Greek Territorial Problem: From the Armistice to Versailles (November 1918 – June 1919)" (PhD diss., Yale University, 1963).
7 See, for example, Vasil Radoslavov, *Bulgariia i svetovnata kriza* (Sofia: Sava Todorov, 1923), chap. 1; Radoslavov's book was also published in German the same year as *Bulgarien und die Weltkrise*; Hall, "Bulgaria in the First World War," 301.

8 William N. Medlicott, *The Congress of Berlin and After: A Diplomatic History of the Near Eastern Settlement, 1878-1880* (Hamden: Archon Books, 1963); Eric Weitz has pointed out the role of the Congress of Berlin in the long term transformation within international relations from a focus on dynastic legitimacy and state-sovereignty to population politics, as demonstrated by the creation of states linked to specific national groups (Romanians, Serbians, Bulgarians). See Weitz, "From the Vienna to the Paris System."
9 Radoslavov, *Bulgariia i svetovnata kriza*, 2.
10 On the Balkan Wars, see Richard C. Hall, *The Balkan Wars, 1912-1913: Prelude to the First World War* (London and New York: Routledge, 2000).
11 Anne Christine Holden, "Bulgaria's Entry into the First World War: A Diplomatic Study, 1913-1915" (PhD diss., University of Illinois at Urbana-Champaign, 1976), 184; see also Richard C. Hall, *Bulgaria's Road to the First World War* (Boulder and New York: East European Monographs; distributed by Columbia University Press, 1996). Hall's study focuses on Bulgarian diplomacy during the period 1911-13.
12 Radoslavov, *Bulgariia i svetovnata kriza*, 132.
13 Zlatanski to the Royal Legation in Vienna, no. 2390, 2 December 1917. TsDA, f. 304k: Bulgarska legatsiia vuv Viena, op. 1, a.e. 1570, l. 185–6.
14 "Kriegsziele Bulgariens," November 1917, 1, 47–9. NARA, RG 242, T 120, roll 1796, D 822566 ff.
15 Taen informatsionen biuletin na Ministerstvoto, 6 March 1918. TsDA, f. 176k, op. 3, a.e. 850, l. 48.
16 On Ferdinand, see Constant, *Foxy Ferdinand*.
17 Czernin to Demblin (for His Majesty), no. 8, 10 November 1917; Demblin to Czernin, no. 9, 10 November 1917. HHStA, PA XL, K 57-1: Vertreter des Ministeriums des Äußern bei Seiner Majestät (1917–1918).
18 Petur H. Petrov, ed., *Nauchna ekspeditsiia v Makedoniia i Pomoravieto, 1916 g.* (Sofia: Universitetsko izdatelstvo "Sv. Kliment Okhridski," 1993), 17.
19 Vladeva, "Brest-Litovskiiat mir i Bulgariia," 53–4.
20 Liubomir Miletich, "Puteshestvie iz Makedoniia." In Petrov, ed., *Nauchna ekspeditsiia v Makedoniia i Pomoravieto, 1916 g.*, 134–5.
21 Dimitur G. Gadzhanov, "Miusiulmanskoto naselenie v novoosvobodenite zemi." Ibid., 279. Emphasis in the original.
22 Ibid., 201. South Slavic languages form a dialect continuum.
23 Aleksandrov, *Brest-Litovskiiat miren dogovor 1918 g.*, 191.
24 Toshev to Radoslavov, no. 2831, 13 November 1917; Rizov to Radoslavov, no. 2261, 17 November 1917. TsDA, f. 176k, op. 3, a.e. 602, l. 16 and 19.
25 Toshev to Radoslavov, no. 2876, 20 November 1917. TsDA, f. 176k, op. 3, a.e. 602, l. 22.

26 Mérey to Czernin, no. 52, 15 December 1917. HHStA, PA I, K 1052.
27 Otto Czernin to Czernin, no. 105, 19 December 1917. HHStA, PA I, K 1052.
28 Markov, *Goliamata voina i bulgarskata strazha*, 161.
29 *Mirnye peregovory v Brest-Litovske*, iv.
30 Ganchev to Radoslavov, no. 2246, 22 December 1917. TsDA, f. 313k, op. 1, a.e. 2463, l. 35. The Dobrudja Question refers to Bulgaria's claim to the whole province, including the Danube delta, which went substantially beyond the border rectification in Northern Dobrudja promised by Germany and Austria-Hungary to Sofia in the secret military convention from September 1915. Northern Dobrudja had an ethnically mixed population, with a Romanian plurality and sizable Tatar, Bulgarian, and German minorities.
31 Radoslavov to Ganchev, unnumbered, 23 December 1917. TsDA, f. 313k, op. 1, a.e. 2463, l. 36–38.
32 Popov to Radoslavov, no. 2251, 23 December 1917. TsDA, f. 313k, op. 1, a.e. 2463, l. 61.
33 Kühlmann to Grünau (for Hertling), no. 2, 25 December 1917. NARA, RG 242, T 120, roll 1791, D 816664.
34 Radoslavov to Ganchev, unnumbered, 24 December 1917. TsDA, f. 313k, op. 1, a.e. 2463, l. 62–63.
35 The view of the Macedonians as a nation, separate from their Bulgarian, Serbian, and Greek neighbours was first developed in Krste Misirkov, *Za makedontskite raboti* (Sofia: Pechatnitsa na "Liberalnii klub," 1903). This work is also notable as the first attempt to create a Macedonian literary language based on the standardization of the westernmost vernacular. Although this view ultimately prevailed after the Second World War, it is unclear how popular the concept of a Macedonian nation was in the 1910s.
36 Popov to Radoslavov, unnumbered, 24 December 1917. TsDA, f. 313k, op. 1, a.e. 2463, l. 79–84; Protokoll. Bei einer in Brest-Litovsk am 24. Dezember stattgehbsten Besprechung zwischen 1.) Seiner Exzellenz dem öesterreichisch-ungarischen Minister des Auswärtigen, Herrn Grafen Czernin, 2.) Seiner Exzellenz dem Staatssekretär des Auswärtigen Amts, Herrn von Kühlmann, 3.) Seiner Exzellenz dem bulgarischen Justizminister, Herrn Popow, ... NARA, RG 242, T 120, roll 1797, D 814800-D 814801; The telegram Hoffmann referred to is most likely one from the self-professed National Council of the Dobrudja to the German Foreign Ministry, dated 17 December 1917, in which the executive of this council (all Bulgarian names, which probably reflects its entire ethnic composition) expressed the wish to unite the province with Bulgaria according to the right to national

self-determination. It appears verbatim in Bussche to Rosenberg, no. 216, 16 January 1918. NARA, RG 242, T 120, roll 1796, D 822317.
37 Anastasov to Radoslavov, unnumbered, 24 December 1917. TsDA, f. 313k, op. 1, a.e. 2463, l. 91.
38 Radoslavov, *Bulgariia i svetovnata kriza*, 195.
39 Quoted in Mazower, *The Balkans*, 39.
40 Popov to Radoslavov, no. 2253, 24 December 1917. TsDA, f. 313k, op. 1, a.e. 2463, l. 66–71.
41 Radoslavov to Ganchev, unnumbered, 25 December 1917. TsDA, f. 313k, op. 1, a.e. 2463, l. 95.
42 Anastasov to Radoslavov, unnumbered, 25 December 1917. TsDA, f. 313k, op. 1, a.e. 2463, l. 72–4.
43 Wheeler-Bennett, *The Forgotten Peace*, 120–1.
44 Radoslavov, *Bulgariia i svetovnata kriza*, 196. Popov to Radoslavov, unnumbered, 25 December 1917. TsDA, f. 313k, op. 1, a.e. 2463, l. 98–101.
45 General Headquarters (Zhekov) to Radoslavov, no. 8634, 26 December 1917. TsDA, f. 176k, op. 3, a.e. 602, l. 84.
46 Zhekov to Radoslavov, no. 8654, 26 December 1917. TsDA, f. 313k, op. 1, a.e. 2463, l. 119–120.
47 Zhekov to Radoslavov, no. 8660, 26 December 1917. TsDA, f. 176k, op. 1, a.e. 602, l. 83.
48 Otto Czernin to the Foreign Ministry, no. 702, 26 December 1917. HHStA, PA I, K 1078.
49 Otto Czernin to Czernin, no. 705, 27 December 1917. HHStA, PA I, K 1080.
50 Ganchev to Radoslavov, no. 2265, 29 December 1917. TsDA, f. 313k, op. 1, a.e. 2464, l. 43.
51 Tomislav Z. Longinović, *Vampire Nation: Violence as Cultural Imaginary* (Durham: Duke University Press, 2011), 51.
52 On the importance of narratives, especially of national victimhood, in the formation of state policy in the Balkans, see Jelena Subotić, "Stories States Tell: Identity, Narrative, and Human Rights in the Balkans," *Slavic Review* 72, no. 2 (Summer 2013):306–26.
53 Ludendorff, *Ludendorff's Own Story*, 2:192–4.
54 Lersner to the Foreign Ministry, no. 1953, 22 December 1917. NARA, RG 242, T 120, roll 1796, D 822293.
55 Pallavicini to Czernin, no. 105, 22 December 1917. "Die thrazische Frage." HHStA, PA I, K 1053.
56 Otto Czernin to Czernin, no. 6, 16 January 1918. "Die 'thrazische Frage' vom bulgarischen Standpunkt aus." HHStA, PA I, K 1053.
57 Aleksandrov, *Brest-Litovskiiat miren dogovor 1918 g.*, 220.

58 Popov to Radoslavov, no. 476, 26 December 1917. TsDA, f. 313k, op. 1, a.e. 2463, l. 151–3.
59 Radoslavov to Ganchev, unnumbered, 27 December 1917. TsDA, f. 313k, op. 1, a.e. 2463, l. 154.
60 Anastasov to Radoslavov, no. 44762, 30 December 1917. TsDA, f. 313k, op. 1, a.e. 2463, l. 157.
61 Popov to Radoslavov, unnumbered, 27 December 1917. TsDA, f. 313k, op.1, a.e. 2463, l. 129–130.
62 "La paix entre la Bulgarie et la Russie." *L'Echo de Bulgarie*, 29 December 1917.
63 Czernin to Otto Czernin, no. 449, 30 December 1917. HHStA, PA I, K 1052.
64 Otto Czernin to Czernin, no. 711, 31 December 1917. HHStA, PA I, K 1052.
65 Markov, *Goliamata voina i bulgarskata strazha*, 165–6.
66 Popov to Radoslavov, unnumbered, 6 January 1918. TsDA, f. 313k, op. 1, a.e. 2463, l. 185–187.
67 Razgovor s Popov, 12 January 1918. TsDA, f. 313k, op. 1, a.e. 2465, l. 25–9.
68 Popov to Radoslavov, no. 16, 19 January 1918. TsDA, f. 313k, op. 1, a.e. 2465, l. 186–8.
69 Popov to Radoslavov, no. 17, 20 January 1918. TsDA, f. 313k, op. 1, a.e. 2465, l. 189–190.
70 Ganchev to Dobrovich (for His Majesty), no. 2328, 21 January 1918. TsDA, f. 313k, a.e. 2464, l. 40–1.
71 Rizov to Radoslavov, no. 158, 22 January 1918. TsDA, f. 313k, op. 1, a.e. 2463, l. 287–8.
72 Rizov to Radoslavov, no. 303, 25 January 1918. TsDA, f. 313k, op. 1, a.e. 2464, l. 44.
73 Toshev to the Foreign Ministry, no. 2, 27 February 1917. TsDA, f. 176k, op. 3, a.e. 849, l. 177.

6 The Second Treaty of Brest-Litovsk and After

1 Trotsky, *My Life*, 381.
2 Rech' na III Vserossiiskom s'ezde sovetov rabochikh, soldatskikh i krest'ianskikh deputatov. In Leon Trotsky, *Sochineniia*, vol. 17: *Sovetskaia Respublika i kapitalisticheskii mir*, part 1: *Pervonachal'nyi period organizatsii sil* (Moscow and Leningrad: Gosudarstvennoe Izdatel'stvo, 1926), http://magister.msk.ru/library/trotsky/trotl631.htm.
3 Mikhutina, *Ukrainskii Brestskii mir*, 175.
4 Trotsky, *The History of the Russian Revolution to Brest-Litovsk*, 135; Iurii Felshtinskii makes a similar assessment in Felshtinskii, *Krushenie mirovoi revoliutsii*, 229.

5 Trotsky to Lenin, unnumbered, 31 January 1918. Houghton Library, MS Rus 13, box 1, T 7.
6 Hohenlohe to Csáky, no. 56, 29 January 1918; Hohenlohe to Czernin, no. 57, 30 January 1918. HHStA, PA I, K 1079.
7 "On the History of the Question of the Unfortunate Peace. Theses on the Question of the Immediate Conclusion of a Separate and Annexationist Peace." In V.I. Lenin, *Collected Works*, vol. 26 (Moscow: Progress Publishers, 1965), 442–4.
8 Ibid., 444–50.
9 Debo, *Revolution and Survival*, 78.
10 Mikhutina, *Ukrainskii Brestskii mir*, 175.
11 "The Immediate Tasks of the Soviet Government." In V.I. Lenin, *Collected Works*, vol. 27 (Moscow: Progress Publishers, 1965), 237, 241.
12 Felshtinskii, *Krushenie mirovoi revoliutsii*, 10–11.
13 "On the History of the Question of the Unfortunate Peace. Theses on the Question of the Immediate Conclusion of a Separate and Annexationist Peace." In Lenin, *Collected Works*, 26:450. Emphasis added.
14 Summing-up Speech at the Congress, January 18 (31). Ibid., 26:482.
15 Karl Radek, "Lenin," in *In Defence of the Russian Revolution: A Selection of Bolshevik Writings*, ed. Al Richardson (London: Porcupine Press, 1995), 75–6.
16 "Afterword to the Theses on the Question of the Immediate Conclusion of a Separate and Annexationist Peace." In Lenin, *Collected Works*, 26:451–2.
17 N.K. Krupskaia, *Reminiscences of Lenin* (New York: International Publishers, 1970), 448.
18 Trotsky, *My Life*, 380.
19 Leon Trotsky, *Lenin: Notes for a Biographer* (New York: G.P. Putnam's Sons, 1971), 102–4; Trotsky, *My Life*, 381–3.
20 Debo, *Revolution and Survival*, 81.
21 *Sed'moi ekstrennyi s'ezd RKP (b), Mart 1918: Stenograficheskii otchet* (Moscow: Gosudarstvennoe izdatel'stvo politicheskoi literatury, 1962), 15.
22 Rezoliutsiia, priniataia III Vserossiiskim s'ezdom sovetov rabochikh, soldatskikh i krest'ianskikh deputatov po voprosu o mire. In Trotsky, *Sochineniia*, 17, part 1: http://magister.msk.ru/library/trotsky/trotl632.htm.
23 *Sed'moi ekstrennyi s'ezd RKP (b), Mart 1918*, 111.
24 Felshtinskii, *Krushenie mirovoi revoliutsii*, 234.
25 Mikhutina, *Ukrainskii Brestskii mir*, 179.
26 Makarenko, "Bolsheviki i Brestskii Mir," 11–12.
27 Chaprashikov to Radoslavov, no. 58, 28 January 1918. TsDA, f. 176k, op. 3, a. e. 1041, l. 32–3.

28 Hempel to the Foreign Ministry (and the delegation in Brest-Litovsk), no. 43, 28 January 1918. HHStA, PA I, K 1053.
29 Paul von Hindenburg, *Out of My Life*, vol. 2 (London and New York: Harper & brothers, 1921), 334.
30 Bussche to Rosenberg, no. 465, 2 February 1918. NARA, RG 242, T 120, roll 1787, D 815338.
31 The Royal Legation in Constantinople to the Ministry of Foreign Affairs and Confessions in Sofia, no. 65, 18 February 1918. TsDA, f. 176k, op. 3, a. e. 847, l. 37.
32 Czernin to the Foreign Ministry (for His Majesty), no. 222, 30 January 1918. HHStA, PA I, K 1077.
33 Demblin (from his Majesty) to Czernin, no. 32, 30 January 1918. HHStA, PA I, K 1079.
34 Gyula Andrássy, *Diplomacy and the War* (London: J. Bale, 1921), 180–1.
35 Bihl, *Österreich-Ungarn und die Friedensschlüsse von Brest-Litovsk*, 95.
36 May, *The Passing of the Hapsburg Monarchy, 1914–1918*, 2:514.
37 Proekt deklaratsii posle pereryva 18–30 ianvaria 1918 g. In Trotsky, *Sochineniia*, 17, part 1: http://magister.msk.ru/library/trotsky/trotl633.htm.
38 Trotsky, *My Life*, 385.
39 Trotsky to Lenin, unnumbered, 31 January 1918. Houghton Library, MS Rus 13, box 1, T 7.
40 Karakhan to Lenin and Stalin, unnumbered, 2 February 1918. Houghton Library, MS Rus 13, box 1, T 8.
41 Wireless Message Addressed to All. Special to the Peace Delegation in Brest-Litovsk; Wireless Message Addressed to All. In Lenin, *Collected Works*, 26:510–11.
42 Hoffmann, *The War of Lost Opportunities*, 224.
43 Diary entry for 2 February 1918. Czernin, *In the World War*, 246.
44 *Proceedings of the Brest-Litovsk Peace Conference*, 136–8.
45 Diary entry for 2 February 1918. Czernin, *In the World War*, 246.
46 Trotsky, *My Life*, 377.
47 Fokke, "Na stsene i za kulisami," 187.
48 Mittag to the Foreign Ministry, no. 270, 5 February 1918. HHStA, PA I, K 1053.
49 Ugron to the Foreign Ministry, no. 122, 7 February 1918. HHStA, PA I, K 1053.
50 Protokol peregovorov v imperskoi kantseliarii mezhdu predstaviteliami Germanii i Avstro-Vengrii, 5 February 1918. *Sovetsko-germanskie otnosheniia*, 277–89; Besprechung der Reichsleitung mit Graf Czernin und General Ludendorff (Berlin). Werner Hahlweg, ed., *Der Friede von Brest-Litovsk*, 492; Diary entry for 5 February 1918. Czernin, *In the World War*, 247; Ludendorff, *The General Staff and Its Problems*, 2:546.

51 Protokol peregovorov v imperskoi kantseliarii mezhdu predstaviteliami Germanii i Avstro-Vengrii, 5 February 1918. *Sovetsko-germanskie otnosheniia*, 289–97.
52 Gusztav Gratz and Richard Schüller, *The Economic Policy of Austria-Hungary during the War in Its External Relations* (New Haven: Yale University Press, 1928), 103–4.
53 Ibid., 104–5; Diary entry for 7 February 1918. Czernin, *In the World War*, 247–9.
54 Debo, *Revolution and Survival*, 100–1.
55 Gratz and Schüller, *The Economic Policy of Austria-Hungary during the War in Its External Relations*, 105–7.
56 Hoffmann, *The War of Lost Opportunities*, 225.
57 Kühlmann to Hertling, no. 30, 10 February 1918. NARA, RG 242, T 149, roll 334, N/A. Emphasis in the original.
58 Hindenburg to *Ober Ost*, no. 27231, 7 February 1918. NARA, RG 242, T 120, roll 1792, N/A.
59 Czernin to Demblin (for His Majesty), no. 25, 10 February 1918. HHStA, PA I, K 1079. A copy of the Kaiser's telegram to Kühlmann and Hoffmann is attached.
60 Telephone conversation between Count Demblin and Ambassador von Wiesner. HHStA, PA I, K 1079.
61 Hoffmann, *The War of Lost Opportunities*, 225–6.
62 Hertling to Kühlmann, no. 1433, 10 February 1918. NARA, RG 242, T 120, roll 1798, D 823428.
63 Grünau to Kühlmann, no. 1436, 10 February 1918. NARA, RG 242, T 120, roll 1798, D 823430-D 823431.
64 Grünau to Kühlmann, no. 1440, 10 February 1918. NARA, RG 242, T 120, roll 1798, D 823432-D 823433.
65 *Proceedings of the Brest-Litovsk Peace Conference*, 171–3.
66 Fokke, "Na stsene i za kulisami," 206–7.
67 Czernin to Demblin (for His Majesty), no. 23, 10 February 1918. HHStA, PA I, K 1053.
68 Kühlmann, *Erinnerungen*, 546.
69 Kühlmann to Hertling, no. 32, 10 February 1918. NARA, RG 242, T 120, roll 1789, D 817710-D 817718.
70 Aus den Erinnerungen des Grafen Karl von Hertling. Baumgart and Repgen, eds., *Brest-Litovsk*, 74.
71 Zapis' soveshchaniia kaizera Vil'gel'ma s predstaviteliami imperskogo pravitel'stva i Verhovnogo glavnokomandovaniia v Gomburge, 13 February 1918. *Sovetsko-germanskie otnosheniia*, 322–9; Aus den Erinnerungen Payers. Baumgart and Repgen, *Brest-Litovsk*, 78; Ludendorff, *Ludendorff's Own Story*, 2:185.

72 Doklad v Petrogradskom Sovete. In Trotsky, *Sochineniia*, 17, part 1: http://magister.msk.ru/library/trotsky/trotl646.htm.
73 Trotsky, *Lenin*, 105–6.
74 Schüller to the Foreign Ministry, no. 416, 17 February 1918. NARA, RG 242, T 120, roll 1788, D 816079-D 816080.
75 Hoffmann and Kühlmann to Schüller, no. 671, 18 February 1918. NARA, RG 242, T 120, roll 1788, D 816081-D 816082.
76 Czernin to Hohenlohe, unnumbered, 19 February 1918. HHStA, PA I, K 1053.
77 Hohenlohe to Czernin, no. 108, 20 February 1918. HHStA, PA I, K 1053.
78 Arz to Czernin, no. 1064, 20 February 1918. HHStA, PA I, K 1053.
79 Diary entry for 22 February 1918. Max Hoffmann, *War Diaries and other Papers*, vol. 2 (London: M. Secker, 1929), 207.
80 Speeches at the Evening Sitting of the Central Committee of the R.S.D.L.P. (B.) February 18, 1918. In Lenin, *Collected Works*, 26:522–4.
81 "The Revolutionary Phrase"; "The Itch"; "Peace or War"; "Where Is the Mistake?"; "An Unfortunate Peace"; "A Painful but Necessary Lesson"; "Strange and Monstrous." In Lenin, *Collected Works*, 27:2–29, 36–41, 51–2, 62–6, 68–75, quotation on 51.
82 Debo, *Revolution and Survival*, 135. Emphasis in the original.
83 Draft Wireless Message to the Government of the German Reich. In Lenin, *Collected Works*, 26:525.
84 Hoffmann to the Council of People's Commissars, unnumbered, 19 February 1918. NARA, RG 242, T 120, roll 1788, D 816095; Diary entry for 20 February 1918. Hoffmann, *War Diaries and other Papers*, 2:206.
85 Kühlmann to Schüller, no. 583, 21 February 1918. NARA, RG 242, T 120, roll 1788, D 816110-D 816113.
86 Report at the Meeting of the All-Russia C.E.C. February 24, 1918. In Lenin, *Collected Works*, 27:43–7, quotation on 47.
87 Soobshchenie o priniatii TsIKom germanskikh usloviiakh mira. In Trotsky, *Sochineniia*, 17, part 1: http://magister.msk.ru/library/trotsky/trotl653.htm.
88 Telegramma M.A. Spiridonovoi mestnym sovetam krest'ianskikh deputatov ob otpore germanskim voiskam. V.V. Shelokhaev, ed., *Partiia levykh sotsialistov-revoliutsionerov: Dokumenty i materialy 1917–1925 gg. v triokh tomakh*, vol. 1: *Iiul' 1917 – mai 1918* (Moscow: ROSSPĖN, 2000), 180–1.
89 Deklaratsiia fraktsii Levykh S.-R. VTsIK po povodu ratifikatsii mirnogo dogovora Chrezvychainym S'ezdom Sovetov. Ibid., 1:182.
90 I. Leontiev, "Ocherk vozniknoveniia partii Levykh Sotsialistov-revoliutsionerov." In ibid., 1 695–700; for more on the Left SRs' opposition to signing the treaty, see Iurii Felshtinskii, *Bol'sheviki i Levye Esery: Oktiabr' 1917 – iiul' 1918* (Paris: YMCA-Press, 1985), 110–26.

91 Kühlmann to the Foreign Ministry, no. 2, 26 February 1918. NARA, RG 242, T 120, roll 1788, D 816180-D 816181.
92 Toshev to Radoslavov, unnumbered, 27 February 1918. TsDA, f. 176k, op. 3, a. e. 849, l. 11.
93 Aufzeichnung über die internen Besprechungen der zu den Friedensverhandlungen mit Russland entsendeten Delegationen des Vierbundes in Brest-Litowsk vom 26.II bis 1.III.1918. HHStA, PA I, K 1082: Brester Kanzlei.
94 Reynolds, *Shattering Empires*, 194.
95 *Mirnye peregovory v Brest-Litovske*, 213–21, quotation on 214.
96 Ibid., 229.
97 Wheeler-Bennett, *The Forgotten Peace*, 270–1.
98 Karl Radek, *Krushenie germanskogo imperializma i zadachi mezhdunarodnogo rabochego klassa: Doklad prochitannyi 2-go oktiabria v Moskovskom Sovetskom teatre* (Moscow: Izdatel'stvo Vserosiiskogo Tsentral'nogo Ispolnitel'nogo Komiteta Sovetov R., S., K. i K. Deputatov, 1918), 36–7.
99 Makarenko, "Bolsheviki i Brestskii mir," 18; Felshtinskii, *Krushenie mirovoi revoliutsii*, 15.
100 Ritter, *The Sword and the Scepter*, 4:114–15.
101 *Texts of the Russian "Peace": (With Maps)* (Washington: Government Printing Office, 1918), 13–24.
102 Ibid., 127, 151.
103 Trotsky, *My Life*, 390.
104 Felshtinskii, *Krushenie mirovoi revoliutsii*, 286–7.
105 "Das Ende eines Reiches." *Arbeiter Zeitung*, 5 March 1918.
106 Velychenko, "Ukrainian Anticolonialist Thought in Comparative Perspective," 365.
107 Joshua Sanborn, *Imperial Apocalypse: The Great War and the Destruction of the Russian Empire* (Oxford: Oxford University Press, 2014).
108 See Ignác Romsics, *The Dismantling of Historic Hungary: The Peace Treaty of Trianon, 1920* (Boulder: East European Monographs, 2002).
109 On the dynamics in the Don region, see Udo Gehrmann, "Turbulenzen am stillen Don. Zur deutschen Kriegsziel- und Ostpolitik in der Zeit des Brest-Litovsker Friedens," *Jahrbücher für Geschichte Osteuropas* 41, no. 3 (1993):394–421.
110 Hoffmann, *The War of Lost Opportunities*, 236–7.
111 Forgách to the Foreign Ministry, no. 673, 13 July 1918. HHStA, PA X, K 153.
112 See I.K. Kobliakov, "Bor'ba Sovetskogo gosudarstva za sokhranenie mira s Germaniei v period deistviia Brestskogo dogovora (mart-noiabr' 1918g.)," *Istoriia SSSR* no. 4 (1958):3–26.

113 Political Report of the Central Committee, March 7. In Lenin, *Collected Works*, 27:105–6.
114 Nota stats-sekretaria vedomstva inostrannykh del polnomochnomu predstavitel'stvu RSFSR v Germanii, 12 June 1918. *Sovetsko-germanskie otnosheniia*, 553.
115 Razgovor po priamomu provodu (Ioffe, Karakhan, Trotsky, Lenin). Houghton Library, MS Rus 13, box 1, T 20. A doctored version of this document, which omits entirely Trotsky's reply, appears in *Sovetsko-germanskie otnosheniia*, 554–6.
116 Report by Minister in Moscow Chaprashikov from 22 June 1918. TsDA, f. 176k, op. 3, a. e. 838: Taen informatsionen biuletin na Ministerstvoto, l. 382.
117 Gustav Hilger and Alfred G. Meyer, *The Incompatible Allies: A Memoir-History of German-Soviet Relations, 1918–1941* (New York: Macmillan, 1953), 2–6; see also Lutz Hafner, "The Assassination of Count Mirbach and the 'July Uprising' of the Left Socialist Revolutionaries in Moscow, 1918," *Russian Review* 50, no. 3 (July 1991):324–44.
118 De Pottere to Burián, no. 10, 8 July 1918. "Die Ermordung des Grafen Mirbach." HHStA, PA X, K 151: Entwicklung des russischen Reiches zu einer Pluralität von Staaten (1917–1918).
119 I.V. Stalin – G.K. Ordzhonikidze, 17 iiulia 1918 g. A. V Kvashonkin, *Bol'shevistskoe rukovodstvo*, 44–5.
120 Hilger and Meyer, *The Incompatible Allies*, 9–10; Riezler to Chicherin, unnumbered, 9 August 1918. HHStA, PA X, K 150: Entwicklung des russischen Reiches zu einer Pluralität von Staaten (1917–1918).
121 De Pottere to Burián, no. 106, 18 October 1918. HHStA, PA X, K 150.
122 Charles A. Kupchan, *How Enemies Become Friends: The Sources of Stable Peace* (Princeton: Princeton University Press, 2010), 2.

Conclusion: Brest-Litovsk and Europe's Twentieth Century

1 E.J. Hobsbawm, *The Age of Extremes: The Short Twentieth Century, 1914–1991* (London: Michael Joseph, 1994).
2 Mark Mazower, *Dark Continent: Europe's Twentieth Century* (New York: Vintage Books, 1998), x.
3 "The Russian Empire was not sui generis. Neither, we may posit, was the way it ended. It is better to use as broad a definition for decolonization as we do for imperialism or empire. Thus, if an empire is a relationship of political control imposed by an imperial society over the effective sovereignty of another political society, then decolonization is the process by which that relationship comes to an end, regardless of the pattern of

settlement or form of domination involved." Joshua Sanborn, "War of Decolonization: The Russian Empire in the Great War," in *The Empire and Nationalism at War*, ed. Eric Lohr et al., vol. 2 of Russia's Great War and Revolution, 1914–1922 (Bloomington: Slavica Publishers, 2014), 49–72, quotation on 51–2.

4 Trauttsmandorff to Burián, 21 May 1918. "Beilage: K. u. k. Armeeoberkommando. Nachrichtenabteilung. 'Politische Lage in Russland. Standort, am 17. Mai 1918.' HHStA, PA X, K 150.

5 On the role of Habsburg POWs in the dissolution of the Austro-Hungarian Empire, see István Deák, *Beyond Nationalism: A Social and Political History of the Habsburg Officer Corps, 1848–1918* (New York: Oxford University Press, 1990).

6 "History of The Communist Party of the Soviet Union (Bolsheviks)," https://www.marxists.org/reference/archive/stalin/works/1939/x01/ch07.htm#7.

7 "Gorbachev at the United Nations," *C-SPAN.org*, http://www.c-span.org/video/?5292-1/gorbachev-united-nations.

Bibliography

Unpublished Sources

Houghton Library, Harvard University, Cambridge, Massachusetts
  MS Rus 13: Leon Trotsky Soviet Papers
  MS Rus 13.1: Leon Trotsky Exile Papers
National Archives and Records Administration, College Park, Maryland
  Record Group 59: Records of the Department of State, microcopy M 367: Records of the Department of State Relating to World War I and Its Termination, 1914–1929
  Record Group 84: Records of Foreign Service Posts. Diplomatic Posts. Austria, vol. 449.
  Record Group 242: Foreign Records Seized Collection
  Microcopy no. T 120: Records of the German Foreign Office Received by the Department of State
  Microcopy no. T 149: German Foreign Ministry Archives, 1867–1929
Österreichisches Staatsarchiv, Abteilung Haus-, Hof- und Staatsarchiv, Vienna, Austria
  Politisches Archiv I: Allgemeines
  523-2-4: Beziehungen Erzherzog Wilhelms zu ukrainischen Notabilitäten (1918.05)
  818-1 o): Lebensmittelnot von Mitte Jänner 1918 und die damit zusammenhängende Ausstandsbewegung (1918.01–1918.02)
  956-2 t): Friedensverhandlungen mit Russland (1917.11–1918)
  1041-2 Krieg 58: Angelegenheiten der Ukraine (1918.01–1918.10)
  1052-2 Krieg 70: Friedensverhandlungen mit Russland, Ukraine, Rumänien, (1917–1918)

1053-1 1): Hauptverhandlung in Brest mit den Delegierten Russlands (1918.01–1918.02)
1077-1082: Brester Kanzlei (1917–1918)
Politisches Archiv X: Rußland
150-153: Russland, Liasse XI: Entwicklung des russischen Reiches zu einer Pluralität von Staaten (1917–1918)
154-1-2 8): Tätigkeit Erzherzog Wilhelms in der Ukraine und seine Abberufung, 1918.06–1918.10
Politisches Archiv XL: Interna
57-1: Vertreter des Ministeriums des Äußern bei Seiner Majestät (1917–1918)
261: Korrespondenz des k. u. k. Ministers des Äußern mit dem Ministerium (1911–1918)
262: Telegramme an Grafen Demblin (1917–1918)
263: Telegramme von Grafen Demblin (1917–1918)
Tsentralen Durzhaven Arkhiv, Sofia, Bulgaria
Fond 176k: Ministerstvo na vunshnite raboti i izpovedaniiata
Fond 304k: Bulgarska legatsiia vuv Viena
Fond 313k: Vasil Radoslavov
Verein für Geschichte der Arbeiterbewegung, Vienna, Austria
Chronologisches Archiv
Lade 15, Mappe 27: Jännerstreik 1918
Partei-Archiv vor 1934
Mappe 2: Sitzungsprotokolle Parteivorstand etc., 27.7.1916–15.11.1921
Mappe 27: Entwurf Organisationsstatut Arbeiterwehr. Feldschutzdienst. Von Bernaschek an Fritz Adler gesandte Unterlagen Geschichte der Arbeiterräte in Ober-Österreich.
Sozialdemokratische Parteistellen
Karton 149, Mappe 1078: Steiermark

Published Primary and Secondary Sources

Adams, Arthur E. "The Great Ukrainian Jacquerie." In *The Ukraine, 1917–1921: A Study in Revolution*, edited by Taras Hunczak, 247–71. Cambridge: Distributed by Harvard University Press for the Harvard Ukrainian Research Institute, 1977.
Akhtamzian, Abdulkhan A. "O Brest-Litovskikh peregovorakh 1918 goda." *Voprosy istorii*, no. 11 (November 1966):32–46.
Aksakal, Mustafa. *The Ottoman Road to War in 1914: The Ottoman Empire and the First World War*. Cambridge: Cambridge University Press, 2008.

Aleksandrov, Valentin. *Brest-Litovskiiat miren dogovor 1918 g.: Voennostrategicheski prichini i mezhdunarodnopravni posleditsi*. Sofia: Voenno izdatelstvo, 2009.
Andrássy, Gyula. *Diplomacy and the War*. London: J. Bale, 1921.
Antonov-Ovseenko, V.A. *Zapiski o Grazhdanskoi voine*. 2 vol. Moscow: Gosudarstvennoe Izdatel'stvo, 1924.
Arens, Olavi. "The Estonian Question at Brest-Litovsk." *Journal of Baltic Studies* 25, no. 4 (1994):305–31.
B. O. "Würzburg und Wien." *Der Kampf: Sozialdemokratische Monatsschrift* 10, no.11–12 (November–December 1917):320–28.
Bailey, Sydney D. "Brest-Litovsk: A Study in Soviet Diplomacy." *History Today* 6, no. 8 (1956):511–21.
Baranowski, Shelley. *Nazi Empire: German Colonialism and Imperialism from Bismarck to Hitler*. Cambridge: Cambridge University Press, 2011.
Bauer, Otto. *Die Österreichische Revolution*. Vienna: Wiener Volksbuchhandlung, 1923.
Baumgart, Winfried. "Brest-Litowsk und Versailles. Ein Vergleich zweier Friedensschlüsse." *Historische Zeitschrift* 210, no. 3 (June 1970):583–619.
– *Deutsche Ostpolitik 1918: Von Brest-Litowsk bis zum Ende des Ersten Weltkrieges*. Vienna: Oldenbourg, 1966.
Baumgart, Winfried, and Konrad Repgen, eds. *Brest-Litovsk*. Göttingen: Vandenhoeck & Ruprecht, 1969.
Berend, Iván T. *The Crisis Zone of Europe: An Interpretation of East-Central European History in the First Half of the Twentieth Century*. Cambridge and New York: Cambridge University Press, 1986.
Bihl, Wolfdieter. *Österreich-Ungarn und die Friedensschlüsse von Brest-Litovsk*. Vienna: Böhlau, 1970.
Borowsky, Peter. *Deutsche Ukrainepolitik 1918 unter besonderer Berücksichtigung der Wirtschaftsfragen*. Lübeck and Hamburg: Mathiesen Verlag, 1970.
– "Germany's Ukrainian Policy during World War I and the Revolution of 1918-19." In *German-Ukrainian Relations in Historical Perspective*, 84–95. Edmonton and Toronto: Canadian Institute of Ukrainian Studies Press, 1994.
Butakov, Iaroslav. *Brestskii mir: Lovushka Lenina dlia kaizerovskoi Germanii*. Moscow: Veche, 2012.
Cambon, Jules, Austen Chamberlain, John W. Davis, and Richard von Kühlmann. *The Permanent Bases of Foreign Policy: France, Great Britain, Germany and the United States*. New York: Council on Foreign Relations, 1931.
Chervinkiv-Koroliov, I.I. "Pro zmovu nimets'koho imperializmu z Tsentral'noiu Radoiu u Brest-Lytovsku v 1918 r." *Ukrains'kyi istorychnyi zhurnal*, no. 5 (May 1983):17–28.

Chickering, Roger. *We Men who Feel most German: A Cultural Study of the Pan-German League, 1886–1914*. Boston: Allen & Unwin, 1984.
Chubarian, A.O. *Brestskii Mir*. Moscow: Gospolitizdat, 1964.
Cobban, Alfred. *National Self-Determination*. New York: Oxford University Press, 1945.
Constant, Stephen. *Foxy Ferdinand, Tsar of Bulgaria*. New York: Franklin Watts, 1980.
Czernin, Ottokar. *In the World War*. New York: Harper & brothers, 1920.
Deák, István. *Beyond Nationalism: A Social and Political History of the Habsburg Officer Corps, 1848–1918*. New York: Oxford University Press, 1990.
Debo, Richard K. *Revolution and Survival: The Foreign Policy of Soviet Russia, 1917–18*. Toronto: University of Toronto Press, 1979.
– *Survival and Consolidation: The Foreign Policy of Soviet Russia, 1918–1921*. Montreal: McGill-Queen's University Press, 1992.
Degras, Jane Tabrisky, ed. *Soviet Documents on Foreign Policy*. Vol. 1. London: Oxford University Press, 1951.
Deutsch, Julius. "Radikale Strömungen." *Der Kampf: Sozialdemokratische Monatsschrift* 11, no. 2 (February 1918):71–8.
DiNardo, R.L. *Breakthrough: The Gorlice-Tarnów Campaign, 1915*. Santa Barbara: Praeger, 2010.
Dornik, Wolfram, ed. *Die Ukraine zwischen Selbstbestimmung und Fremdherrschaft 1917–1922*. Graz: Leykam, 2011.
Dornik, Wolfram, and Stefan Karner, eds. *Die Besatzung der Ukraine 1918: Historischer Kontext, Forschungsstand, wirtschaftliche und soziale Folgen*. Graz, Vienna, and Klagenfurt: Verein zur Förderung der Forschung von Folgen nach Konflikten und Kriegen, 2008.
Doroshkevich, V. and N. Voloshyn. "Nezalezhnist' Ukrainy: Nova sproba. Zaglian'mo do radianskikh dzherel." *Literaturna Ukraina*, no. 3 (1991).
Dowler, Wayne. *Russia in 1913*. DeKalb: Northern Illinois University Press, 2010.
Dowling, Timothy C. *The Brusilov Offensive*. Bloomington: Indiana University Press, 2008.
Farrar, L.L. "Carrot and Stick: German Efforts to Conclude a Separate Peace with Russia, November 1914 – December 1915." *East European Quarterly* 10, no. 2 (1976):153–79.
Fedyshyn, Oleh S. *Germany's Drive to the East and the Ukrainian Revolution, 1917–1918*. New Brunswick: Rutgers University Press, 1971.
Felshtinskii, Iurii. *Bol'sheviki i Levye Esery: Oktiabr' 1917 – iiul' 1918*. Paris: YMCA-Press, 1985.
– *Krushenie mirovoi revoliutsii. Brestskii mir. Okriabr' 1917 – noiabr' 1918*. London: Overseas Publications Interchange, 1991.

Fischer, Fritz. *Germany's Aims in the First World War*. New York: W.W. Norton, 1967.
Flanner, Karl. *Nieder mit dem Krieg! Für sofortigen Frieden!: Der grosse Jännerstreik in Wiener Neustadt*. Wiener Neustadt: Verein Museum und Archiv für Arbeit und Industrie im Viertel unter dem Wienerwald, 1997.
Fokke, D.G. "Na stsene i za kulisami Brestskoi tragikomedii: Memuary uchastnika Brest-Litovskih mirnykh peregovorov." *Arkhiv Russkoi Revoliutsii* 20 (1930).
Frei, Bruno. *Die roten Matrosen von Cattaro: Eine Episode aus dem Revolutionsjahre 1918*. Vienna: Verlag der Wiener Volsbuchhandlung, 1927.
Galántai, József. *Hungary in the First World War*. Budapest: Akadémiai Kiadó, 1989.
Gatrell, Peter. *Russia's First World War: A Social and Economic History*. New York: Pearson/Longman, 2005.
Gehrmann, Udo. "Turbulenzen am stillen Don. Zur deutschen Kriegsziel-und Ostpolitik in der Zeit des Brest-Litovsker Friedens." *Jahrbücher für Geschichte Osteuropas* 41, no. 3 (1993): 394–421.
Geiss, Imanuel. *Der polnische Grenzstreifen 1914–1918: Ein Beitrag zur deutschen Kriegszielpolitik im Ersten Weltkrieg*. Hamburg and Lübeck: Moll-Winter, 1960.
Golczewski, Frank. *Deutsche und Ukrainer 1914–1939*. Paderborn: Schöningh, 2010.
Gratz, Gusztav, and Richard Schüller. *The Economic Policy of Austria-Hungary during the War in Its External Relations*. New Haven: Yale University Press, 1928.
Grebler, Leo, and Wilhelm Winkler. *The Cost of the World War to Germany and to Austria-Hungary*. New Haven: Yale University Press, 1940.
Guthier, Steven L. "The Popular Base of Ukrainian Nationalism in 1917." *Slavic Review* 38, no. 1 (Spring 1979):30–47.
Hafner, Lutz. "The Assassination of Count Mirbach and the 'July Uprising' of the Left Socialist Revolutionaries in Moscow, 1918." *Russian Review* 50, no. 3 (July 1991):324–44.
Hai-Nyzhnyk, Pavlo. *UNR ta ZUNR: Stanovlennia orhaniv vlady i natsional'ne derzhavotvorennia: 1917–1920 rr*. Kiev: Shchek, 2010.
– "Vikradennia bankira A. Dobroho v kvitni 1918 roku (rekonstruktsiia ta analiz podii)." *Naukovi zapiski: Seriia pedagohichni ta istorychni nauky*, no. 120 (2014):212–28.
Hahlweg, Werner. *Der Diktatfrieden von Brest-Litowsk 1918 und die Bolschewistische Weltrevolution*. Münster: Aschendorff, 1960.
–, ed. *Der Friede von Brest-Litowsk: Ein unveröffentlichter Band aus dem Werk des Untersuchungsausschusses der deutschen verfassunggebenden Nationalversammlung und des deutschen Reichstages*. Düsseldorf: Droste, 1971.

Halecki, Oscar. *Borderlands of Western Civilization: A History of East Central Europe*. New York: The Ronald Press, 1952.
Hall, Richard C. "Bulgaria in the First World War." *Historian* 73, no. 2 (2011):300–15.
– *Bulgaria's Road to the First World War*. East European Monographs, no. 460. Boulder and New York: East European Monographs; distributed by Columbia University Press, 1996.
– *The Balkan Wars, 1912–1913: Prelude to the First World War*. London and New York: Routledge, 2000.
Hallas, Duncan. *The Comintern*. London: Bookmarks, 1985.
Hanisch, Ernst. *Der grosse Illusionist: Otto Bauer (1881–1938)*. Vienna, Cologne, and Weimar: Böhlau, 2011.
Haselsteiner, Horst. "The Habsburg Empire in World War I: Mobilization of Food Supplies." In *East Central European Society in World War I*, edited by N.F. Dreisziger, Béla K. Király, and Albert A. Nofi, 87–102. Boulder: Social Science Monographs, 1985.
Hautmann, Hans. "Vienna: A City in the Years of Radical Change 1917–1920." In *Challenges of Labour: Central and Western Europe, 1917–1920*, edited by Chris Wrigley, 87–104. London and New York: Routledge, 1993.
Healy, Maureen. *Vienna and the Fall of the Habsburg Empire: Total War and Everyday Life in World War I*. Cambridge: Cambridge University Press, 2004.
Hilger, Gustav, and Alfred G. Meyer. *The Incompatible Allies: A Memoir-History of German-Soviet Relations, 1918–1941*. New York: Macmillan, 1953.
Hindenburg, Paul von. *Out of My Life*. 2 vols. London and New York: Harper & brothers, 1921.
Hirniak, Nikifor. *Polkovnik Vasyl Vyshyvanyi*. Winnipeg: D. Mykytiuk, 1956.
"History of The Communist Party of the Soviet Union (Bolsheviks)." https://www.marxists.org/reference/archive/stalin/works/1939/x01/ch07.htm#7.
Hnatevich, Bohdan, ed. *Ukrains'ki Sichovi Stril'tsi 1914–1920*. Lviv: Slovo, 1991.
Hobsbawm, E.J. *The Age of Extremes: The Short Twentieth Century, 1914–1991*. London: Michael Joseph, 1994.
Hoffman, Jerry Hans. "The Ukrainian Adventure of the Central Powers, 1914–1918." PhD diss., University of Pittsburgh, 1967.
Hoffmann, Max. *The War of Lost Opportunities*. 2 vols. New York: International Publishers, 1925.
– *War Diaries and Other Papers*. 2 vols. London: M. Secker, 1929.
Holden, Anne Christine. "Bulgaria's Entry into the First World War: A Diplomatic Study, 1913–1915." PhD diss., University of Illinois at Urbana-Champaign, 1976.

Holquist, Peter. *Making War, Forging Revolution: Russia's Continuum of Crisis, 1914–1921*. Cambridge: Harvard University Press, 2002.

Höppner, Siegfried. "Der Januarstreik im Jahre 1918 in Wien und Niederösterreich und die Sozialdemokratische Partei Österreichs." *Wissenschaftliche Zeitschrift der Humboldt-Universität zu Berlin* 7, no. 1 (January 1957):61–8.

Hopwood, Robert F. "Interalliance Diplomacy: Count Czernin and Germany, 1916–1918." PhD diss., Stanford University, 1965.

Horak, Stephan M. *The First Treaty of World War I: Ukraine's Treaty with the Central Powers of February 9, 1918*. Boulder: East European Monographs, 1988.

Hornykiewicz, Theophil, ed. *Ereignisse in der Ukraine 1914–1922, Deren Bedeutung und historische Hintergründe*. 3 vols. Philadelphia: W.K. Lypynsky East European Research Institute, 1966.

Hull, Isabel V. *Absolute Destruction: Military Culture and the Practices of War in Imperial Germany*. Ithaca: Cornell University Press, 2005.

Hunczak, Taras. "The Ukraine under Hetman Pavlo Skoropadskyi." In *The Ukraine, 1917–1921: A Study in Revolution*, edited by Taras Hunczak, 61–82. Cambridge: Distributed by Harvard University Press for the Harvard Ukrainian Research Institute, 1977.

Kamburov, Gencho. "Raznoglasiia v Chetvorniia suiuz pri pregovorite v Brest-Litovsk i Bukuresht prez 1918 g." *Istoricheski pregled* 27, no. 3 (June 1971):48–58.

Keynes, John Maynard. *The Economic Consequences of the Peace*. New York: Harcourt, Brace and Howe, 1920.

Khrystiuk, Pavlo. *Zamitky i materialy do istorii ukrains'koi revoliutsii*. 4 vols. Vienna: Sotsiologichnyi ukrains'kyi instytut, 1921.

Kitchen, Martin. *The Silent Dictatorship: The Politics of the German High Command under Hindenburg and Ludendorff, 1916–1918*. New York: Holmes & Meier Publishers, 1976.

Kobliakov, I.K. "Bor'ba Sovetskogo gosudarstva za sokhranenie mira s Germaniei v period deistviiia Brestskogo dogovora (mart-noiabr' 1918g.)." *Istoriia SSSR*, no. 4 (1958):3–26.

Komjáthy, Miklósné, ed. *Protokolle des Gemeinsamen Ministerrates der Österreichisch-Ungarischen Monarchie (1914–1918)*. Budapest, Akadémiai Kiadó, 1966.

Kondrat'ev, N.D. *Rynok khlebov i ego regulirovanie vo vremia voiny i revoliutsii*. Moscow: Nauka, 1991.

Krupskaia, N.K. *Reminiscences of Lenin*. New York: International Publishers, 1970.

Ksenofontov, Igor' Nikolaevich. *Mir, kotorogo khoteli i kotoryi nenavideli: Dokumental'nyi reportazh*. Moscow: Izd-vo polit. lit-ry. 1991.

Kuchabsky, Vasyl. *Western Ukraine in Conflict with Poland and Bolshevism, 1918–1923*. Edmonton and Toronto: Canadian Institute of Ukrainian Studies, 2009.

Kühlmann, Richard von. *Erinnerungen*. Heidelberg: Verlag Lambert Schneider, 1948.

Kupchan, Charles A. *How Enemies Become Friends: The Sources of Stable Peace*. Princeton: Princeton University Press, 2010.

Kvashonkin, A.V., ed. *Bol'shevistskoe rukovodstv: Perepiska 1912-1927*. Seriia "Dokumenty sovetskoi istorii." Moscow: ROSSPĖN, 1996.

Lenin, V.I. *Collected Works*. 45 vols. Moscow: Progress Publishers, 1960–70.

Lilla, Joachim. "Innen-und aussenpolitische Aspekte der Austropolnischen Lösung 1914–1916." *Mitteilungen des Österreichischen Staatsarchivs* 30 (January 1977):221–50.

Liulevicius, Vejas G. *War Land on the Eastern Front: Culture, National Identity and German Occupation in World War I*. Cambridge: Cambridge University Press, 2000.

Lloyd George, David. *Memoirs of the Peace Conference*. 2 vols. New York: H. Fertig, 1972.

Longinović, Tomislav Z. *Vampire Nation: Violence as Cultural Imaginary*. Durham: Duke University Press, 2011.

Lory, Bernard. "Une guerre invisible? La mémoire de la Premiere Guerre mondiale en Bulgarie." *Guerres mondiales et conflits contemporains* 57, no. 228 (October 2007):37–49.

Ludendorff, Erich. *Ludendorff's Own Story*. 2 vols. New York and London: Harper & brothers, 1920.

– *The General Staff and Its Problems: The History of the Relations between the High Command and the German Imperial Government as Revealed by Official Documents*. 2 vols. London: Hutchinson, 1920.

Lutz, Ralph Haswell, ed. *Fall of the German Empire, 1914–1918*. 2 vols. Stanford: Stanford University Press, 1932.

MacMillan, Margaret. *Paris 1919: Six Months That Changed the World*. New York: Random House, 2002.

Magnes, Judah L. *Russia and Germany at Brest-Litovsk: A Documentary History of the Peace Negotiations*. New York: The Rand School of Social Science, 1919.

Magocsi, Paul Robert. *Historical Atlas of East Central Europe*. Vol. 1 of *A History of East Central Europe*. Seattle: University of Washington Press, 1995.

Makarenko, Pavel Vasil'evich. "Bol'sheviki i Brestskii mir." *Voprosy istorii*, no. 3 (March 2010):3–21.

Manela, Erez. *The Wilsonian Moment: Self-Determination and the International Origins of Anticolonial Nationalism*. Oxford: Oxford University Press, 2007.

Mandel, David. *The Petrograd Workers and the Fall of the Old Regime: From the February Revolution to the July Days, 1917*. New York: St. Martin's Press, 1983.

Markov, Georgi. *Goliamata voina i bulgarskata strazha mezhdu sredna Evropa i Orienta, 1916–1919*. Sofia: Akademichno izdatelstvo "Prof. Marin Drinov," 2006.

Martin, Terry. *The Affirmative Action Empire: Nations and Nationalism in the Soviet Union, 1923–1939*. Ithaca: Cornell University Press, 2001.

May, Arthur James. *The Passing of the Hapsburg Monarchy, 1914–1918*. 2 vols. Philadelphia: University of Pennsylvania Press, 1966.

Mayer, Arno J. *Political Origins of the New Diplomacy, 1917–1918*. New Haven: Yale University Press, 1959.

– *Politics and Diplomacy of Peacemaking: Containment and Counterrevolution at Versailles, 1918–1919*. New York: Vintage, 1969.

Mazower, Mark. *Dark Continent: Europe's Twentieth Century*. New York: Vintage Books, 1998.

– *The Balkans: A Short History*. New York: Modern Library, 2000.

Meckling, Ingeborg. *Die Aussenpolitik des Grafen Czernin*. Munich: R. Oldenbourg, 1969.

Medlicott, William N. *The Congress of Berlin and After: A Diplomatic History of the Near Eastern Settlement, 1878–1880*. 2nd ed. Hamden: Archon Books, 1963.

Medrzecki, Wlodzimierz. "Germany and Ukraine between the Start of the Brest-Litovsk Peace Talks and Hetman Skoropadskyi's Coup." *Harvard Ukrainian Studies* 23, no. 1/2 (June 1999):47–71.

Melgunov, Sergei P. *Legenda o separatnom mire (kanun Revoliutsii)*. Paris, 1957.

"Memuary Vilhelma Habsburha, Polkovnika USS: Avtobiografiia," n.d. http://www.parafia.org.ua/biblioteka/istoriya-mova/ukrajinskyj-patriot-iz-dynastiji-habsburhiv/dokumenty-1-2-memuary-ertshertsoha-vilhelma-habsburha-lotrinhena/.

Mikhutina, Irina V. *Ukrainskii Brestskii mir: Put' vykhoda Rossii iz Pervoi mirovoi voiny i anatomiia konflikta mezhdu Sovnarkomom RSFSR i pravitel'stvom ukrainskoi Tsentral'noi Rady*. Moscow: Izdatel'stvo Evropa, 2007.

Milow, Caroline. *Die ukrainische Frage 1917–1923 im Spannungsfeld der europäischen Diplomatie*. Wiesbaden: Harrassowitz Verlag, 2002.

Mirnye peregovory v Brest-Litovske s 22/9 dekabria po 3 marta (18 fevralia) 1918 g. Vol. 1: *Plenarnye zasedaniia, zasedaniia politicheskoi komissii*. Moscow: Izdanie Narodnogo komissariata inostrannykh del, 1920.

Mommsen, Wolfgang J. "The Debate on German War Aims." In *German Imperialism, 1914–1918: The Development of a Historical Debate*, 195–218. New York: John Wiley & Sons, 1972.

Neck, Rudolf. *Arbeiterschaft und Staat im Ersten Weltkrieg 1914–1918 (A. Quellen).* Vol. I: *Der Staat (2. vom Juni 1917 bis zum Ende der Donaumonarchie im November 1918.* Veröffentlichungen der Arbeitsgemeinschaft für Geschichte der Arbeiterbewegung in Österreich 3. Vienna: Europa-Verlag, 1968.

Nowak, Karl Friedrich. *The Collapse of Central Europe.* London: K. Paul, Trench, Trubner, 1924.

Pajewski, Janusz. "Friedensaktionen in den Anfängen des I. Weltkriegs." *Acta Poloniae Historic,* no. 70 (1994):111–26.

Panaiotov, Panaiot. *Bulgaro-suvetski otnosheniia i vruzki, 1917–1923.* Sofia: Durzhavno izdatelstvo nauka i izkustvo, 1982.

Petrov, Petur H., ed. *Nauchna ekspeditsiia v Makedoniia i Pomoravieto, 1916 g.* Sofia: Universitetsko izdatelstvo "Sv. Kliment Okhridski," 1993.

Pidhainy, O.S. *The Formation of the Ukrainian Republic.* Toronto and New York: New Review Books, 1966.

Plaschka, Richard Georg. *Cattaro-Prag, Revolte und Revolution: Kriegsmarine und Heer Österreich-Ungarns im Feuer der Aufstandsbewegungen vom 1. Februar und 28. Oktober 1918.* Graz and Cologne: Verlag Hermann BohlausNachf, 1963.

– "The Army and Internal Conflict in the Austro-Hungarian Empire, 1918." In *East Central European Society in World War I,* edited by N.F. Dreisziger, Béla K. Király, and Albert A. Nofi, 338–53. Boulder: Social Science Monographs, 1985.

Plaschka, Richard Georg, Horst Haselsteiner, and Arnold Suppan. *Innere Front: Militärassistenz, Widerstand und Umsturz in der Donaumonarchie 1918.* Vol. 1 of Zwischen Streik und Meuterei. Vienna: Verlag für Geschichte und Politik, 1974.

Polic, Branko. "Brestlitovski mir: Prijelomni trenutak Oktobarske revolucije." *Politicka misao* 14, no. 3 (June 1977):467–92.

Proceedings of the Brest-Litovsk Peace Conference: The Peace Negotiations between Russia and the Central Powers 21 November, 1917 – 3 March, 1918. Washington, D.C.: Government Printing Office, 1918.

Radek, Karl. *Krushenie germanskogo imperializma i zadachi mezhdunarodnogo rabochego klassa: Doklad prochitannyi 2-go oktiabria v moskovskom sovetskom teatre.* Moscow: Izdatel'stvo Vserosiiskogo Tsentral'nogo Ispolnitel'nogo Komiteta Sovetov R., S., K. i K. Deputatov, 1918.

– "Lenin." In *In Defence of the Russian Revolution: A Selection of Bolshevik Writings,* edited by Al Richardson, 76–87. London: Porcupine Press, 1995.

Radoslavov, Vasil. *Bulgariia i svetovnata kriza.* Sofia: Sava Todorov, 1923.

Rauchensteiner, Manfried. *The First World War and the End of the Habsburg Monarchy, 1914–1918.* Vienna, Cologne, and Weimar: Böhlau, 2014.

Read, Christopher. *From Tsar to Soviets: The Russian People and Their Revolution, 1917–1921*. New York: Oxford University Press, 1996.

Renner, Karl. "Die taktische Streit." *Der Kampf: Sozialdemokratische Monatsschrift* 11, no. 1 (January 1918):18–30, quotations on 23–24.

Reshetar, John Stephen. *The Ukrainian Revolution, 1917–1920: A Study in Nationalism*. Princeton: Princeton University Press, 1952.

Reynolds, Michael A. *Shattering Empires: The Clash and Collapse of the Ottoman and Russian Empires, 1908–1918*. Cambridge: Cambridge University Press, 2011.

Ritter, Gerhard. *The Sword and the Scepter: The Problem of Militarism in Germany*. Vol. 4 of *The Reign of German Militarism and the Disaster of 1918*. 4 vols. Coral Gables: University of Miami Press, 1969.

Romsics, Ignác. *The Dismantling of Historic Hungary: The Peace Treaty of Trianon, 1920*. Boulder: East European Monographs, 2002.

Sanborn, Joshua. *Imperial Apocalypse: The Great War and the Destruction of the Russian Empire*. Oxford: Oxford University Press, 2014.

– "War of Decolonization: The Russian Empire in the Great War." In *The Empire and Nationalism at War*, edited by Eric Lohr, Vera Tolz, Alexander Semyonov, and Mark Von Hagen, 49–72. Vol. 2 of Russia's Great War and Revolution, 1914–1922. Bloomington: Slavica Publishers, 2014.

Sed'moi ekstrennyi s'ezd RKP (b), Mart 1918: Stenograficheskii otchet. Moscow: Gosudarstvennoe izdatel'stvo politicheskoi literatury, 1962.

Shanafelt, Gary W. *The Secret Enemy: Austria-Hungary and the German Alliance, 1914–1918*. Boulder: East European Monographs, 1985.

Shelokhaev, V.V., ed. *Partiia levykh sotsialistov-revoliutsionerov: Dokumenty i materialy 1917–1925 gg. v triokh tomakh*. Vol. 1 of *Iiul' 1917 – mai 1918*. 3 vols. Politicheskie partii Rossii. Konetd XIX-pervais tret' XX veka. Moscow: ROSSPEN, 2000.

Simonenko, R.G. *Brest: Dvobii viini i miru*. Kiev: Politvydav Ukrainy, 1988.

Skocpol, Theda. *States and Social Revolutions: A Comparative Analysis of France, Russia, and China*. Cambridge and New York: Cambridge University Press, 1979.

Skoropadsky, Pavlo. *Spohady: Kinets' 1917 – hruden' 1918*. Kiev and Philadelphia: Institut ukrains'koi akheohrafii ta dzhereloznanstva im. M.S. Hrushevs'koho, 1995.

Smith, S.A. *Red Petrograd: Revolution in the Factories, 1917–1918*. Cambridge and New York: Cambridge University Press, 1983.

Smolii, V.A., V.F. Verstiuk, Valerii Skal'skii, Volodymyr Holovchenko, Ruslan Pyrig, Tetiana Ostashko, and V.F. Soldatenko. *Narysy istorii ukrains'koï revoliutsii 1917–1921 rokiv*. 2 vols. Kiev: Naukova dumka, 2011.

Snyder, Timothy. *The Red Prince: The Secret Lives of a Habsburg Archduke*. New York: Basic Books, 2008.

Sobolev, Genadii. *Taina "nemetskogo zolota."* St. Petersburg: Izdatel'skii dom Neva, 2002.
Soldatenko, V.F. *Grazhdanskaia voina v Ukraine (1917–1920 gg.)*. Moscow: Novyi khronograf, 2012.
– *Revoliutsiina doba v Ukraini (1917–1920 roky): Lohika piznannia, istorychni postati, kliuchovi episody*. Kiev: Parlament'ske vyd-vo, 2011.
– *Revoliutsiini al'ternatyvy 1917 roku i Ukraina*. Proekt "Naukova knyha." Kiev: Naukova dumka, 2010.
– *Ukraina v Revoliutsiinu dobu: Istorychni ese-khroniky: U 4-kh tomakh*. 4 vols. Kiev: Svitogliad, 2010.
– *Ukrains'ka revoliutsiia Kontseptsiia ta istoriohrafiia*. Kiev: Poshukovo-vydavnyche ahenstvo "Knyha pam'iati Ukrainy, 1997.
Sovetsko-germanskie otnosheniia ot peregovorov v Brest-Litovske do podpisaniia Rapall'skogo dogovora. Moscow: Izdatel'stvo politicheskoi literatury, 1968.
Steglich, Wolfgang. *Die Friedenspolitik der Mittelmächte, 1917/18*. Wiesbaden: F. Steiner, 1964.
Steiner, Herbert. "Otto Bauer und der Kampf um den Frieden 1917–1918." *Zeitgeschichte* 15, no. 4 (January 1988):135–41.
Steinwedel, Charles. "To Make a Difference: The Category of Ethnicity in Late Imperial Russian Politics, 1861–1917." In *Russian Modernity: Politics, Knowledge, Practices*, edited by David L. Hoffmann and Yanni Kotsonis, 67–86. New York: St. Martin's Press, 2000.
Stone, Norman. *The Eastern Front, 1914–1917*. New York: Penguin Books, 1998.
Strachan, Hew. *The First World War*. 1st American ed. New York: Viking, 2004.
Subotić, Jelena. "Stories States Tell: Identity, Narrative, and Human Rights in the Balkans." *Slavic Review* 72, no. 2 (Summer 2013):306–26.
Sydorenko, Alexander. "Ukraine at Brest-Litovsk." *Ukrainian Quarterly* 24, no. 2 (June 1968):117–28.
Tatishchev, A.A. *Zemli i liudi: v gushche pereselencheskogo dvizheniia, 1906–1921*. Moscow: Russkii put', 2001.
Texts of the Russian "Peace": (With Maps). Washington: Government Printing Office, 1918.
Texts of the Ukrainian "Peace": (With Maps). Washington: Government Printing Office, 1918.
Thompson, John A. "Wilsonianism: The Dynamics of a Conflicted Concept." *International Affairs* 86, no. 1 (January 2010):27–47.
Tilly, Charles. *From Mobilization to Revolution*. Reading: Addison-Wesley, 1978.
Tratstsiak, S.A. *Brėstski mir i hramadska-palitychnyia pratsėsy ŭ Belarusi: Listapad 1917 – studzen' 1919 h*. Minsk: Belaruskaia navuka, 2009.

Trotsky, Leon. *Lenin: Notes for a Biographer*. New York: G.P. Putnam's Sons, 1971.
– *My Life: An Attempt at an Autobiography*. Mineola: Dover Publications, 2007.
– *Sochineniia*. Vol. 3, part 2, *Istoricheskoe podgotovlenie Oktiabria: Ot Oktiabria do Bresta*. Moscow and Leningrad: Gosudarstvennoe Izdatel'stvo, 1925.
– *Sochineniia*. Vol. 17, part 1, *Sovetskaia Respublika i kapitalisticheskii mir: Pervonachal'nyi period organizatsii sil*. Moscow and Leningrad: Gosudarstvennoe Izdatel'stvo, 1926.
– *The History of the Russian Revolution to Brest-Litovsk*. London: G. Allen & Unwin, 1919.
– *The Permanent Revolution; Results and Prospects*. London: New Park, 1962.
Tunstall, Graydon A. *Blood on the Snow: The Carpathian Winter War of 1915*. Lawrence: University Press of Kansas, 2010.
Um Friede, Freiheit und Recht: Der Jännerausstand des niederösterreichischen Proletariats. Vienna: Verlag der Wiener Volksbuchhandlung Ignaz Brand, 1918.
Utkin, Anatolii. *Unizhenie Rossii: Brest, Versal', Miunkhen*. Moscow: Eksmo Algoritm, 2004.
Velychenko, Stephen. *State Building in Revolutionary Ukraine: A Comparative Study of Governments and Bureaucrats, 1917–1922*. Toronto: University of Toronto Press, 2011.
– "Ukrainian Anticolonialist Thought in Comparative Perspective. A Preliminary Overview." *Ab Imperio: Studies of New Imperial History and Nationalism in the Post-Soviet Space*, no. 4 (2012):339–71.
Vernadsky, V.I. *Dnevniki 1917–1921: Oktiabr' 1917 – ianvar' 1920*. Kiev: Naukova dumka, 1994.
Verstiuk, V.F. "Ukrains'ka Tsentral'na Rada i ukrainizatsiia viis'kovykh chastyn rossiis'koi armii." *Ukrainski istorichni zhurnal*, no. 3 (2012):4–27.
Vladeva, Liliana V. "Brest-Litovskiiat mir i Bulgariia." *Izvestiia na durzhavnite arkhivi*, no. 72 (1996):47–61.
Von Hagen, Mark. "The Entangled Eastern Front in the First World War." In *The Empire and Nationalism at War*, edited by Eric Lohr, Vera Tolz, Alexander Semyonov, and Mark Von Hagen, 9–48. Vol. 2 of Russia's Great War and Revolution, 1914–1922. Bloomington: Slavica Publishers, 2014.
– "The Great War and the Mobilization of Ethnicity in the Russian Empire." In *Post-Soviet Political Order: Conflict and State Building*, edited by Barnett R. Rubin and Jack Snyder, 34–57. London and New York: Routledge, 1998.
Vynnychenko, Volodymyr. *Vidrozhdennia natsii*. 3 vols. Kiev and Vienna: Dzvin, 1920.

Vyshyvanyi, Vasyl. "Ukrains'ki Sichovi Stril'tsi z vesni 1918 r. do perevorotu v Avstrii." In *Polkovnik Vasyl Vyshyvanyi*, 45–56. Winnipeg: D. Mykytiuk, 1956.
Wade, Rex A., ed. *Documents of Soviet Foreign Policy: The Triumph of Bolshevism, 1917–1919*. Vol. 1 of Documents of Soviet History. Gulf Breeze: Academic International Press, 1991.
Wargelin, Clifford F. "A High Price for Bread: The First Treaty of Brest-Litovsk and the Break-up of Austria-Hungary, 1917–1918." *The International History Review* 19, no. 4 (November 1997):757–88.
– "Bread, Peace, and Poland: The Economic, Political, and Diplomatic Origins of Habsburg Policy at Brest-Litovsk, 1914–1918." PhD diss., University of Wisconsin at Madison, 1994.
– "The Austro-Polish Solution: Diplomacy, Politics, and State Building in Wartime Austria-Hungary 1914–1918." *East European Quarterly* 42, no. 3 (Fall 2008):253–73.
– "The Economic Collapse of Austro-Hungarian Dualism, 1914–1918." *East European Quarterly* 34, no. 3 (Fall 2000):261–89.
Weitsman, Patricia A. *Dangerous Alliances: Proponents of Peace, Weapons of War*. Stanford: Stanford University Press, 2004.
Weitz, Eric D. "From the Vienna to the Paris System: International Politics and the Entangled Histories of Human Rights, Forced Deportations, and Civilizing Missions." *The American Historical Review* 113, no. 5 (December 2008):1313–43.
Wheeler-Bennett, John Wheeler. *The Forgotten Peace: Brest-Litovsk, March 1918*. New York: Morrow, 1939.
Wildman, Allan K. *The End of the Russian Imperial Army*. 2 vols. Princeton: Princeton University Press, 1980.
Windischgrätz, Lajos von. *My Memoirs*. Boston and New York: Houghton Mifflin, 1921.
Winkler, Ernst. *Der grosse Jänner-Streik 1918: Ein Kampf für Brot, Frieden und Freiheit*. Wiener Neustadt: Druck- und Verlagsanstalt Gutenberg, 1968.
Winnicki, Zdzisław. *Rada regencyjna Królestwa Polskiego i jej organy (1917–1918)*. Wrocław: Wektory, 1991.
Yekelchyk, Serhy. "A Long Goodbye: The Legacy of Soviet Marxism in Post-Communist Ukrainian Historiography." *Ab Imperio: Studies of New Imperial History and Nationalism in the Post-Soviet Space*, no. 4 (2012):401–16.
Zeman, Z.A.B, ed. *Germany and the Revolution in Russia, 1915–1918: Documents from the Archives of the German Foreign Ministry*. London: Oxford University Press, 1958.
Zetterberg, Seppo. *Die Liga der fremdvölker Russlands 1916–1918: Ein Beitrag zu Deutschlands antirussischem Propagandakrieg unter den Fremdvölkern Russlands im Ersten Weltkrieg*. Helsinki: Finnische Historische Gesellschaft, 1978.

Index

Adler, Fritz, 80–1, 91, 105, 108, 114
Adler, Viktor, 85, 89–90, 103–4, 111–12, 114
Albania, 162–3
Aleksandrov, Valentin, 164, 175
Altvater, Vasilii, 24, 26–8, 30–1
Ambrosius, Lloyd E., 49
Anastasov, Todor, 167, 169
Anatolia, 31, 37, 50
Andrássy, Gyula the Elder, 33
Andrássy, Gyula the Younger, 194
Antonov-Ovseenko, Vladimir A., 125, 131
Arbeiter Zeitung, 17, 87, 214; Great January Strike and, 89–94, 102–3, 105, 108, 116
Ardahan, 37, 210–11, 213
Arens, Olavi, 33–4
Armee Oberkommando (AOK: Austro-Hungarian High Command), 13, 22, 99, 102, 119, 137, 155, 207, 244n8
armistice of 1917, 31, 40; armistice negotiations, 21–31; Bolshevik "Declaration of Peace" and, 15–21; contrasted with 11/18 armistice, 21–2

Arz von Straußenburg, General Arthur, 106, 207
Austria-Hungary: Austro-Marxism, 44, 91, 108–9, 119; Austro-Polish Solution, 32–4, 56, 59, 98, 103–4, 132–3, 214; Bolshevik peace proposal and, 17; Brest-Litovsk Treaty and, 5, 10; effect of November Revolution on, 83–4, 91; food riots in, 80, 83, 86–7, 89; food shortages in, 6, 79–84, 88, 93, 95–102, 104, 112, 117, 132–4; Great January Strike of 1918 in, 39, 81–3, 87–95, 102–19, 185, 222; internal unrest within, 17–18, 77, 80–1, 85, 95, 104, 106–7, 114, 118–19; mutiny of sailors of, 117–18; potential for revolution in, 118–19, 120, 183, 185, 188, 222, 244n9; POWs and, 55; relationship with Bolsheviks, 39, 193–4, 201, 206–7; relationship with Germany, 15, 32–3, 43, 54–6, 73, 76, 85, 198–9, 219, 239n51; relationship with Ukraine, 10, 119, 128, 131–2, 193, 204, 222; self-determination and, 45, 131; threat of signing separate peace

by, 32, 43, 54–6, 76, 193, 238n42;
Treaty of Trianon and, 215; war
aims of, 32–3, 53–4, 56, 193, 197–8.
See also Central Powers; Habsburg
Empire; Quadruple Alliance
Austro-Hungarian High Command
(*Armee Oberkommando*, AOK), 102,
119, 137, 155, 207;
armistice with Russia, 13–14; Great
January Strike and, 244n8
Austro-Marxism, 44, 91, 108–9. *See
also* SDAPÖ
Austro-Polish Solution, 32–4, 56, 98,
103–4, 132, 214
Avramov, Roman, 60–1

Ballhausplatz, 6, 22, 133, 165, 217
Balogh, Adalbert, 224
Battle Group Archduke Wilhelm, 152
Battle of Gorlice-Tarnow, 12
Battle of Masurian Lakes, 12
Battle of Tannenberg, 12
Batum, 37, 210–11, 213
Bauer, Otto, 90–1, 119, 247n40,
247n41
Baumgart, Winfried, 9–10
Bavaria, 98, 189, 229n15
Beneš, Edvard, 69
Berend, Iván T., 4–5, 225n4
Bethmann-Hollweg, Theobald von,
9, 13, 34, 65, 198–9
Bey, Nessimy, 42, 50, 64, 128
Bihl, Wolfdieter, 194, 238n40
Bismark, Otto von, 65, 134, 160
Bitsenko, Anastasia, 24
Bohemia, 69, 79, 102, 104, 111, 116, 139
Bolsheviks, 37–9, 184–91, 223;
armistice of 1917 and, 22–30;
Austrian communists and, 91;
effect of Brest-Litovsk treaty

on, 214–15, 224; first encounters
with Central Powers, 28;
following the First World War,
216; foreign policy of, 5, 23,
28–9, 39, 57; French Revolution
and, 188; Great January Strike
and, 82, 101; historiography of,
191, 217; hosting of Petrograd
negotiations, 57–61; imperialism
and, 219; international revolution
and, 37–40, 49, 57, 61, 68, 77–8,
119, 126, 183–9, 192, 194–5, 199,
208, 214; Left SRs, 192, 210,
218; Marxism and, 38, 49, 57;
November Revolution and, 14; as
party-state machine, 187; peace
proposal offered by, 14–21, 25,
40; propaganda activities of, 25,
28–9, 57, 59–60, 78, 183, 211–12;
relationship with Austria, 39,
193–4, 201, 206–7; relationship
with Bulgarians, 57, 60–1, 161,
165, 168–9, 176, 178, 181, 183;
relationship with Germany, 183,
185–6, 190; renewal of hostilities
with Germany, 207–8, 223; seen
as German agents, 18, 184, 189,
229n24; self-determination and,
42–4, 46–7, 68, 196; signing
of Brest-Litovsk Treaty by,
210–12, 223; "socialism in one
country" and, 186–7; strategy at
Brest-Litovsk Conference, 184,
191–7, 199, 214, 222; surrender
to Germany of, 209–11; terms
acceptable to, 39–40; Ukraine
and, 7, 124, 155, 183, 193, 196–7,
204; Ukrainian Bolsheviks, 125,
135; use of workers and peasants
as diplomats, 24, 27–8, 231n46;

violations of Brest-Litovsk Treaty by, 217–18; withdrawal from negotiations by, 202–4. *See also* Russia; Soviet Union
Bolshevism, German strategy at Brest-Litovsk negotiations and, 9; in Ukraine, 125
Borowsky, Peter, 67–8
Bosnia-Herzegovina, 56
Brest-Litovsk, city of, 41
Brest-Litovsk Peace Conference, 3–4, 221–2; Austrian internal unrest and, 82, 84–6, 89, 92–4, 99, 102, 104–7, 117–19; Bolshevik strategy at, 184, 191–7; Bolshevik withdrawal from, 202–3; Bulgarian involvement in, 159, 164–70, 179–82; Christmas celebrated at, 50–1; discussions over separate peace with Ukraine, 123–4, 126–7; dispute over location, 66; effect of Austrian strike on, 105–6; final phase of negotiations: Feb-March 1918, 203–12, 223; first phase of negotiations: December 1917, 47–57, 77; historiography of, 10, 159; languages used at, 237n20; Polish representation at, 73–5, 197; refusal of Entente powers to join, 65, 67–8, 77; Russian peasants used as diplomats, 24, 27–8, 231n46; second phase of negotiations: January 1918, 65–77; third phase of negotiations: February 1918, 191–203; Ukrainian delegation to, 125–7, 222; use of academics at, 176
Brest-Litovsk Treaties, 4, 212–16; armistice preceding, 21–31; Bolshevik violations of, 217–18; Bulgarian signing of, 164; coalition warfare and, 6; contrasted with Treaty of Trianon, 215; contrasted with Treaty of Versailles, 8–9, 215; decolonization and, 215, 223; effect of on Habsburg Empire, 6–7, 223–4; effect of on Ottoman Empire, 8; effect of on Russian empire, 213–15; effect of on Ukraine, 7, 120, 214; German war aims and, 213; historiography of, 8–10, 212–13, 217; Imperial collapse and, 4, 7, 11, 120, 215, 222; importance of, 4, 11, 223; international revolution and, 119, 220; main provisions of, 213–14; Russian signing of, 211–12; self-determination and, 5–6, 42–4, 77, 221–2; signed by Bolsheviks, 210–12, 223; Soviet-Central Power conflict following, 216, 219; Soviet interpretations of, 10, 213, 217; Soviet renunciation of, 219; Ukrainian signing of, 4, 10, 136, 156, 201, 223; Ukrainian treaty of Brest-Litovsk, 10, 120, 135–7, 156, 201, 223; Ukrainization and, 121–2, 151, 157; vilification of, 212–13
Britain, 19, 52, 160, 183, 202, 205; armistice of 1917 and, 30; British war aims, 66; as imperial power, 202, 215; Ukraine and, 126
buffer states, 5
Bukharin, Nikolai, 10, 188–90, 208, 223
Bukovina, 99, 130–1
Bulgaria, 8, 181–2; armistice of 1917 and, 26–7; Austrian food shortages and, 99–101; Bolshevik peace proposal and, 17–19, 164–6; conflict with Ottoman

Empire, 160, 162, 166–8, 173–5, 181; Dobrudja and, 17, 21, 99–101, 161, 165–8, 172–5, 177, 179–81, 263n30, 263n36; "dream of Byzantium" and, 8, 159–60, 162, 164, 167, 170, 172, 174–5, 181–2, 261n4; foreign policy of, 159, 161–2; Ioffe Program and, 165, 168, 172, 175; Macedonia and, 17, 99–100, 161–4, 166–8, 170; national unification and, 19, 159, 162–4, 166, 169–72, 181; participation in Brest-Litovsk Peace Conference, 159, 164–70, 179–82; participation in Petrograd negotiations, 57–8, 60–1; relationship with Bolsheviks, 57, 60–1, 161, 165, 168–9, 176, 178, 181, 183; relationship with Central Power allies, 161–3, 166–7, 173–5, 178–82; relationship with Russia, 173, 176–8; relationship with Ukraine, 177–82; self-determination and, 164, 172–3, 175–6, 181–2; sense of victimization and, 173–4, 179; Treaty of San Stefano, 160–3, 172, 176, 181, 212; war aims of, 21, 50, 160–8, 172–3, 179. *See also* Central Powers; Quadruple Alliance

Burián, István, 134, 154, 199

Cambon, M. Jules, 233n77
Central Powers: armistice of 1917 and, 13–14, 20–3, 25–7, 31, 40; Bolshevik peace proposal and, 5, 15–21; Bolsheviks and, 191–4, 198–9, 205, 219–20, 223; Bolshevik surrender and, 210–11; collapse of, 224; defeat of, 181; first encounter with Bolsheviks, 28; Ioffe Program and, 50; military strategy of, 12; participation in Petrograd negotiations, 57–61; position at beginning of treaty negotiations, 43; reaction to Bolshevik withdrawal from negotiations, 203–5; reaction to Ioffe Program, 51–2, 103; self-determination and, 16, 44, 77; separate peace with Ukraine, 10, 29, 120, 135–7, 201; Skoropadskyi and, 146; war aims of, 21, 31–7; withdrawal of from Ukraine, 151. *See also* Austria-Hungary; Austro-Hungarian High Command; Bulgaria; German High Command; Germany

Chaprashikov, Stefan, 58, 60–1, 191–2
China, 45
Christmas Truce, 20
Churchill, Winston, 3
coalition warfare, 6, 15
Cobban, Alfred, 42
collective security, 49
Comintern (Communist International), 57
Committee for the Salvation of Ukraine, 143–4
Congress of Berlin, 33, 160–1, 171, 173, 262n8
Constant, Stephen, 261n4
Coudenhove, Max von, 96
Courland, 5, 13, 69–70, 107, 232n70, 238n42; German occupation of, 33–4, 36, 46, 50, 52–3, 69–70; independence of, 72, 77, 90, 242n93; Russian loss of, 12–13, 16, 53, 209, 213
"crisis zone," 5, 225n4
Croatia-Slavonia, 56

Csáky von Kererzek und Adorjan, Emerich, 22, 39
Csicserics, Maximilian von, 54
Czapp, Karl von, 111–12
Czechoslovakia, 69, 139
Czernin, Otto, 99–101, 100–1, 165, 171, 175, 177
Czernin von und zu Chudenitz, Count Ottokar, 49–56; agitated behavior of, 54, 130; armistice of 1917 and, 29–30, 32–3; Austrian food shortages and, 83, 96–9; Austrian war aims and, 32–3, 53, 232n70; Bolshevik peace proposal and, 15–18; Bulgarian war aims and, 164–71, 175, 179; Christmas speech of, 43, 51, 62, 66–7, 170; conference of 5 February and,197–9; conflict with Germans, 55–6, 198–9; conflict with Ottoman Empire, 50; Great January Strike and, 82, 85, 92, 94, 103, 108, 112, 114, 117; as leader of Brest-Litovsk delegation, 41–2, 53, 166; photo of, 71; Polish self-determination and, 73–5; reaction to Bolshevik withdrawal from negotiations, 204, 206–7; reaction to Ioffe Program, 51–4, 103; relationship with Bolsheviks, 39, 49, 192–7, 200–1, 216–17; relationship with Kühlmann, 236n3, 238n42; Russian Revolution and, 13; self-determination and, 67; Ukraine and, 127–8, 130–5, 192, 196

Daimler Motor Works, 86–7
Dean, Martin, 56
Debo, Richard K., 49, 187, 190, 200, 208
decolonization, 215, 223, 271n3

"Decree on Peace," 15–20, 25, 40; armistice following, 21–31; Central Powers' reactions to, 15–21, 164; Ioffe Program and, 48; main tenets of, 43; "no annexations" clause of, 18–19, 48, 50, 53, 164–6; offered by Bolsheviks, 14
Demblin, Count August, 59, 97, 106–7
De Pottere, Georg, 219
Deutsch, Julius, 109
Dimitrov, Georgi, 57
Dobrudja, 6, 170–5, 263n30; Bulgaria and, 17, 21, 99–101, 161, 165–8, 172–5, 177, 179–81, 263n30, 263n36
Dobryi, Abram, 143–4
Domes, Franz, 81, 86, 93, 111
Dontsov, Boris, 150
Doroshenko, Dmytro, 147–8
Dual Monarchy. See Austria-Hungary
Dukhonin, Nikolai, 19–20
Dzerzhinskii, "Iron" Feliks, 218

Eastern Front, 3, 106; armistice of 1917 and, 12–13, 21, 40; Kerensky Offensive, 14; map of, xix; renewal of hostilities along, 206–9, 223; unofficial armistices along, 20
economic freedom, principle of, 48, 52
Eichhorn, Field-marshal Hermann von, 143–4, 150
Ellenbogen, Wilhelm, 85–6, 90–1, 103
Entente Powers, 12; armistice of 1917 and, 30; Bolshevik peace proposal and, 16, 18; refusal to join Brest-Litovsk conference, 65, 67–8, 77; relationship with Russia, 215–16; relationship with Ukraine, 126; self-determination and, 46, 65–6. See also Britain; France; Russia

Esterházy, Móric, 83, 96
Estonia, 33–4, 205, 207–8, 223;
  Bolshevism in, 216; national
  movements in, 34, 36, 139;
  proposed union with Germany,
  70; Russian evacuation of, 33,
  201–2, 208–9; self-determination
  and, 69

Favoriten, 92–3, 105, 107, 111, 115–16
February Revolution of 1917, 8, 13,
  36, 215; effect of on Ukraine, 122;
  self-determination and, 46; strikes
  and, 88
Fedyshyn, Oleh S., 10, 123, 146
Felshtinskii, Iurii, 187, 191
Ferdinand, Maximilian Karl, 19,
  61, 100, 162–3, 170–2, 181, 261n4;
  abdication of, 159–60
Finland, 36, 195, 205, 208–9, 213–14,
  216
First World War, 12; following
  Bolshevik withdrawal from
  negotiations, 206–8; food shortages
  and, 95; impact of ideology on,
  221; as imperialist war, 14; Italian
  front, 106, 149, 162–3; Kerensky
  Offensive, 14; unofficial armistices
  during, 20. *See also* Eastern Front;
  Western Front
Fischer, Fritz, 9, 160, 213, 226n9
Fischer Controversy, 9
Flanner, Karl, 87
Floridsdorf, 92–3
Flotow, Baron, 88, 103–4
Fokke, Colonel Dzhon, 23–4, 26, 28,
  30–1, 51, 126, 135, 197, 203, 231n46
Forgách von Ghymes und Gacs,
  Count Johann, 143, 146, 154, 217
Fourteen Points, 48–9, 66

France, 19, 183; armistice of 1917
  and, 30; as imperial power, 72,
  215; relationship with Russia,
  215–16; Ukraine and, 126
French Revolution, 188, 205, 208

Galicia, 79, 109, 130–3, 152; food
  production in, 79, 99; Poland and,
  32, 73; Ukraine and, 103, 128,
  130–3, 204, 222
Ganchev, Colonel Petur, 22, 26, 130,
  165–6, 169–72, 180
Gautsch, Baron, 76
German High Command (*Oberste
  Heeresleitung*, OHL): ambitions
  of, 33–4; armistice of 1917 and,
  22; armistice with Russia, 13–14;
  German constitutional crisis
  and, 62–5; military culture
  of, 35; opposition to Austro-
  Polish Solution, 32–3; reaction
  to Bolshevik withdrawal from
  negotiations, 205–6, 223; reaction
  to Ioffe Program, 53–5; renewal
  of hostilities with Russia,
  206–9, 223; Ukraine and, 137,
  143; ultimatum issued by, 192;
  ultimatum to Russia and, 76; war
  aims of, 32
Germany: Austrian food shortages
  and, 97–9, 101; Bolshevik
  violations of Brest-Litovsk Treaty
  and, 217–18; borders of, 225n1;
  conference of 5 February in,
  197–9; constitutional crisis in,
  62–5; Dobryi Affair and, 143–4;
  encirclement of, 35–6; potential
  for revolution in, 183, 185–6,
  188, 208; reaction to Bolshevik
  withdrawal from negotiations,

204–6; relationship with Austria, 15, 32–3, 43, 54–6, 73, 76, 85, 198–9, 219, 239n51; relationship with Bolsheviks, 183, 185–6, 190, 195, 218–19; relationship with Poland, 63–4; relations with other Central Powers, 15, 32–3, 43, 198–9; response to Bolshevik peace proposal, 15, 18–19; strategic position of, 35–6; strikes in, 185; territories occupied by, 19; threat of signing separate peace by, 13, 33, 134; war aims of, 34–6, 197–8, 213; wartime government of, 62. *See also* Central Powers; German High Command; Quadruple Alliance

Golczewski, Frank, 126, 137, 153

Gorbachev, Mikhail, 224

Gorky, Maxim, 60–1

Gratz, Gustav, 199–200

Great January Strike (1918), 7, 39, 81–3, 87–95, 102–19, 185, 222, 244n9; Brest-Litovsk negotiations and, 104–6; ending of, 113–18; food riots and, 82, 87; growth and spread of, 88–95, 102–12; immediate background and outbreak of, 83–8; map of, xix; Ukrainian annexations and, 132

Great War. *See* First World War

Greece, 50, 158, 161–2, 168, 173, 182

Groener, Wilhelm, 143

Guthier, Steven L., 139

Habsburg Empire. *See* Austria-Hungary

Habsburg, Wilhelm, Archduke von: Austro-Polish Solution and, 32, 104; Bolshevik peace proposal and, 15–18; food shortages and, 82, 96, 101; implications of Brest-Litovsk Treaty for, 6–7, 11; Poland and, 73, 112; relationship with Germany, 32; revolution in, 7, 119; self determination within, 15, 131; Treaty of Trianon and, 215; Ukrainian annexations and, 130–1, 134–5, 204; Ukrainization and, 121, 146, 151–6; war aims of, 56

Hádik, Janos, 83, 96–7, 99

Hahlweg, Werner, 9

Hai-Nyzhnyk, Pablo, 125, 139, 141, 145

Hakki Pasha, Prince Ibrahim, 47, 56, 211, 237n20

Halych-Volhynia, Kingdom of, 132

Hanusch, Ferdinand, 111

Haselsteiner, Horst, 278

Healy, Maureen, 80, 82–3

Hellferich, Karl, 219

Hempel, 59, 192

Hertling, Count Georg Friedrich von, 54; armistice of 1917 and, 34; Bulgarian war aims and, 174; German war aims and, 34; negotiations regarding Bolsheviks, 198–9; Polish self-determination and, 73; reaction to Bolshevik peace proposal, 18; ultimatum to Russia and, 202

Hess, Moses, 44

Hetmanate, 144, 146–51, 155, 214. *See also* Ukraine

Hindenburg, Field-marshal Paul von, 34–5, 53–5, 64–5, 76, 192, 201; ultimatum to Russia and, 76

Hobsbawm, Eric, 221

Höfer, General Anton, 86, 88, 111–12

Hoffman, Jerry, 123, 128
Hoffmann, Major-General Max von: agitated behavior of, 54; armistice of 1917 and, 22, 24–9, 31, 33; Bolsheviks and, 28; Bulgarian war aims and, 167, 179–80; on conflict following Bolshevik withdrawal from war, 203, 207, 216; criticism of, 92, 104; Czernin's Christmas speech and, 62; German constitutional crisis and, 63–5; as leader of Brest-Litovsk delegation, 42; memoirs of, 170; opposition to ultimatum to Russia, 76; photo of, 71; Polish self-determination and, 75; reaction to Bolshevik peace proposal, 18; reaction to Bolshevik withdrawal from negotiations, 204; surrender of Bolsheviks and, 209; Ukrainian annexations and, 130–1; Ukrainian independence and, 128, 130
Hohenlohe-Schillingsfurst, Prince Gottfried zu, 17, 67, 85, 97–8, 206
Hohenzollern Empire, 3, 7, 11, 44, 119, 184
Holden, Anne Christine, 161
Holquist, Peter, 4
Holubovych, Vsevolod, 113, 129–30, 143, 145, 180
Hönning, Baron, 98
Horak, Stephan M., 10
Hroch, Miroslav, 138–9, 256n68
Hull, Isabel V., 35
Hunczak, Taras, 146
Hungary. *See* Austria-Hungary

Imperial collapse: Brest-Litovsk Treaty and, 4, 7, 11, 120, 215; of Russia, 5, 8, 120, 122–3, 214–16, 222; self-determination and, 182

Imperialism: The Highest State of Capitalism (Lenin, 1920), 14
indigenization *[korenizatsiia]* policy, 7, 121, 138, 157
Ioffe, Adolf: agitated behavior of, 54; armistice of 1917 and, 22–5, 27, 30; Bulgarian war aims and, 168; Great January Strike and, 92; as leader of Brest-Litovsk delegation, 42, 56, 235n96; negotiations with Central Powers, 52–3; presentation of Ioffe Program by, 47–8; secrecy of Brest-Litovsk negotiations and, 47; views on self-determination, 168–9, 176. *See also* Ioffe Program
Ioffe Program, 47–51, 67, 85, 103, 164–5, 190; Central Powers' response to, 51–2, 165, 168, 172, 175, 181; six points of, 42–3
Italy, 30, 56, 167, 174; armistice of 1917 and, 30; Italian front, 106, 149, 162–3

Kaledin, Ataman Alexie, 124–5, 195
Kamenev, Lev, 22, 24, 30, 203
Kant, Immanuel, 44
Karl Franz Joseph, 54; Austrian food shortages and, 83, 96–7, 134–5; Austrian unrest and, 106–7; Bolshevik peace proposal and, 15–6, 29; Poland and, 59; relationship with Bolsheviks, 193–4; Ukraine and, 152, 154–5
Kars, 37, 210–11, 213
Kerensky Offensive, 14
Kholm (Chelm), 130–2, 135, 204, 222
Khrystiuk, Pavlo, 121, 135, 137, 142
Kolushev, A., 174
Komornyi, O., 145
Krupskaia, Nadezhda, 189
Krylenko, Nikolai, 20, 30

Kucharzewski, Jan, 73–4, 133
Kühlmann, Baron Richard von:
armistice of 1917 and, 34; Austrian food shortages and, 97; Bolshevik violations of Brest-Litovsk Treaty and, 217–18; Bolshevik withdrawal from war and, 203–6; Bulgarian war aims and, 165–7, 169–73, 175, 179–80; conference of 5 February and, 197–9; conflict with Ottoman Empire, 50; debates with Trotsky, 68–72; dismissal of, 233n78; draft treaty proposed by, 56; German constitutional crisis and, 63–5; German war aims and, 198–9; Ioffe Program and, 50–1, 55; as leader of Brest-Litovsk delegation, 42, 47, 166; negotiating strategy of, 67; photo of, 71;Polish border strip and, 34; Polish self-determination and, 73–5; Popov and, 178–9; reaction to Bolshevik peace proposal, 18–20; relationship with Czernin, 236n3, 238n42; relationship with German military, 202, 240n77; secrecy of Brest-Litovsk negotiations and, 47; self-determination and, 68–70; Ukraine and, 127–8, 130, 192, 196; ultimatums to Russia and, 76, 201–2, 217; use of term "security" by, 35, 233n77
Kupchan, Charles A., 219–20
Küstenland, 56, 79, 89, 99, 117

Landwehr von Pragenau, General Ottokar, 96–8
Latvia, 34, 69, 139, 190, 216
League of Russia's Foreign Peoples, 122
Left SRs, 192, 210, 218

Lenin, Vladimir Il'ich, 185–91, 208–9; anti-war sentiment of, 14; Austro-Marxism and, 91–2; Bolshevik withdrawal from negotiations and, 206–8; Brest-Litovsk Treaty as victory for, 10, 224; as head of state, 187, 189; international revolution and, 37, 49, 185–8, 208; nationalism and, 7, 45; renewal of hostilities with Germany and, 207–9; seen as German agent, 18, 184, 189, 229n24; self-determination and, 43–6; strategy at Brest-Litovsk negotiations, 9; surrender of Bolsheviks and, 209; Trotsky and, 189–91, 206; violations of Brest-Litovsk Treaty and, 217–18
Leopold, Prince of Bavaria, 25, 47, 50, 181
Levytskyi, Mykola, 113, 124
liberal internationalism, 43, 49, 221
Linz, 84, 109, 111
Lithuania, 13, 107, 200, 238n42; German occupation of, 33–4, 36, 46, 50, 52, 63, 202, 233n70; independence of, 53, 72, 77, 90, 242n93; Polish- Lithuanian Commonwealth, 72, 133; Russian loss of, 12–13, 16, 53, 209, 213, 216; self-determination and, 46
Liubynskyi, Mykola, 113, 124, 129, 131, 196–7; Dobryi Affair and, 144
Liulevicius, Vejas G., 63
Livonia, 33–4, 69–70, 190, 198, 201–2, 205, 207–9, 213–14, 223
Lloyd George, David, 48, 66, 72, 221
London, Treaty of, 56
Longinović, Tomislav Z., 173
Lubomirski, Zdzisław, 133

Ludendorff, General Erich: Austro-Hungarian war aims and, 198; Bulgarian war aims and, 174; Czernin's Christmas speech and, 62; German constitutional crisis and, 63–5; German war aims and, 36; negotiations with Bolsheviks, 199; reaction to Bolshevik peace proposal, 18–19; reaction to Bolshevik withdrawal from negotiations, 205; reaction to Ioffe Program, 53; strategy at Brest-Litovsk negotiations, 9; use of term "security" by, 35

Macedonia, 160, 168, 263n35; Bulgaria and, 17, 99–100, 161–4, 166–8, 170
Makarenko, Pavel Vasil'evich, 191
Mandel, David, 88
Manela, Erez, 42–3
Markov, Georgi, 165, 177
Martin, Terry, 138, 219
Marx, Karl, 44
Marxism, 38, 45; Austro-Marxism, 44, 91, 108–9, 119; Bolshevik understanding of, 38, 49, 169; international revolution and, 57
Masaryk, Thomaš, 69
May, Arthur James, 194
Mayer, Arno J., 42
Mazower, Mark, 160, 221
Medrzecki, Wlodzimierz, 135–6
Melgunov, Sergei P., 12
Mérey von Kapos-Meré, Kajetan, 22, 29–30, 32, 165
Mikhutina, Irina V., 10, 24, 146, 185, 187, 191
Mirbach, Count Wilhelm von, 58–9, 61, 218

Montenegro, 56
Moonsound Islands, 26–7, 30–1, 200, 202, 213
Moravia, 79, 85, 104, 111, 116

Narkomindel (*Narodnyi komissar inostrannykh del*, Russian people's commissar for foreign affairs), 30, 68, 75, 190–2, 194, 197, 199–200; armistice of 1917 and, 30; Trotsky as, 38, 66, 184–5, 205
Narodno Subraine, 161, 171, 177
nationalism, 45
national statehood, 158, 182, 222; contrasted with international revolution, 126, 178; Ukrainian, 138, 141, 150–1
national unification: Bulgaria and, 19, 159, 162–4, 166, 169–72, 181
nation state consolidation, 8, 158, 160
nation state formation, 8, 120, 122, 158
New Diplomacy, 42–3
Nicholas II, 13
Nikolaevich, Nikolai, 73
non-interference principle, 16, 30, 50, 127
November (October) Revolution of 1917, 14, 31, 36, 40; effect of on Austria-Hungary, 83–4, 91
Nowak, Karl Friedrich, 55

Oberndorff, Alfred von, 180, 192
Odessa, 137, 144–5
Ordjonikidze, Sergo, 218
Ostrowski, Jósef, 133
Ottoman Empire, 8, 158; Bolshevik peace proposal and, 17–19; Bolshevik surrender and, 210–11; conflict with Bulgaria, 160, 162, 166–8, 173–5, 181; demands of, 50;

implications of Brest-Litovsk Treaty for, 11; relationship with Ukraine, 128; relations with Germany, 18–19; self-determination and, 45; war aims of, 37

Pallavicini, Margrave Johann von, 18, 37, 174
Paris Peace Conference, 5, 8, 226n6; self-determination and, 43, 48, 68–9, 72, 222; use of academics at, 176
Pasha, Hakki, 47, 56, 211, 237n20
Pasha, Talaat, 37, 71, 174, 179; photo of, 71
Pasha, Zekki, 22
Peace of Tilsit, 208, 213, 217
Penfield, Frederick C., 13, 80–1
Persia, 45
Petrograd negotiations (1917–18), 57–61
Pichon, Stéphen, 65
Piłsudski, Jozef, 22
Plaschka, Richard Georg, 90, 244n8
Pokorny, Hermann, 22
Poland, 72–4; Austrian food shortages and, 98; Austro-Polish Solution, 32–4, 56, 98, 103–4, 132–3, 214; German war aims and, 34, 50, 240n74; independence of, 112; Polish border strip, 34, 63–4, 198; Polish-Lithuanian Commonwealth, 72, 133; "Polish Question," 34, 63–4, 72, 181; potential for revolution in, 59; Russian loss of, 12, 16; Trotsky's trip to, 197; Ukrainian annexations and, 130–5, 204, 222
Polish- Lithuanian Commonwealth, 72, 133

Polosov, Mykhailo, 113
Popov, Hristo: Bulgarian war aims and, 50, 165–8, 179–80; Kühlmann and, 178; participation in Brest-Litovsk negotiations, 42, 165–71, 176, 180; photo of, 71; recall of, 180–2; relationship with Russia, 176–8; Ukrainian independence and, 128–9; views on self-determination, 168–9, 176
Prisoners of War (POWs), 57, 84, 223–4; reimbursement for costs of, 52, 55, 213
property qualification, 70
Provisional Government (Russian), 13–14, 46, 122
Prussia. See Germany
Putilov Works, 88

Quadruple Alliance, 12; armistice negotiations and, 27; Bolshevik peace proposal and, 16, 19; Bulgaria and, 164, 171, 175; Dobrudja Question and, 181–2; dysfunctional nature of, 101; relationship with Ukraine, 120, 127–8, 134–5. See also Austria-Hungary; Bulgaria; Central Powers; Germany; Ottoman Empire

Rada, Ukrainian, 121–2; Austro-German military intervention and, 7; Dobryi Affair and, 143–4; historiography of, 125, 129; land socialization and, 141–2, 150, 157; relationship with Bolsheviks, 124–6, 129, 135, 137, 184, 196–7; relationship with Central Powers, 129, 142–4, 204,

222; representation at Brest-Litovsk negotiations, 126, 128; Ukrainian independence and, 129; Ukrainian language and, 140–1, 148; Ukrainization and, 7, 121–2, 138–40; urban centres and, 144–5. *See also* Ukraine

Radek, Karl, 44, 188, 213, 219

Radoslavov, Vasil, 161; Austrian food shortages and, 100–1; Bolshevik peace proposal and, 19; Brest-Litovsk peace conference and, 165–6, 169–70, 180–1; Bulgarian/Russian cooperation and, 176–7; Bulgarian war aims and, 161–2; fall of Radoslavov government, 159–60; Ioffe Program and, 165; Petrograd negotiations and, 60–1; Ukrainian independence and, 130

Rákosi, Mátyás, 224

Rauchensteiner, Manfried, 54, 82

Reichsrat, 80, 88, 104, 112, 132, 142, 206

Renner, Karl, 86, 88, 90–3, 103, 108–9, 111, 114

Reynolds, Michael A., 37, 211

Riga, 14, 26, 200, 202

Ritter, Gerhard, 9, 213

Rizov, Dimitur, 164, 180

Romania, 56, 61, 146, 161, 181, 193, 210; armistice with Central Powers, 13–14, 20–1; Bulgaria and, 21, 50, 166, 173–4, 263n30; as food source, 7, 96, 98–101, 118

Rosenberg, Friedrich Hans von, 22, 24, 42, 127–8, 130, 179, 202, 210–11

Ross, Colin, 141–2

Russia: armistice of 1917 and, 13–14, 20–1, 26–7, 31, 40; borders of, 225n1; effect of Brest-Litovsk treaty on, 213–14, 224; February Revolution in, 8, 13, 36, 215; following the First World War, 216; food shortages in, 95; hosting of Petrograd negotiations, 57–8, 61; imperial collapse in, 5, 8, 120, 122–3, 214–16, 222; military defeats of, 12, 206–8; November (October) Revolution in, 14, 31, 36, 40; Poland and, 73; post-revolution conditions in, 58–9; Provisional Government and, 13–14, 46, 122; relationship with Bulgaria, 173, 176–8; relationship with Ukraine, 122–4, 126, 129, 131, 135, 137, 196; relation with Ottoman Empire, 37, 50; renewal of hostilities with Germany, 206–8, 223; self-determination and, 16, 45–6, 67, 70, 75; signing of Brest-Litovsk by, 4; territorial fragmentation of, 5, 12–13, 16, 40, 53, 67, 158, 209, 211, 213–14, 216; Ukrainian army and, 149–50; Ukrainian treaty of Brest-Litovsk and, 10; war aims of, 46–7. *See also* Bolsheviks; Soviet Union

Russian Civil War, 24

Sanborn, Joshua, 215, 223

San Stefano, Treaty of, 160–3, 172, 176, 181, 212

Schlieffen Plan, 12

Schönfeld, Eduard, 86–7, 104–5

Schüller, Richard, 199

Schwarzenstein, Philip Alfons Mumm von, 143, 148

Scientific Expedition in Macedonia and the Pomoravie, 163

SDAPÖ – *Sozialdemokratische Arbeiterpartei Österreichs*, 17, 81, 84–6, 89, 91, 103–4, 108–9, 111, 113, 115
security, concept of, 35, 233n77
Seidler von Feuchtenegg, Ernst, 101, 106, 108, 111–12, 117, 132, 134, 206–7; Austrian food shortages and, 89, 96, 98
Seitz, Karl, 85, 89–91, 93, 103, 111, 113–14
self-determination, 5–6, 11, 42–3, 66, 69, 77, 182, 222; applied to Russian empire, 67; in Baltic regions, 69–70; Bolshevik peace proposal and, 15–16; Brest-Litovsk Treaty and, 5–6, 42–4, 77, 221; Bulgaria and, 164, 168, 172–3, 175–6, 181–2; Central Powers' use of, 67–8, 77; challenges in applying, 72; declarations of independence and, 242n93; as demand of strikers, 185; Entente powers and, 65–6; February Revolution and, 46; Hungarian objections to, 55; Imperial collapse and, 182; importance of to negotiations, 55, 66; Ioffe Program and, 47–8, 51–3; Lenin's views on, 43–6, 49, 75; non-interference and, 16; origins of, 44–7; Paris Peace Conference and, 43, 48, 68–9, 72, 222; plebiscites on, 70–2, 241n92; Poland and, 73–5; as Russian war aim, 46; Trotsky's stance on, 104, 129; Ukrainian annexations and, 130–1, 133; Ukrainian independence and, 129, 196; Wilson and, 43–4, 48, 66, 69, 221, 237n18
Sendler, General von, 101

Serbia, 56, 67, 146, 202; Bulgarian war aims and, 50, 100, 161, 163–6, 173
Sevriuk, Oleksandr, 113, 129, 131
Short Course in the History of the All-Union Communist Party (Stalin, 1938), 10
Silesia, 34, 63, 79, 116
Skalon, Vladimir, 30–1
Skocpol, Theda, 118
Skoropadskyi, Hetman Pavlo, 7, 144, 146–51, 153–5, 157, 214
Snyder, Timothy, 151
Social Democratic Workers' Party of Austria (*Sozialdemokratische Arbeiterpartei Österreichs*, SDAPÖ), 17
Sokolnikov, Grigorii, 22, 209, 211–12
Soldatenko, Valerii F., 120, 125
Soviet Union, 219, 224; Ukraine and, 7–8. *See also* Bolsheviks; Russia
Sovnarkom (*Soviet narodnykh kommissar*, Council of People's Commissars), 61, 125, 210, 218
Spiridonova, Maria, 210
Stalin, Josef, 10, 135, 186–7, 218
Stashkov, R., 27, 30, 231n46
Steglich, Wolfgang, 9
Steiner, Herbert, 91
Steinwedel, Charles, 156
Strachan, Hew, 15
Straußenburg, Arz von, 106
Stürgkh, Karl von, 80–1
Styria, 85, 102, 111
Sublime Porte, 18, 37, 160, 174, 210
Suppan, Arnold, 90
Szeptycki, Stanisław, 98

Tantilov, Petar, 100–1
Tatishchev, Aleksei, 147

Thrace, 8, 158, 162, 174–5
Thurn, Duglas von, 98
Tilly, Charles, 95
Tito, Josip Broz, 87
Toggenburg, Count, 111–12, 117
Toshev, Andrei, 19, 100, 164, 210, 236n3, 247n40
Treaty of Brest-Litovsk. *See* Brest-Litovsk Treaties
Trianon, Treaty of, 215
Trotsky, Leon, 76–7, 184–5, 191–203; armistice of 1917 and, 23, 30; Bolshevik withdrawal from war and, 202–3, 206, 223; Bulgarians and, 165; debates with Kühlmann, 68–72; Great January Strike and, 92, 185; international revolution and, 37–8, 49, 77, 184–5, 214; Lenin and, 189–91, 206; negotiations with Austrians, 199–200; negotiations with Central Powers, 191–203; "no war, no peace" policy of, 184–5, 188–92, 194, 200, 206, 216, 223; Poland and, 74–5, 197; post-*glasnost* rehabilitation of, 10; self-determination and, 44, 45–6, 68–71, 104, 129, 199; stalling tactics of, 75–6; surrender of Bolsheviks and, 209; "treacherous" behavior of, 10, 234n91, 235n96; Ukraine and, 129, 135, 196–7; violations of Brest-Litovsk Treaty and, 218
Turkestan, 45

Ukraine, 7–8, 156–7; Archduke Wilhelm and, 146, 151–7; Bolsheviks and, 7, 124, 155, 183, 193, 196–7, 204; Dobryi Affair, 143–4; effect of February Revolution on, 122; foreign policy of, 125–6, 131–2; Hetmanate in, 144, 146–51, 153, 155, 214; independence of, 128–30, 138, 157, 213, 223; land socialization in, 141–2, 153, 157; relationship with Austria, 10, 119, 128, 131–2, 193, 204, 222; relationship with Bulgaria, 177–82; relationship with Central Powers, 10, 122–30, 132–8, 143, 150, 156–7, 204–5, 222; relationship with Entente nations, 126; relationship with Russia, 122–4, 126, 129, 131, 135, 137, 196; separate peace signed by, 10, 29, 120, 135–7, 201; signing of Brest-Litovsk by, 4, 10, 136, 156, 201, 223; as source of grain, 93, 96, 101–2, 132–5, 137, 183, 193; territorial claims of, 103, 130–5, 204; Ukrainian army, 149, 152; Ukrainian Bolsheviks, 125, 135; Ukrainian language, 121, 138–41, 147–8; Ukrainian Revolution, 120–3, 125, 135, 141, 153; Ukrainization policies, 7–8, 121–2, 138–41, 144–6, 148–9, 151–7; West Ukrainian People's Republic, 132, 156; Wilhelm von Habsburg and, 146, 151–6; withdrawal of Central Powers from, 151. *See also* Rada
Ukrainian language, 121, 138–41, 147–8
Ukrainian Sich Sharpshooters (*Ukrains'ki Sichovi Stril'tsi*, USS), 152–4, 156
Ukrainization policies, 7–8, 121–2, 138–41, 144–6, 157; Archduke Wilhelm and, 151–6; of Skoropadskyi regime, 148–9
Union for the Liberation of Ukraine (*Soiuz vyzvolennia Ukrainy*), 122

United States, 30. *See also* Wilson, Woodrow

Vasyl'ko, Mykola, 142
Velychenko, Stephen, 148–9, 215
Vernadsky, Vladimir, 140, 147
Versailles, Treaty of, 216, 226n6; contrasted with Brest-Litovsk Treaty, 8–9, 215
Verstiuk, Vladislav, 120–2
Viennese workers' council, 105, 108, 113–14, 116
Vladeva, Liliana, 163
Von Hagen, Mark, 4, 73
Von Ugron, Stephan, 133
Vynnychenko, Volodymyr, 126–7, 135–6
Vyshyvanyi, Vasyl. *See* Wilhelm, Archduke von Habsburg

Wargelin, Clifford F., 79–80, 134
Wassilko, Nikolaus von, 142
Wedel, Botho von, 19, 106
Weitsman, Patricia A., 6
Wekerle, Sandor, 32, 55–6, 83, 134
Weltpolitik, 36
Western Front, 3, 18, 20, 109

Westphalian System of international relations, 16
West Ukrainian People's Republic, 132, 156
Wheeler-Bennett, John W., 8–9, 25, 170, 212–13
Wiener Neustadt, 86–94, 104–5, 113–14, 116–18, 185
Wilhelm, Archduke von Habsburg, 151–2, 205; Ukraine and, 7, 146, 151–7
Wilhelm, Kaiser II, 96, 162–3, 201; German constitutional crisis and, 63–5; German war aims and, 34, 36; Ukraine and, 148, 154–5
Wilhelmstraße, 6, 22, 64, 123, 210
Wilhelm von Hohenzollern, xviii
Wilson, Woodrow, 5, 48–9, 221; Fourteen Points and, 48–9, 66; self-determination and, 43–4, 48, 66, 69, 221, 237n18
Windischgrätz, Lajos von, 99
World War I. *See* First World War

Yekelchyk, Serhy, 159

Zhekov, Nikola, 170–1, 177